30 Mock Tests

for

Olympiad

CLASS 7

Science | Mathematics | English
Logical Reasoning | GK | Cyber

DISHA™
Publication Inc

DISHA Publication Inc.

45, 2nd Floor, Maharishi Dayanand Marg,
Corner Market, Malviya Nagar, new Delhi –110017
Tel: 49842349/ 49842350

Typeset By

DISHA DTP Team

Buying books from DISHA

Just Got A Lot More Rewarding!!!

We at DISHA Publication, value your feedback immensely and to show our apperciation of our reviewers, we have launched a review contest.

To participate in this reward scheme, just follow these quick and simple steps:
- Write a review of the product you purchase on Amazon/Flipkart.
- Take a screenshot/photo of your review.
- Mail it to *disha-rewards@aiets.co.in*, along with all your details.

Each month, selected reviewers will win exciting gifts from DISHA Publication. Note that the rewards for each month will be declared in the first week of next month on our website.

https://bit.ly/review-reward-disha.

Write To
Us At
feedback_disha@aiets.co.in

CONTENTS

English

Mathematics

Science

General Knowledge

Unlock your child's
HIDDEN GENIUS!
with Olympiad Champs

ENGLISH

OLYMPIAD Mock Test 1

Name : ___________

Number of Questions : 45

Max. Marks : 45

Time : 2 Hours

There is no negative marking in the test.

DIRECTIONS (Qs. 1 to 12): Choose the best word/phrase to complete each sentence.

1. I wish it _________rain! It's too hot.
   - (a) will
   - (b) would
   - (c) will not
   - (d) does not

2. The principal spoke separately to _________ student.
   - (a) every
   - (b) each
   - (c) any
   - (d) some

3. He was so _________asleep that it was tough to wake him up.
   - (a) fast
   - (b) late
   - (c) sound
   - (d) deeply

4. We regret that we cannot comply _________ your request.
   - (a) at
   - (b) to
   - (c) for
   - (d) with

5. She is _________ M. A. in Geography.
   - (a) a
   - (b) the
   - (c) an
   - (d) no article

6. This is the ____building in the world.
   - (a) taller
   - (b) tallest
   - (c) longer
   - (d) longest

7. The thief broke _________ when the police started interrogating him.
   - (a) down
   - (b) up
   - (c) into
   - (d) up to

8. My dog _________whenever he hears any noise at the door.
   - (a) barks
   - (b) barking
   - (c) bark
   - (d) barkingly

9. Joey wanted so _____ gifts on Christmas.
   - (a) much
   - (b) many
   - (c) very
   - (d) all

10. _______ man is _________ mortal.
    - (a) The, no article
    - (b) A, the
    - (c) The, a
    - (d) No article, the

11. I _________ to reach airport by 9:00, otherwise I will miss my flight.
    - (a) must
    - (b) might
    - (c) may
    - (d) have

12. You _____ be so rude! Why don't you say thanks and please once in a while?
    - (a) have to
    - (b) must
    - (c) must not
    - (d) might

DIRECTIONS (Qs. 13 to 15): How many words are misspelt in the following sentences?

13. I met him during my holyday with my family.
    - (a) 1
    - (b) 2
    - (c) 3
    - (d) None of these

14. I will weer this suite for today's meeting.
    (a) 1　　　　(b) 2
    (c) 3　　　　(d) None of these
15. This is not my book; I just borrowed it.
    (a) 1　　　　(b) 2
    (c) 3　　　　(d) None of these

DIRECTIONS (Qs. 16 to 18): The sentences given below may or may not contain an error. If there is an error, choose that part of the sentence that contains error. If there is no error, choose 'd'.

16. This is not mine house; it is their house. (a)/I have just come here (b)/to stay for sometime.(c)/No error(d)
17. I read (a)/this book (b)/everyday before I go to sleep.(c)/ No error(d)
18. He introduced him (a)/as the manager (b)/of the company. (c)/ No error (d)

DIRECTIONS (Qs. 19 to 24): Choose the best words to complete each sentence.

19. One should accept life's misfortunes as well as its joys. One should _________.
    (a) take the bitter with the sweet.
    (b) take the sour with the sweet.
    (c) take the spicy with the sour.
    (d) take the bitter pill.
20. My friends ____me I would not like the movie, on the contrary, I enjoyed it.
    (a) told　　　　(b) tell
    (c) said　　　　(d) ordered
21. You can lead the _________.
    (a) way　　　　(b) away
    (c) road　　　　(d) street
22. Do not open this letter; it is a/an _______ letter.

    (a) private　　　　(b) fragile
    (c) priceless　　　　(d) secret
23. The Harappan script cannot be_____. so we cannot tell much about it.
    (a) deciphered　(b) written
    (c) found　　　　(d) formed
24. He was offered a _______ –driven car by his company.
    (a) chauffeur　(b) man
    (c) robot　　　　(d) woman

DIRECTIONS (Qs. 25 to 30): Read the passage given below and fill in the blanks with appropriate words. Choose the answers from the options given below.

Greece reached a desperately-needed bailout deal (25)_______the Eurozone aftermarathon talks, (26)____a historic agreement (27)______prevent the country out of the European single currency. The agreement means that the Greek government(28)______now go way beyond a reform proposal it submitted (29)_____week. It has to make (30)_____more changes to pensions, energy, labour and product markets and scale up the programme of privatisation.

25. (a) in　　　　(b) with
    (c) at　　　　(d) on
26. (a) on　　　　(b) in
    (c) at　　　　(d) during
27. (a) to　　　　(b) for
    (c) of　　　　(d) in
28. (a) must　　　　(b) could
    (c) would　　　　(d) can

29. (a) coming   (b) last   30. (a) many   (b) few
    (c) earlier   (d) past   (c) very   (d) much

DIRECTIONS (Qs. 31 to 35): Read the itinerary given below and answer the questions that follow.

E-Ticket SM Receipt and Itinerary
YOUR ELECTRONIC TICKET WAS ISSUED
This Document is for reference only.
Your electronic airline ticket is stored in our computer system. As with all airline ticket, your electronic licked is not transferable.
Thank you for choosing United Airlines.
If you need to change your booking request, please visit united. com.
Click here to print this document print-e-receipt.
Issued: Tue, Feb 05, 2006/LAX
United record locator. VP6588
Name : John Smith
Total Price: USD 2.00
Sat, Jul 26, 2008- Palm Springs, CA (PSP) to San Francisco, CA (SFO)

United 6374	Depart: PSP	Non-stop	Booking class: S	Flight Confirmed
	07:00 AM	1h 26m	Economy	02A
	Arrive: SFD	Bombandher CR J-200	500 Award miles No Meal	
		421 miles traveled	Service	

Sat, Jul 26, 2008- San Francisco, CA (SFO) to Belling, China (PEK)

United 880	Depart: SFO	Non-Stop	Booking class: H	Flight: Confirmed
	11:08 AM	12h 19m	Economy	37A
	Arrive PEK	Boeing 747-400	5,914 Award miles	
	02:25 PM	5,914 miles traveled	Lunch, Lunch	
	Next day Jul 27			

Mon, Sep. 15, 2008-Belling, China (PEK) to San Francisco, CA (SFO)

United 888   Depart: PEK   Non-Stop   Booking Class: V   Flight:

Confirmed

	11:08 AM	11h 39m	Economy	38A
	Arrive: SFO	Boeing	5,914 Award	
		747-400	miles	
	08:39 PM	5,914 miles	Lunch, Lunch	
		traveled		

Mon, Sep. 15, 2008- San Francisco, CA (SFO) to Palm Springs, CA (PSP)

United 5930   Depart: SFO   Non-stop   Booking class: T   Flight:
                                                                  Confirmed

	01 : 15 AM	1h 20 m	Economy	02A
	Amine PSP	BomBardfer:	50D Award	
		CR J-200	miles	
		421 miles	No Meal	
		traveled	Service	

Additional Information: Check-In Information

Please note that valid, government-issued photo identification must be presented at chock-in.

For international travel. Please review the documentation requirements for the country on your linenery. You must present these document and this e-receipt at check-in.

Payment Details

MPVISA xxxxxxxxxxxxxxxx560

| **Total Payment** | USD 2,000 |
| Billing/Delivery Information | USD 2,000 |

---

31. This itinerary shows that the payment was made in___________.

   (a) Indian currency

   (b) American Dollar

   (c) European Currency

   (d) Dinar

32. Which of the following is false?

   (a) The traveller is travelling from Palm Spring to San Francisco on the 26th of July.

   (b) The traveller is travelling from San Francisco to China on 26th of July in the evening.

    (c) The traveller is travelling from Beijing to San Francisco on the 15th of September.

    (d) The traveller is travelling from San Francisco to Palm Springs on the 15th of September.

33. If someone wants to change his booking request what will he do?

    (a) He will go to the office of the airlines.

    (b) He will have to call the airlines.

    (c) He will have to visit the site of the airlines.

    (d) He cannot change the booking.

34. What are the requirements that are mentioned in the itinerary to be presented at the check-in?

    (a) A passport size photo.

    (b) Your credit cards.

    (c) A government issued photo-id.

    (d) Your bank account details.

35. Find out a word from the itinerary that means the opposite of lavish.

    (a) economy

    (b) issue

    (c) information

    (d) delivery

DIRECTIONS (Qs. 36 to 45): Which is the best response to use in everyday conversation?

36. Initially I found the city very crowded, but now I guess ____________.

    (a) I can stay

    (b) I got used to it.

    (c) I am used to it.

    (d) I am accustomed.

37. Mr. Harrison started his new job yesterday. Now________for six days a week.

    (a) used to work

    (b) will not work

    (c) would work

    (d) had worked

38. When I lived near that park, I __________everyday.

    (a) used to go the beach

    (b) used to playing

    (c) used to play

    (d) used to played

39. Where were you? Why were you so late to open the door?

    (a) I was watching TV when you came in.

    (b) I did not hear the doorbell.

    (c) When did you come?

    (d) I was watching TV when you called.

40. Peter: Hurray! We won the football match.

    Henry: _________________________

    Peter: Thanks, It's all because of our team's hard work.

    (a) wow! But not so great!

    (b) Oops! You won!

    (c) Congratulations!

    (d) Congratulations! But your performance was not good.

41. Tom: _________________________

    Siya: Yes, please hold on for a minute.

    (a) Hello, can I speak to George?

    (b) Hello, can I come to your house?

    (c) Hi, I am speaking to you.

    (d) Hello, but My mom is not well.

42. Roger: Can you please be quiet? I am studying.

    James: _________________________

    (a) So what? I cannot keep quiet.

    (b) I am also talking to my friend.

    (c) Sure, sorry for disturbing you.

    (d) Yuck! It's not worth doing.

43. Ginni: why are so late? What took you so long?

    Ryan: _________________________

    (a) We were waiting for you.

    (b) We halted to buy some fruits.

    (c) why were you waiting?

    (d) We ought to be late.

44. Shyam: Sir, I think that is a better idea.

    Sir: _________________________

    (a) You have no right to talk to me like that.

    (b) You cannot say anything.

    (c) Okay, let's consider that one too!

    (d) Okay, but let's focus on this first.

45. Yatin: I am happy to win the first prize.

    Gautam: _________________________

    (a) But why? I was not too happy.

    (b) You ought to be happy.

    (c) I can't say anything.

    (d) You cannot be happy.

Name : __________

Number of Questions : 45

Max. Marks : 45

Time : 2 Hours

There is no negative marking in the test.

DIRECTIONS (Qs. 1 to 12): Fill in the blanks with the most appropriate option given below.

---

1. Horses are often fed on _______.
   - (a) cheff
   - (b) chaff
   - (c) chuff
   - (d) chiff

2. The X-ray showed a __________ of the knee.
   - (a) flannel
   - (b) fracture
   - (c) wound
   - (d) blood

3. Kial might venture into education. This is a __________.
   - (a) possibility
   - (b) order
   - (c) suggestion
   - (d) announcement

4. The government has to work hard to provide internet in every home. It _______ succeed in doing it soon.
   - (a) must
   - (b) might
   - (c) has
   - (d) can

5. They _______ have come out of their house, once they felt the earthquake.
   - (a) can
   - (b) should
   - (c) would
   - (d) will

6. They _______ shift into their new flat.
   - (a) might
   - (b) may
   - (c) must
   - (d) could

7. India _______ pay attention to its infrastructure, if it wants to compete with the developed countries.
   - (a) must
   - (b) might
   - (c) would
   - (d) could

8. India features _______ on every list of polluted countries.
   - (a) prominently
   - (b) dominantly
   - (c) clearly
   - (d) randomly

9. Non-violence _______ non-alignment were cornerstone of India's foreign policy.
   - (a) but
   - (b) and
   - (c) or
   - (d) either

10. After the recent developments, India has become a force to reckon _______.
    - (a) with
    - (b) by
    - (c) of
    - (d) at

11. A person who measures angles is called _______.
    (a) surveyor
    (b) aviator
    (c) geometrist
    (d) scaler

12. A test to discover something new is _______.
    (a) discovery   (b) innovation
    (c) invention   (d) experiment

13. What is the meaning of 'pig in a poke'?
    (a) A deal that is made without first examining it.
    (b) A deal made with proper research.
    (c) A deal made without methodology
    (d) A deal made without consideration

DIRECTIONS (Qs. 14 to 16): How many words are wrongly spelt used in the sentences given below.

14. The mussel in his rite am is quite painfull.
    (a) 1   (b) 2
    (c) 3   (d) 4

15. Our teacher tought us about gravity.
    (a) 1   (b) 2
    (c) 3   (d) 4

16. Miners are not allowed to vot.
    (a) 1   (b) 2
    (c) 3   (d) 4

DIRECTIONS (Qs. 17 to 19): The sentences given below may or may not contain an error. If there is an error, choose that part of the sentence that contains error. If there is no error, choose 'd'.

17. He have (a)/all the luxuries (b)/of life. (c)/No error (d)

18. India has loose (a)/the match (b)/ against China. (c)/ No error (d)

19. The concert ended (a)/from a (b)/ high note. (c)/No error (d)

DIRECTIONS(Qs. 20 to 30): Read the following sentences and fill in the blanks with the most appropriate answer.

20. There are thousands of mice ____________the grain.
    (a) replenishing
    (b) destroying
    (c) disturbing
    (d) sowing

21. The thief was _______by the police.
    (a) arrested   (b) attested
    (c) freed   (d) alarmed

22. The audience clapped loudly _________ she finished her song.

    (a) before   (b) since

    (c) while   (d) when

23. At last I felt released; free to move anywhere and to brush aside fear. What is the meaning of 'brush aside'?

    (a) To comb

    (b) Set something aside

    (c) To treat something as unimportant

    (d) None of these

24. You can't walk _________ when I am talking to you.

    (a) away   (b) on

    (c) out   (d) to

25. Northern Railways _________ for the delay caused.

    (a) rejoiced   (b) rejected

    (c) dejected   (d) apologised

26. Jeremy has been taking many lectures _________, so he does not get free time.

    (a) late much   (b) so many

    (c) lately   (d) hardly

27. Why did you take so much time to reach home? You _________ have been so late.

    (a) should   (b) should not

    (c) must   (d) may

28. What a_________ excuse! I expected you to have completed your work.

    (a) lame   (b) perfect

    (c) plausible   (d) great

29. Take up only the amount of work that you can complete. Do not_________________________

    (a) bite off more than you can chew.

    (b) try to hit two stones with the same arrow.

    (c) try to bell a cat.

    (d) hit yourself.

30. It may be easy to _________ freedom, however, it is tough to maintain it.

    (a) accomplish (b) achieve

    (c) activate   (d) complete

DIRECTIONS (Q. 31 to 35): Read the following passage and answer the questions that follow. Choose the answers from the options given below.

Indian Nobel Prize winning physicist Subramanyam Chandrashekhar discovered the calculation used to determine the future of a dying star. The Indian astrophysicist independently discovered and improved upon the accuracy of the calculation on 1930, at the age of 19.

If the star's mass is less than the Chandrashekhar's limit, it will shrink into a white dwarf and if greater, the star will explode becoming a supernova.

The currently accepted value of the limit is about 1.39M.

31. Which country did Subramanium Chandrashekhar belong to?

    (a) India   (b) Russia

    (c) USA   (d) Germany

32. Which of the following is correct?

    (a) If the star's mass is greater than Chandrashekhar's limit, it will become a white dwarf.

    (b) If the mass of the star is lesser than the Chandrashekhar's limit, it will become a white dwarf.

    (c) If the star's mass is lesser than the Chandrashekhar's limit, it will become a supernova.

    (d) If the star's mass is equal to the Chandrashekhar's limit, it will become a supernova.

33. Find out a word from the passage that means precision.

    (a) Independently

    (b) Accuracy

    (c) Discovered

    (d) Determine

34. What is the value of Chandrashekhar's limit?

    (a) 1.39 M   (b) 1.20 M

    (c) 1.40M   (d) None of these

35. What happens to a star that explodes?

    (a) It forms meteors.

    (b) It forms meteoroids.

    (c) It forms asteroids.

    (d) It becomes a supernova.

DIRECTIONS (Qs. 36 to 45): Choose from the given options the most appropriate response to use in everyday conversation.

36. CONVERSATION ON A PLANE

    Q. Passenger: Excuse me, will you show my seat to me, please?

    Airhostess: _________________

    Passenger: Thank you. May I have a glass of water?

    (a) Please show me your boarding pass. This way please. Here it is.

    (b) I can't tell you.

    (c) I have no idea.

    (d) It must be somewhere.

37. Sunny: Are they coming?

    David: _____________________.

    (a) No, they are not coming with us.

    (b) They don't have time to come.

    (c) They will reach within half an hour.

    (d) Who has called them?

38. Robin: What is the time?

    Frazer: _________________

    (a) Nobody can tell.

    (b) It's quarter past eight.

    (c) Why don't you carry a watch?

    (d) It can be good or bad.

39. Ram: Who all are left in the contest?

    Shyam:_____________________

    (a) He is the only one left in the contest.

    (b) No one has won.

    (c) All have lost the game.

    (d) It's a tough decision.

40. What are you doing?

    (a) I am eating food.

    (b) I am having food.

    (c) I am consuming food.

    (d) I am not eating food.

41. Paul: Did you listen to the Prime Minister's speech?

    Smith:_____________

    Paul: Did you listen to what he spoke about debt relief in developing countries?

    (a) Yes, I listened to the whole speech.

    (b) No I didn't get time.

    (c) It was quite a difficult job.

    (d) He was not audible.

42. An incident where a son has a fight with his peer and he hits him - what should be the reaction of a mother?

    (a) It is not good to be violent; you must try to resolve through talks.

    (b) Well done, I expected this from you.

    (c) You should have not hit him so badly.

    (d) Beware! He may turn against you.

43. Saira: I am having a terrible stomach ache.

    Ruhi: _____________________

    (a) How does it feel like?

    (b) You must see a doctor immediately.

    (c) I can't say anything about it.

    (d) Is it really terrible?

44. Manager: How's the response to the event?

    Employee: _______________

    Manager: Great! I expected it to be a hit.

    (a) I can't tell you right now.

    (b) It's going good but the response is not good.

    (c) It's going good.

    (d) Let's keep our fingers crossed.

45. Johnson: I have made a big cake because I am expecting friends.

    Smith: _____________________

    Johnson: Sure, even you can join in.

    (a) Why are they coming?

    (b) Great! Can I also join?

    (c) Great! But nobody is coming.

    (d) Thanks for inviting me too!

Name : __________

Number of Questions : 50

There is no negative marking in the test.

Max. Marks : 50

Time : 2 Hours

DIRECTIONS (Qs. 1 to 12): Read the sentences given below and fill in the blanks with the most appropriate words. Choose the answers from the options given below.

1. The man and his wife were ______ on the coast.
   - (a) voyaging
   - (b) touring
   - (c) ticketing
   - (d) flying

2. Sam is sweeping all the fallen __________in the garden.
   - (a) leaves
   - (b) leaf
   - (c) trees
   - (d) benches

3. He has ______the books on the two top shelves.
   - (a) stacked
   - (b) stocked
   - (c) stored
   - (d) preserved

4. He __________up the dirty water on the floor.
   - (a) mopped
   - (b) boomed
   - (c) drank
   - (d) dried

5. It was useless to _____waiting for a delayed train.
   - (a) kept
   - (b) keep
   - (c) not
   - (d) accept

6. The officer was annoyed to ________corruption in his office.
   - (a) see
   - (b) feel
   - (c) know
   - (d) mind

7. I ______known him for a long time.
   - (a) have
   - (b) had
   - (c) have been
   - (d) had been

8. Water in my house is ______, you can have it directly from the tap.
   - (a) treatable
   - (b) untreatable
   - (c) drinkable
   - (d) curable

9. Sam's handwriting is _________; he himself can't read it.
   - (a) flexible
   - (b) inflexible
   - (c) legible
   - (d) illegible

10. Bob _____trying to climb a mountain. But he couldn't.
    - (a) is
    - (b) was
    - (c) were
    - (d) are

11. James and I ______making pasta for dinner.
    - (a) are
    - (b) am
    - (c) were
    - (d) is

12. Animals_______be bathed in rivers or canals.
    - (a) should
    - (b) should not
    - (c) may
    - (d) might

DIRECTIONS (Qs. 13 to 15): How many words are wrongly used in the sentences given below?

13. What root did you take to mine house?

    (a) 1   (b) 2

    (c) 3   (d) None

14. Blood is returned to the hurt in this vain.

    (a) 1   (b) 2

    (c) 3   (d) None

15. The mare declared a holiday on Monday.

    (a) 1   (b) 2

    (c) 3   (d) None

DIRECTIONS (Qs. 16 to 18): The sentences given below may or may not contain an error. If there is an error, choose that part of the sentence that contains error. If there is no error, choose 'd'.

16. Where are (a)/he going? (b)/ He will get late. (c)/No error (d)

17. I cannot tolerate (a)/unnecessarily (b)/waste of time (c)/No error (d)

18. With only three (a)/days left of the session, (b)/ the government have to pass the law. (c)/No error (d)

DIRECTIONS (Qs. 19 to 30): Read the following sentences and fill in the blanks by choosing the most appropriate options given below.

19. Do you have _____money left to buy sweets?

    (a) any   (b) little

    (c) much   (d) many

20. Meg fell from the horse yesterday, so she ________ to the hospital.

    (a) go   (b) is going

    (c) went   (d) goes

21. Mary told him what______ (happen) to his dog, so he______ (run) home to see how to see how it ________ (be).

    (a) had happened , ran, was

    (b) have happened, ran, was

    (c) had happened, ran , is

    (d) had happened, run, is

22. I would like to have some________ information.

    (a) farther   (b) further

    (c) better   (d) rare

DIRECTIONS (Qs. 23 to 30): Read the passage given below and fill in the blanks by choosing the most appropriate options given below.

The idea (23)_____traffic lights in the 1800's (24)____a system was required to control the ever increasing flow of horse-drawn traffic. In 1868 (25) _____ London, a signal (26) ____installed at the intersection of George Street and Bridge street, near parliament. (27) ________ provided pedestrians a safe crossing. The system installed a semaphore (system of sending messages by holding the arms- or two flags/ poles- in certain positions according to (28) _____alphabetic code) involved a tall post with moveable arms. When the arms (29) _____ positioned sideways, it meant to stop. After dark, a gaslight was lit at the top. A green tinted light meant go, (30) _____ red meant stop.

23. (a) of   (b) for

    (c) in   (d) by

24. (a) while   (b) when

    (c) hence   (d) then

25. (a) in   (b) at

    (c) on   (d) of

26. (a) were   (b) got

    (c) was   (d) have

27. (a) It   (b) This

    (c) Who   (d) And

28. (a) a   (b) an

    (c) the   (d) it

29. (a) are   (b) were

    (c) was   (d) is

30. (a) but   (b) while

    (c) when   (d) and

DIRECTIONS(Qs. 31 to 35): Read the following piece of information and answer the questions that follow. Choose the answers from the options given below.

WESTERN GHATS

SENSITIVE AREA

Ecologically Sensitive Area (ESA) may be reduced to nearly **50,000 sqkm** from **56,825 sqkm**

Original proosal (as per kastuirangan panel) was to keep it at **59,940 sqkm**

It was reduced to **56,825 sqkm** on Kerala's request under UPA rule (March 2015 draft notification)

• Agriculture, plantation and sand mining (with certain condition will be allowed within ESA

• Excessive mining, big construction and highly polluting industries will not be allowed in ESA

• **Western Chats is spread over six states** - Gujarat, Maharashtra, Goa, Karnataka, Tamil Nadu & Kerala- extending over a horizontal distance of about 1,500 km along the western coast

31. What is the full form of ESA?

    (a) Economically Sensitive Area

    (b) Ecologically Sensitive Area

    (c) Environmentally Sensitive Area

    (d) None of these

32. What activities will not be allowed in ESA?

    (a) Agriculture, plantation and sand mining

    (b) Excessive mining, big construction

    (c) Housing and playing

    (d) None of these

33. Over how many states Western Ghats are spread?

    (a) 6   (b) 5

    (c) 12   (d) 3

34. What does the word horizontal mean?

    (a) Parallel to the ground

    (b) Right angle

    (c) Across

    (d) Vertical

35. What is the meaning of sustainable development?

(a) A development that does not exhaust earth's natural resources and can be sustained.

(b) A development that keeps the environment into consideration.

(c) A development that wants to preserve the future also.

(d) All of these

DIRECTIONS (Qs. 36 to 40): Read the infographic chart given below and answer the questions that follow.

STATOISTIC

JUST A TRICKLE

FLOOD MANAGEMENT - XL AND XLL PLAN

(IN ₹ CR)

WORKS APPROVED

The arrival of monsoon is often followed by stories of deadly floods that state subject and food control schemes are passed executed and largely funded by state governments. The Centre provides technical advice and financial assistance to the states an analysis of the planning and implementation of flood programmes reveals a not very bright picture. During the xi and xii Plan periods, only 57% of the 517 approved flood control works were completed and only 36% of the estimated ₹ 12,00 crore was actually released during this period

Total	AMDS Released (% of cost)			Work completed		(% of approved)
32	-	2,383	Assam	-	141	-	88
35	-	2,261	West Bengal	-	18	-	33
49	-	1,818	Bihar	-	47	-	87
32	-	13,365	Himachal Pradesh	-	7	-	14
37	-	1,050	Utrta Pradesh	-	29	-	21
9	-	638	Tamil Nadu	-	5	-	NA
59	-	571	J&K	-	42	-	19
24	-	366	**Sikkim**	-	45	-	47
48	-	303	Uttarakhand	-	21	-	38
43	-	280	Kerala	-	4	-	NA
44	-	232	Odisha	-	68	-	88
27	-	174	Haryana	-	1	-	NA
6	-	153	Punjab	-	5	-	NA
5	-	140	Puducherry	-	1	-	NA
83	-	109	Manipur	-	22	-	NA
92	-	107	Arunachal Pradesh	-	21	-	52
61	-	295	Others	-	40	-	NA
57		12,243	ESTIMATED COST		TOTAL-517	57

36. The chart shows the value in terms of ____________.

(a) lakhs　　　(b) crores

(c) thousands　(d) hundreds

37. Flood management comes within the management of____________.

(a) centre

(b) states

(c) union territory

(d) people

38. Which of the following is false?

(a) Assam has the largest number of works that have been completed.

(b) Kerala has the largest number of works that have been approved.

(c) Puducherry and Haryana have equal number of approved works.

(d) None of these

39. How many flood control initiatives have been approved?

(a) 12,000　　　(b) 517

(c) 2283　　　(d) 2,261

40. Which word in the given infographic chart means lethal?

(a) Deadly　　(b) Submerge

(c) Trickle　　(d) Bright

DIRECTIONS (Qs. 41 to 50): Choose the most appropriate option to complete the dialogues given below.

41. Geeta: Did it rain last night?

Ram: ____________________

Geeta: Is the thunderstorm over now?

(a) Yes, it had been raining all night.

(b) No, it did not rain at all.

(c) Yes, only a little bit.

(d) No, It is only drizzling

42. Hemant: What is the weather right now?

Reka:____________________

(a) I can't see.

(b) I can't forecast.

(c) Find yourself.

(d) The Sun is appearing on the horizon.

43. Salesman: Welcome to our store.

    Customer: ___________________

    Salesman: We have a large variety of cups from Korea.

    (a) I want a vase.

    (b) I want to buy cups.

    (c) I have come here for window shopping.

    (d) I don't want anything from your shop.

44. To ask the way to the bus stop you should say: ___________________

    (a) Please, I beg your pardon to show me the way.

    (b) Excuse me, would you tell me the way to the bus stop?

    (c) Show me the way to the bus stop.

    (d) I know the way to the bus stop.

45. Which___________________will you join after passing school?

    (a) university

    (b) school

    (c) office

    (d) hostel

46. **Meeting an injured friend**

    Abid: Hello, Zoya! How are you feeling today?

    Zoya: ___________________

    (a) I don't know.

    (b) Much better, Abid. Thanks for coming to see me.

    (c) Better but not good.

    (d) Why do you want to know?

47. **Opening an account in the bank.**

    Bank employee: Good Morning, Madam. What can I do for you?

    Client: ___________________

    (a) I want to open a Savings account.

    (b) I want to deposit some money.

    (c) I want to withdraw some money.

    (d) I was looking for a job.

48. Bank Employee: Yes, madam! may I have your surname first?

    Client:___________________

    (a) My name is Reema.

    (b) My surname is Handa.

    (c) I stay in defence colony.

    (d) I can mail you my details.

49. Soham: Can I go out to play now?

    Teacher: ___________________

    (a) Sorry, but you can.

    (b) Of course, you can't.

    (c) Of course, you are not allowed.

    (d) Sorry, you can't go now.

50. Mary: Would you mind holding my child for a moment?

    Fauzia: ___________________

    (a) I'd love to.

    (b) Certainly not.

    (c) Pardon me.

    (d) No, not at all.

Name : _________

Number of Questions : 50

Max. Marks : 50

Time : 2 Hours

There is no negative marking in the test.

DIRECTIONS (Qs. 1 to 12): Read the sentences and fill in the blanks with the most appropriate option given below.

1. Illegal imitation means _______.
   - (a) forgery
   - (b) copy
   - (c) artificial
   - (d) look alike

2. I would have bought it, if it were _______ expensive.
   - (a) less
   - (b) few
   - (c) fewer
   - (d) lesser

3. My office hours are very_______, I have to arrive exactly on time.
   - (a) inflexible
   - (b) flexible
   - (c) changeable
   - (d) unchangeable

4. Try to_______ smoking, you will feel better.
   - (a) quit
   - (b) improve
   - (c) take
   - (d) think about

5. Parents must keep an eye ____ their children, otherwise they tend to lose track.
   - (a) on
   - (b) at
   - (c) in
   - (d) to

6. The various schemes are formulated to_______ women.
   - (a) control
   - (b) weaken
   - (c) slacken
   - (d) empower

7. 'You must go to bed now.' What kind of statement is this?
   - (a) Order
   - (b) Announcement
   - (c) Suggestion
   - (d) Permission

8. Before we assert our rights, we ____ fulfil our duties.
   - (a) may
   - (b) can
   - (c) must
   - (d) might

9. We must wear seat belts ____ driving.
   - (a) when
   - (b) while
   - (c) during
   - (d) on

10. We must eat balanced diet to avoid _____nutrition.
   - (a) under
   - (b) over
   - (c) mal
   - (d) dis

11. The whole nation paid homage _______ Dr. A.P.J. Abdul Kalam.
   - (a) for
   - (b) of
   - (c) by
   - (d) to

12. We planted________ during the tree plantation drive.
    (a) flowers   (b) seeds
    (c) fruits   (d) saplings

13. The school conducted ________ orientation programme for the students of class 7 and 8.
    (a) a   (b) an
    (c) the   (d) no article

14. The rescuers found no sign of the ship _____ had sunk in the sea.
    (a) that   (b) which
    (c) who   (d) it

15. It did not take long _____the two friends to be back in harmony.
    (a) to   (b) for
    (c) of   (d) by

DIRECTIONS (Qs. 16 to 18): How many words are wrongly used in the sentences given below?

16. He gave me a lone of 50,000.
    (a) 1   (b) 2
    (c) 3   (d) None

17. The cheif took a paper and stuk it firmly over the center of his belt.
    (a) 1   (b) 2
    (c) 3   (d) 4

18. The captian told us to remain calm.
    (a) 1   (b) 2
    (c) 3   (d) None

DIRECTIONS (Qs. 19 to 21): The sentences given below may or may not contain an error. If there is an error, choose that part of the sentence that contains error. If there is no error, choose 'd'.

19. He is going (a)/ everyday (b)/to his office by car. (c)/ No error (d)

20. He ran (a)/very fastly to reach (b)/ the examination centre.(c)/ No error (d)

21. Nobody has (a)/ been able to reach a Sun.(b)/ It is very hot there. (c)/ No error (d)

DIRECTIONS(Qs. 22 to 30): Read the sentences given below and fill in the blanks with the most appropriate answer.

22. They all ___________their old books to the orphanage.
    (a) gave   (b) donated
    (c) distributed   (d) divided

23. Rohan and Soham are my brother's two sons. They are my__________.
    (a) nephews   (b) siblings
    (c) cousins   (d) friends

24. He _______negotiations and attacked our country.
    (a) made   (b) broke off
    (c) dismissed   (d) spoiled

25. Now let's _______the deal.
    (a) open   (b) make
    (c) close   (d) drop

26. This is a very different kind of work that you are telling me to do. This is a ________whatever I have done up till now.
    (a) different   (b) far cry from
    (c) complex   (d) baffling

27. You _______reserve a seat in advance, they get full easily.
    (a) has to   (b) have to
    (c) had to   (d) may

28. He can't see _____. He is blind.
    (a) anything   (b) anyone
    (c) someone   (d) something
29. Expectations that the markets will remain depressed have prompted major producers to _____ their projects.
    (a) down   (b) drop
    (c) expand   (d) aggravate
30. Lambert Glacier _______ East Antarctica holds the world record for being the World's largest glacier.
    (a) on   (b) at
    (c) in   (d) with

DIRECTIONS (Qs. 31 to 35): Read the notice given below and answer the questions that follow.

NOTICE

INTERNATIONAL SCHOOL

NOTICE

INTER - SCHOOL CULTURAL FIESTA

15TH March, 2017

An inter-school cultural fiesta is going to be organised in the Lovely International School on 20th March 2017. The events include competitions in poster making, choreography, dance and dramatics. Winners will be awarded with attractive prizes. Students interested in participating may get their names registered with the undersigned latest by 17th March, 2017.

Rahul

Incharge

Cultural Committee

31. What is the meaning of fiesta?
    (a) Name of the competition
    (b) Festival
    (c) Meeting
    (d) Celebration
32. What are the programmes that are included in the competition?
    (a) Poster making
    (b) Singing
    (c) Debate
    (d) Rangoli making
33. What is the last date for registering for the competition?
    (a) Before or by 17th March
    (b) On 17th March
    (c) Anytime between 15th to 17th March.
    (d) 15th March
34. The event will be held in _______.
    (a) International School
    (b) Lovely International School
    (c) auditorium of the International School
    (d) the garden of the International School
35. Culture means _______ that we produce and the methods we use to produce them.
    (a) language
    (b) behaviour
    (c) customs
    (d) all of the above

DIRECTIONS (Qs. 36 to 40): Look at the advertisement given below and answer the questions that follow. Choose the answers from the options given below.

HERO PLANT A TREE

It's cool to plant a tree. Literally.

That's right, trees deflect sunlight and reduce the heat island effect caused by pavements and building in cities. In fact, every single tree provides ambient cooling equivalent to air conditioners. Now imagine the effect of 1 lakh trees. As a part of the effort to combat pollution and restore the environment of delhi NCR, we have organised Hero Moto Corp - Times of India Green executed by DDA with the aim of planting no less then 1 lakh trees. It's time to give back to the environment some of what we've taken

Join the Drive and plant 1 lakh trees! Be there on 30th August, anytime between 7AM to 4 PM at Tilpat Valley, Block M, Devli, near IGNOU.

36. Which of the following statements about trees is true?
    (a) They deflect sunlight.
    (b) A single tree provides cooling equal to 10 air conditioners.
    (c) They help in reducing pollution.
    (d) All of the above

37. What do you think is the purpose of this advertisement?
    (a) To promote its products
    (b) To promote tree plantation
    (c) To promote Delhi's development
    (d) None of these

38. Heat island means urban area having higher average temperature, what can be the reason for it?
    (a) Absorption and retention of heat.
    (b) Industries and factories polluting air
    (c) Various types of fuels that add to the heat
    (d) All of the above

39. What is the timing of the programme?
    (a) Anytime on 30th August
    (b) Anytime between 7 a.m. to 4 p.m. on 29th August
    (c) Anytime between 7 a.m. to 4 p.m. on 30th August
    (d) Any day between 7 a.m. to 4 p.m.

40. What will this drive help in?
    (a) Producing more carbon dioxide
    (b) Planting more trees
    (c) Reducing environmental pollution
    (d) Deforestation

DIRECTIONS (Qs. 41 & 42): Choose the must appropriate option to complete the dialogues given below.

41. Julie: Mr.Shyam, is it your first trip to Tokyo?
    Shyam:_______________
    (a) No, this is my last trip.
    (b) Yes, everything is new to me.
    (c) I have no idea.
    (d) It seems so old.

42. Patient: I feel dizzy and there is a throbbing pain in my head.
    Doctor:_________________
    Patient: Not really.
    Doctor: How long has it been like this?
    (a) Have you ever had this before?
    (b) Have you been out?
    (c) Are you getting admitted?
    (d) Do you think I can treat you?

DIRECTIONS (Qs. 43 to 45): Given below is a conversation between two classmates who are seeing each other after a long time. Fill in the blanks with appropriate sentences.

Maggi: Hello, Rosy, it has been a long time since we met.

Rosy _________________

Maggi: I am Maggi, your old classmate.

Maggi: I have not seen you for a long time. What have you been doing all these years.

Rosy _____________________

Maggi: I am a teacher in JP School.

Rosy: Oh, my children also go to the same school.

Maggi: _____________________

Rosy: My sons are in 7th standard.

Maggi: It is nice. Are they twins?

Rosy: Yes, they are twins.

Maggi: That's great!

43. (a) Hello, I could hardly recognise you.
    (b) Who are you?
    (c) I don't know you.
    (d) We are strangers.

44. (a) I am not doing anything.
    (b) I had been working in an MNC. What about you?
    (c) Why should I tell you?
    (d) I still have no idea.

45. (a) Why do they go to the same school?
    (b) In which class do your children study?
    (c) What are their names?
    (d) How do they go to school?

DIRECTIONS (Qs. 46 to 50): Choose the most appropriate options to complete the dialogues given below.

---

46. **Conversation between a mother and her son in a market**

    Mother: Dennis, I need to buy some vegetables. What do you want?

    Dennis: _____________________

Mother: That stall has fresh fruits and vegetables.

(a) You can buy anything.
(b) I want to buy fruits.
(c) I want some toys.
(d) I want to eat fruits.

47. **At a petrol station**

    Boy at the petrol station: Good Morning, what can I do for you?

    Mrs. Vinita: _________________

    (a) Fill the tank up.
    (b) Clean my car.
    (c) Nothing, I just came to have a look.
    (d) I want to sell my car.

48. Smita: Are you free next weekend?

    Anita: _____________________

    Smita: I am holding a party next weekend. Please come.

    (a) Why
    (b) I will not tell.
    (c) Of course, what's up?
    (d) I am never free.

49. **Telephonic Conversation**

    Sam: Who's calling?

    Siya: _____________________

    Sam: Speaking, what can I do for you?

    (a) Is it 554488993?
    (b) I am Siya. May I speak to Sam?
    (c) I can't tell you.
    (d) That's not important.

50. Paul: How do you spend your free time?

    Smith: _____________________.

    (a) I waste my time.
    (b) I go out with my friends.
    (c) I don't get any free time.
    (d) I keep working.

OLYMPIAD
Mock Test 5

Name : __________

Max. Marks : 50

Number of Questions : 50

Time : 2 Hours

There is no negative marking in the test.

DIRECTIONS(Qs. 1 to 10): Read the sentences given below and fill in the blanks choosing the most appropriate option.

1. We _____ not oppose you , if you say so.
   - (a) could
   - (b) will
   - (c) ought to
   - (d) need

2. He lived in frugality. What does it mean?
   - (a) He lived luxuriously.
   - (b) He lived splendidly.
   - (c) He spent economically.
   - (d) He spent lavishly.

3. His performance in the competition was _____ than mine.
   - (a) good
   - (b) similar
   - (c) better
   - (d) best

4. 'Shall we reserve tables at Raffles then?' What kind of statement is this?
   - (a) A suggestion
   - (b) A warning
   - (c) A permission
   - (d) An announcement

5. You _______ enrol into yoga classes. They will definitely help you.
   - (a) should
   - (b) could
   - (c) may
   - (d) might

6. You ________ start early otherwise you might get stuck in a jam.
   - (a) have to
   - (b) may
   - (c) can
   - (d) might

7. I have travelled almost the whole of India, now I am _____ Gangtok.
   - (a) in
   - (b) on
   - (c) at
   - (d) of

8. How _____ chairs do we need for the meeting?
   - (a) much
   - (b) many
   - (c) several
   - (d) an

9. We could arrange only a _____ sponsors for tomorrow's show.
   - (a) few
   - (b) little
   - (c) several
   - (d) less

10. Glaciers all over the world _____ melting at an alarming rate.
    - (a) were
    - (b) are
    - (c) was
    - (d) have

DIRECTIONS (Qs. 11 to 13): How many words are wrongly spelt in the sentences given below?

11. You seem to be a miser who loves to horde money.
    - (a) 1
    - (b) 2
    - (c) 4
    - (d) None

12. Air is composed of only a small percentage of oxigen.
    - (a) 1
    - (b) 2
    - (c) 3
    - (d) 4

13. Her coching was based on instintive thinking.
    - (a) 1
    - (b) 2
    - (c) 3
    - (d) None

DIRECTIONS (Qs. 14 to 17): The sentences given below may or may not contain an error. If there is an error, choose that part of the sentence that contains error. If there is no error, choose 'd'.

14. You'd best take a taxi (a)/ otherwise (b)/ you'll be late. (c)/ No error (d)

15. She knows (a)/some new medicine (b)/ for cure cancer. (c)/No error (d)

16. He uses various (a)/techniques to (b)/ reduce stress. (c)/No error (d)

17. He fell off (a)/the ladder (b)/ while try to reach the terrace. (c)/ No error (d)

DIRECTIONS (Qs. 18 to 30): Read the sentences given below and fill in the blanks with the most appropriate options given below.

18. _____grade to the next level of technology.
    - (a) Up
    - (b) Down
    - (c) Dis
    - (d) Un

19. Her salary was not _____to help her repay her loans.
    - (a) full
    - (b) complete
    - (c) enough
    - (d) more

20. This liquid kills germs, it is an_____.
    - (a) interseptic
    - (b) anti-septic
    - (c) imseptic
    - (d) in-septic

21. The whole drama came to an ___.
    - (a) ending
    - (b) end
    - (c) new juncture
    - (d) climax

22. You must _____out of business.
    - (a) go
    - (b) come
    - (c) decide
    - (d) keep

23. It's too late, you don't have a choice now. Don't you know that_______?
    - (a) beggars can't be choosers
    - (b) paupers can't choose
    - (c) hobson's choice
    - (d) you can't speak of the devil

24. I will start up a new enterprise that will help me to complete my other project, too. This way I will, __________
    - (a) kill two birds with one stone.
    - (b) do my business peacefully.
    - (c) make a piece of cake.
    - (d) wouldn't be caught dead.

25. It takes ______to tango.
    - (a) two
    - (b) all
    - (c) togetherness
    - (d) a lot

26. He was trying to find out the details of his case which backfired; and curiosity killed the________.
    (a) cat   (b) mouse
    (c) dog   (d) Goose

27. These tickets should be ______us when we go for the show.
    (a) between   (b) with
    (c) amongst   (d) bought

28. This parcel ____________delivered by tomorrow afternoon.
    (a) should have been
    (b) should be
    (c) should be doing
    (d) could be

29. That painting doesn't seem to be real. It________ an imitation.
    (a) could be   (b) must
    (c) could have   (d) may

30. I saw her crying. She must be really ______.
    (a) angry   (b) upset
    (c) annoyed   (d) gay

DIRECTIONS (Qs. 31 to 35): Read the passage given below and answer the questions that follow. Choose the answers from the options given below.

RR Public School, DD Puram dedicated a month to recognise and acknowledge the noble work of doctors. The initiative was undertaken to pay tribute to the hard work of the legendary physician and the second chief minister of West Bengal, Dr. Bidhan Chandra Roy, whose birthday is celebrated as the Doctor's Day.

A special assembly was conducted where Dr.Tarikh, Professor and Head of the Department of Paediatrics, L. L. Medical College threw light on the importance of hygiene and health. He also briefed students about common diseases and ways to keep them at bay in the current weather.

31. Which day is celebrated as the Doctor's Day?
    (a) 24th October
    (b) Dr. Bidhan Chandra Roy's birthday
    (c) Dr. A.P.J. Kalam's birthday
    (d) Dr. Radhakrishnan's birthday

32. What do you mean by legendary?
    (a) Great   (b) Best
    (c) Worst   (d) Well-known

33. What is meant by 'keep them at bay'?
    (a) Keeping handy
    (b) Keep them close by
    (c) Maintain a distance
    (d) To prevent something from coming near you

34. Paediatricians treat ________.
    (a) children
    (b) feet
    (c) legs
    (d) pulmonary system

35. Why do you think hygiene is important?
    (a) To prevent development of infections and illnesses.
    (b) To maintain a good life standard.
    (c) To prevent body odour.
    (d) All of these

DIRECTIONS (Qs. 36 to 40): Read the passage given below and answer the questions from the options given below.

(1) A survey was conducted on student preferences with respect to the most popular means of

communication among them. Surprisingly, the student didn't seen much interested in traditional means of communication. Only 7% were interestedin writing letter to their friends or kins as compared to those who preferred e-mails.

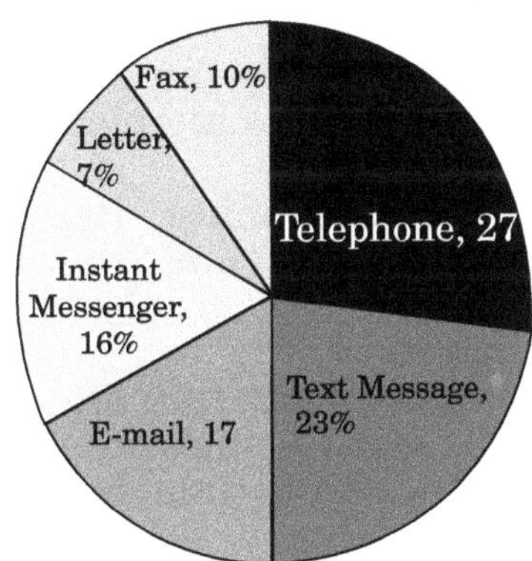

(2) However, the chief competition is between users of Instant Messenger and those of Emails. The users fo fax line as a medium of communication are only margin. There are supporters of text messaging also. Overall, the survey has a mixed response from the students.

(3) The student informed that out of the choices given in the survey questionnaire, they have indicated the most preferred option. But, most of the students are of the view that video calling need to be mentioned in the questionnaire as it is the most effective and most popular means of communication. Further, voice messages are teh second most preferred means of communication.

36. Which means of communication is liked by exactly one-tenth of the student?

(a) Letter   (b) Fax

(c) E-mail   (d) Letters

37. How much of the student prefer either of telephones or text messages as medium of communication?

(a) Option 1 

(b) Option 2

(c) Option 3

(d) Option 4

38. What is the overall response of the student to the survey?
(a) Biased
(b) Unbiased
(c) Mixed
(d) None of these

39. What is the correct order of the medium of communication is decreasing order of preference?
(a) Voice message, Text message, Instant messager, Fax
(b) Text message, Instant messenger, Voice message, Fax
(c) Instant Messenger, Fax, Voice message, Text message
(d) Text message, Instant Messenger, Fas, Voice message

40. Pick out the word or phrase from the passage which means opposite to 'gradual' (used in Para 2).
(a) Chief   (b) Instant
(c) Marginal   (d) Mixed

DIRECTIONS (Qs. 41 to 50): Choose the most appropriate option to complete the dialogues given below.

---

41. Teacher: Have you finished writing your exam?
Student: ___________________
   (a) 5 more minutes are required.
   (b) You can take the paper from the other students.
   (c) Please, can I get 5 more minutes?
   (d) Can't you give me 5 more minutes?

42. Sahil: I am taking my children to the museum tomorrow. Do you want to send your kids?
Samir: Great! But they have to be picked up from school.
Sahil: ___________________
   (a) You pick them up on time.
   (b) That's okay we can go in a car.
   (c) That's not a problem, I can pick them up.
   (d) Then see you tomorrow.

43. Rahim: We are going out for a week; can you water my plants in my absence?
Neighbour: ___________________
   (a) I can't. That's not my job.
   (b) Sure, I'd love to.
   (c) I will come with you.
   (d) It's not that easy.

44. Snehlata: Thank you for your warm hospitality.
Dennis: ___________________
   (a) I am generally hospitable.
   (b) It was nothing at all. It was pleasure being with you.
   (c) I will come with you.
   (d) Only I can tell how boring it was.

45. **Converstation at a shop**
Customer: Do you deal in ethnic wear also?
Salesman: ___________________
   (a) Yes. We have ethnic wear from all parts of the world.
   (b) That's good can you tell me what is that?
   (c) Of course. But our jeans are the best.
   (d) I'll just get them from the other shop.

46. Avi: Will you take my photograph, Mr. George?
Mr. George: ___________________
   (a) Of course not, it is not such a pleasure.
   (b) Yes, please buy me a camera.
   (c) Of course. It is my pleasure.
   (d) Thank you.

47. Adrian: Good evening, Bob. You have come just on time.
Bob: ___________________
   (a) I had to.
   (b) Thanks for inviting me.
   (c) I was going somewhere else.
   (d) I did not have time, but still I came.

48. Mr. Morgan: Your house is very beautiful
Brian: ___________________
   (a) Excuse me, it is beautiful.
   (b) Thank you for your praise.
   (c) Of course! It is beautiful.
   (d) No, it is not so beautiful.

At the entertainment park

Good evening. You are welcome. The entrance fee for each person is Rs. 300.
Bimal: (49)___________________?

Yes, Sir. Let me finish what I am going to say. For the fees that we charge, we give a welcome drink along with snacks.

Bimal: I see, where can we get the (50) ___________________?

49. (a) It is strange that you charge us before we enter.
   (b) Of course, you can't charge entrance fees.
   (c) Sorry, I will not pay you entrance fees.
   (d) It is beyond my capacity to understand what you are saying.

50. (a) food   (b) drinks
   (c) place to sit (d) exit

MATHEMATICS

OLYMPIAD
Mock Test 1

Name : _________

Number of Questions : 50

Max. Marks : 50

Time : 2 Hours

There is no negative marking in the test.

1. What should be placed in the empty space $\underset{\smile}{?}$ so that the sum of the fractions on each side of the triangle is same ?

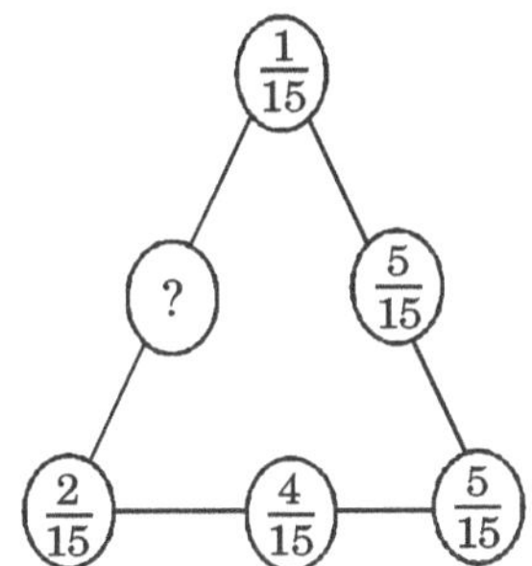

   (a) $\dfrac{7}{15}$
   (b) $\dfrac{9}{15}$
   (c) $\dfrac{6}{15}$
   (d) $\dfrac{8}{15}$

2. Out of $-7, 5, -3, 1, 4, 7$ find a pair whose sum is -2 and 2 respectively?
   (a) $(-3, 1)$ and $(-5, 7)$
   (b) $(7, 4)$ and $(-5, -3)$
   (c) $(-7, 5)$ and $(4, -3)$
   (d) $(-3, -7)$ and $(1, 4)$

3. The product of $\left(\dfrac{4p}{5} - 3\right)$ and $\left(\dfrac{5p}{8} - 6\right)$ is

   (a) $\dfrac{p^2}{2} + \dfrac{267}{40}p - 18$

   (b) $\dfrac{p^2}{2} - \dfrac{267}{40}p - 18$

   (c) $\dfrac{p^2}{2} + \dfrac{267}{40}p + 18$

   (d) $\dfrac{p^2}{2} - \dfrac{267}{40}p + 18$

4. 'n' litres of water was poured into a tank and it was still e% empty. How much water must be poured into the tank in order to fill it to the brim?

   (a) $\dfrac{ne}{100+e}$
   (b) $\dfrac{100-e}{ne}$
   (c) $\dfrac{ne}{100-e}$
   (d) $\dfrac{100+e}{ne}$

5. If $\div$ means $+$, $-$ means $\div$, $\times$ means $-$ and $+$ means $\times$, then

   $$\dfrac{(36\times4)-8\times4}{4+8\times2+16\div1} = ?$$

   (a) 0
   (b) 8
   (c) 12
   (d) 16

6. The points, P, Q, R, S, T, U, A and B on the number line are such that, TR = RS = SU and AP = PQ = QB. Name the rational numbers

represented by P, Q, R and S.

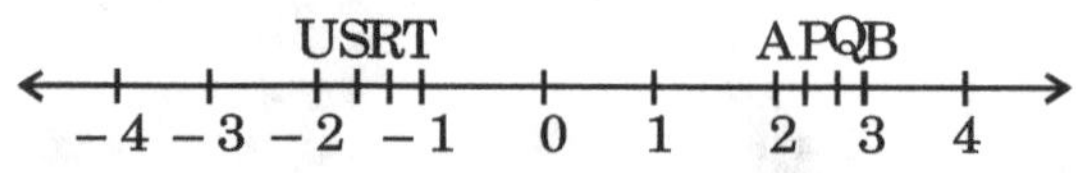

(a) $\dfrac{7}{3}, \dfrac{8}{3}, \dfrac{-4}{3}, \dfrac{-5}{3}$

(b) $\dfrac{-7}{3}, \dfrac{-8}{3}, \dfrac{-4}{3}, \dfrac{-5}{3}$

(c) $\dfrac{-7}{3}, \dfrac{-8}{3}, \dfrac{4}{3}, \dfrac{5}{3}$

(d) $\dfrac{7}{3}, \dfrac{8}{3}, \dfrac{4}{3}, \dfrac{5}{3}$

7. If $2805 \div 2.55 = 1100$,
   then $280.5 \div 25.5 =$ _____
   (a) 1.1   (b) 1.01
   (c) 0.11   (d) 11

8. A shopkeeper sold two watches for ₹ 425 each, gaining 10% on one and losing 10% on the other. Then, he
   (a) neither gains nor loses
   (b) gains 1%
   (c) loses 1%
   (d) None of these

9. The difference between circumference and radius of a circle is 37 m. The circumference of that circle is
   (a) 7 m   (b) 44 m
   (c) 154 m   (d) None of these

10. Mean of following frequency distribution table is :

Ages in years	14	15	16	17	18
No. of boys	5	8	15	10	2

   (a) 15.9 yrs   (b) 17 yrs
   (c) 14.9 yrs   (d) 16.9 yrs

11. In the figure CD is parallel to AB. The value of y is :

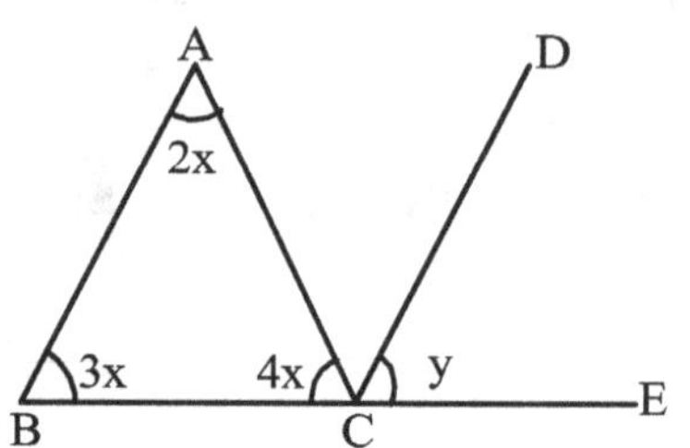

   (a) 50°   (b) 60°
   (c) 55°   (d) 65°

12. If $\dfrac{x-1}{x+1} = \dfrac{5}{7}$, then the values of x is.
   (a) 8   (b) 7
   (c) 6   (d) 9

13. In the given figure, it is given that $l \parallel m$, t is a transversal. Then the value of x is

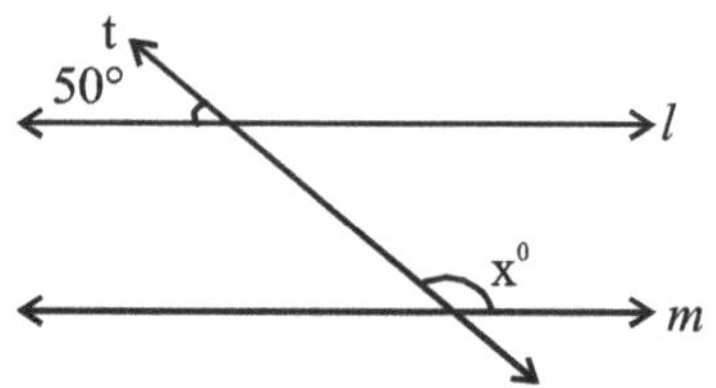

   (a) 130°   (b) 50°
   (c) 120°   (d) None of these

14. If the radii of two concentric circles are 15 cm and 13 cm respectively, then the area of the circulating ring in sq. cm will be
   (a) 176   (b) 178
   (c) 180   (d) 200

15. If Ram used 3 litres of oil daily, what per cent of oil in the 36 litre tank would be used in 10 days?
   (a) 83.33%   (b) 85%
   (c) 75.75%   (d) 73.33%

16. A man can row at 8 kmph in still water. If the river is running at 2 kmph, it takes him 48 minutes to row to a place and back. How far is the place ?
    (a) 1 km   (b) 2 km
    (c) 3 km   (d) 4 km

17. Consider the statements given below :
    (i)   A set of numbers can have more than one mode.
    (ii) Median is always equal to mean
    (iii) While drawing a bar graph, scale is not of much importance.
    (iv) In a given data, arranged in ascending or descending order the median gives us the middle observation.
    (v)   The data $6, 4, 3, 8, 9, 12, 13, 9$ has mean 9.

    Which of the above statements is/ are correct?
    (a) only (iv) and (v)
    (b) only (i) and (iv)
    (c) only (ii), (iii) and (v)
    (d) All the statements are correct

18. Which of the following statements is/are correct about integers?
    (i)   For every integer a, we have $a \div 1 = a$.
    (ii) For all non-zero integers a and b, $a \times b$ is always greater than either a or b.
    (iii) The greater the integer, the lesser is its negative.
    (a) (i) & (ii)   (b) (i) (ii) & (iii)
    (c) (ii) & (iii)   (d) (i) & (iii)

19. The median of the following data $46, 64, 87, 41, 58, 77, 35, 90, 55, 33, 92$ is
    (a) 87   (b) 77
    (c) 58   (d) 60.2

20. Which of the following statement is true?
    (a) If in a triangle, two angles are equal to $60°$, then it is equilateral.
    (b) If the angles of a triangle are in the ratio $1: 1: 2$ then it is a right angled isosceles triangle.
    (c) If the angles of a triangle are in the ratio $1: 2 : 3$ then it is a right angled triangle.
    (d) All the given statements are true.

21. By what rational number should we multiply $\dfrac{-15}{56}$ to get $\dfrac{-5}{7}$.
    (a) $\dfrac{-3}{8}$ (b) $\dfrac{3}{8}$
    (c) $\dfrac{8}{3}$ (d) $\dfrac{-8}{3}$

22. Ram and Shyam are ranked 13th and 14th respectively in a class of 23. What are their ranks from the last respectively?
    (a) $10^{th} : 11^{th}$
    (b) $11^{th}; 12^{th}$
    (c) $11^{th} ; 10^{th}$
    (d) None of these

23. Match column-I with column-II and select the correct answer using the code given below the columns.

| **Column-I** | **Column-II** |
| (Expression) | (Coefficient of x) |

(A) $4x - 3y$ (p) y^2
(B) $8 - x + y$ (q) -1
(C) $y^2 x - y$ (r) $-5z$
(D) $2z - 5xz$ (s) 4

(a) $A \to (s), B \to (r), C \to (p), D \to (q)$

(b) $A \to (p), B \to (q), C \to (r), D \to (s)$

(c) $A \to (s), B \to (q), C \to (p), D \to (r)$

(d) None of these

24. In $\triangle ABC$, $AD \perp BC$, $\angle B = \angle C$ and $AB = AC$. State by which property $\triangle ADB \cong \triangle ADC$?
(a) SAS property
(b) SSS property
(c) RHS property
(d) ASA property

25. The mean of first 10 natural numbers is

(a) $\dfrac{5}{2}$ (b) $\dfrac{11}{2}$

(c) $\dfrac{13}{2}$ (d) 5

26. Sarita is in 11th place from the top in a group of 45 girls. If we start counting from the bottom, what will be her place?
(a) 36th
(b) 34th
(c) 35th
(d) Cannot be determined

27. Which of the following figures has only one line of symmetry?

(a)    (b)

(c) 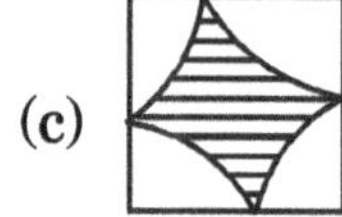   (d) 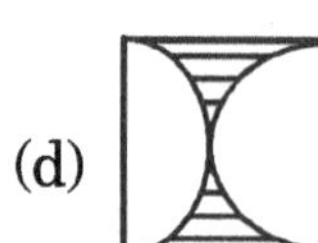

28. The total cost of three prizes is ₹ 2550. If the value of second prize is $\dfrac{3}{4}$ th of the first and the value of 3rd prize is $\dfrac{1}{2}$ of the second prize, find the value of first prize.
(a) ₹ 900   (b) ₹ 1500
(c) ₹ 1200   (d) ₹ 450

29. At what rate of interest per annum will a sum double itself in 8 years, if calculated as per Simple Interest formula.

(a) 25%   (b) $6\dfrac{1}{4}\%$

(c) $12\dfrac{1}{2}\%$ (d) None of these

30. Choose the simplest form of ? $(x^{-1} + y^{-1})^{-1}$.

(a) $x + y$ (b) $\dfrac{xy}{x + y}$

(c) xy (d) $\dfrac{x + y}{xy}$

31. Perimeter of an equilateral triangle is $\left(x + \dfrac{y}{2} + \dfrac{z}{3} \right)$ cm. Choose the length of its side.

(a) $\left(3x + \dfrac{y}{2} + z\right)$ cm

(b) $\left(2x + y + \dfrac{2z}{3}\right)$ cm

(c) $\left(\dfrac{x}{3} + \dfrac{y}{6} + \dfrac{z}{9}\right)$ cm

(d) $\left(\dfrac{x}{4} + \dfrac{y}{8} + \dfrac{z}{12}\right)$ cm

32. In the following figure if AB = AC, then find $\angle x$.

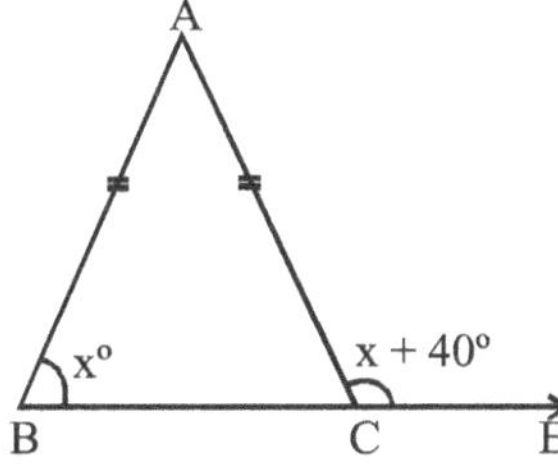

(a) 80°　　　　　　(b) 70°
(c) 60°　　　　　　(d) 110°

33. The perimeter of a trapezium is 52 cm and its both non-parallel sides are equal to 10 cm and its altitude is 8 cm. Its area is
(a) 128 cm^2　　　(b) 112 cm^2
(c) 118 cm^2　　　(d) 124 cm^2

34. Which of the following statements is/are correct?
(i) A rational number is said to be positive if its numerator and denominator are either both positive integers or both negative integers.
(ii) In the number line for integers, every number on the right is greater than all the numbers on its left.
(iii) Associative property holds both in addition and in subtraction.
(a) (i) only
(b) Either (i) & (iii) or (ii)
(c) (i), (ii) & (iii)
(d) (i) & (ii)

35. A three centimetre sized cube has been painted red on all its sides. It is cut into one centimetre sized cubes. How many cubes will be there with only one side painted red ?
(a) 4　　　　　　　(b) 6
(c) 1　　　　　　　(d) 9

36. What should be added to $-3p + 7q - 16$ to get the sum 8?
(a) 8　　　　　　　　　(b) $-3p + 7q + 8$
(c) $3p - 7q + 8$　　(d) $3p - 7q + 24$

37. In a quadrilateral PQRS, if $\angle P = \angle R = 100°$ and $\angle S = 75°$ What is the measure of $\angle Q$?
(a) 50°　　　　　　　(b) 85°
(c) 120°　　　　　　(d) 360°

38. In $6(2a - 1) + 8 = 14$, the value of 'a' is
(a) –1　　　　　　　(b) $3\dfrac{1}{12}$

(c) $1\dfrac{3}{12}$　　　　　　(d) +1

39. On solving $(x - y)(x + y) + (y - z)(y + z) + (z - x)(z + x)$
(a) 0　　　　　　　(b) 1
(c) -1　　　　　　(d) 2

40. Count the number of cubes in the given figure.

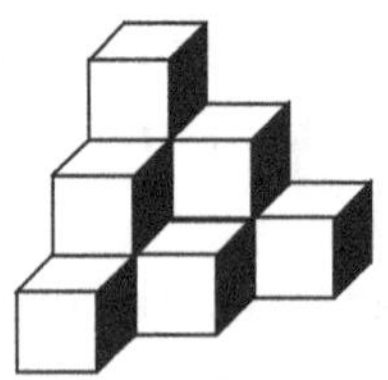

(a) 14   (b) 12
(c) 10   (d) 8

41. The ratio of two numbers is a : b. If one of them is x, then other is

(a) $\dfrac{ab}{x}$ (b) $\dfrac{b}{ax}$

(c) $\dfrac{b}{a+b}x$ (d) $\dfrac{bx}{a}$

42. **Assertion (A) :** The quotient of two integers is always a rational numbers.

Reason (R) : $\dfrac{1}{0}$ is not rational number.

(a) A is true and R is correct explanation of A.

(b) A is false and R is the correct explanation of A.

(c) A is true and R is false.

(d) Both A and R are false.

43. If ab = 63, bc = 99 and ca = 77 then select option correctly showing the value of a.

(a) 4   (b) 5
(c) 6   (d) 7

44. A plot is in the form of a rectangle ABCD having semi-circle on BC as shown in figure. The semi-circle portion is grassy while the remaining plot is without grass. The area of the plot without grass where AB = 60 m and BC = 28 m is

:

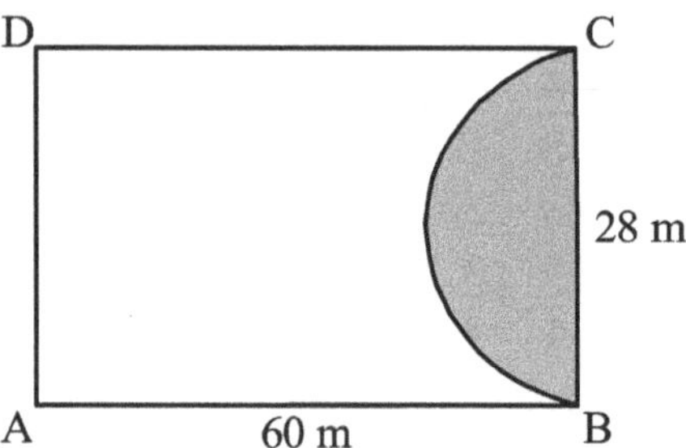

(a) 3722 m^2

(b) 1372 m^2

(c) 926 m^2

(d) None of these

45. In a $\triangle$PQR, PQ = PR and $\angle$Q is twice that of $\angle$P. Then $\angle$Q =

(a) 72°   (b) 36°
(c) 144°   (d) 108°

46. How many bricks 20 cm by 10 cm will be needed to pave the floor of a room 25 m long and 16 m wide?

(a) 18000   (b) 20000
(c) 22000   (d) 24000

47. Area of shaded square formed by joining the mid-points of the sides of a square with area 16 m^2 is

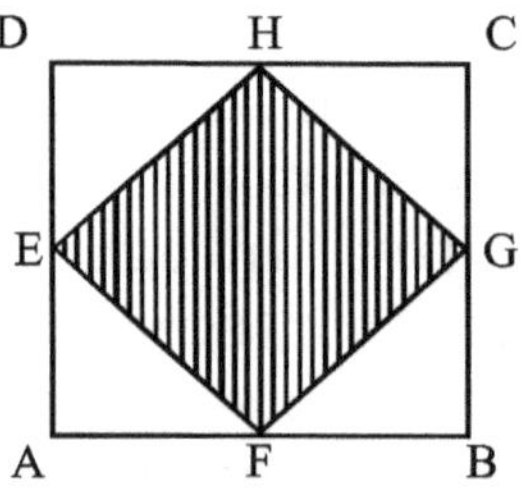

(a) 16 m^2 (b) 4 m^2
(c) 10 m^2 (d) 8 m^2

DIRECTIONS (Qs. 48 to 50) : Read the following graph and answer the questions given below :

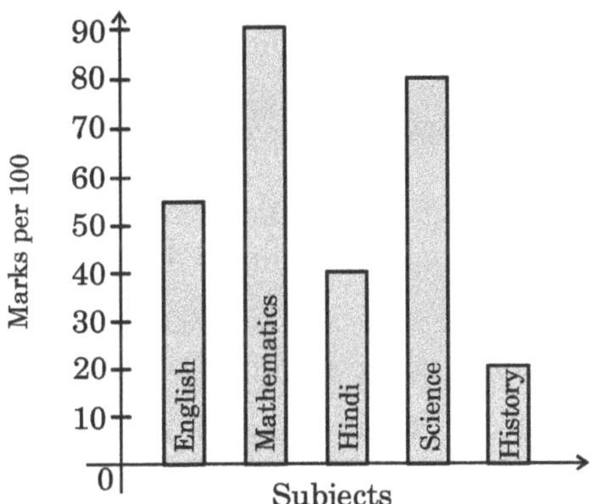

48. At what subject is the student sharp ?

    (a) English

    (b) Mathematics

    (c) Science

    (d) History

49. What is the percentage obtained by the student ?

    (a) 80%

    (b) 63%

    (c) 57%

    (d) 90%

50. What is the ratio of the highest marks to the lowest marks obtained by the student ?

    (a) 2 : 11

    (b) 9 : 2

    (c) 2 : 9

    (d) 11 : 2

OLYMPIAD
Mock Test 2

Name : _________

Number of Questions : 50

There is no negative marking in the test.

Max. Marks : 50

Time : 2 Hours

1. Choose the correct option whether the statements are true (T) or false (F).
   (i) Mean of the data is always from the given data.
   (ii) Median of the data may or may not be from the given data.
   (iii) Mode of the data is always from the given data.
   (a) FFT   (b) FTT
   (c) TFT   (d) FTF

2. Reshma uses $\frac{3}{4}$m of cloth to stitch a shirt. Number of shirts she can make with $2\frac{1}{4}$m cloth is:
   (a) 4   (b) 2
   (c) 5   (d) 3

3. Identify the simplest value of $7 - 7 \times 7 + 7 \div 7$.
   (a) 1   (b) -41
   (c) 2   (d) -5

4. Sum of four consecutive odd numbers is 144. What is the product of the greatest and the smallest number?
   (a) 1287   (b) 1295
   (c) 1221   (d) 1365

5. In the given figure, it is given that AB || CD. ∠BAO = 108° and ∠OCD = 120° then ∠AOC =

   (a) 120°   (b) 72°
   (c) 132°   (d) 150°

6. If angles P, Q, R and S of the quadrilateral PQRS, taken in order, are in the ratio 3 : 7 : 6 : 4, then PQRS is a
   (a) rhombus
   (b) parallelogram
   (c) trapezium
   (d) kite

7. Walking $\frac{7}{6}$th of his usual rate, a boy reaches his school 4 minutes early. Find his usual time to reach the school.
   (a) 40 min.   (b) 32 min.
   (c) 28 min.   (d) 48 min.

8. If $\frac{2}{x} + 3y = 15$ and $\frac{5}{x} - 4y = 3$, then value of x is

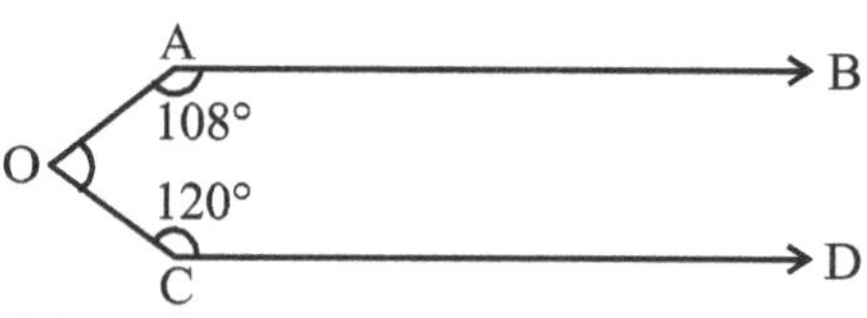

   (a) 1/2   (b) 2
   (c) 1/3   (d) 3

9. The figure having only one line of symmetry in the following is

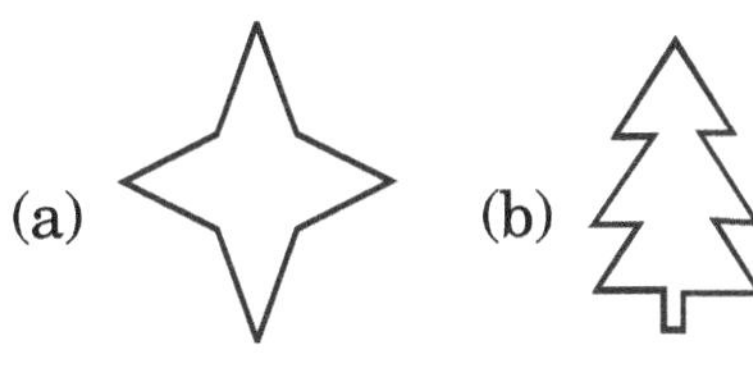

(a)   (b)

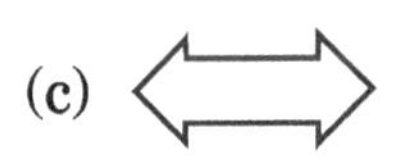

(c)   (d)

(a) 60   (b) 8

(c) 25   (d) 30

10. In a class of 60, the number of girls are twice that of boys. Kamal ranked seventeenth from the top. If there are nine girls ahead of Kamal, how many boys are after him in rank?

(a) 3   (b) 7

(c) 12   (d) 23

11. The sum of two rational numbers is –8. If one of the rational numbers is $\dfrac{-17}{9}$, then the other is:

(a) $\dfrac{-27}{7}$ (b) $\dfrac{-55}{9}$

(c) $\dfrac{-46}{7}$ (d) $\dfrac{9}{55}$

12. Two vessels contain mixtures of water and milk in the ratio 1 : 2 and 2 : 5. These mixtures of two vessels are mixed in the ratio 1 : 4. The ratio of water and milk in the resulting mixture is :

(a) 32 : 17   (b) 41 : 79

(c) 31 : 74   (d) 47 : 74

13. If the rent for grazing 40 cows for 20 days is ₹370, how many cows can graze for ₹111 for 30 days ?

14. In triangle ABC, if AB = AC and AB = (7 x – 5) cm, BC = (4x + 9) cm and CA = (3x + 23) cm. Find the value of BC.

(a) 44 cm   (b) 40 cm

(c) 37 cm   (d) 32 cm

15. The greatest possible length which can be used to measure exactly the lengths 4 m 95 cm, 9 m and 16 m 65 cm is:

(a) 45 cm   (b) 96 cm

(c) 1665 cm   (d) 45 m

16. If a commission of 20% is given on retail price, the profit is 60%. The profit percentage when the commission is increased by 5% of the retail price will be:

(a) 27%   (b) 44%

(c) 50%   (d) 78%

17. First, third and the fourth terms of a proportion are 6, 12 and 36. Then the second term is

(a) 12   (b) 18

(c) 16   (d) 108

18. In what time will ₹ 72 become ₹ 81 at $6\dfrac{1}{4}\%$ p.a. SI?

(a) $1\dfrac{1}{2}$ year   (b) $2\dfrac{1}{2}$ years

(c) 2 years   (d) None of these

19. Rakesh is on 9th position from upwards and on 38th position from downwards in a class. How many students are in the class?

(a) 47   (b) 45

(c) 46   (d) 48

20. The value of $25x^2 + 16y^2 + 40xy$ at $x = 1$ and $y = -1$ is

(a) 81   (b) -49

(c) 1   (d) None of these

21. A bag contains an equal number of one rupees, 50 paise and 25 paise coins, respectively. If the total value is ₹ 35, how many coins of each type are there?

(a) 20   (b) 5

(c) 17   (d) 23

22. What value of y would make expressions $4y + 5$ and $-y + 15$ equal?

(a) 1   (b) -2

(c) 2   (d) 1

23. **Assertion (A) :** Every whole number is a natural number.

Reason (R) : 0 is not a natural number.

(a) A is false and R is the correct explanation of A.

(b) A is true and R is the correct explanation of A.

(c) A is true and R is false.

(d) Both A and R are true.

24. Indian Cricket Team won 4 more matches than it lost with New Zealand. If it won $\dfrac{3}{5}$ of its total matches, how many matches did India play?

(a) 8   (b) 12

(c) 16   (d) 20

25. At what rate percent by simple interest, will a sum of money double itself in 5 years 4 months ?

(a) 10%   (b) 25%

(c) 20.01%   (d) 18.75%

26. If the numerator of a fraction be increased by 15% and its denominator be diminished by 8%, the value of the fraction is $\dfrac{15}{16}$. The original fraction is:

(a) $\dfrac{2}{3}$ (b) $\dfrac{3}{4}$

(c) $\dfrac{7}{4}$ (d) $\dfrac{9}{2}$

27. Which of the following are true about algebraic expressions?

(i) Algebraic expressions are formed from variable and constants.

(ii) Expressions are made up of terms.

(iii) A term is a product of factors.

(iv) The coefficient is the numerical factor in the term.

(a) i and ii   (b) All are correct

(c) i & iii only   (d) iii & iv only

28. If cost price of 110 apples is equal to the selling price of 100 apples, then what is the profit percentage?

(a) 0   (b) 5

(c) 10   (d) 25

29. Select from the alternatives the box that can be formed by folding the sheet shown in figure (X)

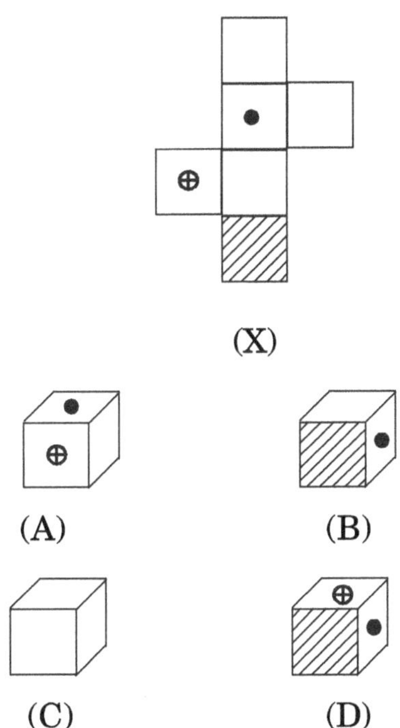

(X)

(A)   (B)

(C)   (D)

(a) A only

(b) A and C only

(c) A , C and D only

(d) A, B, C and D

30. Which of the following is/are true ?

(i) Every natural number is a whole number and vice-versa.

(ii) Every negative integer is less than zero.

(iii) 0 is a whole number and it is neither negative nor positive.

(a) (i), (ii) & (iii)

(b) (ii) & (iii)

(c) (i) & (ii)

(d) None of these

DIRECTIONS (Qs. 31 to 33) : Read the graph carefully and answer the following questions.

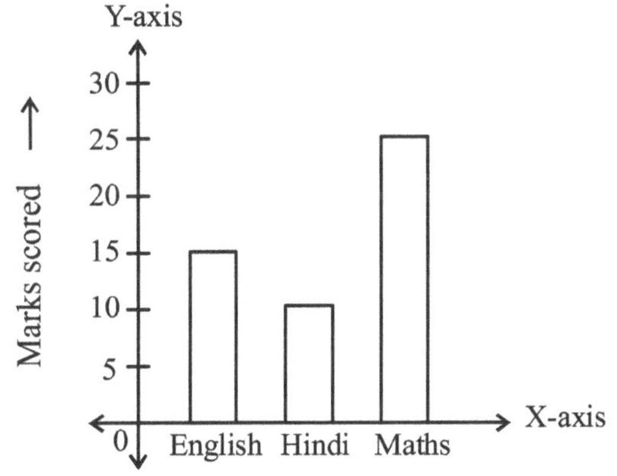

31. The horizontal line in the graph is called

(a) X-axis   (b) Y-axis

(c) line   (d) None of these

32. The vertical line in the graph is called

(a) Y-axis   (b) X-axis

(c) ray   (d) None of these

33. Highest marks are scored in which subject?

(a) English   (b) Hindi

(c) Maths   (d) None of these

34. The mean of 10 observations was calculated as 40. It was detected on re-checking that the value of 45 was wrongly copied as 15. The correct mean is:

(a) 96 (b) 52 (c) 43 (d) 27

35. The product of two decimals is 1.5008. If one of them is 0.56, what is the other ?

(a) 2.86 (b) 26.8

(c) 2.68 (d) 0.268

36. A car is purchased for ₹ 80,000. Its value depreciates every year by 20%. The value of the car at the end of 2 years will be:

(a) ₹ 51,200 (b) ₹ 37,160

(c) ₹ 24,120 (d) ₹ 47,100

37. The simple interest on ₹ 2400 at 6% per annum for 146 days will be:

(a) ₹ 97.40 (b) ₹ 42.60

(c) ₹ 82.10 (d) ₹ 57.60

38. Four circles of radius 1 cm each are placed in such a way on a plane paper that each touches the other. Find the area (cm^2) of the space left in between the four circles.

$$(\pi = 3.16)$$

(a) 0.82 (b) 0.84

(c) 0.86 (d) 0.88

39. Arrange the following numbers in descending order. $-2, \dfrac{4}{-5}, \dfrac{-11}{20}, \dfrac{3}{4}$

(a) $\dfrac{3}{4} > -2 > \dfrac{-11}{20} > \dfrac{4}{-5}$

(b) $\dfrac{3}{4} > \dfrac{-11}{20} > \dfrac{4}{-5} > -2$

(c) $\dfrac{3}{4} > \dfrac{4}{-5} > -2 > \dfrac{-11}{20}$

(d) $\dfrac{3}{4} > \dfrac{4}{-5} > \dfrac{-11}{20} > -2$

40. The mean of x, $x + 3$, $x + 6$, $x + 9$ and $x + 12$ is

(a) $x + 6$ (b) $x + 3$

(c) $x + 9$ (d) $x + 12$

41. In a trapezium whose parallel sides measure 24 cm and 15 cm and the distance between them is 10 cm. Find the area of trapezium.

(a) 215 cm^2 (b) 205 cm^2

(c) 195 cm^2 (d) 295 cm^2

42. A circular grass plot, whose diameter is 70 m, contains a gravel walk 5 m wide round it, 15 m from the edge. The cost to turf the grass plot at ₹ 2 per m^2 will be

(a) ₹ 5300 (b) ₹ 6600

(c) ₹ 7100 (d) ₹ 8760

43. If x and 8 are in the same ratio as that of 8 and 16, then x is:

(a) 6 (b) 7

(c) 4 (d) 8

44. ₹ 800 amounts to ₹ 920 in 3 years at simple interest. If the interest is increased by 3%, it would amount to:

(a) ₹ 120 (b) ₹ 192

(c) ₹ 800 (d) ₹ 992

45. Mean of ages of 20 students is 10 years. 5 students with mean age of 15 years leave the class. Mean of ages of the remaining students will be:

(a) 4 yrs (b) 5.66 yrs

(c) 6.25 yrs (d) 8.33 yrs

46. Five students were tested in English and Hindi and the marks obtained by them were as under:

	A	B	C	D	E
English	55	60	82	65	75
Hindi	21	25	86	90	99

Which subject has a better median value:

(a) Hindi (b) English

(c) Both (d) None of these

PASSAGE

A rectangular park is of dimensions 90 m by 80 m. Four paths pass through the park such that two paths each of width 2 m are parallel to the breadth and two paths each of width 3 m are parallel to the length.

47. Total area of the two roads along the length is

(a) 270 m^2 (b) 810 m^2

(c) 540 m^2 (d) 504 m^2

48. Total area of the two roads along the breadth is

(a) 320 m^2 (b) 160 m^2

(c) 230 m^2 (d) 270 m^2

49. Total area of the four roads is

(a) 386 m^2 (b) 836 m^2

(c) 863 m^2 (d) 368 m^2

50. Area of the remaining portion of the park is

(a) 6364 m^2 (b) 6463 m^2

(c) 6634 m^2 (d) 6346 m^2

OLYMPIAD
Mock Test 

Name : _________

Number of Questions : 50

Max. Marks : 50

Time : 2 Hours

There is no negative marking in the test.

1. Out of a pair of complementary angles, one is two-third of the other. Find the angles.
   (a) 36°, 54°   (b) 40°, 50°
   (c) 35°, 55°   (d) 32°, 58°

2. If the mean of 26, 28, 25, x, 24 is 27, find the value of x.
   (a) 50   (b) 36
   (c) 32   (d) 18

3. Next three consecutive numbers in the pattern 11, 8, 5, 2, --, --, -- are
   (a) 0, –3, – 6
   (b) – 1, – 5, – 8
   (c) – 2, – 5, – 8
   (d) – 1, – 4, – 7

4. Simplify: $\dfrac{8}{-15}+\dfrac{7}{20}-\dfrac{-11}{35}+\dfrac{1}{5}$.

   (a) $\dfrac{-71}{149}$ (b) $\dfrac{-191}{312}$

   (c) $\dfrac{214}{224}$ (d) $\dfrac{139}{420}$

5. H.C.F. and L.C.M. of two numbers are 16 and 240, respectively. If one of the numbers is 48, then the other number will be:
   (a) 24   (b) 48
   (c) 80   (d) 96

6. Find the value of $\dfrac{3^{12+n}\times 9^{2n-7}}{3^{5n}}$

   (a) $\dfrac{1}{9}$ (b) $\dfrac{1}{2}$

   (c) 4   (d) 8

7. If A + B = 2C and C + D = 2A, then
   (a) A + C = B + D
   (b) A + C = 2D
   (c) A + D = B + C
   (d) A + C = 2B

8. In how much time would the simple interest on a certain sum be 0.125 times the Principle at 10% per annum ?
   (a) $1\dfrac{1}{4}$ Years   (b) $1\dfrac{3}{4}$ Years
   (c) $2\dfrac{1}{4}$ Years   (d) $2\dfrac{3}{4}$ Years

9. Bhanu borrowed a certain sum of money at 12% per annum for 3 years and Madhuri borrowed the same sum at 24% per annum for 10 years. Find the ratio of their amounts.

(a) $1:3$ (b) $2:1$

(c) $2:3$ (d) $2:5$

10. In the given figure, it is given that D and E are the mid-points of AB and AC respectively. If $\angle A = 80°$, $\angle C = 35°$, then $\angle EDB =$ _______

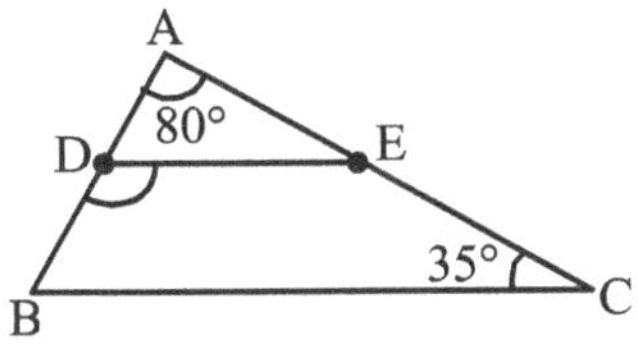

(a) $120°$ (b) $160°$

(c) $70°$ (d) $115°$

11. By what number should we multiply 4^{-3} so that the product may be equal to 64?

(a) 4^5 (b) 2^{12}

(c) 2^6 (d) None of these

12. $AB = 8$ cm, $BC = 12$ cm and $AK = 4$cm. The area of $\triangle ABC$ is :

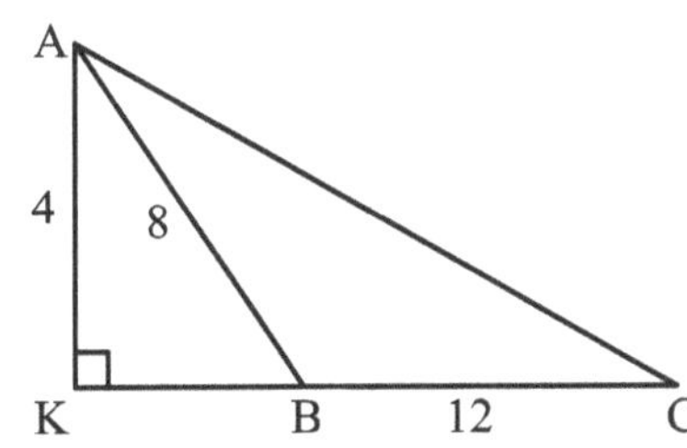

(a) 16 cm^2 (b) 12 cm^2

(c) 24 cm^2 (d) 32 cm^2

13. Kajol has ₹ 75. This is $\dfrac{3}{8}$ of the amount she earned. She earned:

(a) ₹ 140   (b) ₹ 180

(c) ₹ 200   (d) ₹ 210

14. Salary of a Person is increased by 20%, then it is decreased by 20%. Change in his salary is

(a) 4 % decrease

(b) 4 % increase

(c) 8 % decrease

(d) 20 increase

15. The smallest number of five digits exactly divisible by 16, 24, 36 and 54.

(a) 16038   (b) 10638

(c) 10236   (d) 10368

16. One litre of water is mixed with 3 litres of sugar solution containing 4% of sugar. What is the % of sugar in the solution?

(a) 4%   (b) 3%

(c) 6%   (d) None of these

17. The mean of 5 observations is 15. If mean of the first three observations is 14 and that of the last three is 17 then the third observation is

(a) 18   (b) 17

(c) 51   (d) 75

18. If each of the dimensions of a rectangle is increased by 100% its area is increased by

(a) 100%   (b) 200%

(c) 300%   (d) 400%

19. A hill, $101\dfrac{1}{3}$ m in height, has $\dfrac{1}{4}$th of its height under water. The height of the hill visible above the water is:

    (a) 104 m   (b) 89 m

    (c) 57 m   (d) 76 m

20. The ratio between two numbers is 3 : 5. If each number is increased by 4, the ratio becomes 2 : 3. The numbers are:

    (a) 9, 15   (b) 12, 20

    (c) 15, 25   (d) 18, 30

21. Choose the simplest ratio of $4^{3.5}$: 2^5 ?

    (a) 2:1   (b) 4:1

    (c) 7:5   (d) 7:10

22. If $x = -8$, then $x|x|$ equals to _____.

    (a) 64   (b) -64

    (c) 0   (d) 8

23. The angles of a quadrilateral are 1 : 4 : 2 : 3. The quadrilateral is a

    (a) parallelogram

    (b) square

    (c) trapezium

    (d) rectangle

24. A rectangle has __________

    (a) one line of symmetry.

    (b) two lines of symmetry.

    (c) three lines of symmetry.

    (d) None of these.

25. The difference between the length and breadth of a rectangle is 23 m. If the perimeter is 206 m, then the area is

    (a) 1520 m^2 (b) 2520 m^2

    (c) 2420 m^2 (d) None of these

26. In a class test in English, 10 students scored 75 marks, 12 scored 60 marks, 8 scored 40 marks and 3 scored 30 marks. The mode for their scores is

    (a) 75   (b) 30

    (c) 60   (d) 25

27. Three dice are shown, The first two display alphabets in a certain sequence. Find that sequential rule and fill the blank spaces in the third dice from the four alternatives provided.

Sequence of letters :

A B C D E F G H I J K L M

N O P Q R S T U V W X Y Z

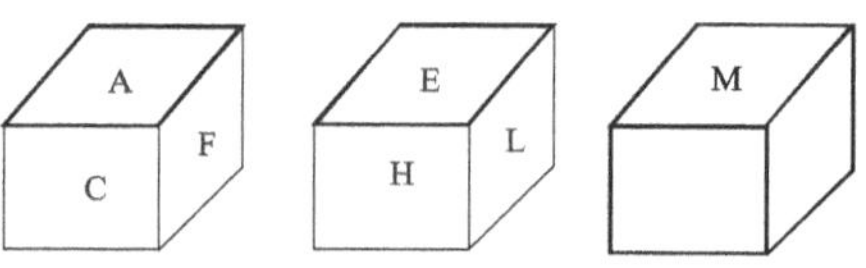

    (a) Q, L   (b) Q, V

    (c) P, S   (d) H, Q

28. The median of observations 11, 12, 14, 18, $x + 2$, 20, 22, 25, 61 arranged in ascending order is 21. The value of x is:

    (a) 17   (b) 19

    (c) 23   (d) 29

29. 1 subtracted from one-third of a number gives 1. The number is:

    (a) 6   (b) 2

    (c) 11   (d) 14

30. Sum of $\dfrac{7}{-18} + \dfrac{5}{-12} + \dfrac{-9}{-16}$ is:

    (a) $\dfrac{35}{144}$ (b) $\dfrac{-9}{49}$

    (c) $\dfrac{-35}{144}$ (d) $\dfrac{-21}{104}$

31. If the radius of two circumference of two circles is 9 : 4, the ratio of their area is.

   (a) 9 : 4 (b) 16 : 81

   (c) 81 : 16 (d) 2 : 3

32. Anmol finds that he is twelfth from the right in a line of boys and fourth from the left, how many boys should be added to the line such that there are 35 boys in the line?

   (a) 19 (b) 13

   (c) 14 (d) 20

33. $\frac{1}{4}$th of $\frac{2}{5}$th of a number is 82. What is the number ?

   (a) 410 (b) 820

   (c) 420 (d) 220

34. Value of x in $\frac{x}{4} + \frac{1}{2} = 4$ is

   (a) +28 (b) −28

   (c) +14 (d) −14

35. $42(4 + 2) = (42 \times 4) + (42 \times 2)$ is an example of

   (a) closure property

   (b) commutative property

   (c) associative property

   (d) distributive property

36. The median of the data:

   3, 11, 7, 2, 5, 9, 9, 2, 10, 15, 7

   (a) 11 (b) 7

   (c) 9 (d) 5

37. What change in percent is made in the area of a rectangle by decreasing its length and increasing its breadth by 5%?

   (a) 2.5% increase

   (b) 0.25% increase

   (c) 0.25% decrease

   (d) 2.5% decrease

38. The CP of 25 articles is equal to the SP of 20 articles. Then gain % is

   (a) 25% (b) 20%

   (c) 30% (d) 50%

39. In what time will ₹ 8000 amounts to ₹ 9620 if time period is 25% of the rate per annum?

   (a) $1\frac{1}{4}$ years (b) $2\frac{1}{4}$ years

   (c) $2\frac{1}{2}$ years (d) None of these

40. The daily consumption of milk of a family is $3\frac{1}{4}$ litres. The quantity of milk consumed by the family during the month of September 2003 is

   (a) 90 litres (b) $100\frac{1}{2}$ litres

   (c) $97\frac{1}{2}$ litres (d) none of these

41. $\frac{a}{b} = \frac{c}{d}$, then $\frac{ma + nc}{mb + nd} =$

   (a) an : bm (b) m : n

   (c) a : b (d) md : án

42. Choose the correct option, whether the statements are True (T) or False (F).

   (i) 5 is the solution of the equation $3x + 2 = 17$.

   (ii) $\dfrac{9}{5}$ is the solution of the equation $4x - 1 = 8$.

   (iii) $\dfrac{3}{2}$ is the solution of the equation $8x - 5 = 7$.

   (a) TTF   (b) FTT

   (c) TFT   (d) FTF

43. In figure, CD intersects the line AB at F, $\angle CFB = 50°$ and $\angle EFA = \angle AFD$. The measure of $\angle EFC$ is:

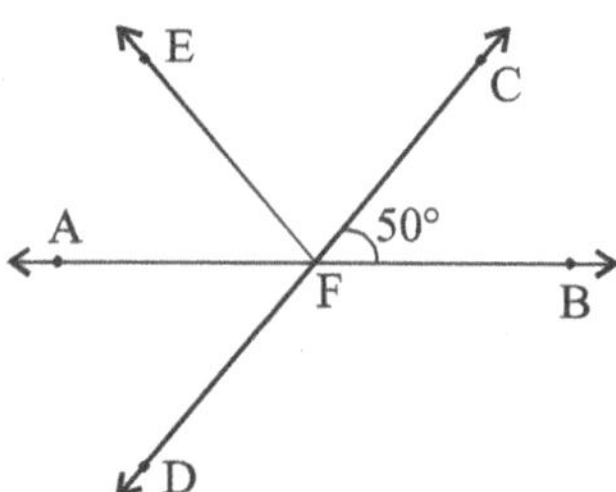

   (a) 80°   (b) 75°

   (c) 50°   (d) 180°

44. In $\triangle PQR$, PQ = PR, $\angle QPR$ is equal to

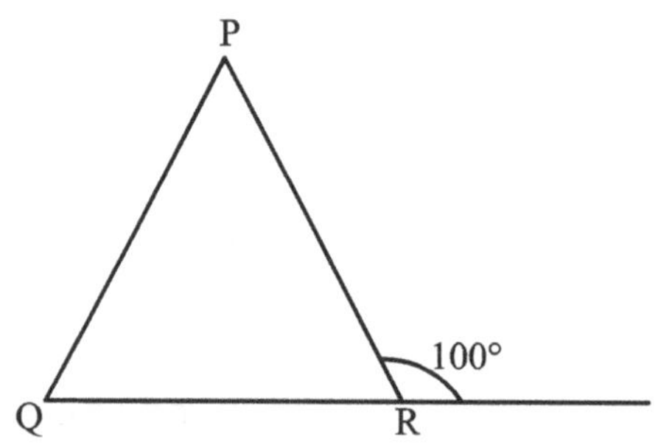

(a) 20°   (b) 30°

(c) 40°   (d) 50°

45. The area of trapezium is 600 cm^2. If the length of one of its parallel sides be 30 cm and altitude is 10 cm then the length of other side is

(a) 15 cm   (b) 10 cm

(c) 40 cm   (d) 90 cm

46. Which of the following properties are not true for a rectangle?

(a) Its diagonals are not equal.

(b) Its diagonals are perpendicular to each other.

(c) The diagonals divide the rectangle into four congruent triangles.

(d) All the above.

47. A wheel of diameter 1.54 m makes 525 revolutions to cover a distance of

(a) 2.541 km

(b) 1.564 km

(c) 980 km

(d) 550 km

DIRECTIONS (Qs. 48 to 50) : Given below is a bar graph showing the heights of six mountain peaks. Read the following graph and answer the questions given below:

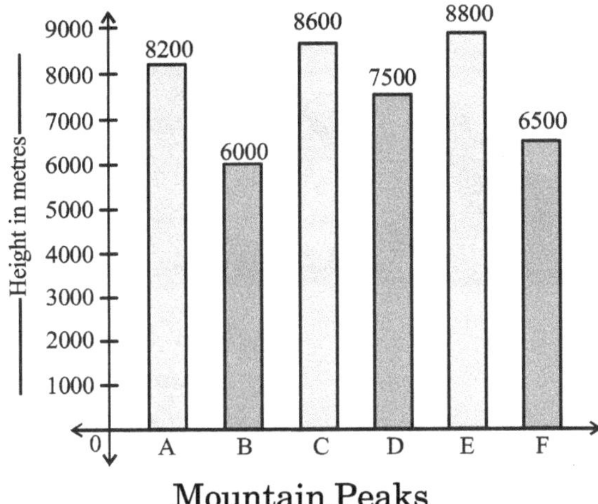

48. Write the ratio of the heights of the highest peak and the lowest peak.

   (a) 22 : 15

   (b) 15 : 22

   (c) 20 : 13

   (d) 13 : 22

49. Which peak is the second highest?

   (a) B

   (b) A

   (c) C

   (d) E

50. When the heights of the given peaks are written in ascending order, then what is the average of the middle two peaks?

   (a) 7950 m

   (b) 7560 m

   (c) 7650 m

   (d) 7850 m

OLYMPIAD
Mock Test 4

Name : ___________
Number of Questions : 50

Max. Marks : 50
Time : 2 Hours

There is no negative marking in the test.

1. If $\dfrac{x}{2} = 3$, then the value of $3x + 2$ is
   (a) 20   (b) 11
   (c) $\dfrac{13}{2}$ (d) 8

2. John borrowed ₹ 75000 from his friend and after one year returned ₹ 80000 to his friend. The interest is:
   (a) ₹ 7200   (b) ₹ 3700
   (c) ₹ 5200   (d) ₹ 5000

3. If $\dfrac{-5}{7} = \dfrac{x}{28}$, the value of x is:
   (a) 20   (b) –20
   (c) 26   (d) 42

4. A person deposits ₹ 25000 in a firm who pays an interest at the rate of 20% per annum. The income he gets, from it annually.
   (a) ₹ 3800   (b) ₹ 4800
   (c) ₹ 6400   (d) ₹ 5000

5. After spending 82% of his monthly income, Raman has ₹ 423 left with him. His monthly income is:
   (a) ₹ 1860   (b) ₹ 2780
   (c) ₹ 2210   (d) ₹ 2350

6. In a mixture of 60 litres, the ratio of milk and water is 2 : 1. What amount of water must be added to make the ratio 1 : 2?
   (a) 36 litres   (b) 60 litres
   (c) 82 litres   (d) 48 litres

7. If $3^x = 500$ then the value 3^{x-2} is
   (a) $\dfrac{100}{9}$ (b) $\dfrac{1000}{9}$
   (c) $\dfrac{500}{9}$ (d) $\dfrac{500}{3}$

8. If Meenakshee pays an interest of ₹ 1500 for 4 years on a sum of ₹ 2500, the rate of interest per annum (p.a.) is:
   (a) 13%   (b) 15%
   (c) 19%   (d) 27%

9. The product of $-2\dfrac{3}{4}$ and $5\dfrac{6}{7}$ is:
   (a) $\dfrac{28}{451}$ (b) $\dfrac{451}{28}$
   (c) $\dfrac{-28}{451}$ (d) $\dfrac{-451}{28}$

10. Divide 15 sweets between Manu and Sonu so that they get 20% and 80% of it respectively. How many sweets does each get?
    (a) M - 3 and S - 12

    (b) M - 11 and S - 4

    (c) S - 3 and M - 12

    (d) S - 11 and M - 4

11. Calculate the value of $1 - (-0.3)^3$.

    (a) 0.1027   (b) 10.27

    (c) 1.027   (d) 0.01027

12. The least number exactly divisible by 12, 15, 20 and 27 is:

    (a) 720   (b) 260

    (c) 540   (d) 940

13. The angle which exceeds its complement by 20° is

    (a) 45°   (b) 55°

    (c) 70°   (d) 110°

14. The value of $\left[\left(\dfrac{1}{4}\right)^2 - \left(\dfrac{1}{4}\right)^3\right] \times 2^6$ is

    (a) 1   (b) 2

    (c) 3   (d) 4

15. Roshan was ranked 11th from the top and 31st from the bottom in a class. How many students are there in the class?

    (a) 42   (b) 43

    (c) 41   (d) 40

16. An improper fraction is

    (a) a fraction that has the numerator less than its denominator.

    (b) a fraction in its simplest form is called an improper fraction.

    (c) a fraction that has the denominator less than its numerator.

    (d) both (a) and (c)

17. The value of $\left[(-2)^{(-2)}\right]^{(-3)}$ is

    (a) 64

    (b) 32

    (c) Cannot be determined

    (d) None of these

18. The circumference of a circle is 100 cm. What is the side of the largest square inscribed in the circle?

    (a) $\dfrac{100\sqrt{2}}{\pi}$ cm   (b) $\dfrac{50\sqrt{2}}{\pi}$ cm

    (c) $\dfrac{100}{\pi}$ cm   (d) $50\sqrt{2}$ cm

19. If p is 95% of q, then what percentage of p is q?

    (a) 105%   (b) 105.3%

    (c) 110%   (d) 115%

20. How many edges does the following figure have?

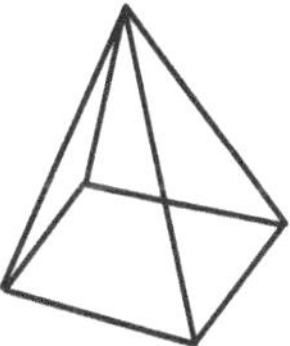

    (a) 12   (b) 8

    (c) 6   (d) 4

21. Raman is 7 ranks ahead of Suman in a class of 39. If Suman's rank is seventeenth from the bottom what is Raman's rank from the top ?

    (a) 14th   (b) 15th

    (c) 16th   (d) 17th

22. A man borrowed ₹ 8000 from a bank at 8% per annum. The amount he has to pay after $4\frac{1}{2}$ years is:

    (a) ₹ 15440   (b) ₹ 21110

    (c) ₹ 10880   (d) ₹ 16440

23. A man sells his scooter for ₹ 3000 making a profit of 20%. How much did the scooter cost him?

    (a) ₹ 1860   (b) ₹ 2270

    (c) ₹ 2200   (d) ₹ 2500

24. In the following fig. if AB = AC and BD = DC, then ∠ADC = C

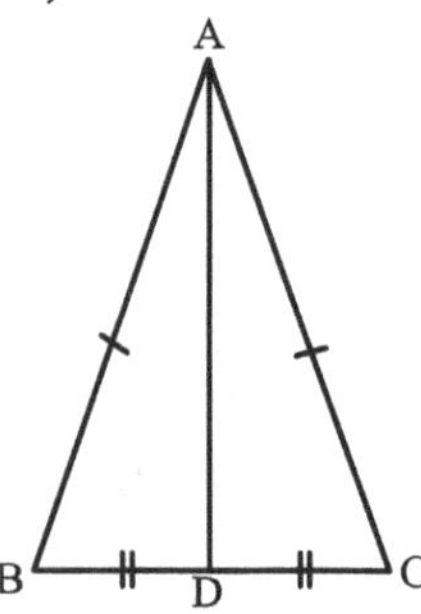

    (a) 60°

    (b) 120°

    (c) 90°

    (d) None of these

25. If the length of both diagonal of a rectangle is 10 cm whereas its length and breadth are positive integers, then the length and breadth of the rectangle are:

    (a) 8 cm, 6 cm   (b) 14 cm, 4 cm

    (c) 6 cm, 4 cm   (d) None of these

26. A : B = 2 : 3, B : C = 5 : 6, then value of A : B : C is

    (a) 15 : 10 : 18   (b) 10 : 18 : 15

    (c) 18 : 15 : 10   (d) 10 : 15 : 18

27. What number should replace the question mark?

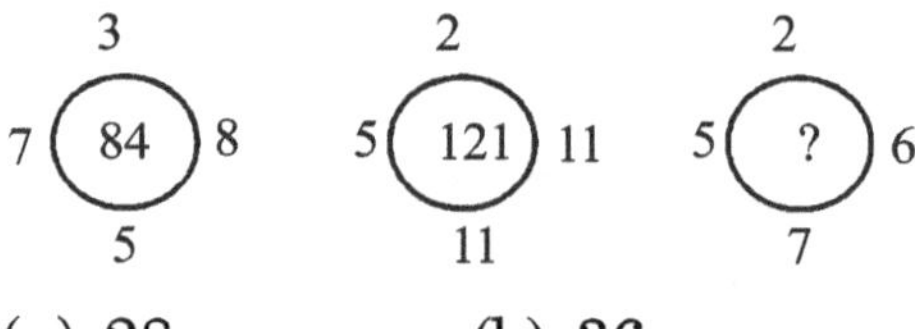

    (a) 28   (b) 36

    (c) 48   (d) 42

28. Count the number of blocks in the given figure.

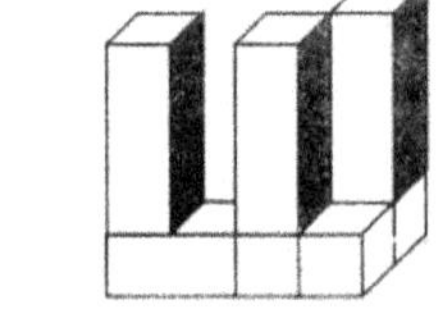

    (a) 6   (b) 7

    (c) 8   (d) 9

29. Solve 5(x − 3) − 7(6 − x) = 24 − 3 (8 − x) − 3.

    (a) x = 6   (b) x = 8

    (c) x = 11   (d) x = 23

30. The mean temperature of Monday, Tuesday and Wednesday is 40°C. The mean temperature of Tuesday, Wednesday and Thursday is 41°C. If the temperature of Thursday is 30°C, then the temperature on Monday is

    (a) 27°C   (b) 30°C

    (c) 25°C   (d) 35°C

31. How long will it take for a boy to run around a square field of area 25 hectares at 10 km per hour?

    (a) 12 min   (b) 14 min

    (c) 16 min   (d) 18 min

32. A windmill has rotational symmetry of order 2×K. Find K

    (a) 1   (b) 2

    (c) 3   (d) 4

33. Divide $125.625 \div 0.5$.

    (a) 251.25   (b) 2512.5

    (c) 25125   (d) 25.125

34. A certain sum of money amounts to ₹ 1560 in 2 years and ₹ 2100 in 5 years. The   te percentage per annum is:

    (a) 8%   (b) 10%

    (c) 15%   (d) 22%

35. If the altitude of an equilateral triangle is $\sqrt{6}$ cm, its area is

    (a) $2\sqrt{3}\,\text{cm}^2$ (b) $2\sqrt{2}\,\text{cm}^2$

    (c) $3\sqrt{3}\,\text{cm}^2$ (d) $6\sqrt{2}\,\text{cm}^2$

36. If $p + \dfrac{1}{p} = a + b$ and $p - \dfrac{1}{p} = a - b$,

    then :

    (a) $ab = 1$ (b) $a = b$

    (c) $ab = 2$ (d) $a + b = 0$

37. Mrs. Kumar is 3 times as old as her daughter. In 5 years' time, the sum of their ages will be 62 years. Daughter's present age is:

    (a) 13 years   (b) 14 years

    (c) 17 years   (d) 19 years

38. A Shopkeeper sells two T.V. sets at the same Price. There is a gain of 20% on one T.V. and loss of 20% on the other. State which of the following Statement is correct?

    (i) The Shopkeeper neither gain nor lose

    (ii) The shopkeeper loses by 2%

    (iii) The shopkeeper gain by 4%

    (iv) The shopkeeper losses by 4%

    (a) Only (i) is correct
    (b) Only (iv) is correct
    (c) Both (i) & (ii) may possible
    (d) Cannot be determined

39. Which of these statements is true?

    (i) General formula for the area of a triangle is $\dfrac{1}{2} \times$ base $\times$ height.

    (ii) Perimeter of any right angled triangle is the sum of the measurment of its boundary

    (iii) Area of an equilateral triangle of side a and area of an isosceles right angled triangle (equal sides = a) is same.

    (a) (i) & (ii)   (b) (i) & (iii)
    (c) (i), (ii) & (iii)   (d) (iii)

40. The mean of 6, y, 7, x and 14 is 8. Then

    (a) $x + y = 13$ (b) $x - y = 13$
    (c) $2x + 3y = 13$ (d) $x^2 + y^2 = 15$

41. A rectangular shaped swimming pool with dimensions 30 m × 20 m has 5 m wide cemented path along its length and 8 m wide path along its width (as shown in figure). The cost of cementing the path at the rate of ₹ 200 per m^2 is:

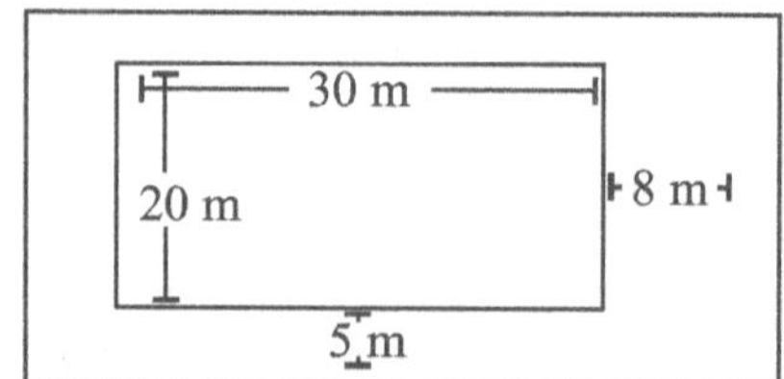

(a) ₹ 214120   (b) ₹ 148240

(c) ₹ 156000   (d) ₹ 914032

42. The area of a circle is 2464 m^2, then the diameter is

(a) 56 m   (b) 154 m

(c) 176 m   (d) None of these

43. The mean, median and mode of four numbers is 8. The smallest number is 7. The numbers are
(a) 7, 7, 8, 8   (b) 7, 8, 8, 8
(c) 7, 8, 8, 9   (d) 8, 8, 8, 8

44. A number is increased by 10% and then reduced by 10%, then the number
(a) doesn't change
(b) decreases by 1%
(c) increases by 1%
(d) None of these

45. The mode of the following data:

Size	1	3	5	7	9
Frequency	6	9	12	3	15

  is
(a) 9   (b) 7
(c) 5   (d) 3

46. Multiply: $\sqrt{3}x^2y^2 - \sqrt{2}x^3y^2$

$$+ \sqrt{2}x^3y^3 \text{ by } - \sqrt{2}x^2y^2$$

(a) $-\sqrt{6}x^4y^4 + 2x^5y^4 + \sqrt{10}x^5y^5$

(b) $\sqrt{6}x^4y^4 - 2x^5y^4 - \sqrt{10}x^5y^5$

(c) $\sqrt{6}x^2y^2 - \sqrt{21}x^3y^2 + \sqrt{2}x^3y^3$

(d) $\sqrt{6}x^4y^4 + 2x^5y^4 + \sqrt{10}x^5y^5$

47. The value of the expression:

$$\left(x - \frac{1}{x}\right)\left(x + \frac{1}{x}\right)\left(x^2 + \frac{1}{x^2}\right) \text{ will be}$$

_______ .

(a) $x^3 - \dfrac{1}{x^3}$ (b) $x^3 + \dfrac{1}{x^3}$

(c) $x^4 - \dfrac{1}{x^4}$ (d) $x^4 + \dfrac{1}{x^4}$

48. How much should $3xy - 4a^2 + 5b^2 + 2$ be increased to get $-5 + 4a^2 + 2b^2 - 7xy$?

(a) $8a^2 + 3b^2 - 11xy + 10$

(b) $8a^2 - 3b^2 - 10xy - 7$

(c) $9a^2 + 5b^2 - 11xy + 2$

(d) $3xy - 4a^2 + 5b^2 + 2$

49. The cross-section of a trough of depth 36 cm is a trapezium ABCD where AB = 50 cm as shown. If the area of ABCD is 2250 cm^2, the length of CD is:

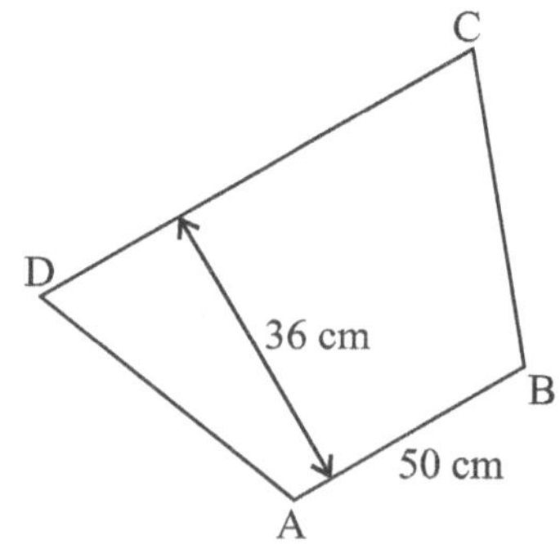

(a) 75 cm   (b) 78 cm   (c)   81 cm   (d)   69 cm

50. Match column I with column II and select the correct answer using the code given below in columns

Column I	**Column II**
(Figure)	**(Perimeter)**
(A) Equilateral triangle	(p) $2\pi \times$ radius
(B) Square	(q) 2 (length + breadth)
(C) Rectangle	(r) $4 \times$ side
(D) Circle	(s) $3 \times$ side

(a) A-s, B-r, C-q, D-p   (b) A-s, B-q, C-r, D-p

(c) A-p, B-q, C-r, D-s   (d) A-r, B-p, C-q, D-s

Name : _________

Number of Questions : 50

Max. Marks : 50

Time : 2 Hours

There is no negative marking in the test.

1. Which of the following equations cannot be formed using the equation x = 7 ?
   (a) 2x + 1 = 15   (b) 7x − 1 = 50
   (c) x − 3 = 4   (d) $\dfrac{x}{7} - 1 = 0$

2. If A : B = 7 : 9 and B : C = 6 : 7 then A : C is
   (a) 2 : 3   (b) 3 : 2
   (c) 1 : 3   (d) 2 : 7

3. Find out the H.C.F. of 3^5, 3^9 and 3^{14}.
   (a) 3^9 (b) 3^{14}
   (c) 3^5 (d) 3^{28}

4. The sum of the present age of A, B and C is 90 years. Six years ago, their ages were in the ratio 1 : 2 : 3. What is the present age of C?
   (a) 46 years   (b) 28 years
   (c) 39 years   (d) 42 years

5. The simple interest on a sum of money is 25% of the principal and the rate per annum is equal to number of years. Find the rate (in percentage).
   (a) 8%   (b) 5%
   (c) 4%   (d) 7%

6. The volume of a cube is 125 cm³. The surface area of cube is:
   (a) 625 cm²   (b) 125 cm²
   (c) 150 cm²   (d) 100 cm²

7. If $\dfrac{5x - 3y}{5y + 3y} = \dfrac{3}{4}$, then value of $\dfrac{x}{y}$ is
   (a) 2:9   (b) 7:2
   (c) 7:9   (d) None of these

8. The value of x in the figure is

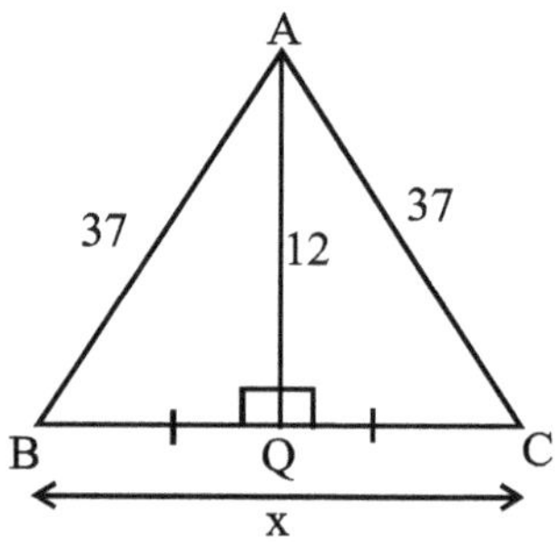

   (a) 35   (b) 70
   (c) 55   (d) 65

9. Match column I with column II and select the correct answer using the given code below the columns:

Column - I (Number)	Column - II (Scientific Notation)
A. 360	(p) 3.6×10^4
B. 36000	(q) 3.6×10^6
C. 3600000	(r) 3.6×10^1

   D. 36   (s) 3.6×10^2

A	B	C	D
(a) p	q	r	s
(b) p	s	q	r
(c) s	p	r	q
(d) s	p	q	r

10. Area of four walls of a room is $77\ m^2$. The length and breadth of the room are 7.5 m and 3.5 m, respectively. The height of the room is :
   - (a) 7.7 m
   - (b) 3.5 m
   - (c) 6.77 m
   - (d) 5.4 m

11. Solve the equation: $\dfrac{t}{t+3} = 1\dfrac{1}{4}$.
   - (a) t = –10
   - (b) t = –15
   - (c) t = –14
   - (d) t = 9

12. Consider the following statements.
   - (i) The ratio of areas of two circles is 4 : 25, if the ratio of their radii is 2 : 5.
   - (ii) If each side of a square is 14 cm, then its area is $98\ cm^2$.
   - (iii) The areas of two circles are in the ratio 25 : 36. The ratio of their circumferences is 5 : 6.

   Which of the statement is True or False?
   - (a) TFT
   - (b) TTF
   - (c) FTT
   - (d) FFT

13. The area of an isosceles triangle with equal sides 5.1 metres and the third side 4.6 metres is
   - (a) 10.47 sq.m
   - (b) 2.86 sq.m
   - (c) 10.45 sq.m
   - (d) None of these

14. The solution of
   $0.2\,(2x – 1) – 0.5\,(3x – 1) = 0.4$ is
   - (a) $\dfrac{1}{11}$
   - (b) $-\dfrac{1}{11}$
   - (c) $\dfrac{3}{11}$
   - (d) $\dfrac{-3}{11}$

15. Which of the following statement (s) is/are true about the area of a circle?
   - (i) Area of a circle is equal to four times the area of a quadrant of same radius.
   - (ii) Area of a circle cannot be divided into two equal parts.
   - (iii) If the measure of diameter of a circle is given we can determine its area.
   - (a) (i) and (ii)
   - (b) (i) and (iii)
   - (c) (i), (ii) and (iii)
   - (d) None of these

16. How many numbers amongst the numbers 9 to 54 are there which are exactly divisible by 9 but not by 3?
   - (a) 8
   - (b) 6
   - (c) 5
   - (d) Nil

17. The perimeter of a circular plot is equal to that of a square plot. What is the ratio of their respective areas?
   - (a) 13 : 11
   - (b) 14 : 11
   - (c) 15 : 11
   - (d) 16 : 11

18. If 2A = 3B = 4C, then A:B:C is:

(a) 2 : 3 : 4   (b) 4 : 3 : 2

(c) 6 : 4 : 3   (d) 3 : 4 : 2

19. In $\frac{2}{3}p - 2\frac{1}{2} = 3\frac{1}{2}$, the value of p is

(a) −9   (b) +6

(c) +9   (d) 0

20. In external bisectors of $\angle B$ and $\angle C$ meet at O. If $\angle A = 50°$, then $\angle BOC$ is equal to :

(a) 65°   (b) 75°

(c) 45°   (d) 40°

21. The ratio of exterior angle to interior angle of a regular polygon is 1:4. Find the number of sides of the polygon.

(a) 15   (b) 10

(c) 20   (d) 30

22. Three sons of a man have ₹ 12, ₹ 15 and ₹ 19 with them. The father asks his sons to give him equal amount so that the money held by the sons now are in continued proportion. The amount taken from each son is:

(a) ₹ 3   (b) ₹ 5

(c) ₹ 7   (d) ₹ 11

23. Original price of a sofa is ₹ 7,000. It is now on sale for ₹ 5,500. What was the percentage decrease in price?

(a) 19.6%   (b) 21.4%

(c) 18.2%   (d) 24.4%

24. If $\dfrac{x}{y} = \dfrac{6}{5}$, then $\dfrac{x^2 + y^2}{x^2 - y^2}$ is

(a) $\dfrac{36}{25}$ (b) $\dfrac{25}{36}$

(c) $\dfrac{61}{11}$ (d) $\dfrac{11}{61}$

25. Which of the following alphabet has no lines of symmetry?

(a) A   (b) B

(c) Q   (d) O

26. If the seventh day of a month is three days earlier than Friday, what day will it be on the nineteenth day of the month?

(a) Sunday   (b) Monday

(c) Wednesday   (d) Friday

27. If $(3x - 4)(5x + 7) = 15x^2 - ax - 28$, then a = __________ .

(a) 1   (b) − 1

(c) − 2   (d) none of these

28. A book was sold for ₹ 27.50 with a profit of 10%. If it were sold for ₹ 25.75, then what would have been the percentage of profit or loss?

(a) Profit 4%   (b) Loss 3%

(c) Profit 3%   (d) Profit 7%

29. Match column I with column II and select the correct answer using the given code below the columns.

Column I	Column II
A. $(3^3)^2$	(p) $(0^{18})^{15}$
B. $(0^6)^{12}$	(q) $(16)^3$
C. $(644^3)^0$	(r) $(9)^3$
D. $(2^2)^6$	(s) $(3^0)^{644}$

    A   B   C   D

(a) r   p   q   s

(b) r   p   s   q

(c) p   q   r   s

(d) p   r   q   s

30 If $-\dfrac{3}{x} = \dfrac{x}{27}$, then the value of "x" is ____.

(a) a rational number

(b) not a rational number

(c) an integer

(d) a natural number

31. Consider the following two situations.

Situation 1: Chance of getting '2' or '5' in a throw of die.

Situation 2: Chance of getting '1', '3' or '5' in throw of die.

Which situation has more chance to occur?

(a) Situation 1

(b) Situation 2

(c) Data insufficient

(d) Both the situations have equal chances

32. Which of the following statements are correct?

(i) Division by zero is not defined.

(ii) − 3 is greater than zero.

(iii)Any number multiplied by zero will give zero.

(iv)0 is an integer.

(a) (i), (ii), (iii) and (iv)

(b) (i) and (ii)

(c) (i), (iii) and (iv)

(d) (iii) and (iv)

33. If $\angle A = (4x + 2)°$, the measure of the complementary of $\angle A$ is equal to

(a) $(178 + 4x)°$ (b) $(88 − 4x)°$

(c) $(4x + 88)°$ (d) $(6x − 178)°$

34. Which number lies opposite to the face 4, if the four different positions of a dice are as in the figures given below.

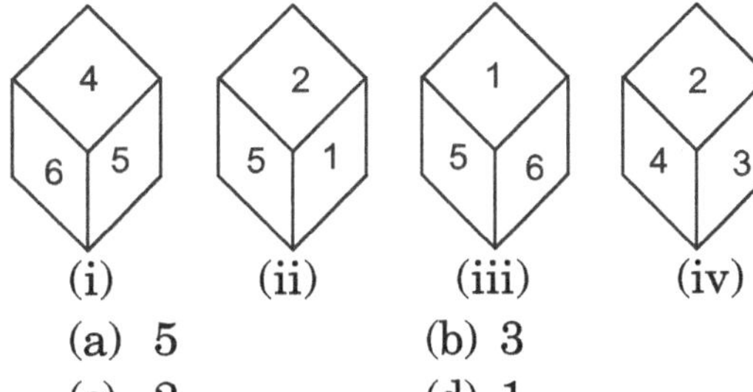

(a) 5   (b) 3

(c) 2   (d) 1

35. Which of the following outcome is possible?

(i) Someone in your class will be absent next week.

(ii) You will become a doctor when you grow up.

(iii)It will snow in Shimla in January.

(a) only (i)

(b) only (ii)

(c) only (iii)

(d) All three outcomes

36. The value of x in the given figure.

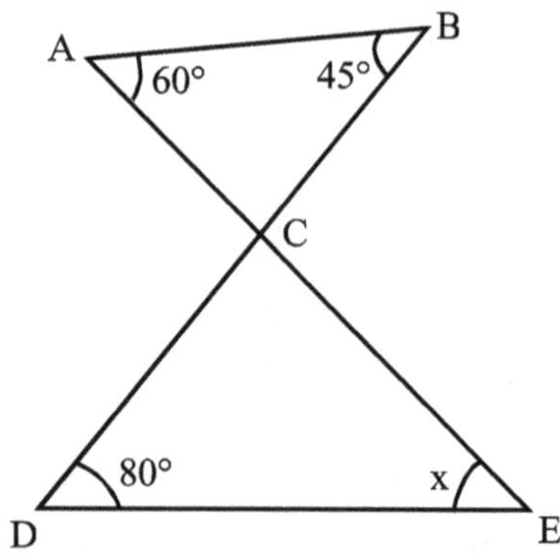

(a) 30°   (b) 25°

(c) 35°   (d) 45°

37. For three rational numbers a, b, c we have a > b and b < c. Which one of the following is true?

   (a) a > c

   (b) b is the smallest rational number

   (c) a < c

   (d) both (a) and (b) are correct

38. If 10% of m is twice the 20% of n, then $m : n$ is equal to

   (a) 2 : 3   (b) 1 : 4

   (c) 4 : 1   (d) 5 : 2

39. If A + D = B + C,

   A + E = C + D,

   2C < A + E and 2A > B + D, then

   (a) A > B > C > D > E

   (b) B > A > D > C > E

   (c) D > B > C > A > E

   (d) B > C > D > E > A

40. Which of the following statements is/are true about the median of a given data?

   (i) It is always equal to mean.

   (ii) It is the value of the variable, which divides the total frequency into 2 parts.

   (iii) The median is always one of the numbers in a data.

   (iv) Median refers to the value which lies in the middle of the data (when arranged in an increasing or a decreasing order).

   (a) (i) & (iv)   (b) (ii), (iii) & (iv)

   (c) (i) & (ii)   (d) only (iv)

41. How many bricks 20 cm by 10 cm will be needed to pave the floor of a room 25 m long and 16 m wide?

   (a) 18000   (b) 20000

   (c) 22000   (d) 24000

42. In figure, ABCD is a parallelogram, in which AB = 8 cm, AD = 6 cm and altitude AE = 4 cm. The altitude corresponding to side AD.

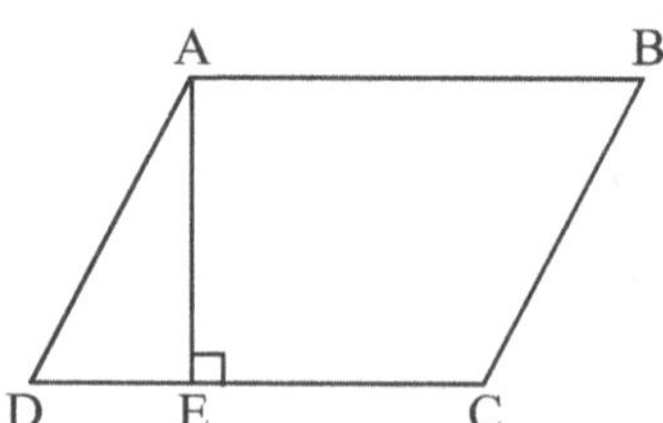

   (a) $\dfrac{5}{4}$ cm   (b) $\dfrac{7}{2}$ cm

   (c) $\dfrac{15}{8}$ cm   (d) $\dfrac{16}{3}$ cm

43. The figure represents a sign board. AD = 8 cm, BC = 6 cm, ME = 4 cm and EN = 3 cm. The area of the sign board is:

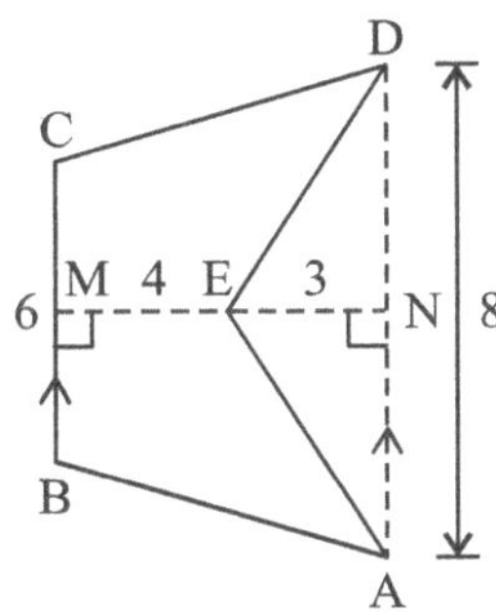

(a) 29 cm^2

(b) 37 cm^2

(c) 39 cm^2

(d) 41 cm^2

44. In an examination, a candidate scores the following percentage of marks. English — 44; Hindi — 58; Maths —74; Physics — 61; Chemistry — 62. If weights 2, 4, 4, 5, 3 respectively are allotted to these subjects, then the candidate's weighted mean percentage is

(a) 61   (b) 61.5

(c) 62   (d) 62.5

45. The condition that makes the following pair of triangles congruent is

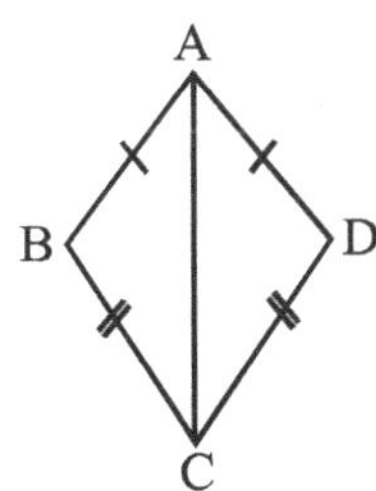

(a) SSS

(b) ASA

(c) SAS

(d) RHS

46. The area of shaded region of the figure given below is

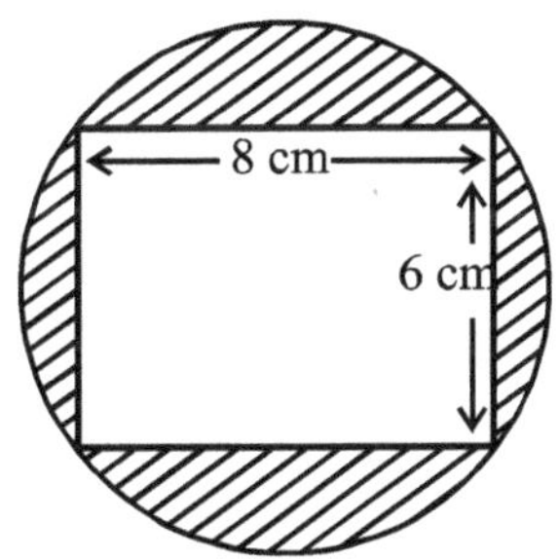

(a) 78.5 cm^2

(b) 30.57 cm^2

(c) 42.8 cm^2

(d) 47 cm^2

47. In the given triangle, the value of x is

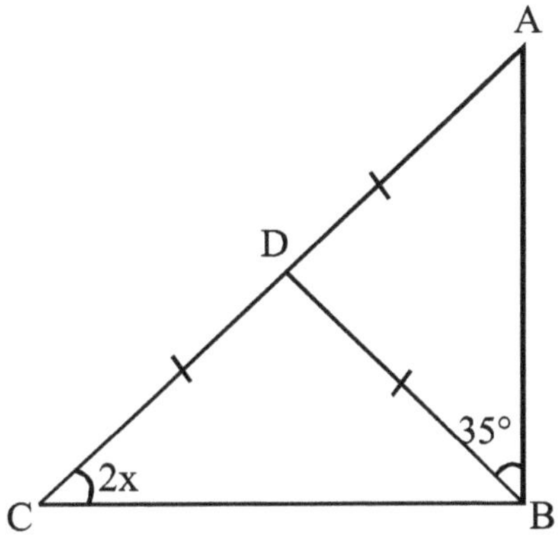

(a) 55°

(b) 110°

(c) 70°

(d) 27.5°

DIRECTIONS (Qs. 48 to 50) : Study the following graph carefully and answer the questions based on it.

Production of rose in various states

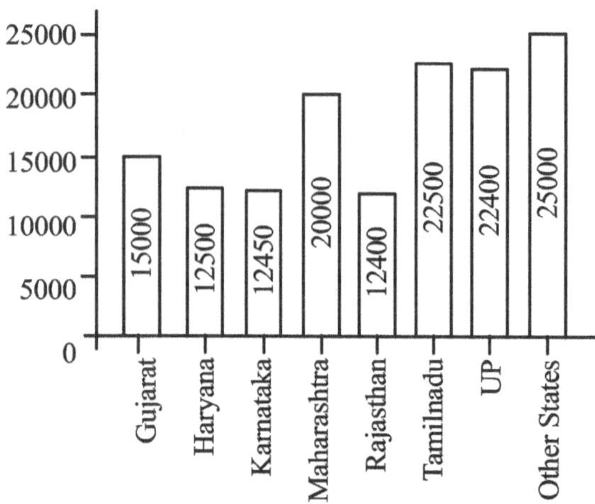

48. Which of the following state(s) contribute(s) less than 10 percent in the total rose production?

(a) Only Rajasthan

(b) Rajasthan, Karnataka

(c) Rajasthan, Karnataka, Haryana

(d) Rajasthan, Karnataka, Haryana and Gujarat

49. What is the approximate average production of roses (in thousands) across all the states?

(a) 21   (b) 20

(c) 19   (d) 18

50. If total percentage contribution of the states having production of roses below twenty thousand is considered, which of the following statements is true?

(a) It is little above 40%

(b) It is exactly 35%

(c) It is below 35%

(d) None of these

OLYMPIAD
Mock Test 1

Name : _________

Max. Marks : 50

Number of Questions : 50

Time : 2 Hours

There is no negative marking in the test.

PHYSICS

1. A marble tile would feel cold as compared to a wooden tile on a winter morning, because the marble tile
   - (a) is a better conductor of heat than the wooden tile.
   - (b) is polished while wooden tile is not polished
   - (c) reflects more heat than wooden tile.
   - (d) is a poor conductor of heat than the wooden tile.

2. The graph given here shows the motion of four runners– P, Q, R and S in a 5 km marathon. Whose motion is the fastest?

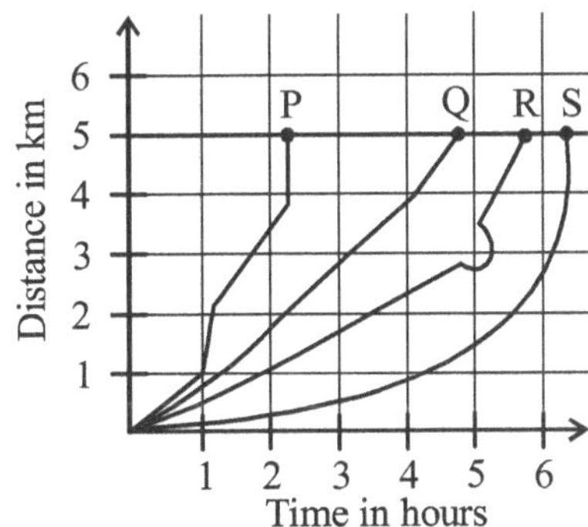

- (a) P
- (b) Q
- (c) R
- (d) S

3. Which canned drink will remain cold the shortest?

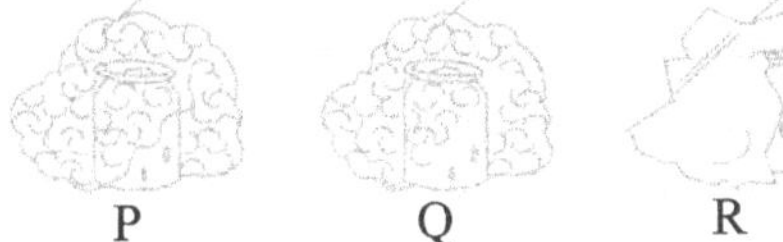

- (a) P
- (b) Q
- (c) R
- (d) Both P and Q

4. What will happen when a magnetic compass is brought near a current carrying wire?
   - (a) It will lose its magnetism.
   - (b) It will deflect the magnetic needle.
   - (c) No effect will occur on the compass.
   - (d) It will deflect fast in East-West direction.

5. Match the column I with column II and select the correct option from the codes given below.

Column I

(A) Concave mirror
(B) Plane mirror
(C) Convex mirror

Column II

(i) Always forms virtual image
(ii) Forms image of same size as that of object
(iii) Forms real images

(a) (A)-(i), (B)-(iii), (C)-(ii)
(b) (A)-(ii), (B)-(iii), (C)-(i)
(c) (A)-(iii), (B)-(ii), (C)-(i)
(d) (A)-(i), (B)-(ii), (C)-(iii)

6. When a body moves around a fixed axis, the body is in......
(a) Rectilinear motion
(b) Circular motion
(c) Rotatory motion
(d) Periodic motion

7. $0°C$ is equal to:
(a) 243K   (b) 234K
(c) 273K   (d) All of these

8. In the given circuit diagram, P and Q are switches.

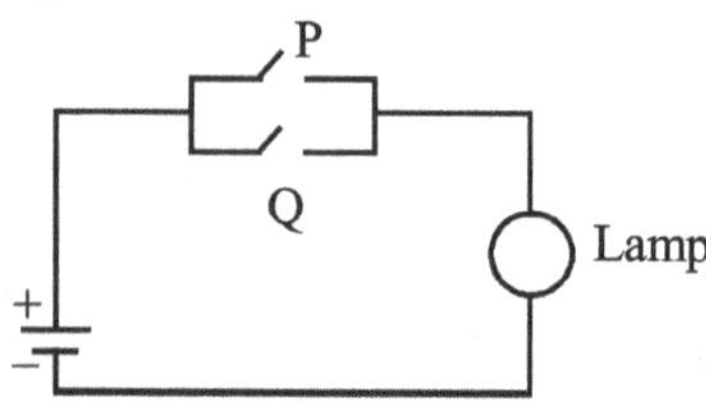

Lamp will glow when
(a) P is open, Q is closed
(b) P is closed, Q is open
(c) Both P and Q are closed
(d) Any of these

9. Dispersion of light by a glass prism takes place because of
(a) difference in wavelengths of the constituents of light
(b) difference in speeds of various constituents of white light.
(c) scattering of light by the surface of the glass prism
(d) only b and a are correct

10. From the diagram given, what is the angle of incidence?

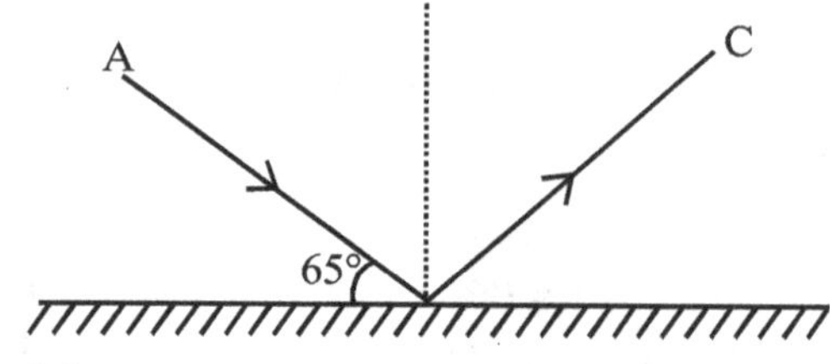

(a) 25°   (b) 50°
(c) 65°   (d) 90°

11. A body covers half of its journey with a speed of 60 m/s and the other half with a speed of 40 m/s. Then average speed during whole journey is
(a) 0   (b) 50 m/s
(c) 48 m/s   (d) 52 m/s

12. When an electric current flows through a copper wire AB as shown in Figure the wire

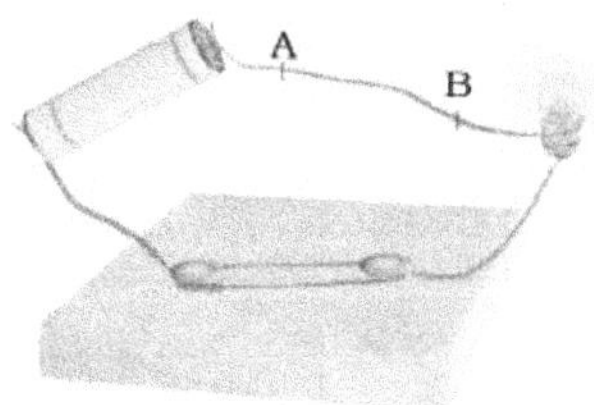

(a) deflects a magnetic needle placed near it
(b) becomes red hot.
(c) gives electric shock.
(d) behaves like a fuse

13. If an object is placed at a distance of 0.5 m in front of a plane mirror, the distance between the object and the image formed by the mirror will be
(a) 2 m (b) 1 m
(c) 0.5 m (d) 0.25 m

14. When a steel rod is heated, it becomes
(a) lighter
(b) heavier
(c) a little longer
(d) a little shorter

15. Match the columns and select the correct option from the codes given below.

Column - I	**Column - II**
(A) Wind carrying water	(i) Thunderstorms
(B) Dark funnel shaped cloud	(ii) Tornado
(C) Moving air	(iii) Monsoon
(D) Develop in India very frequently	(iv) Wind

(a) (A) - (iii), (B) - (ii), (C) - (iv), (D) - (i)
(b) (A) - (ii), (B) - (iv), (C) - (i), (D) - (iii)
(c) (A) - (iv), (B) - (ii), (C) - (iii), (D) - (i)
(d) (A) - (i), (B) - (ii), (C) - (iii), (D) - (iv)

CHEMISTRY

16. Match the following and choose the correct option.

Column I		**Column II**
A.	Quick lime	p.	NaOH
B.	Caustic soda	q.	$Ca(OH)_2$
C.	Baking soda	r.	CaO
D.	Slaked lime	s.	$NaHCO_3$

(a) A - r, B - p, C - s, D - q
(b) A - q, B - s, C - p, D - r
(c) A - p, B - q, C - s, D - q
(d) A - r, B - s, C - q, D - p

17. Which of the following will be observed if an apple slice is left exposed to air ?

(a) It undergoes oxidation and becomes brown in colour.

(b) Appearance of brown colour on the surface of apple slice is caused by a chemical reaction between air and enzymes.

(c) Both of the above are correct.

(d) None of these.

18. Arrange the following in terms of artificial and natural fibres.

Flax, Wool, Acrylic, Nylon, Rayon

(a) Artificial fibres – Wool, Rayon. Natural fibres – Flax, Acrylic, Nylon

(b) Artificial fibres – Nylon, Acrylic, Rayon. Natural fibres – Flax, Wool

(c) Artificial fibres – Flax, Wool. Natural fibres – Acrylic, Rayon, Nylon

(d) Artificial fibres – Nylon, Wool. Natural fibres – Flax, Acrylic, Rayon

19. Study the simplified diagram of the water cycle below.

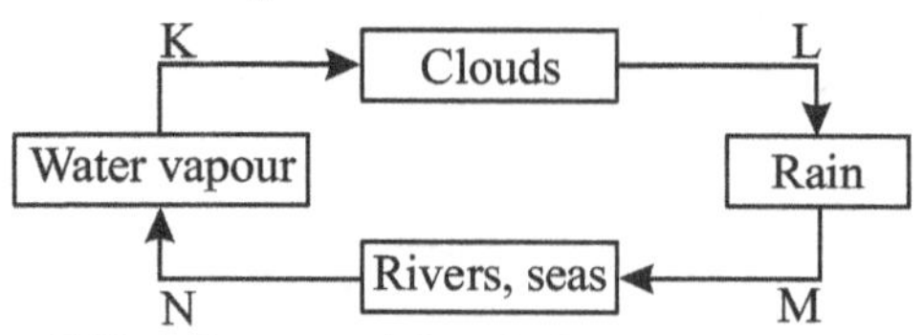

Which part(s) of the water cycle, represented by K, L, M and N, involve(s) a change in the state of water?

(a) N only

(b) K and L only

(c) K and N only

(d) M and N only

20. Read the following statements with reference to soil.

(i) Weathering is a very fast process of soil formation.

(ii) Percolation of water is faster in sandy soils.

(iii) Loamy soil contains only sand and clay.

(iv) Top soil contains the maximum amount of humus.

Choose the correct statements from the above.

(a) (ii) and (iv)   (b) (i) and (iii)

(c) (ii) and (iii)   (d) (i) and (ii)

21. **Assertion (A) :** Breaking of a bone china plate is a physical change.

Reason (R) : When a bone china plate breaks, the pieces cannot be joined to get back the original plate.

(a) Both A and R are true and R is the correct explanation of A.

(b) Both A and R are true but R is not the correct explanation of A.

(c) A is true but R is false.

(d) A is false but R is true.

22. Which part in the given figure represents layer that provides better shelter for living organism.

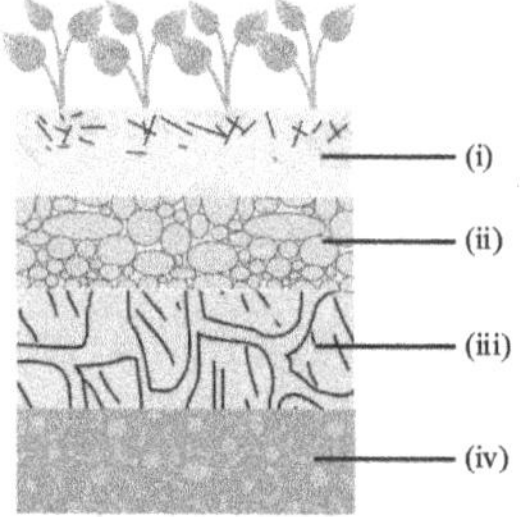

(a) (i) and (ii)   (b) (ii) only

(c) (i) only   (d) (ii) and (iii)

23. The person who remove the fleece of sheep is called

(a) sorter   (b) weaver

(c) dyer   (d) shearer

24. Availability of water and minerals in the soil for maximum absorption by roots is in the-

(a) B-horizon

(b) C-horizon

(c) A-horizon

(d) surface of soil

25. Which of the following is a neutralisation reaction?

(a) $Na_2O + H_2O \rightarrow 2NaOH$

(b) $4Na + O_2 \rightarrow 2Na_2O$

(c) $NaOH + HCl \rightarrow NaCl + H_2O$

(d) $2Ca + O_2 \rightarrow 2CaO$

26. Match the following and choose the correct option.

Column I	Column II
A. A monobasic acid	p. Potash alum
B. A dibasic acid	q. Phosphoric acid
C. A tribasic acid	r. Hydrochloric acid

D. Common salt   s. Sulphuric acid
E. A double salt   t. Sodium chloride
(a) A - r, B - s, C - q, D - t, E - p
(b) A - t, B - s, C - q, D - p, E - r
(c) A - r, B - p, C - q, D - t, E - s
(d) A - t, B - q, C - r, D - p, E - s

27. Match the following and choose the correct option.

Column I	**Column II**
A. Burning of wood	p. Slow change
B. Formation of day and night	q. Periodic change
C. Digestion of food	r. Chemical change
D. Melting of ice	s. Reversible change

(a) A - s, B - q, C - r, D - p
(b) A - q, B - p, C - s, D - r
(c) A - r, B - q, C - p, D - s
(d) A - r, B - p, C - s, D - q

28. Two major sheep-rearing countries of the world are
(a) Australia and India.
(b) South America and Asia.
(c) Australia and New Zealand.
(d) None of them

29. ______________ has the highest water holding capacity.
(a) Sandy soil   (b) Clayey soil
(c) Loamy soil   (d) All of them

30. Vicky packed some hot fried noodles into a container for his lunch break. Before he left for work, he observed the water droplets that had formed in the container. Which of the diagrams given below shows the formation of water droplets in the container correctly?

(a) 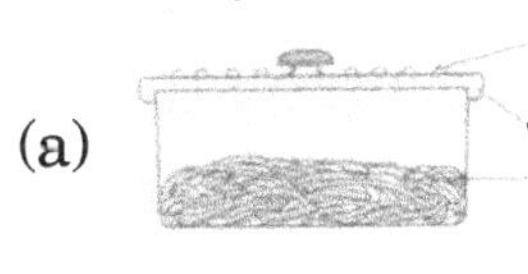

(b) 

(c)
(d)
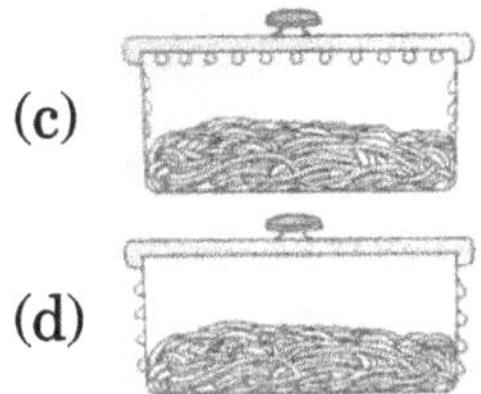

BIOLOGY

31. This bacteria is capable of photosynthesis, is anaerobic or microaerophilic and found in hot springs or stagnant water.
(a) Green bacteria
(b) Cyanobacteria
(c) Iron bacteria
(d) Purple sulphur bacteria

32. Earth's weather is primarily caused by the
(a) drifting of Earth's crustal plates
(b) gravitational attraction of the Moon
(c) uneven heating of the Earth's surface
(d) changing distance between the Earth and the Sun

33. Which of the following statements is/are correct?
    (i) All green plants can prepare their own food.
    (ii) Most animals are autorophs.
    (iii) Carbon dioxide is not required for photosynthesis.
    (iv) Oxygen is liberated during photosynthesis.
    Choose the correct answer from the options below:
    (a) (i) and (iv)
    (b) (ii) only
    (c) (ii) and (iii)
    (d) (i) and (ii)

34. They are pipe-like consisting of a group of specialised cells. They transport food substances and form a two-way traffic in plants. Which of the following terms qualify for the features mentioned above?
    (a) Xylem tissue
    (b) Vascular tissue
    (c) Root hairs
    (d) Phloem tissue

35. The figure given below represents human excretory system. Identify the labelled part in which urine is stored.

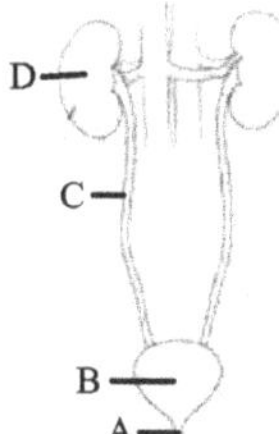

    (a) A
    (b) B
    (c) C
    (d) D

36. Water polluted by various human activities causes a number of water borne diseases. Which of the following is not a water borne disease?

    (a) Cholera
    (b) Typhoid
    (c) Asthma
    (d) Dysentry

37. Read the following environmental conditions of tropical rain forests.
    (i) Hot and humid climate
    (ii) Unequal lengths of day and night
    (iii) Abundant rain fall
    (iv) Abundant light and moisture
    Identify the conditions from the above list that are responsible for the presence of large number of plants and animals in tropical rain forests.
    (a) (i) and (ii)
    (b) (i) and (iii)
    (c) (i), (iii) and (iv)
    (d) (ii) and (iv)

38. Open drain system is the breeding place for which of the following?
    (a) Flies
    (b) Mosquitoes
    (c) Organisms which cause diseases
    (d) All of these

39. Match column I with column II and select the correct option from the codes given below.

Column - I	Column - II
(A) Earthworm	(i) Pulmonary respiration
(B) Human	(ii) Bronchial respiration
(C) Prawn	(iii) Tracheal respiration
(D) Insects	(iv) Cutaneous respiration

    (a) (A) - (i), (B) - (ii), (C) - (iii), (D) - (iv)
    (b) (A) - (iv), (B) - (i), (C) - (ii), (D) - (iii)
    (c) (A) - (iii), (B) - (ii), (C) - (iv), (D) - (i)
    (d) (A) - (iv), (B) - (ii), (C) - (i), (D) - (iii)

40. Which of the following statements is/are correct?
    (a) Climatic conditions in the tropical rain forests are highly suitable for supporting an enormous number and variety of animals.
    (b) Red-eyed frog has developed sticky pads on its feet to help it climb trees on which it lives.
    (c) The bird toucan possesses a long, large beak, which helps it to reach the fruits on branches which are otherwise too weak to support its weight.
    (d) All of these

41. Read the given statements and select the correct option.
    (i) In insects, circulating body fluids serve to distribute oxygen to tissues.
    (ii) Yeasts respire aerobically, therefore, they are used to make wine and beer.
    (iii) Bronchitis is the inflammation of bronchi which may be caused on exposure to air pollutants.
    (iv) On an average, an adult human being at rest, breathes in and out 15-18 times in a minute.
    (v) In a healthy person, maximum capacity of lungs for inhaled air is 1500 mL.
    (vi) Sneezing expels the foreign particles from the inhaled air.
    (a) Statements (i), (ii) & (v) are incorrect, while Statements (iii), (iv) & (vi) are correct.
    (b) Statements (i), (ii) & (iii) are incorrect, while statements (iv), (v) & (vi) are correct.
    (c) Statements (ii) & (v) are incorrect, while statements (i), (iii), (v) & (vi) are correct.
    (d) Statements (ii) & (iv) are incorrect, while statements (i), (ii), (iv) & (v) are correct.

42. Read the given paragraph.
    The ____(i)____ secretes bile juice which is stored in the ____(ii)____. The bile breaks up ____(iii)____ into tiny droplets that can be digested and absorbed more easily. The digestive juices then act on these tiny droplets to form simpler compounds known as ____(iv)____ and ____(v)____.
    Select the option which correctly completes the above paragraph.

	(a)	(b)	(c)	(d)
(i)	Pancreas	Liver	Liver	Small intestine
(ii)	Spleen	Gall bladder	Gall bladder	Spleen
(iii)	Proteins	Starch	Fats	Fats
(iv)	Amino acids	Fructose	Fatty acids	Amino acids
(v)	Glycerol	Maltose	Glycerol	Fatty acids

43. The cells shown in the figure can be found in the blood.
    Which of the following statements is/are correct regarding these cells?

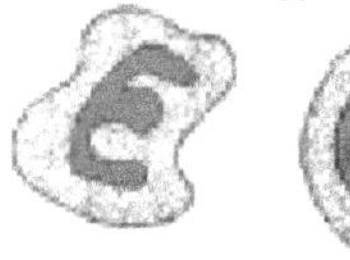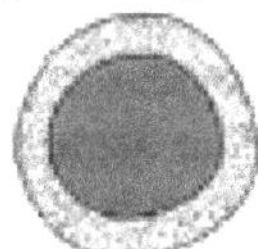

    (i) They do not have nucleus.
    (ii) They help the body to fight against infections.
    (iii) They help the blood to clot.
    (iv) They help to transport oxygen.
    (a) (ii) only
    (b) (i) and (ii)
    (c) (i), (ii) and (iii)
    (d) (i), (iii) and (v)

44. On saturday, Sumit after having his lunch, forgot his lunch box in the school. When he opened it on monday he found that it has some blackish-brown, cottony stuff in it. Which of the following organisms can it most likely be?
    (a) Mushroom
    (b) *Amoeba*
    (c) *Rhizopus*
    (d) Either (a) or (c)

45. The given table lists some plants and their reproductive structures.

Plants	Reproductive structures
Bean plant	Seeds
X	Spores
Onion	Y

    (a) X - Fern, Y - Spores
    (b) X - Pineapple, Y - Suckers
    (c) X - Moss, Y - Underground stems
    (d) X - Moss, Y - Leaves

46. Match column I with column II and select the correct answers using the code given below the columns.

    Column-I
    (A) Food factories of plants
    (B) Cell membrane
    (C) Tiny pores on the surface of leaves surrounded by "guard cells"
    (D) Carbohydrates

    Column-II
    (p) Semi - permeable memebrane
    (q) Leaves
    (r) Complex chemical substances
    (s) Stomata

    (a) A → (p); B → (r); C → (q); D → (s)
    (b) A → (q); B → (p); C → (s); D → (r)
    (c) A → (r); B → (s); C → (p); D → (q)
    (d) A → (s); B → (q); C→ (p); D → (r)

47. Disappearance of the forest will lead to increase in amount of carbon dioxide in air. It is likely to result in
    (a) eutrophication
    (b) global warming
    (c) deforestation
    (d) afforestation.

48. Which of the following adaptations of polar bear are not meant for hunting prey and getting protection from predators?
    (i) White colour of the fur
    (ii) Huge teeth
    (iii) Long hair between the pads on its feet
    (iv) Two thick layers of the fur
    (v) Sharp claws on each foot
    (a) (i) and (v)   (b) (iii) and (iv)
    (c) (ii) and (iii)   (d) (i) and (iv)

49. Which of the following statements is/are true for sexual reproduction in plants?
    (i) Plants are obtained from seeds.
    (ii) Two plants are always essential.
    (iii) Fertilisation can occur only after pollination.
    (iv) Only insects are agents of pollination
    Choose from the options given below.
    (a) (i) and (iii)   (b) (i) only
    (c) (ii) and (iii)   (d) (i) and (iv)

50. What is the function of mucous secreted by the inner lining of stomach ?
    (a) Kills many bacteria
    (b) Makes medium in stomach acidic
    (c) Protects lining of stomach
    (d) All the above

OLYMPIAD
Mock Test 2

Name : __________

Number of Questions : 50

There is no negative marking in the test.

Max. Marks : 50

Time : 2 Hours

PHYSICS

1. Sunil and Rohit start at one end of a street, the origin, run to the other end, then head back. On the way back Sunil is ahead of Rohit. Which statement is correct about the distances run and the displacements from the origin?
   (a) Sunil has run a greater distance and his displacement is greater than Rohit's.
   (b) Rohit has run a greater distance and his displacement is greater than Sunil's.
   (c) Sunil has run a greater distance but his displacement is lesser than Rohit's.
   (d) Rohit has run a greater distance but his displacement is lesser than Sunil's.

2. When the switch of an electric bell is pushed, then
   (a) flow of the current stops through the electromagnet in the bell
   (b) a current starts to flow through the electromagnet
   (c) voltage and current decreases in the electromagnet
   (d) None of these

3. Four boxes made of different materials are left under the Sun for half an hour. Which one of the boxes will be the hottest after half an hour?

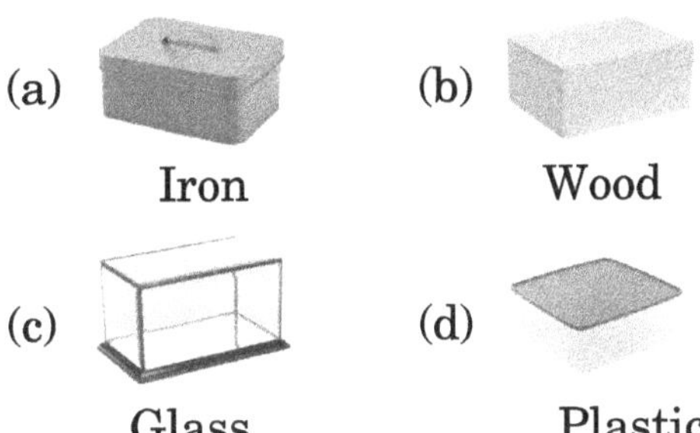

4. Which of the following energy conversions takes place in the figure given here?

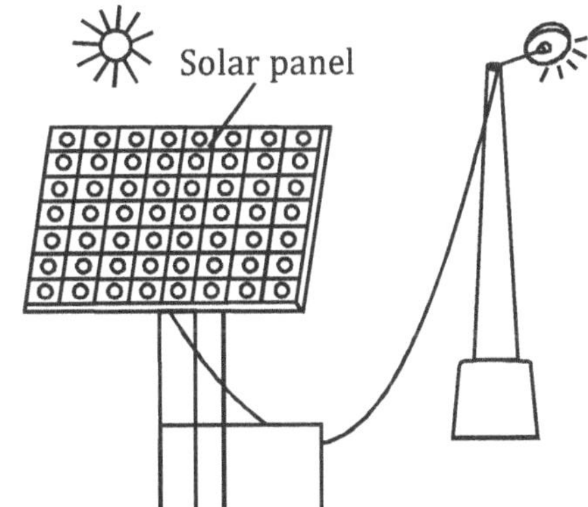

(a) Solar → electrical

(b) Solar → light → heat

(c) Solar → electrical → light

(d) Solar → electrical → light → heat

5. A beggar wrapped himself with a few layers of newspaper on a cold winter night. This helped him to keep himself warm because

(a) friction between the layers of newspaper produces heat.

(b) air trapped between the layers of newspaper is a bad conductor of heat.

(c) newspaper is a conductor of heat

(d) newspaper is at a higher temperature than the temperature of the surrounding.

6. Match the columns and select the correct option from the codes given below.

Column - I   Column-II

(A) Day   (i)   Second

(B) Month   (ii) m/s

(C) Time   (iii) Metre

(D) Speed   (iv) The time from one sunrise to the next

(E) Distance   (v)   One new moon to the next.

	A	B	C	D	E
(a)	(v)	(i)	(ii)	(iii)	(iv)
(b)	(iv)	(v)	(i)	(ii)	(iii)
(c)	(ii)	(iii)	(iv)	(v)	(i)
(d)	(i)	(ii)	(iii)	(iv)	(v)

7. A student tries to magnetise a short steel rod. Which of the following tests will show that he has succeeded?

(a) Both ends of a magnet attract the rod

(b) One end of a magnet repels the rod

(c) The rod picks up a small piece of paper

(d) When freely suspended, the rod points in any direction

8. John performs an experiment in the physics lab for the verification of the laws of reflection. Which one of the following parameters should he measure for the same?

(a) Refractive index of the medium

(b) Angle of incidence and angle of reflection

(c) Cross sectional area of the medium

(d) All of these

9. Thermometers are used to measure the temperature. Thermometer senses the temperature by which one of the following liquid?

(a) Sulfur based fluid

(b) Potassium based fluid

(c) Mercury based fluid

(d) All of these

10. The distance between a plane mirror and the image of an object placed in front of the mirror is 4 m. If now the object is moved 1 m towards the mirror, then the distance between the object and its image in the mirror will be

(a) 3 m   (b) 5 m

(c) 6 m   (d) 8 m

11. When you put a metal key into its metal lock, you find the key is too tight. Which of the following methods will you adopt to make the key fit properly?

(a) Heat the key and lock

(b) Cool the key and heat the lock

(c) Heat the key and cool the lock

(d) Cool the key and lock

12. Two clocks A and B are shown in Figure. Clock A has an hour and a minute hand, whereas clock B has an hour hand, minute hand as well as a second hand. Which of the following statement is correct for these clocks?

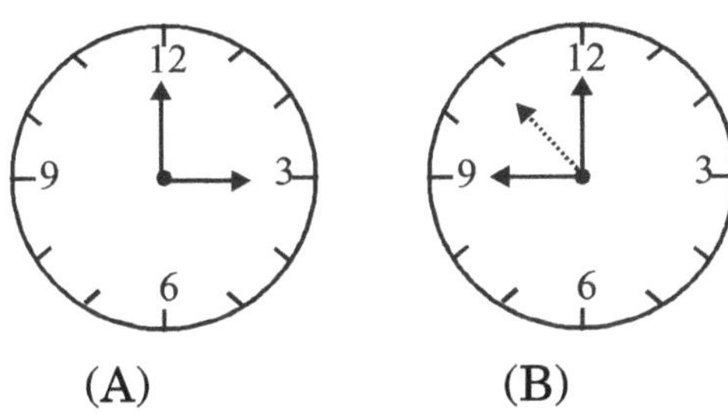

(A)   (B)

(a) A time interval of 30 seconds can be measured by clock A.

(b) A time interval of 30 seconds cannot be measured by clock B.

(c) Time interval of 5 minutes can be measured by both A and B.

(d) Time interval of 4 minutes 10 seconds can be measured by clock A.

13. Choose the statement which is not correct in the case of an electric fuse.

(a) Fuses are inserted in electric circuits of all buildings.

(b) There is a maximum limit on the current which can safely flow through the electric circuits.

(c) There is a minimum limit on the current which can safely flow in the electric circuits.

(d) If a proper fuse is inserted in a circuit it will blow off if current exceeds the safe limit.

14. You are provided with a concave mirror, a convex mirror, a concave lens and convex lens. To obtain an enlarged image of an object you can use either.

(a) concave mirror or convex mirror.

(b) concave mirror or convex lens.

(c) concave mirror or concave lens.

(d) convex mirror or convex lens.

15. How does cyclone decrease the fertility of the soil in the coastal areas?

(a) By flooding the land with saline water

(b) By dissolving soil and rocks

(c) By increasing the water table of the place

(d) By decreasing the water table of the place

CHEMISTRY

16. Choose correct option on the basis of statements (i) and (ii).

(i) When hydrogen burns in oxygen, water is formed.

(ii) When water is electrolysed, hydrogen and oxygen are formed.

(a) (i) is a physical change and (ii) is a chemical change.

(b) (i) is a chemical change and (ii) is a physical change.

(c) Both (i) and (ii) are physical changes.

(d) Both (i) and (ii) are chemical changes.

17. **Assertion (A) :** Coating an iron sheet with a layer of zinc is called galvanisation.

    Reason (R) : The process which converts iron to iron oxide in the presence of moisture and air is called rusting.

    (a) Both A and R are true and R is the correct explanation of A.

    (b) Both A and R are true but R is not the correct explanation of A.

    (c) A is true but R is false.

    (d) A is false but R is true.

18. Lime water is a solution of

    (a) $Ca(OH)_2$ in water.

    (b) $CaCl_2$ in water.

    (c) NaOH in water.

    (d) NaCl in water.

19. Match the following columns and choose the correct answer.

Column-I	Column-II
(A) Reeling	(p) Process of rearing of silkworms for obtaining silk
(B) Wool industry	(q) Anthrax
(C) Shearing	(r) Unwind the threads or fibres of silk from the cocoon
(D) Sericulture	(s) Removing fleece from the body of sheep

    (a) A - s, B - q, C - r, D - p

    (b) A - p, B - s, C - r, D - q

    (c) A - r, B - q, C - s, D - p

    (d) A - r, B - q, C - p, D - s

20. Dark blue is the colour of red litmus on dissolving into which of the following solution?

    (a) Sulphur

    (b) Ammonia

    (c) Oxygen

    (d) Hydrogen

21. Soil has particles of different sizes. Arrange the words given below in increasing order of their particle size.

    Rock, Clay, Sand, Gravel, Silt.

    (a) Rock > Gravel > Sand > Silt > Clay

    (b) Sand > Rock > Gravel > Clay > Silt

    (c) Rock > Sand > Clay > Gravel > Silt

    (d) Rock > Gravel > Clay > Sand > Silt

22. Roshni wanted to buy a gift made of animal fibre obtained without killing the animals. Which of the following would be the right gift for her to buy?

    (a) Woollen shawl

    (b) Silk scarf

    (c) Animal fur cap

    (d) Leather jacket

23. Match column I with column II and choose the correct option.

Column I	Column II
(A) Black soil	(p) Suitable for growth of sugarcane and cotton
(B) Red soil	(q) Less fertile
(C) Alluvial soil	(r) Suitable for cultivation of wheat, rice and sugarcane
(D) Mountain soil	(s) Iron oxide

   (a) A - p, B - s, C - q, D - r
   (b) A - p, B - r, C - s, D - q
   (c) A - p, B - s, C - r, D - q
   (d) A - q, B - s, C - r, D - p

24. Ammonium hydroxide is found in
   (a) window cleaner
   (b) detergents
   (c) soap
   (d) milk of magnesia

25. Which of the following statements is true?
   (a) All substances are either acidic or basic.
   (b) A compound if acidic will turn all indicators to red.
   (c) Lime water turns red litmus to blue.
   (d) Common salt dissolved in water turns blue litmus red.

26. We turn on a bulb and filament changes its colour and becomes bright. Is it chemical change like burning?
   (a) No, filament burn itself but that is not a chemical change.
   (b) Yes, filament burns itself like wood to give light.
   (c) No, filament does not change into something new.
   (d) Yes, filament made up of tungsten changes to its oxide on burning.

27. Which of the following salts is basic in nature?
   (a) NH_4NO_3 (b) Na_2CO_3
   (c) Na_2SO_4 (d) $NaCl$

28. Which of the following set of substances contain acids?
   (a) Grapes, lime water
   (b) Vinegar, soap
   (c) Curd, milk of magnesia
   (d) Curd, vinegar

29. If you perform an experiment bare handed and you realise that your palm has become slippery and slimy. The most probable reason for this is that you have dropped
   (a) sodium hydroxide on your hands.
   (b) hydrochloric acid on your hands.
   (c) sodium chloride on your hands.
   (d) none of these

30. The diagram shows a beaker of water that is being heated.

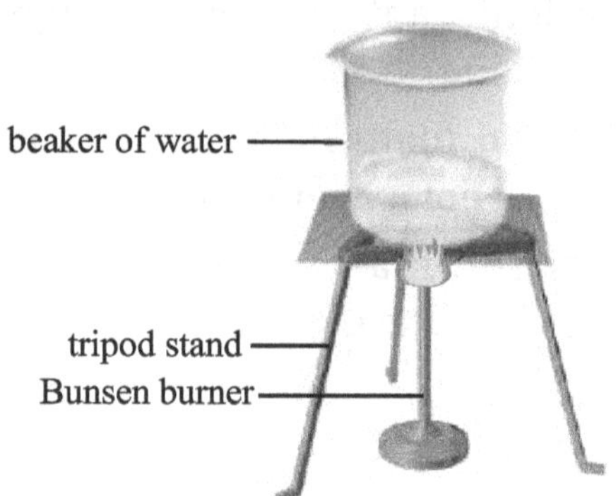

Which of the following statement is not true?

(a) The water in the beaker will lose heat.

(b) The amount of water in the beaker will decrease.

(c) The temperature of the water will increase.

(d) The amount of water vapour in the air will increase.

BIOLOGY

31. Most crops require a lot of nitrogen to synthesize the proteins. The bacterium *Rhizobium* helps some of the crops to get nitrogen. Which of the following statement is incorrect for *Rhizobium*?

(a) It converts atmospheric nitrogen into a soluble form that the plants can absorb.

(b) It can make its own food.

(c) It lives in the roots of leguminous plants like grams, peas, moong etc.

(d) Legiminous plants provide food and shelter to *Rhizobium*.

32. Traditionally in India, the structure called *baolis* is used for storing rainwater. The water collected during monsoon was used during non-monsoon months. It was also used to recharge groundwater. Such type of water conservation is known as ______.

(a) recycling of water

(b) rainwater harvesting

(c) rainwater treatment

(d) none of these

33. The snowshoe rabbit lives in the snowy regions. What best explains the rabbit's white fur colour?

(a) Increased sunlight results in lighter pigmentation and fur colour.

(b) White fur absorbs most of the sunlight that strikes it, keeping the rabbit warm.

(c) White fur is a better insulator against freezing temperature.

(d) White fur makes the rabbit less visible in the snow.

34. In a tall tree, which force is responsible for pulling water and minerals from the soil?

(a) Gravitational force

(b) Transportation force

(c) Suction force

(d) Conduction force

35. Earthworms and frogs breath through their skin because of which the skin of both the organisms are

(a) moist and rough.

(b) dry and rough.

(c) dry and slimy.

(d) moist and slimy.

36. Hydrochloric acid secreted in the stomach is strong enough to kill bacteria that enter along with food, however the inner lining of the stomach is protected from such corrosive action of hydrochloric acid?

    (a) Inner lining of stomach is thick enough to prevent corrosive action of HCl.

    (b) Inner lining of stomach secretes mucus which forms a protective layer over it.

    (c) The glands in the stomach secrete some bases that neutralize the effect of HCl.

    (d) All of the above

37. Chinmay is blowing into a beaker containing limewater through a straw. What will he observe?

    (a) Limewater turns violet.

    (b) Limewater turns yellow.

    (c) Limewater turns milky.

    (d) No change in the colour of limewater.

38. Match Column-I with Column-II and select the correct answer using the codes given below the columns.

Column-I	**Column-II**
(A) Food Pipe	(p) Digestive tract
(B) Alimentary canal	(q) Oesophagus
(C) Stomach	(r) Flattened U shape
(D) Widest part of alimentary canal	(s) Stomach

    (a) A → (p), B → (q), C → (r), D → (s)
    (b) A → (q), B → (r), C → (s), D → (p)
    (c) A → (q), B → (p), C → (r), D → (s)
    (d) A → (r), B → (s), C → (q), D → (p)

39. Select the one that is true about cross pollination

    (a) generally it results in higher yield of plants

    (b) It takes place only in unisexual flowers

    (c) It can fail to occur because of distance barrier

    (d) It requires production of large number of pollen grains.

40. Pollen sacs are found in

    (a) pollen grain   (b) pollen tube

    (c) anther   (d) ovule

41. When a person breathes in, what happens to the diaphragm and to the rib cage?

Diaphragm	**Rib cage**
(a) Becomes flatten	Moves downwards and inwards
(b) Become flatten	Moves outwards and upwards
(c) Becomes more curved	Moves downwards and inwards
(d) Becomes more curved	Moves outwards and upwards

42. Read the following statements with reference to the villi of small intestine.
   (i) They have very thin walls.
   (ii) They have a network of thin and small blood vessels close to the surface.
   (iii) They have small pores through which food can easily pass.
   (iv) They are finger-like projections.
   Identify those statements which enables the villi to absorb digest food.
   (a) (i), (ii) and (iv)
   (b) (ii), (iii) and (iv)
   (c) (iii) and (iv)
   (d) (i) and (iv)

43. Two organisms are good friends and live together. One provides shelter, water, and nutrients while the other prepares and provides food. Such an association of organisms is termed as
   (a) saprophyte   (b) parasite
   (c) autotroph   (d) symbiosis

44. Lila observed that a pond with clear water was covered up with a green algae within a weak. By which method of reproduction did the algae spread so rapidly?
   (a) Budding
   (b) Sexual reproduction
   (c) Fragmentation
   (d) Pollination

45. Given below are some adaptive features of animals:
   (i) Layer of fat under the skin
   (ii) Long, curved and sharp claws
   (iii) Slippery body
   (iv) Thick white fur
   Which of them are the adaptive features of a polar bear?
   (a) (i) only
   (b) (i) and (ii) only
   (c) (i), (ii) and (iii) only
   (d) (i), (ii) and (iv) only

46. A large area of forest was cleared by burning. Which of the following statements is/are correct?
   (i) Rise in soil erosion as soil is directly exposed to wind and rain.
   (ii) The land will have more fresh air as there are lesser tress to take in oxygen.

(iii) Wildlife will easily thrive in the cleared area because more space is available now.

(iv) New trees will grow faster and replace the burnt forest soon as the ash of the burnt trees will make the soil more fertile.

(a) (i) only

(b) (i) and (iv)

(c) (i), (ii) and (iv)

(d) (i), (ii), (iii) and (iv)

47. Arterial blood may be distinguished from venous blood because the latter is

(a) a dull red

(b) a brighter red

(c) thicker

(d) thinner

48. Forests are not responsible for

(a) providing medicinal plants.

(b) maintaining the flow water into the streams.

(c) creating flood conditions.

(d) absorbing rainwater and maintaining water table.

49. Look at the given diagram carefully.

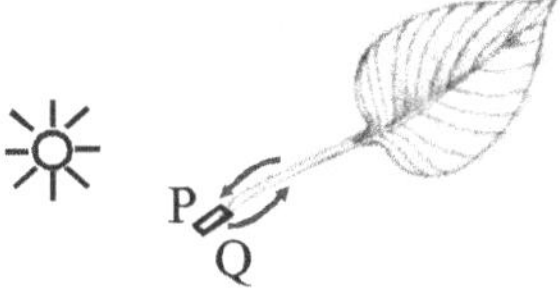

Which of the following correctly matches the substances carried in the direction of arrows P and Q

	P	Q
(a)	Water	Sugar
(b)	Carbon dioxide	Oxygen
(c)	Water vapour	Carbon dioxide
(d)	Sugar	Water

50. Match column-I with column-II and select the correct answer using the codes given below the columns.

Column-I	Column-II
(A) Anemometer	(i) caused by high speed wind and air pressure difference.
(B) Cyclone	(ii) accompanied by reduced pressure.
(C) Increased wind speed	(iii) instrument used to measure wind speed.
(D) Wind movement	(iv) caused due to uneven heating on earth.

(a) A → (iii); B → (ii); C → (i); D → (iv)   (b) A → (iii); B → (i); C → (ii); D → (iv)

(c) A → (iii); B → (iv); C → (i); D → (ii)   (d) A → (iii); B → (ii); C → (iv); D → (i)

OLYMPIAD Mock Test 3

Name : __________

Number of Questions : 50

There is no negative marking in the test.

Max. Marks : 50

Time : 2 Hours

PHYSICS

1. Which one of the following process is involved for heating the liquid inside the pan?
   (a) Conduction (b) Convection
   (c) Radiation (d) All of these

2. Which one of the following is true for the uniform speed
   (a) If speed of the object varies at different intervals of time, the object has uniform speed
   (b) If speed of the object is constant at different intervals of time, the object has uniform speed
   (c) If a moving object suddenly comes to rest, the object has uniform speed
   (d) All of these

3. Three bulbs A, B and C are connected in a circuit as shown in Figure. When the switch is 'ON'

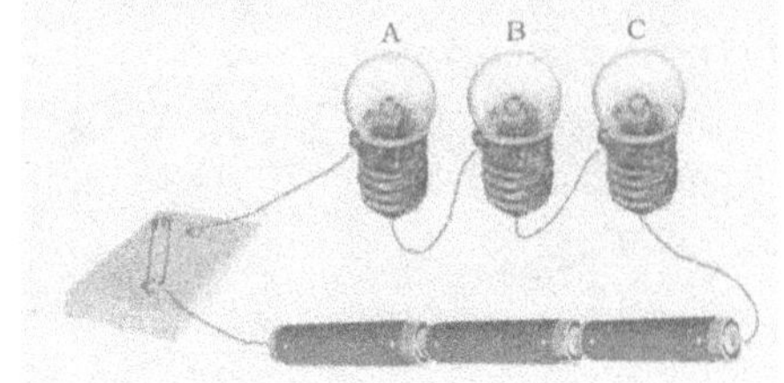

   (a) bulb C will glow first.
   (b) bulb B and C will glow simultaneously and bulb A will glow after sometime.
   (c) all the bulbs A, B and C will glow at the same time.
   (d) the bulbs will glow in the order A, B and C

4. When a person moves closer to a plane mirror, the size of his image in the mirror
   (a) increases
   (b) remains the same
   (c) decreases
   (d) first increases and then decreases.

5. Karan and Johar measured their body temperature. Karan found 98.6 F and Johar recorded 37°C. Which of the following statement is true?
   (a) Karan has a higher body temperature than Johar.
   (b) Karan has a lower body temperature than Johar.
   (c) Both have normal body temperature.
   (d) Both are suffering from fever.

6. The image is formed by a plane mirror is due to the reflection of light. Why an image is called virtual when it is formed by a plane mirror?
    (a) It can be obtained on the screen
    (b) It cannot be obtained on the screen
    (c) Both (a) and (b)
    (d) None of these

7. Which of the following figures does not use the heating effect of current?

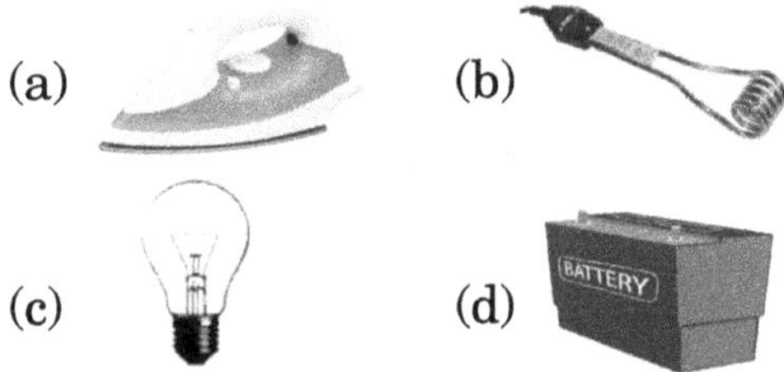

8. A man walks on a straight road from his home to market 2.5km away with a speed of 5 km/h. Finding the market closed, he instantly turns and walks back home with a speed of 7.5 km/h. The average speed of the man over the interval of time 0 to 40 min. is equal to –
    (a) 5 km/h   (b) 25/4 km/h
    (c) 30/4 km/h   (d) 45/8 km/h

9. What is the tendency of hot air?
    (a) It tends to rise and causes a drop in pressure of atmosphere
    (b) It tends to rise and causes an increase in pressure of atmosphere
    (c) It tends to rise but does not cause any change in pressure of the atmosphere
    (d) None of these

10. When a light ray is reflected repeatedly by a set of parallel plane mirrors, the intensity of light rays decreases after some reflections. This is because of
    (a) poor reflection from mirrors
    (b) absorption of some amount of light by mirrors
    (c) dispersion of light when the rays travel through the atmosphere
    (d) scattering of light by the mirrors.

11. Suppose we take two identical size rods (one wooden rod and another iron rod) and wrap each one of them in a piece of paper, and heat, these rods with a candle flame. On being heated, the paper around the iron rod does not burn but the one around wooden rod catches fire. Which of the following is the possible reason for this ?
    (a) Iron being a good conductor, conducts away heat given to paper.
    (b) Wood being an insulator, takes away all the heat.
    (c) In case of iron rod, the candle is near the paper.
    (d) Paper around iron rod is thicker.

12. Figure shows an oscillating pendulum.

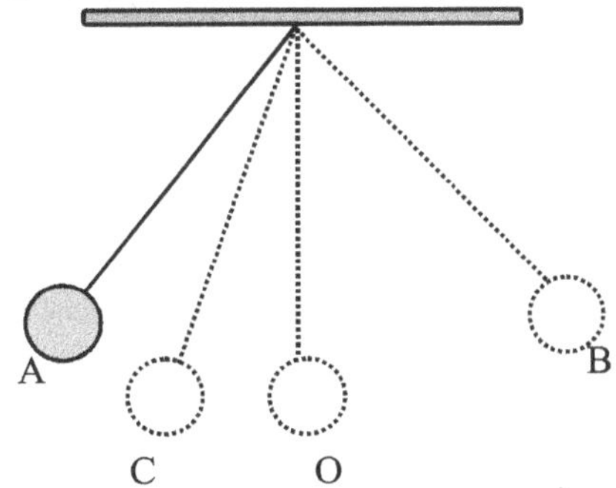

Time taken by the bob to move from A to C is t_1 and from C to O is t_2. The time period of this simple pendulum is

(a) $(t_1 + t_2)$ (b) $2(t_1 + t_2)$

(c) $3(t_1 + t_2)$ (d) $4(t_1 + t_2)$

13. A rainbow can be seen in the sky
    (a) when the sun is in front of us.
    (b) when the sun is behind us.
    (c) when the sun is overhead.
    (d) only at the time of sun rise.

14. The experiment shows that heat causes solids to change their ______________.

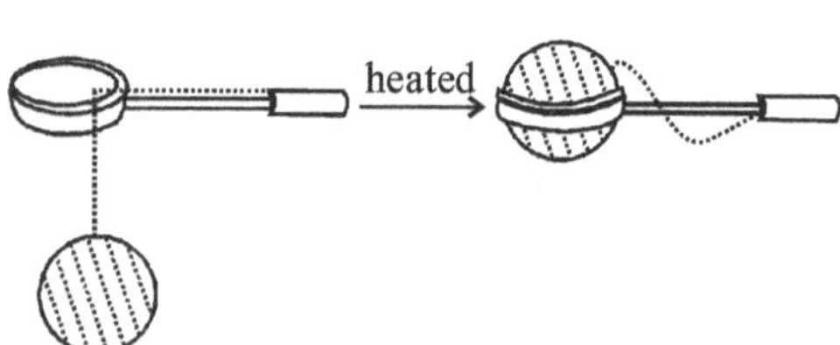

    (a) Sizes   (b) States
    (c) Shapes   (d) Composition

15. Which of the following place is most likely to be affected by a cyclone?
    (a) Mumbai   (b) Puri
    (c) Goa   (d) Porbandar

CHEMISTRY

16. Complete the following equation of rusting of iron.

    Iron(Fe) + A + moisture → B

    (a) A = Oxygen, B = Carbon dioxide
    (b) A = Water, B = Oxygen
    (c) A = Oxygen, B = Rust (iron oxide)
    (d) A = Carbon dioxide, B = Oxygen

17. Liquified Petroleum Gas (L.P.G.) used as kitchen fuel is supplied in the liquid form in the gas cylinders. When it comes out from cylinder it comes out as a gas which burns. Which of the following statements is correct?
    (a) The process of conversion of liquid to gas involves a chemical change.
    (b) The process of burning gas is a chemical change.
    (c) Both the above are correct.
    (d) None of these

18. Match column I that consists of different types of silk with column II having plants on which respective silkworms are reared and select the correct option from the codes given below.

Column I	Column II
(A) Muga silk	(i) Polyanthus
(B) Eri silk	(ii) Sal
(C) Tussar silk	(iii) Castor

    (a) (A) - (i), (B) - (ii), (C) - (iii)
    (b) (A) - (iii), (B) - (ii), (C) - (i)
    (c) (A) - (iii), (B) - (i), (C) - (ii)
    (d) (A) - (i), (B) - (iii), (C) - (ii)

19. Study the flowchart carefully and identify X and Y.

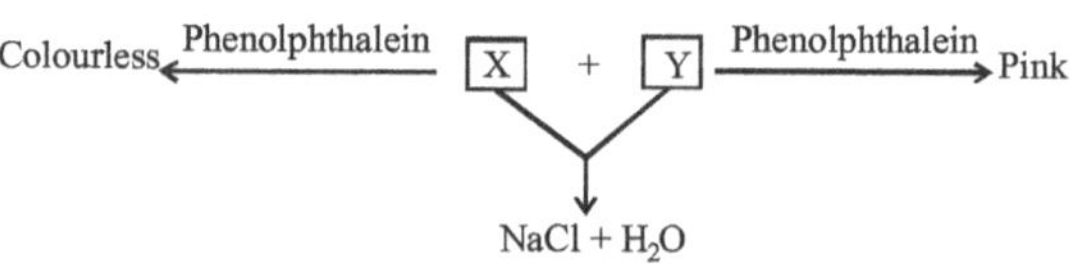

    (a) X = NaOH, Y = NaCl
    (b) X = HCl, Y = NaOH
    (c) X = NaOH, Y = HCl
    (d) X = HCl, Y = H_2O

20. Soil conservation measures are mainly aimed at protecting which of the following?
    (a) Plants
    (b) Top soil
    (c) Subsoil
    (d) Soil organisms

21. Which of the following is an acid-base indicator?
    - (a) Vinegar
    - (b) Lime water
    - (c) Turmeric
    - (d) Baking soda

22. **Assertion (A) :** Soil is formed by weathering of rocks.

    Reason (R) : The process of breaking down of rocks by the action of wind, water and climate is called weathering.
    - (a) Both A and R are true and R is the correct explanation of A.
    - (b) Both A and R are true but R is not the correct explanation of A.
    - (c) A is true but R is false.
    - (d) A is false but R is true.

23. A man digging the ground near a water body found that the soil was moist. As he kept digging deeper and deeper he reached a level where all the spaces between particles of soil and gaps between rocks were filled with water. The upper limit of the layer is called
    - (a) water level.
    - (b) water table.
    - (c) ground water.
    - (d) water limit.

24. On the basis of following features identify the correct fibre
    - I. It is originally a natural product.
    - II. It is obtained from hairs of animals.
    - III. It traps and retains a lot of air and is suitable to wear in winters.
    - (a) Silk
    - (b) Wool
    - (c) Jute
    - (d) Polyester

25. Following are given the steps involved in the processing of fibre into wool. Arrange them in a proper sequence and select the correct option.
    - (i) Rearing
    - (ii) Scouring
    - (iii) Removing burr
    - (iv) Shearing
    - (v) Sorting
    - (vi) Making yarn
    - (vii) Dyeing
    - (a) (i) → (iii) → (v) → (ii) → (vii) → (iv) → (vi)
    - (b) (i) → (iv) → (ii) → (v) → (iii) → (vii) → (vi)
    - (c) (v) → (ii) → (iv) → (iii) → (vii) → (vi) → (i)
    - (d) (ii) → (iii) → (iv) → (i) → (v) → (vii) → (vi)

26. Fill in the blanks by choosing the option with correct words.

    The process of rusting is a ______ change. For rusting, both ______ and ______ are required. The salt present in sea water makes the process of rusting ______.
    - (a) chemical, air, water, faster
    - (b) physical, air, water, slower
    - (c) chemical, air, water, slower
    - (d) physical, air, water, faster

27. Monika categorised the following household items into acids and bases.

Acids	Bases
1. Lemon	4. Baking soda
2. Antacid	5. Vinegar
3. Tea	6. Curd

    Which of them are placed under the wrong category?
    - (a) 3 and 5
    - (b) 2 and 6
    - (c) 3, 4 and 5
    - (d) 2, 5 and 6

28. Carbonic acid, the primary agent of chemical weathering is produced by _______ .
    (a) carbon dioxide dissolved in rainwater.
    (b) plant roots.
    (c) bacteria that feed on plant and animal remains.
    (d) all of the above

29. Which of the following stages in the life history of a silkmoth produces silk fibres?

    (a) 

    (b) 

    (c) 

    (d) None of these

30. Two drops of dilute sulphuric acid were added to 1 g of copper sulphate powder and then small amount of hot water was added to dissolve it (step I). On cooling, beautiful blue coloured crystals got separated (step II). Step I and step II
    (a) are physical and chemical changes respectively.
    (b) are chemical and physical changes respectively.
    (c) both are physical changes.
    (d) both are chemical changes.

31. During the formation of rain, when water vapour changes back to liquid in the form of rain drops
    (a) Heat is absorbed
    (b) Heat is released
    (c) Heat is first absorbed and then released
    (d) There is no exchange of heat

32. Spores are
    (a) asexual reproductive bodies
    (b) sexual reproductive bodies
    (c) covered by delicate coatings
    (d) all the above are correct

33. Match the column - I with column II and select the correct option from the codes given below.

Column-I	Column-II
(A) Chlorophyll	(i) *Rhizobium*
(B) Symbiosis	(ii) Starch
(C) Insectivorous plant	(iii) Lichen
(D) Nitrogen fixing organism	(iv) Mistletoe
(E) Partial parasite	(v) Pitcher plant

    (a) (A) - (i), (B) - (iv), (C) - (iii), (D) - (ii), (E) - (v)
    (b) (A) - (iii), (B) - (v), (C) - (ii), (D) - (i), (E) - (iv)
    (c) (A) - (ii), (B) - (iii), (C) - (v), (D) - (i), (E) - (iv)
    (d) (A) - (v), (B) - (iv), (C) - (i), (D) - (ii), (E) - (iii)

34. Pick from the following one chemical used to disinfect water.
    (a) Chlorine
    (b) Washing soda
    (c) Silica
    (d) Coal

35. The common feature in both the things below is

(a) both can be classified as sea animals.
(b) both can move in water using some fuel.
(c) both have streamlined body.
(d) Nothing is common in them.

36. When we observe the lower surface of a leaf through a magnifying lens we see numerous small openings. Which of the following is the term given to such opening?
(a) Stomata
(b) Lamina
(c) Midrib
(d) Veins

37. Which of the following is a part of inorganic impurities of the sewage?
(a) Pesticides
(b) Urea
(c) Phosphates
(d) Vegetable waste

38. Yeast is used in wine and beer industries because it respires
(a) aerobically producing oxygen.
(b) aerobically producing alcohol.
(c) anaerobically producing alcohol.
(d) anaerobically producing CO_2.

39. Hump of a camel is used to
(a) tread on the desert land
(b) store food
(c) store water
(d) both (b) and (c)

40. The system of a network of pipes used for taking away wastewater from homes or public buildings to the treatment plant is known as
(a) sewers
(b) sewerage
(c) transport system
(d) treatment plant

41. Which of the following gives the correct functions of the xylem and phloem in a green plant?

	Xylem	Phloem
(a)	Transports food, water and minerals	Provides support to the plant
(b)	Transports water, minerals and gases	Provides support to the plant
(c)	Provides support to plant and transports gases	Transports water and minerals
(d)	Provides support to plant and transports water and minerals	Transports food

42. Match the column - I with column II and select the correct option from the codes given below.

	Column-I		Column-II
(A)	Energy value of food is measured in calories.		(i) True
(B)	Starch and sugar are proteins.		(ii) False
(C)	Cellulose can be digested in our digestive system.		
(D)	In absence of peristalsis, food from oesophagus cannot enter stomach.		

(a) (A) - (i), (B) - (ii), (C) - (ii), (D) - (i)
(b) (A) - (ii), (B) - (i), (C) - (ii), (D) - (i)

(c) (A) - (i), (B) - (i), (C) - (ii), (D) - (ii)

(d) (A) - (ii), (B) - (i), (C) - (i), (D) - (ii)

43. Bees that collect nectar from the flower help carry 'X' to other places. Which part of the flower should the bees touch to collect 'X'?

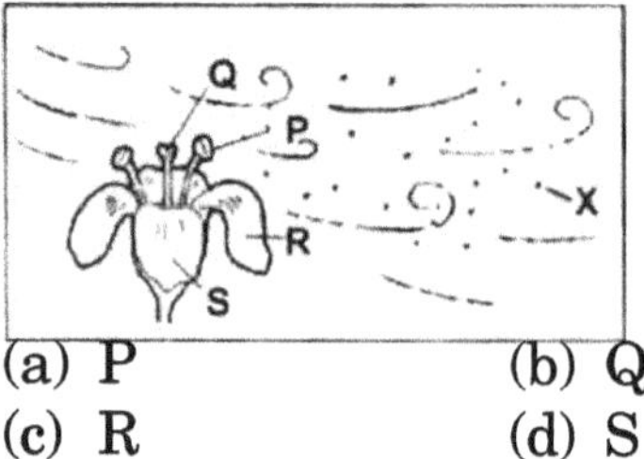

(a) P (b) Q

(c) R (d) S

44. Aquifer

(a) It refers to the place where ground water is stored between the layers of hard rock above water table.

(b) It refers to the place where ground water is stored between the layers of hard rock below the water table.

(c) Both the above are correct.

(d) None of these is correct

45. Neeta went to a wildlife sanctuary where she saw dense vegetation of trees, shrubs, herbs and also a variety of animals like monkeys, birds, elephants, snakes, frogs, etc. The most likely location of this sanctuary is in the-

(a) temperate region

(b) tropical region

(c) polar region

(d) coastal region

46. Which of the following is incorrect?

(a) The tropical rain forests support a wide variety of plants and animals.

(b) We find animals such as ape, bird Toucan, red eyed frogs etc in the regions of tropical rain forests.

(c) The temperature range in the areas of tropical rain forests is 15–40°C.

(d) None of the above is incorrect.

47. Match column I with column II and select the correct answers using the code given below the columns.

Column-I	Column-II
(A) Salivary glands	(p) pepsin
(B) Liver	(q) trypsin
(C) Small intestine	(r) amylase
(D) Stomach	(s) Bile

(a) A → r, B → s, C → q, D → p

(b) A → r, B → q, C → p, D → s

(c) A → s, B → r, C → q, D → p

(d) A → q, B → p, C → s, D → r

48. Mesoglea is present in-

(a) Sponges (b) Hydra

(c) Spirogyra (d) Vaucheria

49. Which of the following pair of teeth differ in structure but are similar in function?

(a) canines and incisors.

(b) molars and premolars.

(c) incisors and molars.

(d) premolars and canines.

50. Which of the following statement is incorrect of penguins?

(a) They huddle together

(b) They cannot swim

(c) They have webbed feet

(d) They have streamlined body

Name : _________

Number of Questions : 50

There is no negative marking in the test.

Max. Marks : 50

Time : 2 Hours

PHYSICS

1. Raman walks to his school which is at a distance of 3 km from his home in 30 minutes. On reaching he finds that the school is closed and comes back by a bicycle with his friend and reaches home in 20 minutes. His average speed in km/h is
   (a) 8.3 (b) 7.5
   (c) 5 (d) 3.6

2. When electric current is flowing through a conductor, then some amount of
   (a) electrical energy is converted into heat energy
   (b) electrical energy is converted into mechanical energy
   (c) mechanical energy is converted into electrical energy
   (d) heat energy is converted into electrical energy

3. Velocity-time graph for a particle moving along a straight line is shown in the figure. Mark the correct statement.

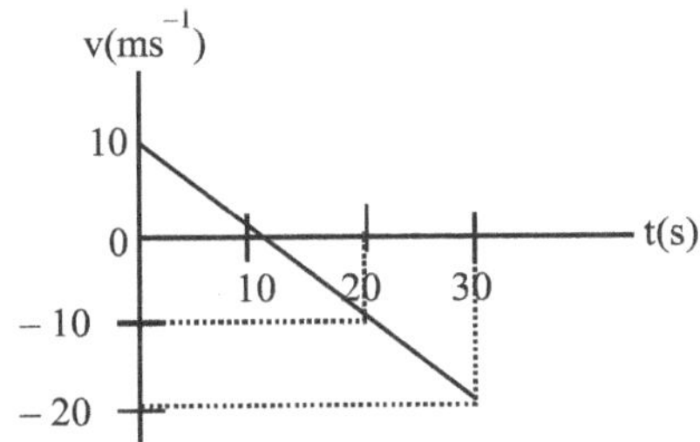

   (a) The particle has never turned around.
   (b) The particle has zero displacement.
   (c) The particle has same average velocity between 0 to 10s and 10 to 20s.
   (d) Both (a) and (b)

4. On holding a stainless steel spoon near our face, we see
   (a) our inverted image on outer side of the spoon
   (b) our erect image on inner side of the spoon
   (c) our inverted image on inner side of the spoon
   (d) our laterally inverted image on inner side of the spoon.

5. The diagram shows an electric bell

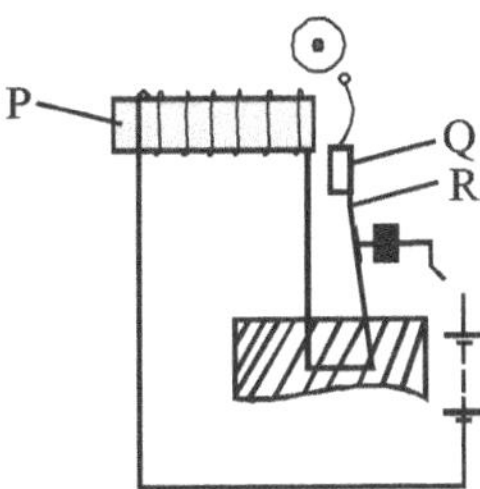

   Which materials would be suitable for the parts labelled P, Q and R?

	P	Q	R
A	soft iron	brass	soft iron
B	soft iron	soft iron	spring steel
C	soft iron	brass	brass
D	spring steel	soft iron	spring steel

   (a) A (b) B
   (c) C (d) D

6. A ray of light consists of seven colours as we can see in a rainbow. How can it be easily shown in the physics lab?
   (a) When a ray of light falls on a transparent glass prism
   (b) When a ray of light falls on a plane mirror
   (c) When a ray of light falls on a spherical mirror
   (d) All of these

7. A cyclist covers 25 km in first hour, 30 km in the second hour and 35 km in the third hour. The cyclist is in __________.
   (a) Uniform motion
   (b) Non-uniform motion
   (c) Cannot be find that the body is in uniform motion or in non uniform motion
   (d) All of these

8. When we touch a steel rod and a paper simultaneously, we feel that the rod is colder because:
   (a) iron being a good conductor conducts more heat from our body
   (b) paper being a good conductor conducts more heat from our body
   (c) more heat flows from the iron to our body
   (d) more heat flows from the paper to our body

9. Speed-distance graph of an object in uniform motion which comes to rest suddenly is

(a)
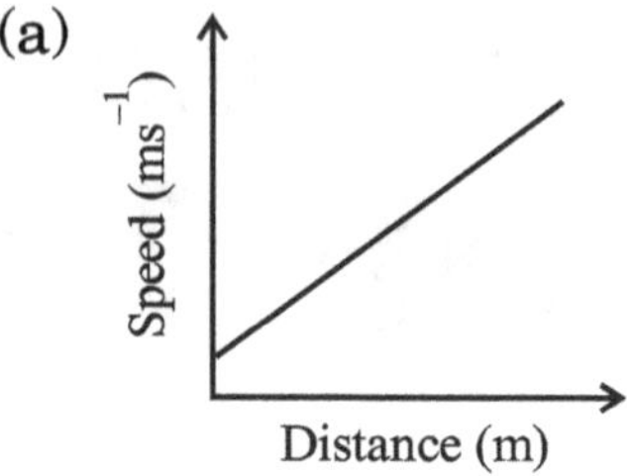

(b)
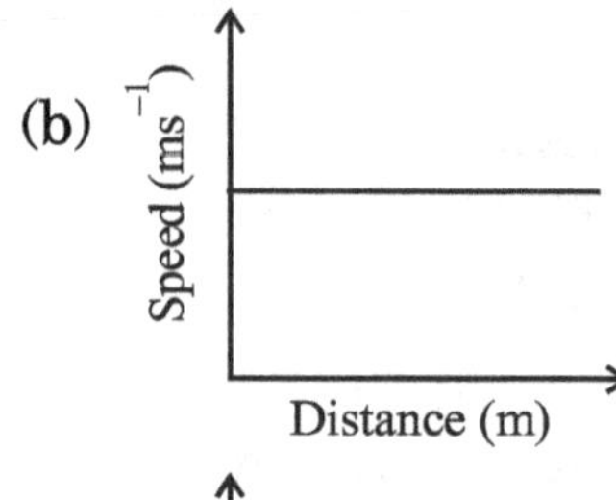

(c)
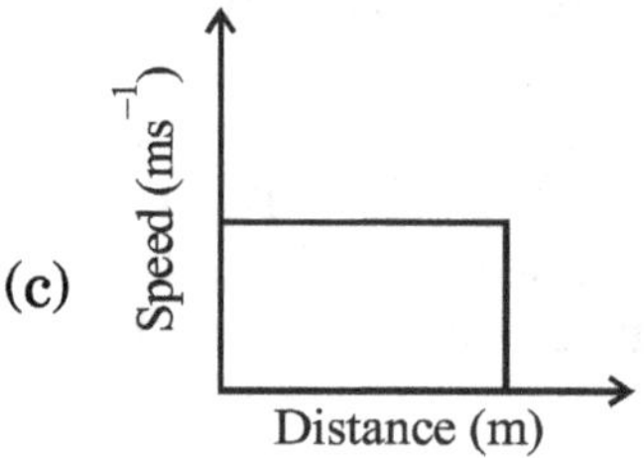

(d)
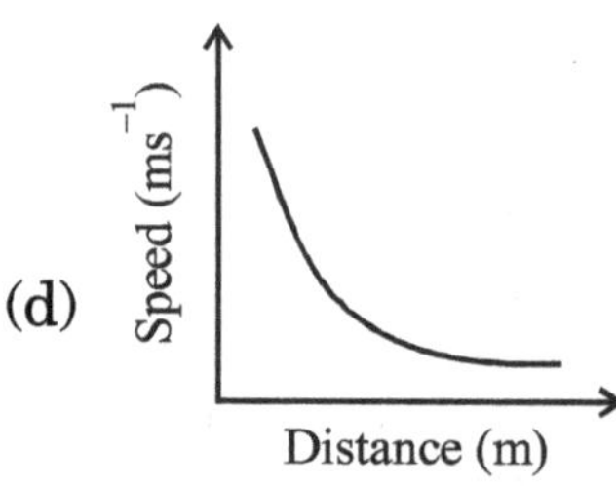

10. Air moves from a region of
    (a) low pressure to high pressure
    (b) high pressure to low pressure
    (c) movement of air is independent of pressure
    (d) None of these

11. Which one of the following statements regarding a rainbow is correct?

(a) It is always seen as a circle.

(b) The order of colours is always (from the top to bottom as seen from the ground) violet, indigo, blue, green, yellow, orange, red.

(c) Its order of colours is always (from the top to bottom as seen from the ground)red, orange, yellow, green, blue, indigo, violet.

(d) The order of colours can be either violet to red or red to violet depending upon the time of the day.

12. Karan has three thermometers as shown in Fig. He wants to measure the temperature of his body and that of boiling water. Which thermometer (s) should he choose?

(i)

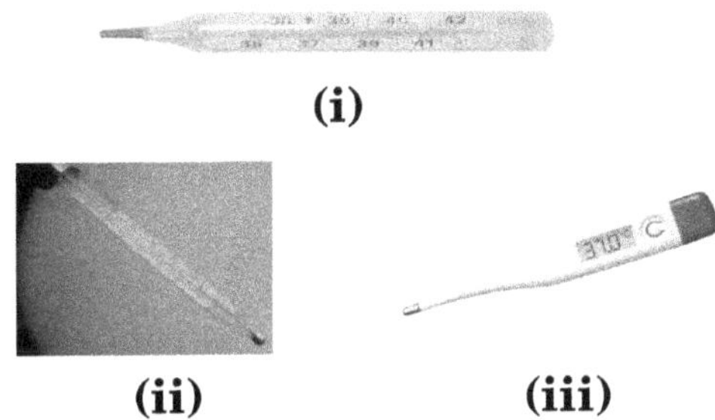

(ii)   **(iii)**

(a) Thermometer (i) or (iii) for measuring body temperature and (ii) for measuring the temperature of boiling water.

(b) Thermometer (i) for measuring temperature of both.

(c) Thermometer (ii) for measuring temperature of both.

(d) Thermometer (iii) for measuring temperature of both.

13. When a switch is in OFF position.

(i) circuit starting from the positive terminal of the cell stops at the switch.

(ii) circuit is open.

(iii)no current flow through it.

(iv)current flows after some time.

Choose the combination of correct answer from the following.

(a) all are correct

(b) (ii) and (iii) are correct

(c) only (iv) is correct

(d) only (i) and (ii) are correct

14. An image formed by a lens is erect. Such an image could be formed by a

(a) convex lens provided the image is smaller than object.

(b) concave lens provided the image is smaller than object.

(c) concave lens provided the image is larger than object.

(d) concave lens provided the image is of the same size.

15. The factor(s) which contribute(s) to the development of cyclones is/are

(i) Wind speed

(ii) Temperature

(iii)Humidity

(a) (i) only

(b) (ii) and (iii) only

(c) (i) and (iii) only

(d) All of these

CHEMISTRY

16. A man painted his main gate made up of iron, to

(i) prevent it from rusting.

(ii) protect it from sun.

(iii)make it look beautiful.

(iv)make it dust free.

Which of the above statement(s) is/are correct?

(a) (i) and (ii)   (b) (ii) and (iii)

(c) only (ii)   (d) (i) and (iii)

17. Wool industry is an important means of livelihood for many people in our country. But sorter's job is risky as sometimes they get infected by a _____________ called _____________ which leads to a fatal lung disease called sorter's disease.
    (a) bacterium, *Bacillus anthracis*
    (b) bacterium, *Escherichia coli*
    (c) fungus, *Salmonella typhimurium*
    (d) virus, *Vibrio anthracis*

18. Ground water is water that fills pores in soil and rock. It is formed when precipitation percolates into the ground. Select the correct statement regarding it.
    (a) An aquifer is above ground layer of water-bearing permeable rocks or unconsolidated materials.
    (b) The area where all available spaces below the ground level are filled with water is called saturated zone.
    (c) The lower level of water under the ground which occupies all the space in soil and rocks is called water table.
    (d) An artesian well is formed if the water table on sides is lower than the middle.

19. Which of the following diagram(s) represents alkalies and bases in the correct form?

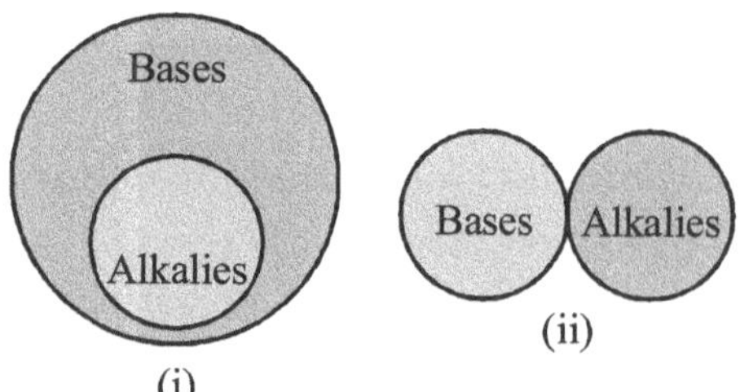

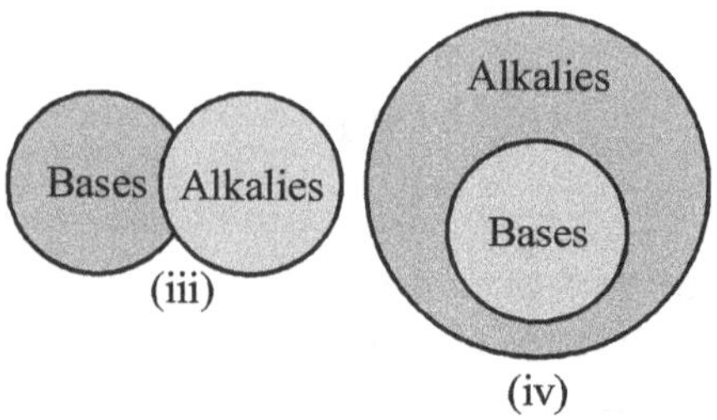

    (a) (i)   (b) (iii)
    (c) (i) and (iv)   (d) (iii) and (iv)

20. Dig up a handful of garden soil and put it in a beaker. Add about 500 mL of water and shake the beaker for a little while. Now allow the soil to settle down. In which order, the soil components will get arranged from (i) to (iv) as shown in the figure?

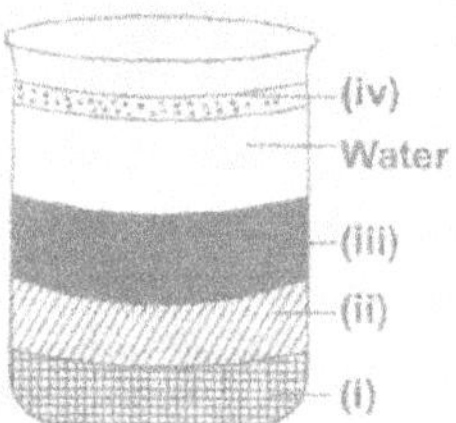

	(i)	(ii)	(iii)	(iv)
(a)	Sand	Silt	Clay	Gravel
(b)	Gravel	Sand	Clay	Humus
(c)	Clay	Gravel	Sand	Humus
(d)	Humus	Gravel	Sand	Clay

21. The shipping industry has to bear huge financial loss because of rusting of ships. The rusting of ships occur because
    (a) the body of ship is always in contact with water.
    (b) the air around the ship is humid.
    (c) presence of salts in sea water speed up the process of rusting.
    (d) all of the above

22. Column-I   Column-II
    A. Top soil   (p) Harder and more compact
    B. Sandy soil   (q) High percolation rate
    C. B-horizon   (r) Dark in colour
    D. Loamy soil   (s) Containing silt.

    (a) A → (r); B→ (q); C → (p); D → (s)
    (b) A →(s); B → (r); C → (q); D → (p)
    (c) A → (p); B → (q); C → (r); D → (s)
    (d) A → (q); B → (r); C → (s); D → (p)

23. The given figure shows the colour changes in test tubes I, II and III, when china rose indicator is added to them. The respective solutions in test tube I, II and III are

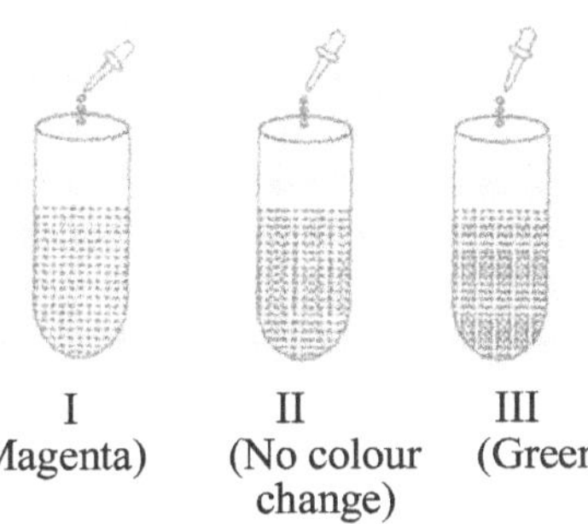

I   II   III
(Magenta)   (No colour   (Green
              change)

    (a) sugar solution, lime water, baking powder
    (b) sugar solution, lemon juice, vinegar
    (c) lime water, sugar solution, lemon juice
    (d) lemon juice, sugar solution, lime water

24. 50 mL of water at 25° C was poured into each of the three containers as shown in the given figure. The containers were then left in a closed room.

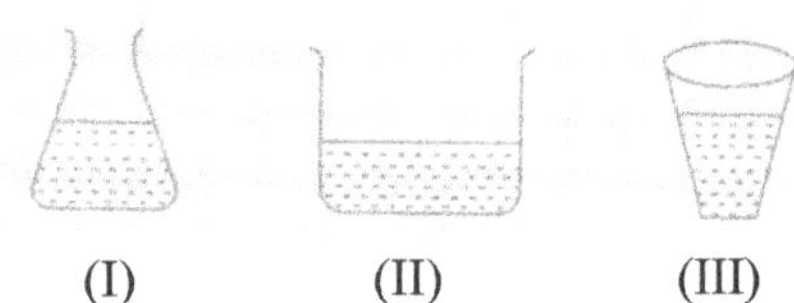

(I)   (II)   (III)

Which of the following graphs correctly shows the volume of water in each container after five hours?

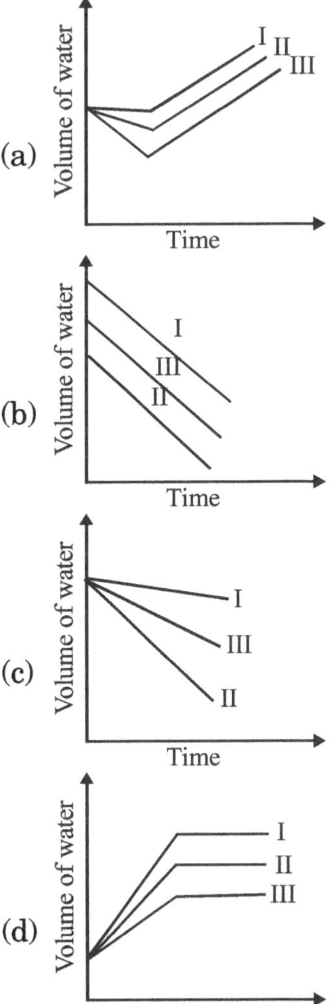

(a)
(b)
(c)
(d)

25. Select the correct match out of the following.

	Sheep breed	Quality of wool	State where found
(a)	Lohi	Brown fleece	Himachal pradesh
(b)	Rampur bushair	Coarse wool	Uttar Pradesh
(c)	Nali	For hosiery	Gujarat
(d)	Bakharwal	For woolen shawls	jammu and Kashmir

26. The given pie charts show the composition of three types of soil samples X, Y and Z. Which of the following is correct regarding these?

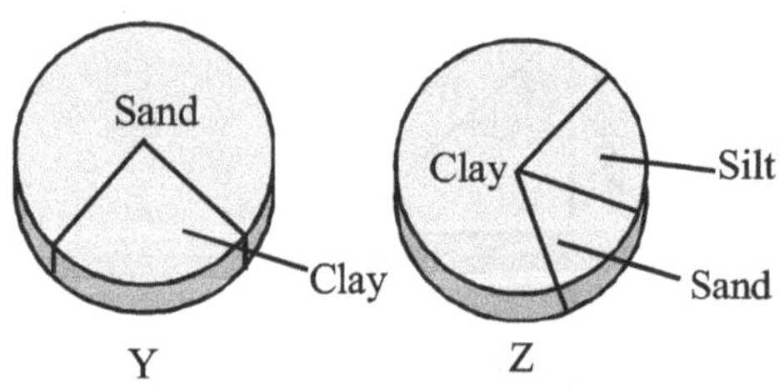

(a) X is unable to hold water or nutrients.
(b) Y is used for pot making.
(c) Z provides good amount of oxygen.
(d) X is best suited for cultivation.

27. Which of the following represents the correct sequence of different phases in the lifecycle of silkworm?

(a) Eggs → pupa → cocoon → caterpillar → adult moth

(b) Eggs → caterpillar → cocoon → pupa → adult moth

(c) Adult moth → eggs → pupa → caterpillar → cocoon

(d) Eggs → adult moth → pupa → cocoon → caterpillar

28. Rima prepared an indicator paper by dipping a paper strip in a solution of X. She put a few drops of an unknown solution Y which contain H^+ ions less than OH^- ions on this paper. She observed that the colour of paper turned yellow. What do you think was solution of X?

(a) Red litmus solution

(b) Phenolphthalein

(c) Methyl orange

(d) Turmeric solution

29. In a pressure-kerosene stove,

(i) we pump kerosene and convert it into vapours.

(ii) the vapours are then ignited.

Which of the following is true about the above statements?

(a) (i) is a chemical change; (ii) is a physical change.

(b) (i) is a physical change; (ii) is a chemical change.

(c) Both (i) and (ii) are physical changes.

(d) Both (i) and (ii) are chemical changes.

30. Match Column-I with Column-II and select the correct answer using the codes given below the columns.

Column-I	Column-II
A. Heat energy is evoled	(p) Physical change
B. Heat energy is absorbed	(q) Chemical change
C. Digestion of food in the body	(r) Exothermic reaction
D. Melting of wax	(s) Endothermic reaction

(a) A → (p); B → (q); C → (r); D → (s)
(b) A → (q); B → (p); C → (r); D → (s)
(c) A → (r); B → (s); C → (p); D → (q)
(d) A → (r); B → (s); C → (q); D → (p)

BIOLOGY

31. Vermi-processing toilet
    (a) is a design of toilet in which human excreta is treated by round worm.
    (b) is a design of toilet in which human excreta is treated by earthworm.
    (c) Both the above are correct
    (d) None of these is correct.

32. In a filtration the plant water is filtered using layers of
    (a) sand and clay.
    (b) clay and fine gravel.
    (c) sand and fine gravel.
    (d) sand, fine gravel and medium gravel.

33. Monu is a poor farmer. He cannot spend money on buying fertilizers. What should he do to increase the fertility of his farmland?
    (a) He should grow eucalyptus trees in his field.
    (b) He should water his field more frequently.
    (c) He should grow pea plants in his field.
    (d) He should grow mustard plants in his field.

34. Read the given statements and select the correct option.
    Statement 1: Chewing breaksdown the food into small pieces and aids in digestion.
    Statement 2: Chewing increases the surface area of food for the saliva to act upon.
    (a) Both statements 1 and 2 are true and statement 2 is the correct explanation of statement 1.
    (b) Both statements 1 and 2 are true and statement 2 is not the correct explanation of statement 1.
    (c) Statement 1 is true but statement 2 is false.
    (d) Both statements 1 and 2 are false.

35. Organisms which prepare food for themselves using simple naturally available raw materials is referred to as
    (a) heterotrophs   (b) autotrophs
    (c) parasites   (d) saprophytes

36. The female part which receives the pollen grains during the pollination will ________.
    (a) turn into the seeds of the fruit
    (b) form the stalk of the fruit
    (c) become flesh of the fruit
    (d) wither and drop off

37. Sometimes when we do heavy exercise, anaerobic respiration takes place in our muscle cells. What is produced during this process?
    (a) Alcohol and lactic acid.
    (b) Alcohol and CO_2
    (c) Lactic acid and CO_2
    (d) Lactic acid only

38. Which of the following is/are products of wastewater treatment?
    (a) Biogas
    (b) Sludge
    (c) Both biogas and sludge
    (d) Aerator

39. The finger-like outgrowth of amoeba helps to ingest food. However, the finger-like outgrowths of human intestine helps to
    (a) digest the fatty food substances.
    (b) make the food soluble.
    (c) absorb the digested food.
    (d) absorb the undigested food

40. Pulmonary _______ carries _______ rich blood from the heart to the lungs and pulmonary _______ carries _______ rich blood from the lungs to the heart.
    Select the option that correctly fills up the blank spaces in the above passage.
    (a) vein, carbon dioxide, artery, oxygen
    (b) vein, oxygen, artery, carbon dioxide
    (c) artery, carbon dioxide, vein, oxygen
    (d) artery, oxygen, vein, carbon dioxide

41. The pharynx actually has two apertures, one opening into the windpipe and the other into the _______. The aperture opening into the windpipe is guarded by _______. It closes the windpipe when you take _______. Select the correct sequence of words to complete the above passage.
    (a) oesophagus, uvula, food
    (b) stomach, epiglottis, water
    (c) oesophagus, epiglottis, food
    (d) liver, uvula, food

42. The organism in the given figure has a flattened body shape. This characteristic helps the organism to

    (a) survive for a long period without food
    (b) fly in the air
    (c) camouflage itself
    (d) crawl between crevices and spaces easily.

43. Which of the following is the correct sequence of human nutrition?
    (a) Ingestion → egestion → digestion → absorption → assimilation.
    (b) Egestion → ingestion → absorption → assimilation.
    (c) Digestion → assimilation → ingestion → absorption → egestion.
    (d) Ingestion → digestion → absorption → assimilation → egestion.

44. Which of the following animals have sticky pads on its feet ?
    (a) Blue eyed frog
    (b) Red eyed frog
    (c) Green eyed frog
    (d) Yellow eyed frog
45. The absorption of nutrients and exchange of respiratory gases between the blood and tissues takes place in-
    (a) veins   (b) arteries
    (c) heart   (d) capillaries
46. Which part of the elephant helps it to keep cool in the hot and humid climate of rain forests ?
    (a) Trunk   (b) Tusk
    (c) Ears   (d) Nose
47. Listed below are the stages of budding in yeast but they are not in the correct order.
    (i)   One of the nuclei enters the bud.
    (ii) A bud forms on the outer surface of a parent cell.
    (iii) The bud breaks away to become a new daughter cell.
    (iv) The nucleus then doubles and divides.
    (v)   A cell wall is formed between the parent cell and the bud.
    Which of the following options has the correct sequence of budding in yeast?
    (a) (i), (ii), (iv), (v), (iii)
    (b) (ii), (i), (v), (iii), (iv)
    (c) (ii), (iv), (i), (v), (iii)
    (d) (iv), (i), (ii), (v), (iii)
48. Cellulose-rich food substances are good source of roughage in human beings because
    (a) human beings do not have cellulose-digesting enzymes.
    (b) cellulose gets absorbed in the human blood and converts into fibres.
    (c) the cellulose-digesting bacteria convert cellulose into fibres.
    (d) cellulose breaks down into smaller components which are egested as roughage.
49. Why did the students place a layer of oil over the water?
    (a) To prevent plant from dying
    (b) To prevent evaporation of water
    (c) To prevent breeding of mosquitoes
    (d) Both (b) and (c)
50. The scaly skin of snakes
    (a) protects them from drying
    (b) helps them to crawl
    (c) makes them beautiful
    (d) Both (a) & (b)

Mock Test

Name : __________

Max. Marks : 50

Number of Questions : 50

Time : 2 Hours

There is no negative marking in the test.

PHYSICS

1. Kamal and Tarun were given one mirror each by their teacher. Kamal found his image to be erect and of the same size whereas Tarun found her image erect and smaller in size. This means that the mirrors of Kamal and Tarun are, respectively

   (a) plane mirror and concave mirror.

   (b) concave mirror and convex mirror.

   (c) plane mirror and convex mirror.

   (d) convex mirror and plane mirror.

2. Which one of the following is not a good conductor of heat?

   (a) Soil   (b) Aluminum

   (c) Tungsten   (d) Steel

3. The displacement-time graphs of two bodies A and B are shown in figure. Which of the following statements is correct?

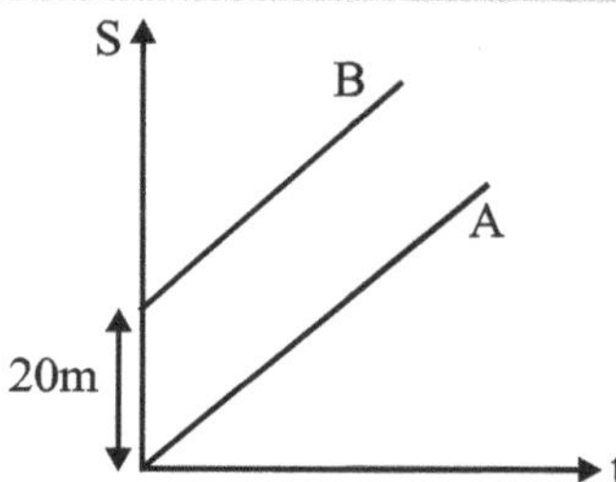

   (a) A is moving faster than B.

   (b) B is moving faster than A.

   (c) B is always 20 m behind A.

   (d) A is always 20 m behind B.

4. A ball is cut into two halves. On the outer surface of one half of the ball, a shiny aluminium foil is pasted. A candle is now placed in front of this shiny surface.

   The image of the candle formed by the shiny surface is:

   (a) virtual and smaller in size

   (b) real and smaller in size

   (c) virtual and bigger in size

   (d) real and bigger in size

5. The graph shows the first five seconds of a car journey.

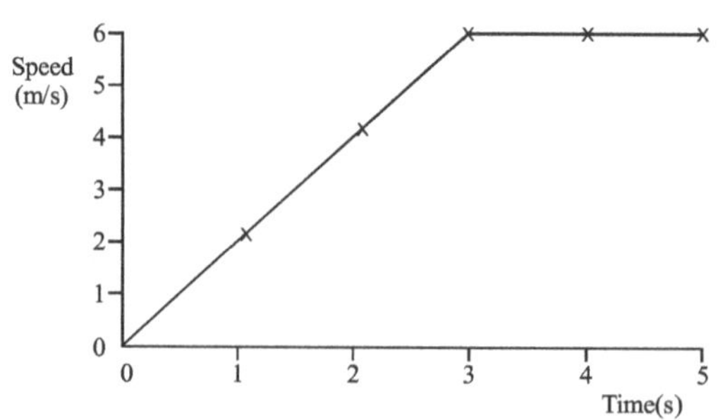

How far did the car travel in the first three seconds?

(a) 6 m   (b) 9 m

(c) 15 m   (d) 18 m

6. The figure shows air-filled bulbs connected by a U-tube partly filled with alcohol. What happens to the levels of alcohol in the limbs X and Y when an electric bulb is placed midway between the painted air filled bulbs and electric bulb is lighted?

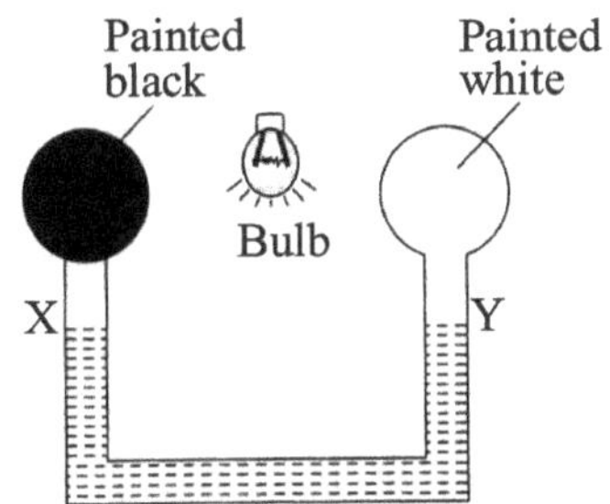

(a) the level of alcohol falls in both limbs.

(b) the level of alcohol in the limb X rises while that in limb Y falls.

(c) the level of alcohol in limb X falls while that in limb Y rises.

(d) there is no change in the levels of alcohol in the two limbs.

7. In which of the following circuit bulb will glow?

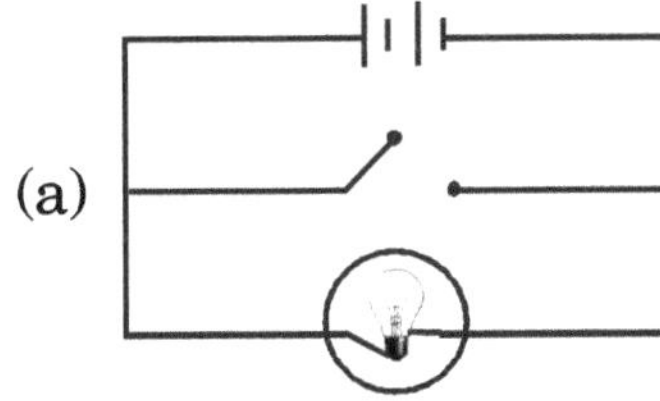

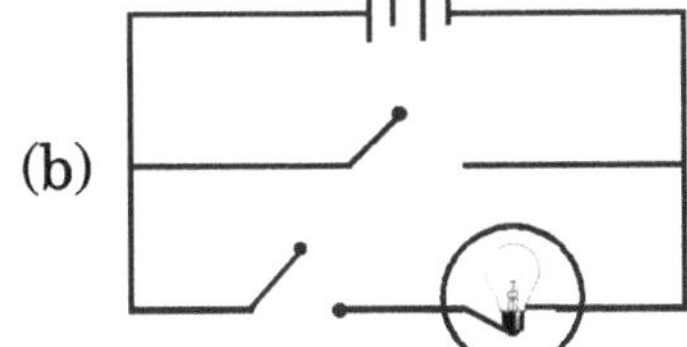

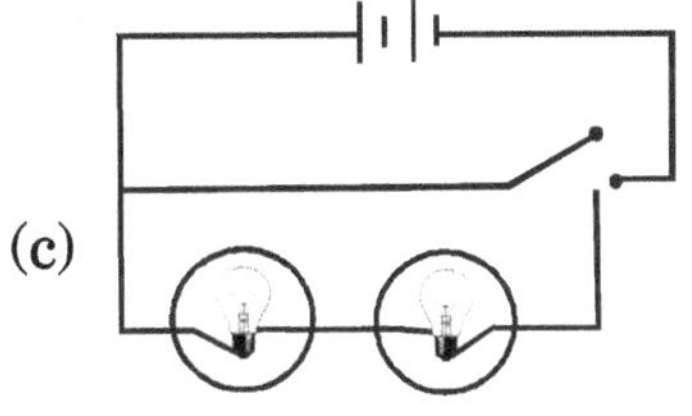

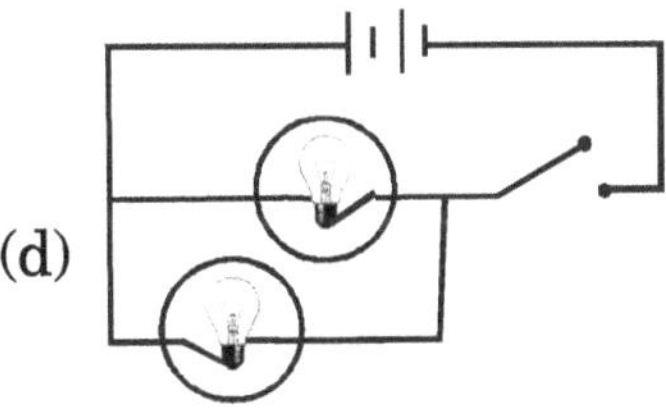

8. Mercury is used as a thermometer substance because

(a) It is very costly

(b) It expands less than glass

(c) It does not wet the wall of the glass tube

(d) None of these

9. Oscillations are set in a simple pendulum whose length is 2m and mass of the bob is 2 kg. Its time period

(a) is always constant

(b) increases slowly

(c) decreases slowly

(d) first increases then decreases

10. Which one of the following is an insulator?

(a) Water

(b) Human body

(c) Dried wood

(d) Iron nail

11. Two blocks of ice when pressed together, join to form one block. This happens because

(a) melting point rises with pressure

(b) melting point falls with pressure

(c) heat is absorbed from outside

(d) heat is rejected to outside.

12. Figure (a-d) shows the readings on four different thermometers. Indicate which of the reading shows the normal human body temperature?

(a)

(b)

(c)

(d)

13. Which of the following can be used to form a real image?
    (a) Concave mirror only
    (b) Plane mirror only
    (c) Convex mirror only
    (d) Both concave and convex mirrors.

14. Which of the following appliances does not use an electromagnet?
    (a) Washing machine
    (b) Refrigerator
    (c) Electric heater
    (d) Electric bell

15. A tornado is
    (a) Uneven heating between two regions
    (b) A violent, twisting funnel of wind
    (c) Strong circulatory winds in the tropical region
    (d) None of these

CHEMISTRY

16. Blacksmith grinds edges of iron axe against a spinning wheel to sharpen it. Sparks of fire and heat is generated. On the basis of this statement choose the correct answer.

(a) It is a physical change as only shape of axe changes.
(b) It is a chemical change as heat is generated.
(c) It is chemical change as iron turns into new metal.
(d) None of these.

17. Fill in the blanks by observing the following chemical process.

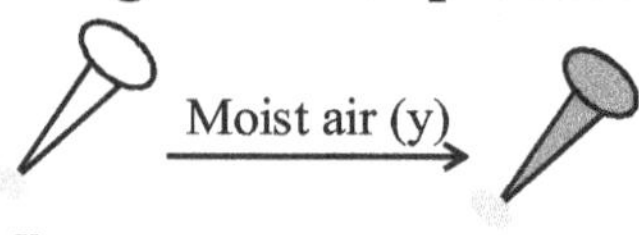

The above process becomes faster when humidity is A and can be prevented by applying a coat of B or by depositing a layer of a metal like C on iron.

(a) x - Mg, y - O_2, z - MgO,
    A - log, B -water, C - copper
(b) x - Ca, y - CO_2, z - $CaCO_3$,
    A - high, B -oil, C -magnesium
(c) x - Fe, y - O_2 & H_2O, z - Fe_2O_3,
    A - high, B - grease, C - zinc
(d) x - Fe, y - H_2O, z - FeO,
    A - low, B - paint, C - zinc

18. Disposal of factory wastes in water bodies has been found to be harmful to water plants and animals. To prevent this the factory owner should

(a) neutralise waste before disposal.
(b) make the waste acidic before disposal.
(c) make the waste basic before disposal.
(d) all of the above are correct.

19. Kanu performed the following experiment by taking few solutions and phenolphthalein indicator. Identify p, q and r in his experiment.

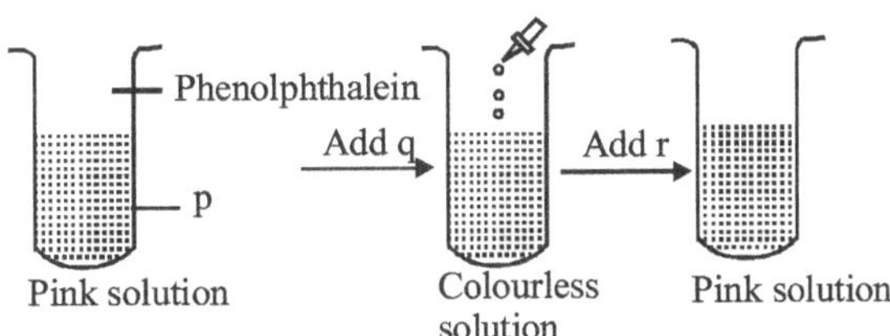

(a) p → Acid, q → Acid, r → Base   (b) p → Base, q → Acid, r → Base

(c) p → Base, q → Base, r → Acid   (d) p → Base, q → Acid, r → Acid

20. Match Column I with Column II and choose the correct option.

Column I

(A) Depositing a layer of zinc on iron

(B) Carbon dioxide

(C) Iron oxide

(D) Dissolving common salt in water

Column II

(i)   Turns lime water milky

(ii) Physical change

(iii) Rust

(iv) Galvanisation

(a) A - (iv), B - (iii), C - (i), D - (ii)   (b) A - (iv), B - (iii), C - (ii), D - (i)

(c) A - (iv), B - (i), C - (iii), D - (ii)   (d) A - (iii), B - (i), C - (ii), D - (iv)

21. Read the following statements.

(A) Both _______ and _______ soils are suitable for growing wheat and gram.

(B) For pulses, _______ soil that drains water easily, is most suitable.

Select the option which correctly fills the blanks in the given statements.

(a) (A) - clayey, loamy, (B)- loamy

(b) (A) - sand, gravel, (B) - clayey

(c) (A) - clayey, sandy, (B) - clayey

(d) (A) - clayey, loamy (B) - sandy

22. Anita took a spoon of turmeric powder and made a paste by adding little water to it. She cut thin strips of a paper and applied this paste on them. After drying she put few drops of given sample solutions (i)-(iv) on these strips.

What would be the changes in the colour she observed?

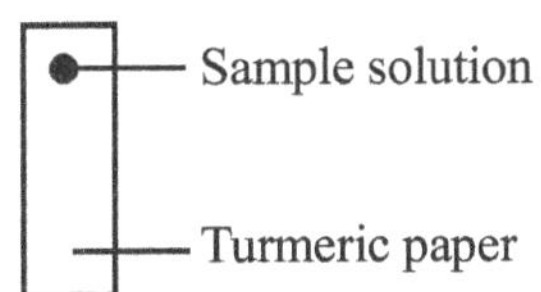

(i)   Orange juice

(ii) Soap solution

(iii) Common salt solution

(iv) Baking soda solution

(a) (i) -Yellow, (ii) - Red, (iii) Yellow, (iv) - Red

(b) (i) -Red, (ii) - Yellow, (iii) Red, (iv) - Yellow

(c) (i) -Red, (ii) - Red, (iii) Yellow, (iv) - Yellow

(d) (i) -Yellow, (ii) - Yellow, (iii) Red, (iv) - Red

23. **Assertion :** Shearing does not harm the sheep.

    Reason : The uppermost layer of the skin is made up of dead cells.

    (a) Both assertion and reason are true and reason is the correct explanation of assertion.

    (b) Both assertion and reason are true and reason is not the correct explanation of assertion.

    (c) Assertion is true but reason is false.

    (d) Both assertion and reason are false.

24. If the percolation rate of water of a particular soil sample is 20 mL/min, then how much time will 200 mL of water take to percolate completely into the soil?

    (a) 800 s   (b) 600 s

    (c) 200 s   (d) 400 s

25. Match the column I with column II and select the correct option from the codes given below.

Column I	Column II
(A) Ammonium hydroxide	(i) Spinach
(B) Tartaric acid	(ii) Window cleaner
(C) Zinc carbonate	(iii) Tamarind
(D) Oxalic acid	(iv) Calamine

    (a) (A) - (ii), (B) - (iii), (C) - (iv), (D) - (i)

    (b) (A) - (iv), (B) - (i), (C) - (ii), (D) - (iii)

    (c) (A) - (ii), (B) - (iii), (C) - (i), (D) - (iv)

    (d) (A) - (iii), (B) - (ii), (C) - (iv), (D) - (i)

26. Read the following and select the correct option.

    Assertion : Forest prevent soil erosion.

    Reason : Canopy formed by crown of leaves of forest trees reduces the force and speed of raindrops.

    (a) Both assertion and reason are true and reason is the correct explanation of assertion.

    (b) Both assertion and reason are true and reason is not the correct explanation of assertion.

    (c) Assertion is true but reason is false.

    (d) Both assertion and reason are false.

27. Burning piece of wool fabric smells like burning hair. This is because both wool and hair are made up of

    (a) proteins

    (b) fats

    (c) vitamins

    (d) carbohydrates

28. Sharp pain caused by an ant bite is due to

    (a) malic acid   (b) nitric acid

    (c) formic acid   (d) lactic acid

29. Some examples of changes are given below:

    A. Cutting a log of wood into pieces.

    B. Breaking down of ozone.

C. Melting of glaciers.
D. Lime water turns milky.
E. Digestion of food.
F. Punching a hole in a paper.

Classify the above change into

I.   Irreversible physical change
II. Chemical change
III. Reversible physical change

(a) I - A, F, II - B, D, E, III - C
(b) I - A, B, E, II - D, F, III - C
(c) I - A, II - B, D, III - C, E, F
(d) I - F, II - C, E, III - A, B, D

30. Read the given passage.

The water-bearing layer of the earth called __P__ is made up of two components __Q__ and __R__. The top level of layer __P__ is called S. When too many tubewells are used in an area, the level of __S__ in that area goes down.

Select the correct sequence of words to fill up the blanks in the above passage.

	P	Q	R	S
(a)	sea	permeable rock	soil	aquifer
(b)	water table	soil	permeable rocks	aquifer
(c)	lake	Permeable rocks	soil	water table
(d)	aquifer	soil	permeable rocks	water table

BIOLOGY

31. The steps of the digestive process are listed below but not in correct order.

    (i)   Water and vitamin absorption begins.

    (ii) Food is liquefied; breakdown of protein begins.

    (iii) Food is moistened; breakdown of starch begins.

    (iv) Proteins, carbohydrates, and fats break down; nutrients are absorbed into the bloodstream.

    Select the option that gives the correct order of these events as food passes through the human digestive tract.

    (a) (ii), (iv), (i), (iii)
    (b) (iv), (ii), (iii), (i)
    (c) (i), (iii), (ii), (iv)
    (d) (iii), (ii), (iv), (i)

32. Muscular cramps after strenuous exercise are due to __________ in muscle cells.

    (a) accumulation of lactic acid
    (b) breakdown of glucose
    (c) slow circulation of blood
    (d) aerobic respiration

33. Which of these is a behavioural adaptation?

    (a) A hognose snake pretends as dead to trick the predator.
    (b) A frog's light-coloured belly makes it harder for a predatory fish to see it against sunlight on the water surface.

(c) The scarlet king snake looks very much like the poisonous coral snake.

(d) A treehopper on a leaf or twig resembles a thorn.

34. This is broomrape bacteria, is parasite on its plants and get its nutrients from the roots of.

(a) viscum album

(b) orobanche ramosa

(c) rawuolfia

(d) bladderwort

35. Refer the given figure. What does it represent?

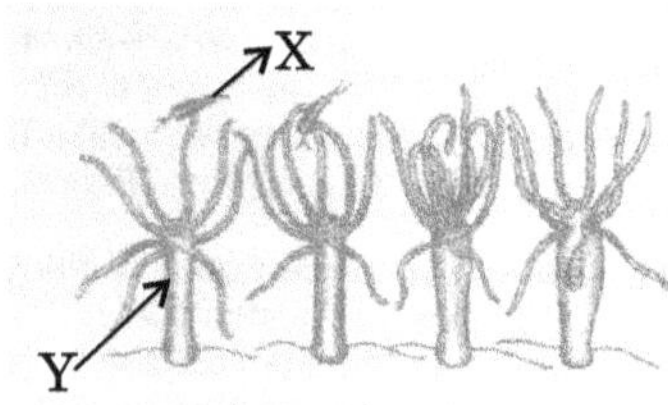

(a) Autotrophic mode of nutrition as the organism Y is obtaining food itself.

(b) Parasitic mode of nutrition as the organism X is being harmed by organism Y.

(c) Symbiotic mode of nutrition as both the organism X and Y are being benefitted in the process.

(d) Predatory mode of nutrition as organism X is being eaten by organism Y.

36. Covering of lungs is called

(a) pericardium

(b) pleural membrane

(c) peritoneum

(d) perichondrium

37. Mr. Khanna had a pond in his garden, filled with all kinds of aquatic plants. He wanted to prevent mosquitoes from breeding in the pond without harming the plant in any way. He could ________.

(i) Add salt into the water

(ii) Add some goldfish into the pond

(iii) Spray a film of oil on the surface of the pond

(a) (i) only

(b) (ii) only

(c) (iii) only

(d) (i), (ii) and (iii)

38. Fish breathe with the help of gills which are richly supplied with blood vessels. The gills help the fish to

(a) take the oxygen from air.

(b) take in oxygen dissolved in water.

(c) absorb nutrients present in water.

(d) release waste substances in water.

39. The term that is used for the mode of nutrition in yeast, mushroom and bread-mould is

(a) autotrophic

(b) insectivorous

(c) saprophytic

(d) parasitic

40. Which of the following is not one of the ways of preventing water pollution?

    (a) Toxic products like plants, automobile oil, polishes, cleaning products should be stored and disposed properly.

    (b) Non-degradable products like disposable plates, glass, plastic, etc. should not be thrown into the drain.

    (c) Farmers should try using natural fertilizers and pesticides.

    (d) Cooking oil, ghee, mayonnaise and fats should be poured down the drains as they will help in greasing the draining pipes and thus making the flow of other wastes easy.

41. Aquatic animals like fish excrete their wastes in gaseous form as

    (a) oxygen   (b) hydrogen

    (c) ammonia   (d) nitrogen

42. Which of the following is a correct statement?

    (a) In winter, the winds flow from the land to the ocean.

    (b) The coastline of India is not vulnerable to cyclones.

    (c) A cyclone is formed by a very high-pressure area with very high speed winds revolving around it.

    (d) None of these

43. Which of the products is not obtained from a forest?

    (a) Honey   (b) Catechu

    (c) Gum   (d) Ginger

44. Choose the correct order of terms that describes the process of nutrition in ruminants.

    (a) swallowing → partial digestion → chewing of cud → complete digestion

    (b) chewing of cud → swallowing → partial digestion → complete digestion

    (c) chewing of cud → swallowing → mixing with digestive juices → digestion

    (d) swallowing → chewing and mixing → partial digestion → complete digestion

45. Read the given statements and select the correct option.

    Statement 1: Doctors use the urine test to diagnose some diseases in the body.

    Statement 2: An examination of urine tells a lot about whether various organs in the body are functioning normally or not

    (a) Both statments 1 and 2 are true and statement 2 is the correct explanation of statement 1.

(b) Both statments 1 and 2 are true and statement 2 is the not the correct explanation of statement 1.

(c) Statement 1 is true but statement 2 is false.

(d) Both statements 1 and 2 are false.

46. Which of the following substances is/are present in a higher percentage in exhaled air than in inhaled air?

(i) Carbon dioxide

(ii) Oxygen

(ii) Water vapour

(iv) Nitrogen

(a) (i) only

(b) (i) and (ii)

(c) (i) and (iv)

(d) (i), (ii), (iii) and (iv)

47. Germination takes place when the

(a) previously dormant embryo is activated

(b) cotyledons emerge above ground

(c) hypocotyl or epicotyl emerges above ground

(d) vascular tissue begins the transport of water and minerals.

48. The coldest region on earth is the-

(a) polar region

(b) tropical region

(c) temperate region

(d) coastal region

49. Select the incorrect statement.

(a) Phloem tubes are only found in the leaves of plants as this is where the sugars are made.

(b) Volume of blood in an average human adult is 10 litres.

(c) Blood contains many more white blood cells than red blood cells.

(d) All of the above

50. Why cannot a turkey fly?

(i) It has underdeveloped wings.

(ii) It is too heavy.

(iii) It has hollow bones.

(iv) It has very few feathers.

(a) (ii) only

(b) (i) and (ii)

(c) (ii) and (iv)

(d) (i), (ii), (iii) and (iv)

Name : _________

Number of Questions : 25

Max. Marks : 25

Time : 1 Hour

There is no negative marking in the test.

1. Proboscis monkey is a reddish brown arboreal Old World monkey that is endemic to Southeast Asian island of Borneo. Which of the following is a prominent feature in a proboscis monkey?

   (a) Tail   (b) Nose
   (c) Ear   (d) Lip

2. The Siberain Huskies were imported form Siberia in Russia to Alaska, where they were initially used as sled animals. Today, these working animals are popular pets as well. What kind of animal is a Siberian Husky?

   (a) Reindeer   (b) Donkey
   (c) Dog   (d) Horse

3. What is the science of classification of animals and plants based on their similar characteristics known as?

   (a) Taxidermy   (b) Sorting
   (c) Taxonomy   (d) Toxicology

4. Washing machine converts

   (a) electrical energy to chemical energy.
   (b) electrical energy to mechanical energy.
   (c) chemical energy to sound energy
   (d) mechanical energy to electrical energy.

5. Match column-I with column-II and select the correct answer using the codes given below the columns.

Column I	Column II
A. Alpaca	(p) Goat
B. Silkworm	(q) Camel
C. Patanwadi	(r) Mulberry
D. Angora	(s) Sheep

   (a) A → (q), B → (r), C → (s), D → (p)
   (b) A → (s), B → (r), C → (p), D → (q)
   (c) A → (p), B → (r), C → (q), D → (s)
   (d) A → (q), B → (r), C → (p), D → (s)

6. Which of the following statements are/ is correct?
   (a) Cutting of wood into pieces is a chemical change.
   (b) Conversion of manure from leaves is a physical change.
   (c) Iron pipes coated with zinc do not rust easily.
   (d) All of the above

7. Lichens are a symbiotic association of *algae* and *fungi*. Which of the following statements is correct with respect to lichens ?
   (a) Fungi supplies water and minerals to cells of algae.
   (b) Algae supplies food to the fungi.
   (c) Fungi supplies water, minerals and food to algae and algae do not supply anything.
   (d) Both (a) and (b) are correct.

8. The main function of the human digestive system is to
   (a) break down food for absorption into the blood.
   (b) exchange oxygen and carbon dioxide in the lungs.
   (c) release energy from sugars within the cells.
   (d) carry nutrients to all parts of the body.

9. Which kind of forest receives heavy rainfall throughout the year and also has day and night equal in duration?
   (a) Evergreen forest
   (b) Tropical rain forest
   (c) Temperate deciduous forest
   (d) Temperate coniferous forest

10. Choose the correct order for travel of air through various organs of respiratory system.
    (a) Nostrils → larynx → trachea
    (b) Nostrils → trachea → larynx
    (c) Nostrils → larynx → lungs
    (d) None of these

11. Vegetative propagation refers to the formation of new plants from which the following existing organs of the old plants?
    (a) Stems, roots, flowers
    (b) Stems, flowers, fruits
    (c) Roots, stems, leaves
    (d) Stems, leaves, flowers

12. Which of the following is a good practice that needs to be followed?
    (a) Cooking oil and paint should not be thrown in a drain.
    (b) Used tea leaves, solid food and cotton should not be thrown in the drain.
    (c) Chemicals like insecticides should not/ be thrown in the drain.
    (d) All of these

13. Place the rulers given below in ascending order of their rule?
    (I)   Humayun   (II)   Jahangir
    (III) Akbar   (IV) Babur
    (V) Aurangzeb   (VI) Shah Jahan
    (a) I,II,III,IV,V,VI (b) I,III,VI,II,IV,V
    (c) IV,I,III,II,VI,V (d) VI,II,I,V,IV,III

14. Democracy is a Government of the people, by the people and for the people.
    (a) It is a correct statement for Democracy.
    (b) It is not the correct statement for democracy.
    (c) This definition belongs to socialism.
    (d) None of these.

15. __________ is the process involved in creating a unique name and image for a product in the consumer's mind, mainly through advertising campaigns with a consistent theme.

(a) Packaging

(b) Labeling

(c) Branding

(d) Retailing

16. A volcano is a

(a) vent in the earth's crust through which molten material erupts suddenly.

(b) opening in the earth's surface through which water comes out.

(c) force that works on the surface of the earth.

(d) None of these

17. This author's first novel was 'Train to Pakistan'. The novel is based on the dark, bitter and barbaric truth of Indian Independence. The novel gives vivid accounts of the massacres of Hindus and Muslims. Who among these has written the novel Train to Pakistan?

(a)    (b) 

Khushwant Singh   Rohinton Mistry

(c)     (d) 

Salman Rushdie   Kiran Desai

18. World Hand Hygiene day was observed annually on May 5. What is the theme for the day for the year 2020?

(a) "Clean Hands - a recipe for health,"

(b) "Clean care for all - it's in your hands"

(c) "SAVE LIVES: Clean your hands"

(d) "Our Hands, Our Future!"

19. Hari Shankar Vasudevan who passed away recently is a renowned __________.

(a) Minimalist

(b) Architect

(c) Physician

(d) Historian

20. Kiara always secures good marks in exams. She studies regularly. This shows that
    (a) She is very creative.
    (b) She is consistent.
    (c) She understands other people's emotions.
    (d) She is flexible.

21. Name the 1st Indian tennis player who has won the Fed Cup heart award 2020 for Asia/Oceania Zone.
    (a) Leander Paes
    (b) Mahesh Bhupathi
    (c) Vijay Amritraj
    (d) Sania Mirza

22. When was International Nurses Day 2022 with the theme "Nurses: A voice to lead- Nursing the World to Health" observed on_______.
    (a) May 12   (b) May 3
    (c) May 17   (d) May 8

23. Which state government has launched "Indira Canteen" for urban poor?
    (a) Karnataka
    (b) Himachal Pradesh
    (c) Puducherry
    (d) Punjab

24. What are the precautions that need to be taken to protect from the coronavirus?
    (a) Cover your nose and mouth when sneezing.
    (b) Add more garlic into your diet.
    (c) Visit your doctor for antibiotics treatment
    (d) Wash your hands after every hour.

25. Which of the following diseases are related to coronavirus?
    (a) MERS
    (b) SARS
    (c) Both (a) and (b)
    (d) Neither (a) nor (b)

Mock Test 

Name : __________

Number of Questions : 25

Max. Marks : 25

Time : 1 Hour

There is no negative marking in the test.

1. This branch of science involves the study of birds eggs, nests and breeding behaviour. Which branch of science is this?
   - (a) Herpetology
   - (b) Oology
   - (c) Ethology
   - (d) Ichthyology

2. The mammal in the picture below is native to the Democratic Republic of the Congo in Central Africa. Despite the zebra-like stripes, it is actually more closely related to giraffes. Identify it.

   - (a) Lemur
   - (b) Slow loris
   - (c) Okapi
   - (d) Quagga

3. Which state is the largest producer of cashews in India?
   - (a) Maharashtra
   - (b) Karnataka
   - (c) Tamil Nadu
   - (d) Odisha

4. Which of these metals is used in electroplating, a process that involves coating an object with a rust-proof substance?
   - (a) Iron
   - (b) Silver
   - (c) Sodium
   - (d) Zinc

5. Nights are cooler in the deserts because
   - (a) sand radiates heat less quickly as compared to earth .
   - (b) the sky is generally clear.
   - (c) sand radiates heat more quickly as compared to earth.
   - (d) the sky is generally cloudy.

6. In an electric motor, there is conversion of

   - (a) chemical energy into electrical energy.
   - (b) electrical energy into mechanical energy.
   - (c) electrical energy into light.
   - (d) electrical energy into chemical energy.

7. Match column-I with column-II and select the correct answer using the code given below the columns.

Column-I	**Column-II**
(A) Anemometer	(p) Caused by high speed wind and air pressure differences.
(B) Cyclone	(q) Accompanied by low pressure.
(C) High wind speed	(r) Instrument used to measure wind speed.
(D) Wind movement	(s) Caused by uneven heating of earth surface.

(a) A → (r), B → (q), C → (p), D → (s)
(b) A → (r), B → (p), C → (q), D → (s)
(c) A → (r), B → (s), C → (p), D → (q)
(d) A → (r), B → (q), C → (s), D → (p)

8. Which of the following is the correct sequence of steps involved in processing of wool?
(a) Sorting → Grading → Shearing → Scouring → Picking of burrs → Dyeing
(b) Shearing → Scouring → Picking of burrs → Grading → Sorting → Dyeing
(c) Scouring → Shearing → Grading → Picking of burrs → Dyeing → Sorting
(d) Shearing → Scouring → Sorting → Picking of burrs → Grading → Dyeing

9. Which of the following causes soil pollution?
(a) Insecticides
(b) Fertilizers
(c) Manure
(d) Both (a) and (b)

10. In the pitcher plant

(a) there is a pitcher like structure
(b) the apex of the leaf forms a lid which can open and close the mouth of the pitcher.
(c) both (a) and (b) are correct
(d) None of these is correct

11. Why is it said that life would be impossible on earth in the absence of photosynthesis?
(a) In the absence of photosynthesis, there would be no food available for us.
(b) Solar energy is the ultimate source of energy.
(c) Solar energy is essential for photosynthesis.
(d) None of these

12. It is secreted by salivary glands and its function is to break down starch into sugars. It is
    (a) pancreatic juice
    (b) bile juice
    (c) saliva
    (d) none of these

13. Polar bear is an animal of Polar region. Which of the following adaptations of polar bear helps it to locate its prey?

    (a) Its very strong sense of smell
    (b) Its long, curved and sharp claws
    (c) Its white fur which is not easily visible in snowy background
    (d) A layer of fat under its skin

14. Which of the following causes a depletion in water table of a place ?
    (a) Constructing foctories and houses
    (b) Making concrete roads
    (c) Deforestation
    (d) All of these

15. Sewage treatment
    (a) is a process of waste water treatment.
    (b) refers to waste water that is released by homes, industries, hospitals etc.
    (c) refers to the rain water that run down the streets during heavy rains.
    (d) (a) & (b) both

16. Moth ki Masjid was built during the reign of______________.

    (a) Qutub-ud-din Aibak
    (b) Iltutmish
    (c) Balban
    (d) Sikandar Lodhi

17. Match the following workers to their professions
    A. Devadasi   I.   Horses
    B. Sculptor   II. Temple
    C. Trader   III. Utensils
    D. Potter   IV. Bronze idols
    (a) A - II, B - IV, C - I, D - III
    (b) A - II, B - III, C - IV, D - I
    (c) A - I, B - II, C - III, D - IV
    (d) A - I, B - IV, C - II, D - III

18. Homer's epic poems lliad and Odyssey are the oldest known literary sources of ______________ mythology.
    (a) Latin
    (b) Greek
    (c) Anglo - Saxon
    (d) Roman

19. V.S. Naipaul is a famous writer who has won both Booker Prize and Nobel Prize in Literature. Which among these is not a literary work of V.S. Naipaul?

(a) Half a life
(b) River of Smoke
(c) A Bend in the River
(d) Magic Seeds

20. The Logo in the given picture is of famous brand of luxury clothing. This brand also sells footwears and fragrances. Identify it.

(a) Burberry
(b) U.S. Polo Assn.
(c) Ralph Lauren
(d) Allen Solly

21. In the game of snooker, how many balls are present on the table at the beginning of game?

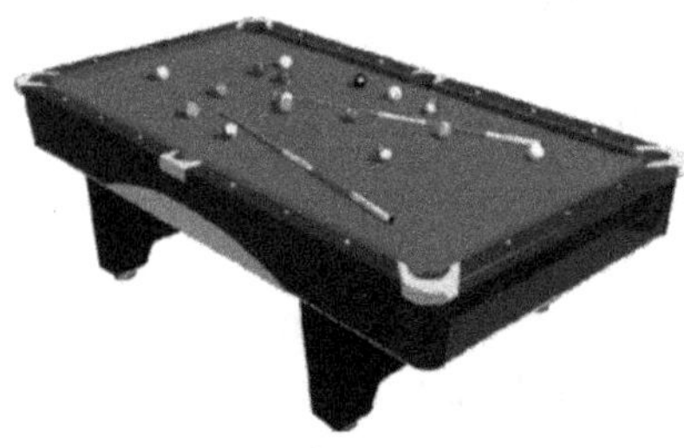

(a) 22
(b) 20
(c) 21
(d) 19

22. What do you understand by the term "Dress code"?
(a) Against the law
(b) Colour coded dresses
(c) Written rules of how one should dress
(d) None of these

23. What is the rank of India in World Economic Forum (WEF)'s global Energy Transition Index (ETI) 2022 which was topped by Sweden?
(a) 79
(b) 66
(c) 59
(d) 87

24. Name the country which has named one of its streets after Indian poet Rabindranath Tagore on his 159th birth anniversary recently.
(a) United Kingdom
(b) United States
(c) UAE
(d) Israel

25. Name the country which has won the 1st edition of FIDE Chess.com online Nations Cup 2020 (India - 5th).
(a) Russia
(b) China
(c) Serbia
(d) Ukraine

Name : _________

Max. Marks : 25

Number of Questions : 25

Time : 1 Hour

There is no negative marking in the test.

1. This endangered species exclusively (99 percent) feeds on bamboo. It is found in China. It has large, distinctive black patches around its eyes, over the ears and across its round body. Name the species.
   (a) Raccoon
   (b) Giant Otter
   (c) Giant Panda
   (d) Brown Eared Pheasant

2. Sharks are killers of the deep seas. Which of the following are the characteristics of the sharks?

   (a) They are bony.
   (b) They are cartilaginous.
   (c) They are mostly warm-blooded.
   (d) Gill slits are covered.

3. Which of the following statements is incorrect?
   (a) Photochemical smog always contains ozone
   (b) Forests are called green lungs because they maintain the balance of oxygen and carbon dioxide in the atmosphere.
   (c) Lead is the most hazardous metal pollutant of automobile exhaust.
   (d) None of these

4. Baking soda or sodium bicarbonate ($NaHCO_3$) is a versatile compound. Which of the following is an example of a chemical property of baking soda?
   (a) Bubbles up when mixed with vinegar
   (b) Allows dough to rise while baking
   (c) Neutralizes odours
   (d) All of these

5. Who discovered the link between electricity and magnetism?

(a) 

Michael Faraday

(b) 

Isaac Newton

(c) 

Einstein

(d) 

Maxwell

6. The movement of cold air from sea towards land during daytime is called
   (a) air breeze
   (b) sea breeze
   (c) land breeze
   (d) None of these

7. The central government has launched India's biggest evacuation plan to bring back Indian citizens stranded in foreign countries. What is the name of the mission?
   (a) Stranded Indians Mission
   (b) Smart India Mission
   (c) Come Back Indians Mission
   (d) Vande Bharat Mission

8. Rain becomes acidic
   (a) because excess of carbon dioxide present in air get dissolved in rain drops to form carbonic acid.
   (b) oxides of nitrogen and sulphur present in air dissolve to form respective acids.
   (c) Both (a) and (b) are correct
   (d) None of these

9. Which one of the following substances is a mixture?
   (a) Copper
   (b) Salt
   (c) Sugar
   (d) Muddy water

10. Which of the following is correct regarding symbiotic relationship?
    (a) A mode of life in which two organisms live in intimate association with each other
    (b) Two organisms live together and share the shelter.
    (c) Two organisms live together and share nutrients.
    (d) All the above are correct.

11. Which statement is FALSE for meteorological department-
    (a) It helps farmers by providing monsoon and rainfall reports.
    (b) It uses satellite data to map pattern of heating and cooling of regions of Earth.
    (c) It calculates temperature of different places
    (d) It does not give national alerts like cyclone etc.

12. Match column I with column II and select the correct answers using the code given below the columns.

Column-I	Column-II
A Fish	(p) Skin and lungs
B Snake	(q) Lungs
C Humans	(r) Cell membrane
D Amoeba	(s) Gills

    (a) A → r, B → p, C → s, D → q
    (b) A → q, B → r, C → p, D → s
    (c) A → s, B → p, C → q, D → r
    (d) A → p, B → q, C → s, D → r

13. Out of the following, select those that would help to reduce water pollution.
    (i) Use of sewers for removal of urban waste
    (ii) Use of unleaded petrol in cars
    (iii) Spraying of pesticides on plants
    (iv) We should not excrete in open.
    (a) (i) and (ii)
    (b) (iii) and (iv)
    (c) (i), and (iv)
    (d) All of these

14. Which of the following process is responsible for release of carbon dioxide by the animals?

    (a) Digestion

    (b) Respiration

    (c) Photosynthesis

    (d) Reproduction

15. Basohli is the art of miniature painting developed in

    (a) Uttar Pradesh

    (b) Karnataka

    (c) Himachal Pradesh

    (d) Gujarat

16. Which of the following was the first state in India to introduce midday meal scheme?

    (a) Andhra Pradesh

    (b) West Bengal

    (c) Bihar

    (d) Tamil Nadu

17. The place in the Earth crust where the earthquake occurs is called the

    (a) epicenter   (b) focus

    (c) boundary   (d) direction

18. Which of the following tree(s) grow in Tropical Rain Forests?

    (a) Mahogany

    (b) Ebony

    (c) Rosewood

    (d) All of them

19. Which among these is not a female protagonist from Shakespeare's works?

    (a) Gertrude   (b) Isabella

    (c) Olivia   (d) Julie

20. This famous Indian form of painting is one of the popular forms of classical painting marked by dense composition, surface richness and use of vibrant colours with embellishment of semi-precious stones, pearls and glass pieces. Identify the form of painting.

    (a) Warli painting

    (b) Tanjore painting

    (c) Madhubani painting

    (d) Rajput painting

21. Benjamin Netanyahu has been sworn as the Prime Minister for the 6th time for which country?

    (a) Ukraine

    (b) Georgia

    (c) Armenia

    (d) Israel

22. When you see a flashing yellow light, while driving then you should_________.

    (a) Speed up and try to cross the signal

    (b) Stop immediately

    (c) Slow down your vehicle

    (d) Continue driving at the same speed

23. Name the person who heads the ICC cricket committee which has recommended the ban of using saliva to shine the ball.

    (a) Rahul Dravid

    (b) Kumar Sangakkara

    (c) Ricky Ponting

    (d) Anil Kumble

24. Name the 1st bank in India to introduce video-KYC facility for Savings Account customers.

    (a) Axis Bank

    (b) YES Bank

    (c) Kotak Mahindra Bank

    (d) IndusInd Bank

25. Match column-I with column-II and select the correct answer using the code given below the columns.

    Column-I

    (A) Wind

    (B) Monsoon

    (C) Thunderstorms

    (D) Tornado

    Column-II

    (p) Wind transporting water

    (q) Moving air

    (r) Dark funnel shaped cloud

    (s) Swift movement of falling water droplets alongwith rising air that creates lightning and sound

    (a) A → (p), B → (q), C → (r), D → (s)

    (b) A → (q), B → (p), C → (r), D → (s)

    (c) A → (q), B → (p), C → (s), D → (r)

    (d) A → (p), B → (q), C → (s), D → (r)

OLYMPIAD
Mock Test 4

Name : __________

Number of Questions : 40

There is no negative marking in the test.

Max. Marks : 40

Time : 2 Hours

1. What is the chemical name of caustic potash?
   - (a) Barium hydroxide
   - (b) Potassium hydroxide
   - (c) Aluminum hydroxide
   - (d) Ammonium hydroxide

2. It is one of the world's oddest looking birds that builds its nest in a burrow. It has a triangular hooked beak and "Sea parrot" is its nickname. Name the bird.
   - (a) Atlantic puffin
   - (b) Albatross
   - (c) Pelican
   - (d) Arctic tern

3. A rainforest is a huge dense lush forest having four distinct layers. Which of the following layers lies above the canopy layer?
   - (a) Forest floor
   - (b) Emergent
   - (c) Understorey
   - (d) Canopy is the uppermost layer

4. The Milky Way is the galaxy that contains our solar system. The solar system is located within the disc, about 27, 000 light years from the Galactic Centre, on the inner edge of one of the spiral-shaped concentrations of gas and dust called the .... arm.

   - (a) Sagittarius
   - (b) Orion
   - (c) Keplerian
   - (d) Auriga

5. Shobit observes the moon which looks like as shown in the picture. How long will it be before Shobit sees the moon in the same phase again?

   - (a) 1 week
   - (b) 1 month
   - (c) 1 year
   - (d) 15 days

6. Which of the following movements fights against the taking over of fertile land for testing of missiles in a thickly populated village in Odisha?

   (a) Chipko Movement

   (b) Baliapal Movement

   (c) Bishnoi Movement

   (d) Appiko Movement

7. Which of the following is the smallest unit?

   (a) hour

   (b) nano second

   (c) microsecond

   (d) light year

8. The direction of flow of heat is

   (a) always from hotter body to a cooler body

   (b) always from cooler body to a hotter body.

   (c) always from a body at a lower temperature to a body at higher temperature

   (d) All of the above

9. Which of the following is used as side view mirror in vehicles?

   (a) Plane mirror

   (b) Concave mirror

   (c) Convex mirror

   (d) None of these

10. A tornado is

   (a) uneven heating between two regions.

   (b) a violent, twisting funnel of wind.

   (c) strong circulatory winds in the tropical region.

   (d) None of these

11. Name the person who has been appointed as the chairman of NABARD recently till July 2022.

   (a) P.V.S Suryakumar

   (b) Govinda Rajulu Chintala

   (c) Shaji K V

   (d) Harsh Kumar Bhanwala

12. Cocoon is-

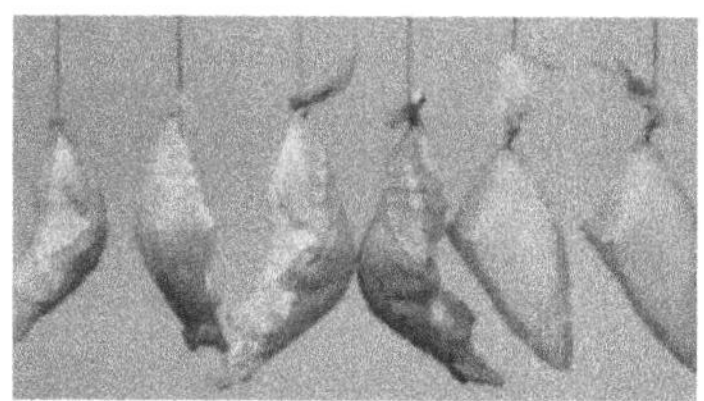

   (a) a caterpillar.

   (b) the fibre cover spun by the silk larva around its body on changing into pupa state.

   (c) a silk moth.

   (d) a variety of silk.

13. Which of the following is a physical change?

   (a) Burning of kerosene

   (b) Tearing of paper

   (c) Heating sugar in a pan

   (d) Heating sulphur with iron fillings to redhot state.

14. While taking a walk in a park, Muskan observed that an insect sat on a pitcher plant (Nepenthes). Immediately the flower opened up and the insect slid down. To which of the following categories does the pitcher plant belongs ?

 (a) Saprophytes

 (b) Insectivorous

 (c) Parasite

 (d) Symbiotic

15. Climate

 (a) refers to average temperature at a place over a long time.

 (b) refers to average rainfall at a place over a long time.

 (c) refers to average weather pattern at a place taken over a long time.

 (d) None of these

16. Which of the following is the correct sequence of air passage during inhalation?

 (a) Nostrils → larynx → pharynx

 → trachea → lungs

 (b) Nostrils → pharynx → larynx

 → trachea → alveoli

 (c) Larynx → nostrils → trachea

 → lungs

 (d) Nasal passage → trachea

 → pharynx → larynx → alveoli

17. Match column I with column II and select the correct answers using the code given below the columns

Column-I	**Column-II**
(A) Kidneys	(p) Air
(B) Heart	(q) Food
(C) Lungs	(r) Blood
(D) Stomach	(s) Wastes

 (a) A → p, B → r, C → s, D → q

 (b) A → s, B → r, C → p, D → q

 (c) A → r, B → p, C → s, D → q

 (d) A → q, B → s, C → p, D → r

18. The Mango department of which Indian state signed MoU with Flipkart to support mango farmers?

 (a) West Bengal (b) Uttar Pradesh

 (c) Gujarat   (d) Karnataka

19. It is the minimum amount of water recommended by United Nations for drinking, washing, cooking and maintaining proper hygiene. It is recommended per person and is

 (a) 20 litres per day.

 (b) 50 litres per day.

 (c) 100 litres per day.

 (d) 200 litres per day.

20. Cyclone Amphan has landfall between Digha in West Bengal and Hatiya island in Bangladesh recently. Name the country which proposed the name Amphan?

 (a) India   (b) Bangladesh

 (c) Thailand   (d) Maldives

21. Ecosystem means
    (a) organisms reacting with one another
    (b) a community of organisms together with the environment in which they live
    (c) abiotic components
    (d) Earth and its atmosphere
22. Identify the Sultanate ruler by the following statements regarding him.
    I.   He was a very knowledgeable person with deep knowledge in philosophy, logic and medicine.
    II. He introduced token currency.
    III. He shifted his capital from Delhi to Daulatabad
    IV. He increased the land revenue on the farmers of Doab
    (a) Alauddin Khilji
    (b) Muhammad bin Tughlaq
    (c) Ghiyasuddin Tughlaq
    (d) Jalaluddin Khilji
23. Din Panah at Delhi was built by

    (a) Akbar   (b) Babur
    (c) Aurangzeb   (d) Humayun
24. Identify the Rajput ruler.
    I.   He build the city of Jaipur.
    II. He was a great astronomer
    III. He erected observatories
    IV. He was the ruler of Ajmer
    (a) Raja Man Singh
    (b) Raja Todar Mal
    (c) Raja Bhoj
    (d) Raja Sawai Jai Singh
25. Hauz-i Sultani or the King's reservoir was a large reservoir built by

    (a) Balban
    (b) Alauddin Khilji
    (c) Iltutmish
    (d) Babur
26. The practice of Sati or the immolation of widows on the funeral pyres of their husbands is associated with
    (a) Kansaris
    (b) Rajputs
    (c) Tamilians
    (d) Manipuris
27. "Governor is the constitutional head of the state"
    (a) It is a correct statement
    (b) President is the head
    (c) Chief Minister is the head
    (d) None of these.
28. What is the main focus of marketing process?
    (a) Storage or warehousing.
    (b) Branding.
    (c) Packaging.
    (d) Need and want.

29. Petroleum and fuel oil is found in which type of rock?
    (a) Igneous
    (b) Sedimentary
    (c) Metamorphic
    (d) None of these

30. Which environmental component includes plants and all living organisms?
    (a) Abiotic
    (b) Biotic
    (c) Non-Living
    (d) Human

31. The process by which water continually changes its form and circulates between oceans, atmosphere and land is know as.
    (a) Water cycle
    (b) Ocean currents
    (c) Tides
    (d) Waves

32. Which regions are called 'Orchards of the World'?
    (a) Mediterranean regions
    (b) Temperate Deciduous regions
    (c) Coniferous regions
    (d) Evergreen regions

33. An India origin academic has been recently awarded the fields Medal which is often called the Nobel Prize of mathematics. He was awarded the prize at the bennial International statistical Institute world statistics Congress in Ottawa, Ontario, Canada. Who is being talked about in the above paragraph?
    (a) C.R. Rao
    (b) Manjul Bhargana
    (c) Akshay Venkatesh
    (d) Narendra Karmarkar

34. Which are the mass communication media ?
    (a) Post and Telegraph
    (b) Radio and Television
    (c) Telephone and Post
    (d) Computer and Newspaper

35. Match column-I with column-II and select the correct answer using the code given below the columns.

Column I   **Column II**
(A) Taj Mahal   (i) Assam
(B) Allahabad   (ii) Yamuna river
(C) Kaziranga   (iii) Arunachal Pradesh
(D) Tawang   (iv) Confluence of the rivers Ganga and Yamuna

Codes:
    (a) A - (i), B - (ii), C - (iii), D - (iv)
    (b) A - (ii), B - (iv), C - (i), D - (iii)
    (c) A - (iii), B- (ii), C - (iv), D - (i)
    (d) A- (iv), B - (iii), C - (ii), D - (i)

36. Which of the following idioms means 'to present a counter argument?
    (a) Devil's Advocate
    (b) Caught between two stools
    (c) Give the benefit of the doubt
    (d) In the heat of the moment

37. Sattriya is one among the eight principal classical Indian dance traditions and the most recent entrant in the classical dance list. It was introduced in 15th century A.D by the great saint Sankaradeva

as a powerful medium for propagation of the Vaishnava faith. To which state does this classical dance form belong?

(a) Manipur
(b) Assam
(c) Odisha
(d) Arunachal Pradesh

38. He was one of the greatest footballers of all times and what makes him even more distinguished were the doctorate degrees he held in philosophy and medicine, a rarity in the football world. Who was this football legend?

(a) The Brazilian, Socrates
(b) The French, Franck Ribery
(c) The Italian, Dino Zoff
(d) The Dutch, Marco Van Basten

39. Who has been appointed as the new Chief Economist and Senior Vice President of world bank group with effect from September 1, 2022?
(a) Intermit Gill
(b) Makhtar Diop
(c) Alison Evans
(d) Gita Gopinath

40. Match column-I with column-II and select the correct answer using the code given below the columns.

Column-I	Column-II
(A) Wind carrying water	(p) Thunderstorms
(B) Dark funnel shaped cloud	(q) Tornado
(C) Moving air	(r) Monsoon
(D) Develop in India very frequently	(s) Wind

(a) A → (r), B → (q), C → (s), D → (p)
(b) A → (p), B → (q), C → (r), D → (s)
(c) A → (q), B → (r), C → (p), D → (s)
(d) A → (s), B → (p), C → (r), D → (q)

Name : __________

Number of Questions : 40

Max. Marks : 40

Time : 2 Hours

There is no negative marking in the test.

1. The bark of cinchona tree is medicinally active containing a variety of alkaloids like quinine and quinidine which are used to cure certain diseases. Which of the following diseases can be cured using quinine?

   (a) Malaria   (b) Dengue

   (c) Pneumonia   (d) Diabetes

2. The smallest fox lives in the deserts of North Africa. It has large ears that radiate body heat and help keep the fox cool. Name this animal.

   (a) Fennec fox   (b) Red fox

   (c) Grey fox   (d) Kit fox

3. What percent of the Earth's water is found in the atmosphere?

   (a) 0.001   (b) 0.003

   (c) 0.02   (d) 0.2

4. In 1774, a British clergyman named Joseph Priestley conducted an experiment in which he focussed sunrays on a tube containing mercuric oxide. This produced a gas which he noticed made candles burn brigthter, thus discovering a gas which is the very essence of life. What gas was it?

   (a) Carbon dioxide

   (b) Nitrogen

   (c) Oxygen

   (d) Helium

5. Match column I with column II and select the correct option from the codes given below.

	Column I		Column II
(i)	Sulphur dioxide in air	(A)	Damage ozone layer
(ii)	CFCs	(B)	Leads to food toxicity
(iii)	Sewage dumped in river	(C)	Prevents photo-synthesis
(iv)	Dust in air	(D)	Produce acid rain
(v)	Excess fertiliser in fields	(E)	Causes water borne diseases

   (a) (i)-(D), (ii)-(A), (iii)-(E), (iv)-(C), (v)-(B)

   (b) (i)-(D), (ii)-(A), (iii)-(C), (iv)-(E), (v)-(B)

   (c) (i)-(B), (ii)-(E), (iii)-(A), (iv)-(C), (v)-(D)

   (d) (i)-(C), (ii)-(B), (iii)-(E), (iv)-(D), (v)-(A)

6. The weak zones of earth's crust which are more prone to earthquakes are called.
   (a) Seismic zones
   (b) Fault zones
   (c) Danger zones
   (d) Both (a) and (b)

7. For his scientific work, he was awarded the Nobel Prize in Chemistry in 1954. In 1962, for his peace activism, he was awarded the Nobel Peace Prize. This makes him the only person to be awarded two unshared Noble Prizes. Who is this incredible gentleman?
   (a) Linus Pauling
   (b) Frederic Joliot
   (c) Richard Feynman
   (d) Aage Bohr

8. An Indian manned spacecraft is being designed to send three people to space in 2022. This spacecraft is being designed by Indian Space Research Organization and will orbit the Earth for up to seven days. Name the spacecraft?
   (a) Chandrayaan-1
   (b) Mangalyaan
   (c) Gaganyaan
   (d) Chandrayaan-2

9. On which lake is India's first and only floating post office located?
   (a) Dal Lake, Srinagar
   (b) Wular Lake, Jammu and Kashmir
   (c) Vembanad Lake, Kerala
   (d) Pushkar Lake, Ajmer

10. Rashtriya Vayoshri Yojana is a scheme for providing physical aids and assisted living devices for senior citizens belonging to BPL category. In which state was it launched first?
    (a) Uttar Pradesh
    (b) Madhya Pradesh
    (c) Andhra Pradesh
    (d) Arunachal Pradesh

11. Water stored in a dam possess

    (a) no energy
    (b) electrical energy
    (c) potential energy
    (d) kinetic energy

12. Which one of the following statements regarding thorny bushes are correct ?
    (I) Thorny bushes are found in the dry desert like regions.
    (II) Tropical deserts are located on the western margins of the continents.
    (III) Thorny bushes have deep roots and small leaves.

    Select the correct answer using the codes given below :

    Codes :
    (a) I, II and III   (b) I and II
    (c) I only   (d) II only

13. Match column I with column II and select the correct answers using the code given below the columns

Column-I	Column-II
A. Autotroph	(p) Mushroom
B. Saprotroph	(q) Bacteria
C. Decomposer	(r) Non green plants & animals
D. Heterotroph	(s) Green plants

(a) A → s, B → p, C → q, D → r
(b) A → p, B → s, C → r, D → q
(c) A → r, B → q, C → p, D → s
(d) A → s, B → p, C → r, D → q

14. Tungsten is used for the manufacture of an electric bulb because

(a) it is malleable.
(b) it is inexpensive.
(c) it has a very high melting point.
(d) it is a good conductor.

15. Typhoon is another name used for cyclone in ________
(a) India
(b) Philippines
(c) Japan
(d) Both (b) and (c)

16. Workers of which fabric industry have maximum possibility of getting infected by anthrax?
(a) silk
(b) cotton
(c) nylon
(d) wool

17. Which medicines are used for treating indigestion?
(a) Antibiotic
(b) Analgesic
(c) Antacids
(d) Antiseptic

18. The Khudol initiative of which Indian state/UT is among the top 10 global initiatives announced by UN for an inclusive fight against the COVID-19.
(a) Sikkim
(b) Ladakh
(c) Odisha
(d) Manipur

19. ________ affect the soil profile and bring changes in soil structure.
(a) Vegetation
(b) Animals
(c) Climatic factors
(d) Fertilizers

20. Which of the following is an insectivorous plant ?

(a) Cuscuta
(b) Amarbel
(c) Venus flytrap
(d) Algae

21. The digestive system consists of
(a) digestive tract.
(b) digestive tract and liver.
(c) digestive tract and pancreas.
(d) digestive tract and the associated glands.

22. Which part of the elephant helps it to keep cool in the hot and humid climate of rain forests ?

   (a) Trunk   (b) Tusk

   (c) Ears   (d) Nose

23. Match column I with column II and select the correct answers using the code given below the columns.

Column-I   Column-II

A. Polar bear (p) Camouflage

B. Frog   (q) Migrate

C. Birds   (r) Fur

D. Chameleon (s) Hibernate

(a) A → r, B → s, C → q, D → p

(b) A → s, B → p, C → r, D → q

(c) A → r, B → q, C → p, D → s

(d) A → p, B → s, C → q, D → r

24. What is the first step involved in treatment of polluted water?

   (a) Chlorination

   (b) Aeration

   (c) Filtration

   (d) None of these

25. An example of temple town is

   (a) Surat   (b) Bhopal

   (c) Hampi   (d) Thanjavur

26. On which river is Kolkata port situated?

   (a) Betul   (b) Tapti

   (c) Hooghly   (d) Ganga

27. The growth of vegetation depends on

   (I) temperature

   (II) moisture

   (III) thickness of soil

   (IV) climate

Select the correct answer

   (a) Only I   (b) Only II

   (c) II and III   (d) I, II, III and IV

28. Name the state/UT which is 1st in the country to release report on conservation of endemic, threatened floras.

   (a) Arunachal Pradesh

   (b) Uttarakhand

   (c) Meghalaya

   (d) Manipur

29. The word sonnet comes from Italian word sonetto. A sonnet is a small song or lyric. How many lines does a sonnet have?

   (a) 18   (b) 12

   (c) 14   (d) They vary

30. In 2005 Vishal Bhardwaj directed a movie 'The Blue Umbrella' inspired by the novel of same name. The film received great critical acclaim. Who was the author of the novel 'The Blue Umbrella'?

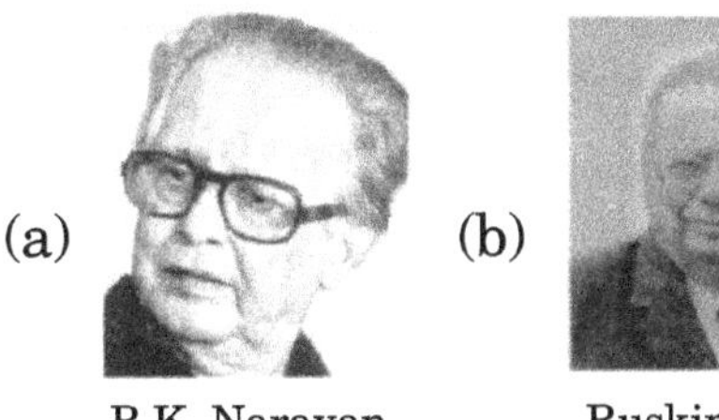
(a)
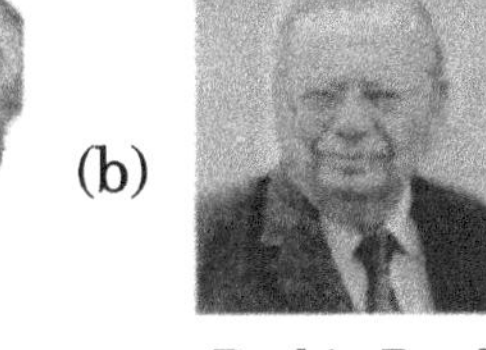
(b)

R.K. Narayan   Ruskin Bond

(c)

(d)

A. J. Cronin   Jane Austen

(c)

(d)

Melanie Brown   Michael Jackson

31. It is the longest running U.S. primetime television show having maximum number of seasons. It was first aired in 1989. Name it.

(a) Lassie

(b) Law and Order

(c) The Simpsons

(d) Friends

32. This singer and song writer has won 200 awards from 448 nominations including six Grammy Awards and thirteen MTV Video Music award along with several other achievements. Name her/him.

(a)

(b)

Lady Gaga   Justin Bieber

33. Padma Shri awardee Balbir Singh who passed away recently is associated with which sports?

(a) Cricket   (b) Tennis

(c) Football   (d) Hockey

34. Who has released the new online Children's book titled 'The Ickabog' recently?

(a) JK Rowling (b) Seuss

(c) Enid Blyton (d) Jeff Kinney

35. Who is the youngest ever UN Messenger of Peace?

(a) Emma Watson

(b) Malala Yousafzai

(c) Haya Bint Al Hussein

(d) Charlize Theron

36. NASA has renamed its Wide Field Infrared Survey Telescope (WFIRST) space telescope after which astronomer?

(a) James C. Fletcher

(b) Kalpana Chawla

(c) Nancy Grace Roman

(d) Sally Ride

37. Ajit Jogi who passed away recently is the 1st Chief Minister of which state/UT?

    (a) New Delhi

    (b) Chhattisgarh

    (c) Puducherry

    (d) Sikkim

38. Which city will host the 2024 Summer Olympics?

    (a) London   (b) Los Angeles

    (c) Paris   (d) New York

39. Name the Bank which has launched 'Vikas Abhaya' scheme to provide relief to MSME borrowers.

    (a) Assam Gramin Vikash Bank

    (b) Jharkhand Gramin Bank

    (c) Kerala Gramin Bank

    (d) Karnataka Vikas Grameena Bank

40. Which metro became India's first metro to have its own FM radio station?

    (a) Kolkata Metro

    (b) Lucknow Metro

    (c) Delhi Metro

    (d) Nagpur Metro

LOGICAL REASONING

OLYMPIAD Mock Test 1

Name : __________

Number of Questions : 25

There is no negative marking in the test.

Max. Marks : 25

Time : 1 Hour

DIRECTIONS (Qs. 1 & 2): In each of the following questions choose the missing term to complete the given series.

1. 1, 4, 2, 8, 6, 24, 22, 88, ?
   - (a) 86
   - (b) 98
   - (c) 90
   - (d) 154

2. 18, 24, 21, 27, ?, 30, 27
   - (a) 33
   - (b) 24
   - (c) 30
   - (d) 21

DIRECTION (Qs. 3): In the following question, there is a series of five figures. In order to continue the series, choose a figure from the options that could be the next term of the series.

3. **Problem Figures**

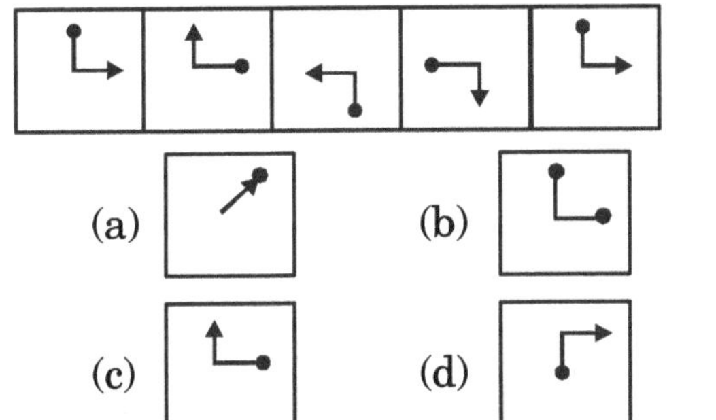

DIRECTION (Qs. 4): In the following question, identify the pattern and find out the missing character.

4. 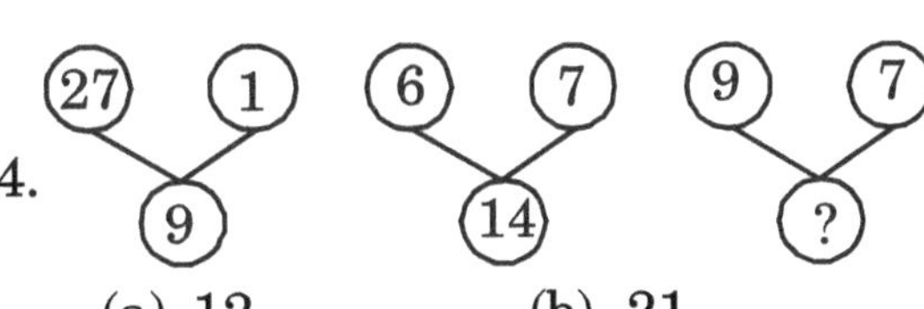
   - (a) 12
   - (b) 21
   - (c) 24
   - (d) 35

5. ACFJ is related to ZXUQ in the same way EGIB is related to______.
   - (a) VTRY
   - (b) WQYR
   - (c) UTRX
   - (d) XPQY

DIRECTIONS (Qs. 6 & 7): In the following questions, select the one which is different from the other three responses.

6. (a) ZKXJ
   (b) CMAL
   (c) TGRF
   (d) FRTK

7. (a) Room
   (b) Chamber
   (c) Veranda
   (d) Cabin

DIRECTIONS (Qs. 8 & 9): Find the missing number/letters.

8. 36, 28, 24, 22 ?
   - (a) 18
   - (b) 19
   - (c) 21
   - (d) 22

9. DA, HE, LI, _?_ , TQ
   (a) PJ (b) PT
   (c) PM (d) PK

10. From the given alternative words, select the word which **cannot** be formed using the letters of the given word:
    MISFORTUNE
    (a) FORT (b) TURN
    (c) SOFT (d) ROAM

11. Which word will appear last in the dictionary?
    (a) laugh (b) latch
    (c) laurels (d) latitude

12. If in a certain code 'LUTE' is written as 'MUTE' and 'FATE' is written as 'GATE', then how will 'BLUE' be written in that code?
    (a) CLUE (b) GLUE
    (c) FLUE (d) SLUE

13. If 'ROSE' is coded as '6821', 'CHAIR' is coded as '73456' and PREACH' is coded as '961473', what will be the code for SEARCH?
    (a) 246173 (b) 214763
    (c) 214673 (d) 216473

DIRECTION (Q. 14) : The four Venn diagrams (a), (b), (c) and (d) are given below. Elements in the following question can be represented by any one of the diagrams. Choose the correct Venn diagram from the options.

14. Man, Worker, Garden

(a) 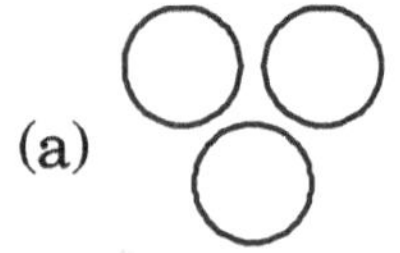

(b) 

(c) 

(d) 

15. Raman is 7 ranks ahead of Manoj in a class of 39. If Manoj's rank is seventeenth from the last, what is Raman's rank from the start?
    (a) 14th (b) 15th
    (c) 16th (d) 17th

16. P is brother of Q, R is mother of P, S is father of R. What is S of Q?
    (a) Maternal grandfather
    (b) Grandson
    (c) Uncle
    (d) Nephew

17. A cat runs 20 m towards East, turns right and runs 10 m. She then turns right and runs 9 m. She again turns left and runs 5 m and then turns left and runs 12 m. Finally she turns left and runs 6 m. Now which direction is the cat facing?
    (a) East (b) North
    (c) West (d) North-East

18. If A stands for +, B stands for –, C stands for ×, then what is the value of (10 C4) A (4 C 4) B 6?
    (a) 60 (b) 50
    (c) 56 (d) 20

DIRECTION (Q. 19) : Find the number of triangles in the given figure.

19. 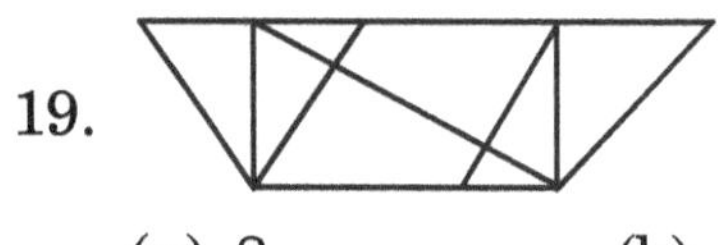
    (a) 8 (b) 10
    (c) 12 (d) 14

DIRECTION (Q. 20) : In the following question, a word is given. Select its correct mirror image, if mirror is placed to the right of the given word.

20. STROKE

    (a) EKORTS   (b) EKORTS

    (c) ƎꓘOЯTꙄ   (d) ROKETS

DIRECTION (Q. 21) : In the following question, choose the correct water image of the given Fig.(X) amongst the four alternatives (a), (b), (c) and (d).

21. 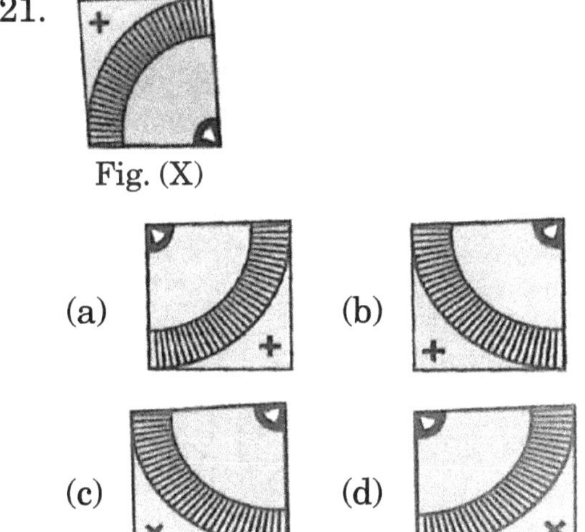

Fig. (X)

(a)   (b)

(c)   (d)

DIRECTION (Q. 22) : In the following question, Fig (X) is exactly embedded in any one of the options and find the option which contains fig. (X) as one of its part.

22. 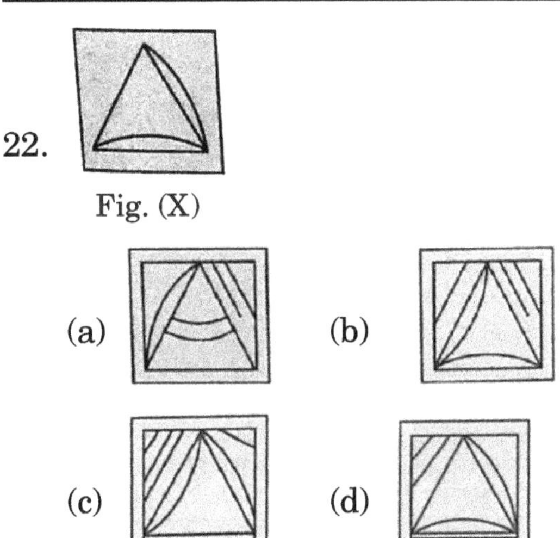

Fig. (X)

(a)   (b)

(c)   (d)

DIRECTION (Q. 23) : In the following question, there are three figures X, Y, and Z of a sheet of paper. Figure X and Y show the two consecutive folds of the sheet. And figure Z shows cuts on the folded sheet. Choose one figure from the options that resembles the unfolded form of the fig. Z.

23. 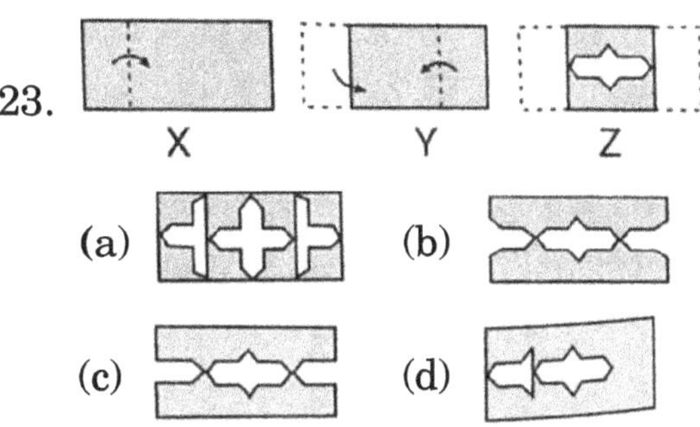

    X   Y   Z

(a)   (b)

(c)   (d)

24. The two positions are of the same dice whose each surface bears a number among 1, 2, 3, 4, 5 and 6. What number is opposite to 1?

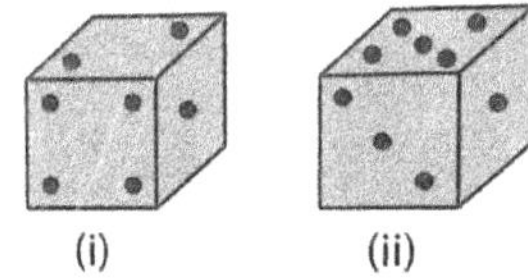

    (i)   (ii)

    (a) 4

    (b) 5

    (c) 6

    (d) Cannot be determined

DIRECTION (Q. 25) : In the following question, find out which of the options completes the figure matrix

25. 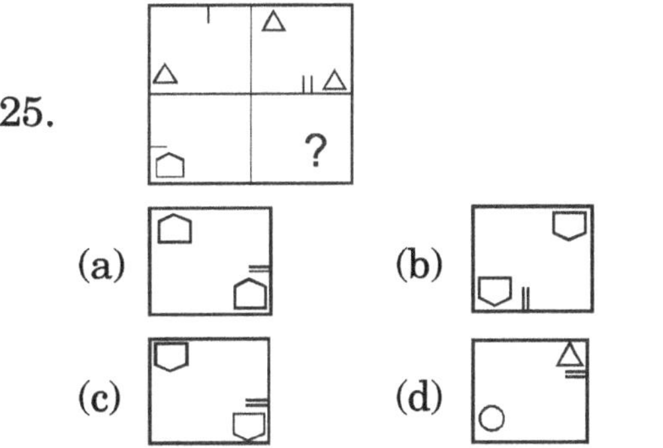

(a)   (b)

(c)   (d)

Mock Test 2

Name : _________

Max. Marks : 25

Number of Questions : 25

Time : 1 Hour

There is no negative marking in the test.

1. Which number space indicates Indian teachers who are also advocates?

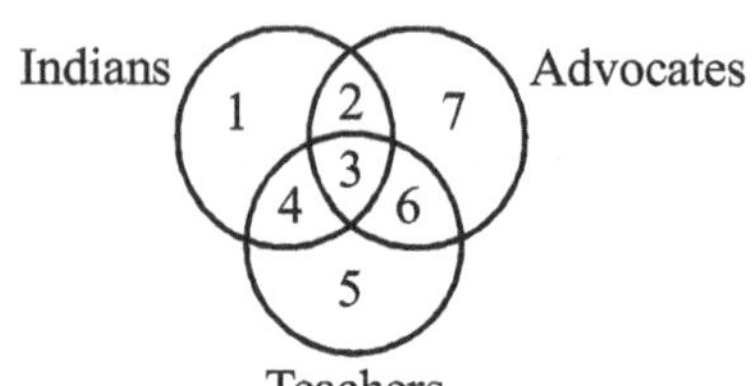

   (a) 2   (b) 3

   (c) 4   (d) 6

2. Five boys A, B, C, D, E are sitting in a park in a circle. A is facing South-West, D is facing South-East, B and E are right opposite A and D respectively and C is equidistant between D and B. Which direction is C facing?

   (a) West   (b) South

   (c) North   (d) East

DIRECTION (Q. 3): From the given answer figures, select the one in which the question figure is hidden/embedded.

3. **Question Figure**

Answer Figures

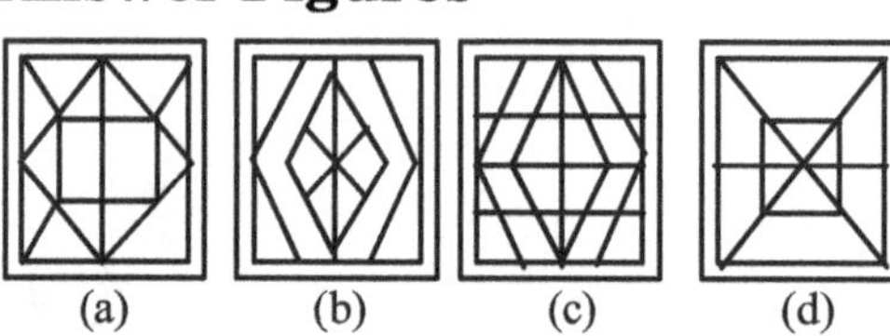

4. How many triangles are there in the given figure?

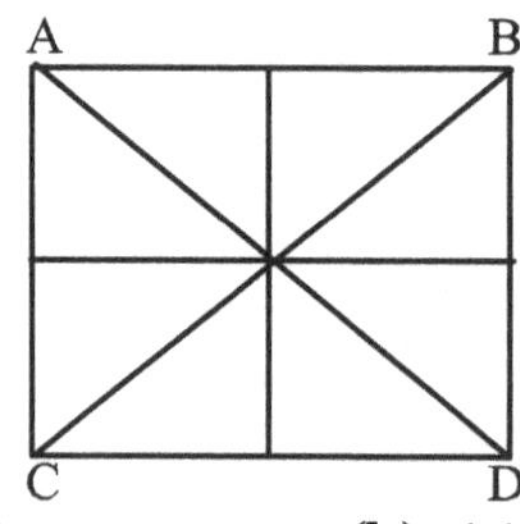

   (a) 16   (b) 14

   (c) 8   (d) 12

5. Arrange the following words in their ascending order, as in a dictionary:

   1. Pick   2. Pith
   3. Pile   4. Perk
   5. Pour

   (a) 4, 1, 2, 3, 5   (b) 4, 1, 3, 2, 5

   (c) 4, 3, 2, 1, 5   (d) 5, 4, 3, 2, 1

DIRECTION (Q. 6) : From the given alternatives select the word which cannot be formed using the letters of the given word.

6. CONTENTION
   (a) TONIC   (b) NOTE
   (c) NATION   (d) NOTION

7. If HONESTY is written as 5132468 and POVERTY as 7192068, how is HORSE written in a certain code?
   (a) 50124   (b) 51042
   (c) 51024   (d) 52014

DIRECTIONS (Qs. 8 & 9) : Find the odd word/number pair from the given alternatives.

8. (a) Division   (b) Addition
   (c) Subtract   (d) Multiplication

9. (a) 47   (b) 17
   (c) 27   (d) 37

DIRECTIONS (Qs. 10 & 11) : In the following questions, select the related word/figure from the given alternatives.

10. Writer : Pen : : ?
    (a) Needle :Tailor
    (b) Artist : Axe
    (c) Painter : Brush
    (d) Teacher : Class

11. 

(a) 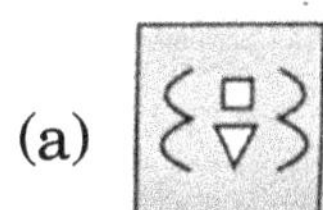   (b) 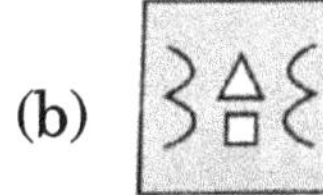

(c) 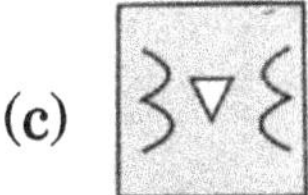   (d) 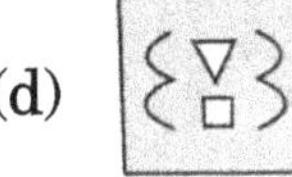

DIRECTION (Q. 12) : Choose a figure from the options which is different from others.

12. (a) 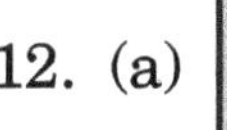   (b) 

    (c)    (d) 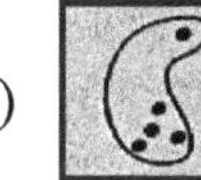
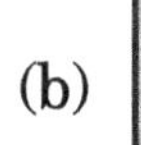

13. If D is the brother of B, how is B related to C?

    To answer this question which of the following statement(s) is/are necessary?

    1. The son of D is the grandson of C.

    2. B is the sister of D.

    (a) Only (1)

    (b) Only (2)

    (c) Either (1) or (2)

    (d) Both (1) and (2)

DIRECTION (Q. 14) : In the following question, from amongst the options select the one which satisfies the same conditions of placement of the dot(s) as in the figure(X).

14. 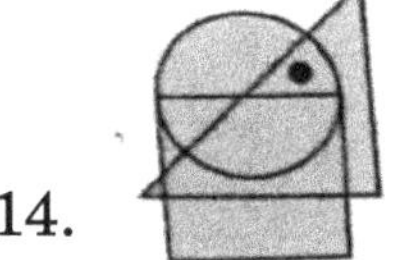

    Fig. (X)

(a) 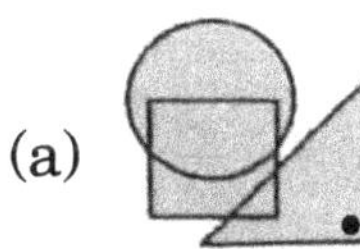   (b) 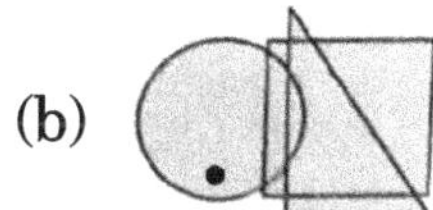

(c) 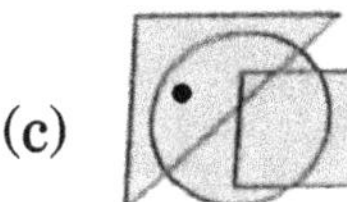   (d) 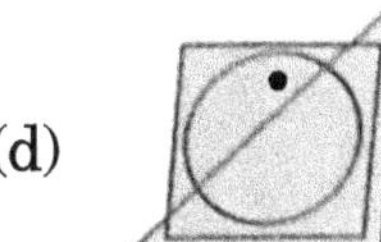

DIRECTION (Q. 15) : In the following question, the sheet of paper shown in the fig(X) is folded to form a box. Choose from amongst the options the boxes that are similar to the box that will be formed.

15.

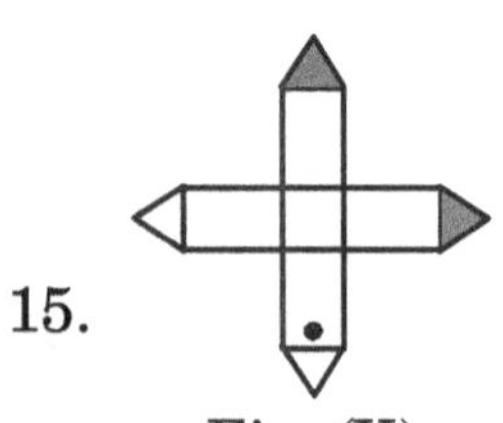

Fig. (X)

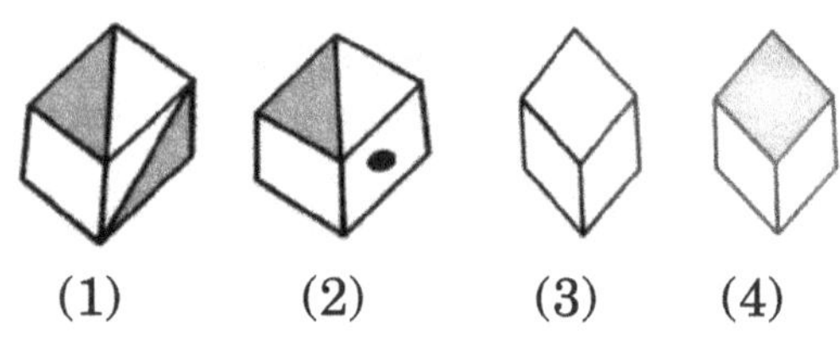

(1)   (2)   (3)   (4)

(a) 1 and 2 only

(b) 2 and 4 only

(c) 2 and 3 only

(d) 1 and 4 only

16. If X is to the South of Y and Z is to the East of Y, in what direction is X with respect to Z?

(a) North-East   (b) North-West

(c) South-West   (d) South-East

17. How many 5's are immediately preceded by 4 but not immediately followed by 3 in the following series?

5 4 3 7 6 5 4 5 3 6 2 4 5 4 5 5 4 3 7 5
6 4 5 5 4 3 5

(a) 2   (b) 3

(c) 4   (d) 5

DIRECTION (Q. 18) : In the following question, there are three figures X, Y and Z of a sheet of paper. Figure X and Y show the two consecutive folds of the sheet. And figure Z shows cuts on the folded sheet. Choose one figure from the option that resembles the unfolded form of the fig.Z.

18.

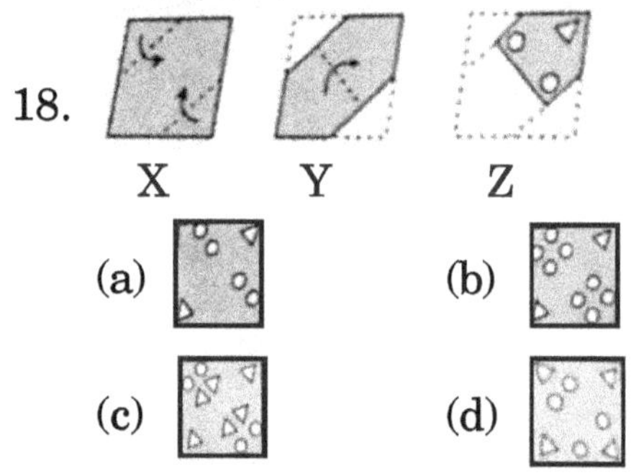

X   Y   Z

(a)   (b)

(c)   (d)

DIRECTION (Q. 19) : In the following question, arrange the given words in a meaningful sequence.

19. 1. Family   2. Locality

    3. Member   4. Community

    5. Country

(a) 3, 1, 4, 5, 2   (b) 3, 2, 1, 4, 5

(c) 3, 1, 4, 2, 5   (d) 3, 1, 2, 5,4

DIRECTION (Q. 20) : In the following question, find out which of the options completes the figure matrix.

20.

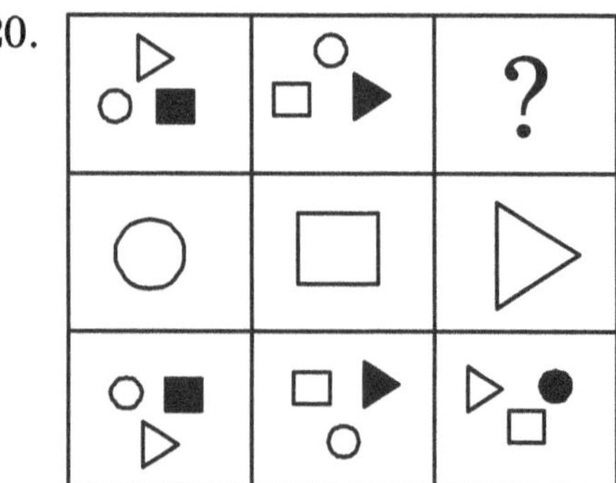

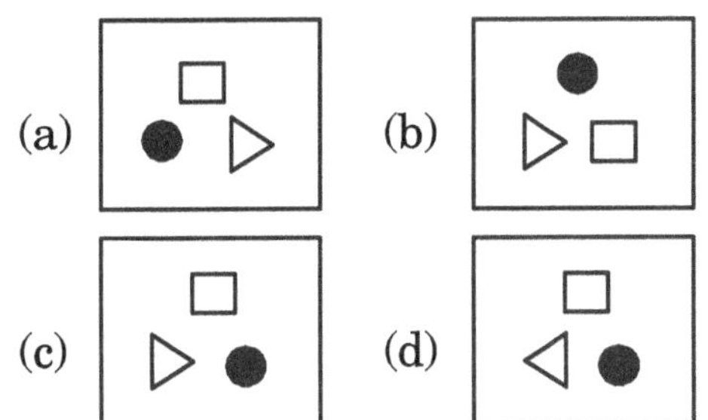

(a)   (b)   (c)   (d)

21. If A denotes ÷, B denotes ×, C denotes + and D denotes –, then the value of 18 B 12 A 4 C 5 D 6 is _______.

(a) 36   (b) 59

(c) 53   (d) 70

DIRECTION (Q. 22): In the following question, select the option in which all the components of the fig. (X) are found?

22.

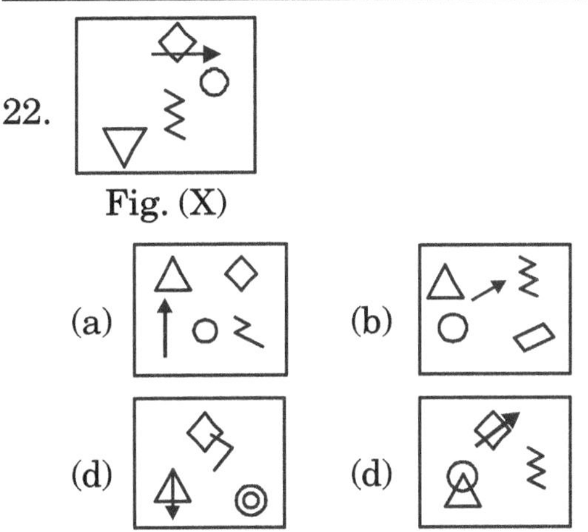

Fig. (X)

(a)   (b)   (d)   (d)

DIRECTION (Q. 23): In the following question, choose the correct image of the given fig.(X) from amongst the options if mirror is placed vertically to the right of each figure.

23.

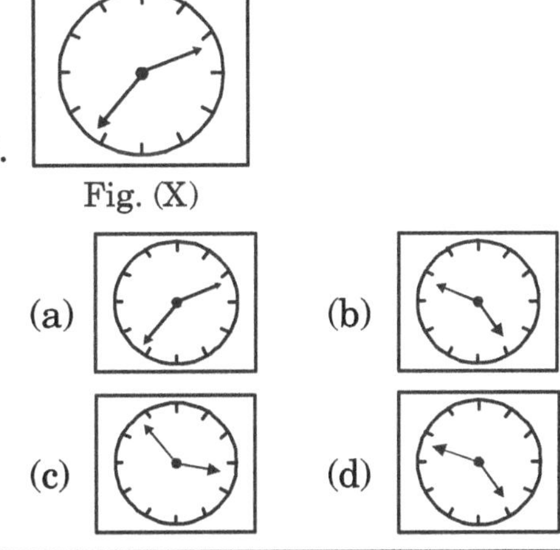

Fig. (X)

(a)   (b)   (c)   (d)

DIRECTION (Q. 24) : In the following question, a word is given. Select its correct water image out of the given options.

24. FAMILY

(a) ꟻAMILY   (b) ꟻAMILY

(c) ꟻAMILY   (d) ꟻAMILY

25. Mohan ranks seventh from the top and twenty eighth from the bottom in a class. How many students are there in the class?

(a) 37   (b) 36

(c) 35   (d) 34

OLYMPIAD
Mock Test 3

Name : ___________

Number of Questions : 25

There is no negative marking in the test.

Max. Marks : 25

Time : 1 Hour

DIRECTIONS (Qs. 1 & 2): In each of the following questions, select the related word/number from the given alternative.

1. Paper : Tree :: Glass : ?
   (a) Window   (b) Sand
   (c) Stone   (d) Mirror
2. 9 : 80 : : 100 : ?
   (a) 901   (b) 1009
   (c) 9889   (d) 9999

DIRECTIONS (Qs. 3 & 4) : In each of the following questions, find the odd number/word from the given alternatives.

3. (a) 49-33   (b) 62-46
   (c) 83-67   (d) 70-55
4. (a) Flute   (b) Violin
   (c) Guitar   (d) Sitar

DIRECTIONS (Qs. 5 & 6): Choose the correct alternative from the given ones that will complete the series.

5. AZ, CX, EV, ? .
   (a) HT   (b) HU
   (c) GS   (d) GT
6. 46, 50, 47, 55, 49, 61, ?
   (a) 54   (b) 52
   (c) 57   (d) 51
7. Arrange the following words according to the dictionary :

A. Tortoise   B. Toronto
C. Torped   D. Torus
E. Torsel
(a) B, E, C, A, D   (b) B, E, C, D, A
(c) B, C, E, A, D   (d) B, C, E, D, A

DIRECTION (Q. 8) : From the given alternatives select the word which cannot be formed using the letters of the given word.

8. TEACHER
   (a) REACH   (b) EATER
   (c) EARTH   (d) TRACTOR
9. In a certain code, '253' means 'books are old'; '546' means 'man is old' and '378' means 'buy good books'. What stands for "are" in that code?
   (a) 2   (b) 4   (c) 5   (d) 6
10. Find the missing number from the given responses:

5	6	12
4	3	4
2	3	?
18	27	96

(a) 4   (b) 5   (c) 3   (d) 6

DIRECTION (Q. 11): There is a certain relationship between the pair of figures on the either side of : : . Identify the relationship and find the missing figure.

11. 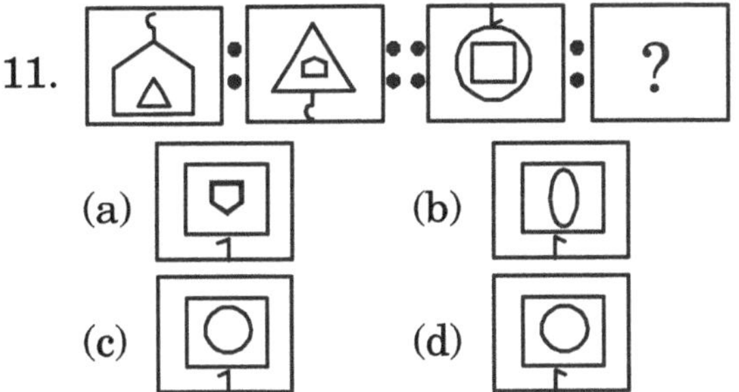

(a) (b)

(c) (d)

DIRECTION (Q. 12): Choose a figure from the options which is different from others.

12. (a) 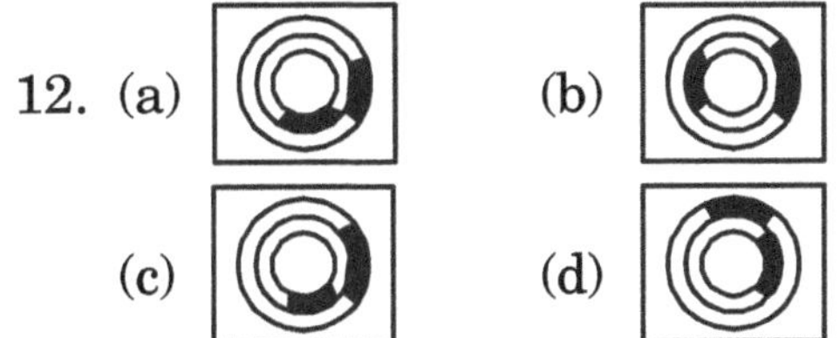 (b)

(c) (d)

13. If 'DELHI' can be coded as 'CCIDD', then how would you code 'BOMBAY'?
(a) AJMTVT   (b) AMJXVS
(c) MJXVSU   (d) WXYZAX

14. How many blocks are there in the given figure?

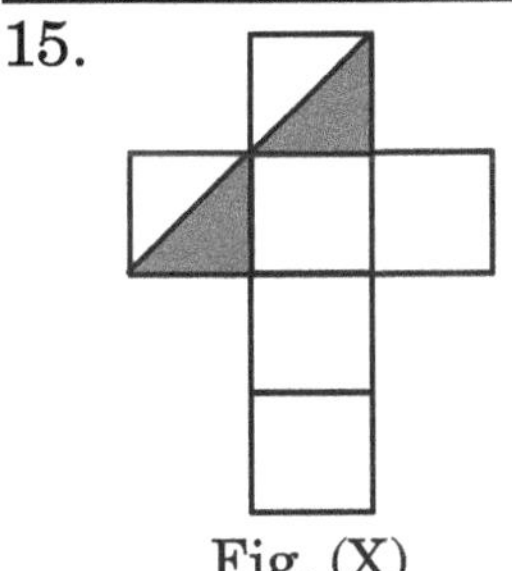

(a) 10   (b) 14
(c) 18   (d) 20

DIRECTION (Q. 15): In the following question, the sheet of paper shown in the fig.(X) is folded to form a box. Choose from amongst the options the boxes that are similar to the box that will be formed.

15.

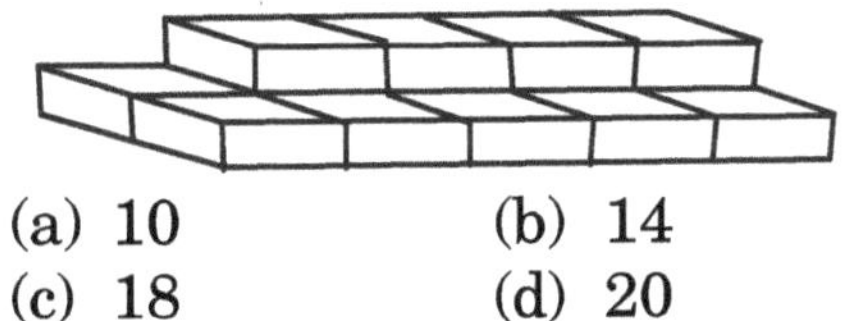

Fig. (X)

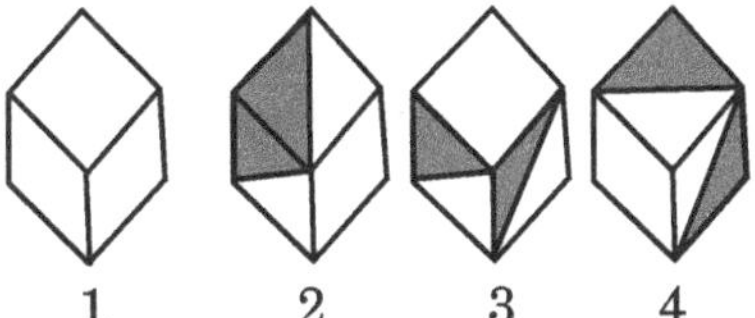

1   2   3   4
(a) 1 and 4   (b) 3 and 4 only
(c) 1 and 2 only   (d) 2 and 3 only

16. Neeta who is the sister-in-law of Anshu, is the daughter-in-law of Riya. Neeraj is the father of Abhishek who is the only brother of Anshu. How is Neeta related to Abhishek if Neeraj and Riya are a married couples?
(a) Mother-in-law (b) Aunt
(c) Wife   (d) None of these

DIRECTIONS (Q. 17): In the following question, there are three figures X, Y, and Z of a sheet of paper. Figure X and Y show the two consecutive folds of the sheet. And figure Z shows cuts on the folded sheet. Choose one figure from the options that resembles the unfolded form of the fig.Z.

17. 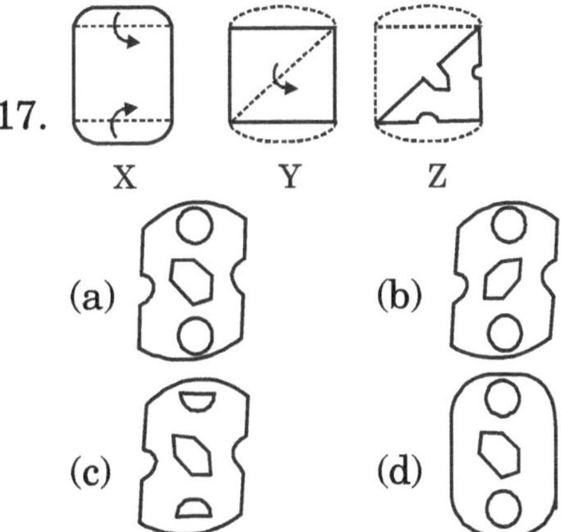

X   Y   Z

(a) (b)

(c) (d)

18. Village W is 20 km to the North of village X. village Y is 18 km to the East of village X. Village Z is 12 km to the West of W. If Manu starts from village Y and goes to village Z via village W, in which direction is he from his starting point?
(a) North-West (b) South
(c) North-East (d) East

DIRECTION (Q. 19): In the following question, find out which of the options completes the figure matrix.

19.
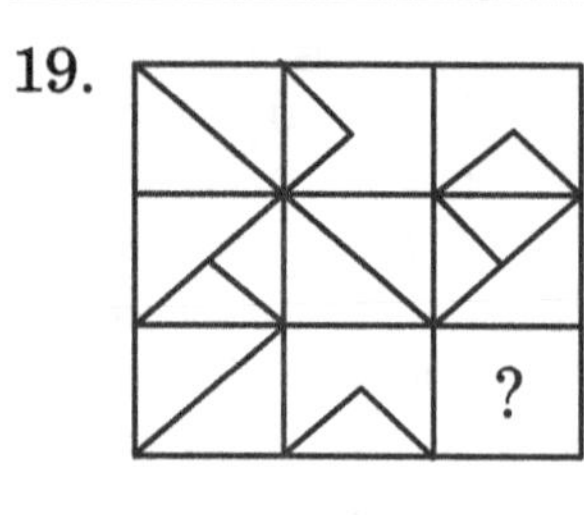

(a) 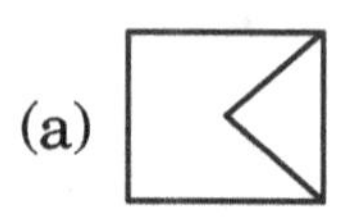   (b) 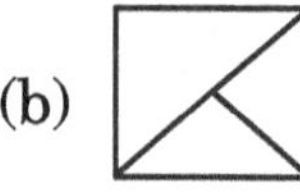

(c)    (d) 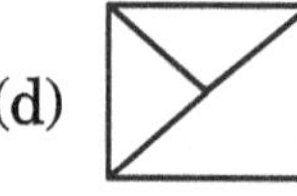

20. Which of the following diagram indicates the best relation between Men, Trees and Living beings?

(a) 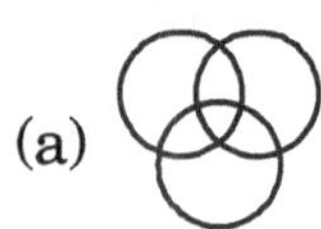   (b) 

(c)    (d) 

DIRECTION (Q. 21): In the following question, a fig. (X) is provided which embeds only one figure out of the options without any orientation. Select the correct option.

21. 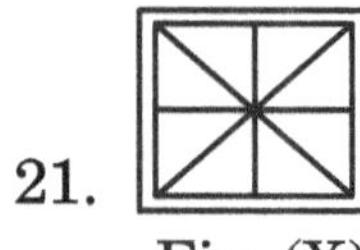

Fig. (X)

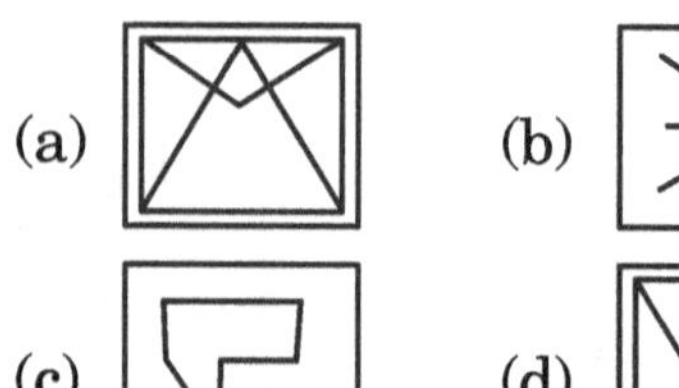

(a)   (b)   (c)   (d)

22. If the first day of a month is Monday, which of the following will be the fifth day from 21st of the month?
 (a) Monday   (b) Tuesday
 (c) Friday   (d) Thursday

23. If P denotes ÷, Q denotes ×, R denotes +, and S denotes –, then, 18 20Q 12P 6R 5S 13 = ?
 (a) 95   (b) 32
 (c) 51   (d) 57

24. Five coaches P, L, R, M, O are in a row. R is to the right of M and left of P. L is to the right of P and left of O. Which coach is in the middle?
 (a) P   (b) L
 (c) R   (d) O

25. Which answer figure completes the form in question figure ?
Question Figure :

Answer figures :

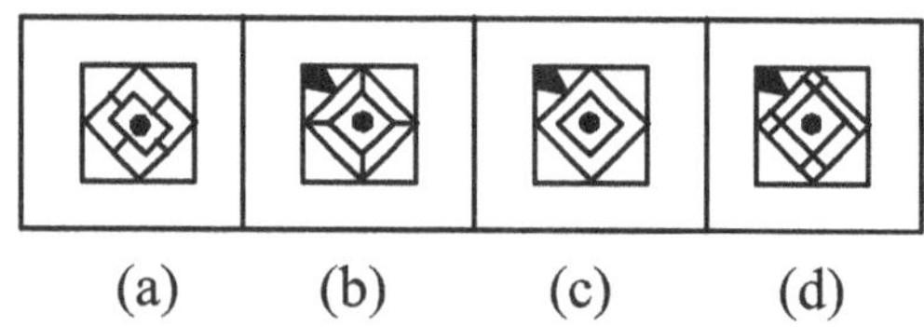

(a)   (b)   (c)   (d)

Mock Test 4

Name : __________

Max. Marks : 40

Number of Questions : 40

Time : 2 Hours

There is no negative marking in the test.

1. In a certain code, FAVOUR is written as EBUPTS. How is DANGER written in that code ?
   (a) CBFFDS   (b) CBMHDS
   (c) EBFHDS   (d) EBHHFS

2. In a certain code, BRAIN is written as $*\% \div \# \times$ and TIER is written as $\$ \# + \%$. How is RENT written in that code ?
   (a) $\% \times \# \$$ (b) $\% \# \times \$$
   (c) $\% + \times \$$ (d) $+ \times \% \$$

DIRECTIONS (Qs. 3 & 4): Choose the odd one out from the given alternatives.

3. (a) Broad : Wide
   (b) Light : Heavy
   (c) Tiny : Small
   (d) Big : Large

4. (a) 3, 4, 8   (b) 6, 2, 9
   (c) 1, 5, 7   (d) 2, 6, 9

5. If + means $\div$, – means $\times$, $\div$ means + and $\times$ means –, then $36 \times 8 + 4 \div 6 + 2 - 3 = ?$
   (a) 20
   (b) 18
   (c) 43
   (d) 50

6. What number should replace the question mark ?

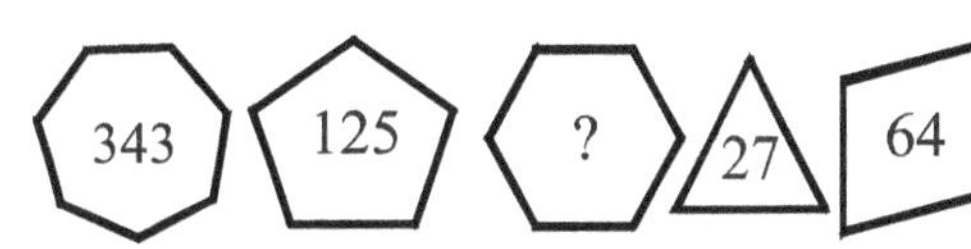

   (a) 216   (b) 316
   (c) 117   (d) 215

7. Mohit is 16th from the top and 12th from the bottom in merit in the class. How many students are there in the class ?
   (a) 29
   (b) 27
   (c) 28
   (d) 25

8. Select from the alternative, the box that can be formed by folding the sheet shown in figure (X) :

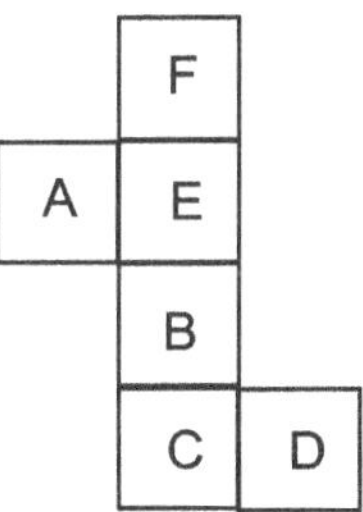

(X)

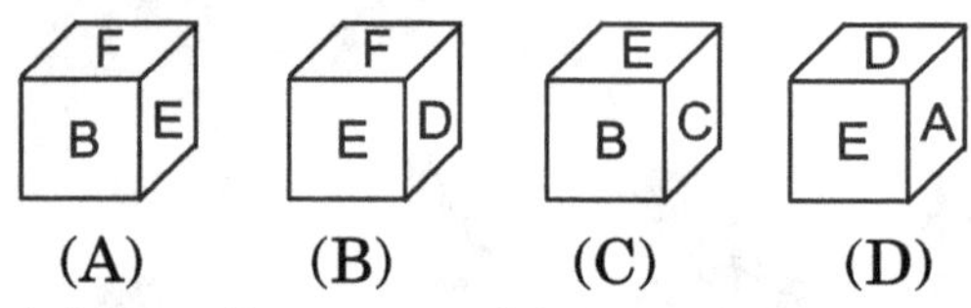

(A)   (B)   (C)   (D)

(a) A only   (b) B only

(c) A and C only (d) A, B, C and D

9. Which one of the given responses would be a meaningful order of the following?

  a. Sentence   b. Word
  c. Chapter   d. Phrase
  e. Paragraph

  (a) d, c, a, b, e   (b) b, c, e, d, a
  (c) c, e, a, d, b   (d) a, c, b, d, e

DIRECTION (Q.10) : In the following questions, a square sheet of paper is folded along the dotted lines and then cuts are made on it. How would the sheet look when opened? Select the correct figure from the given choices.

10.

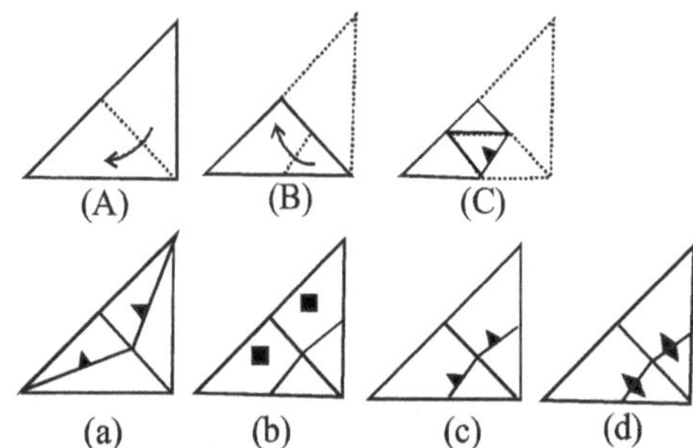

(A)   (B)   (C)

(a)   (b)   (c)   (d)

11. From the given alternatives select the word which cannot be formed using the letters of the given word.

IRREGULARITIES

  (a) REGULAR   (b) TIRED
  (c) TRAILER   (d) IRRIGATE

DIRECTION(Q. 12) : In the following question, you are given a fig. (X) followed by four alternative figures (a), (b), (c) and (d) such that fig. (X) is embedded in one of them. Trace out the alternative

figure which contains fig. (X) as its part.

12.

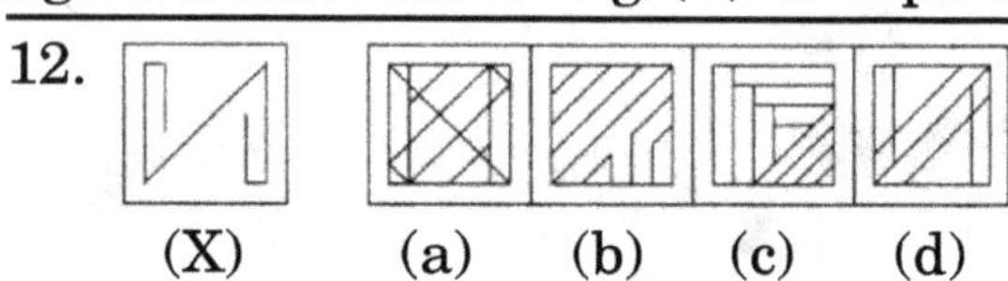

(X)   (a)   (b)   (c)   (d)

13. In this question, from the given alternatives select the word which cannot be formed by using the letters of the given word.

APPROPRIATE

  (a) PIRATE   (b) APPROVE
  (c) PROPER   (d) RAPPORT

14. Arrange the following words as per order in the dictionary.

  (i) Forge   (ii) Forget
  (iii) Forgo   (iv) Forgive
  (v) Format

  (a) (v), (ii), (iv) , (iii), (i)
  (b) (i), (iv), (iii), (ii), (v)
  (c) (iii), (iv), (v), (ii), (i)
  (d) (i), (ii), (iv), (iii), (v)

DIRECTIONS (Qs. 15 & 16): Select the related word/letters from the given alternatives.

---

15. Blue whale : Sea : : ? : Land
  (a) Turtle   (b) Fish
  (c) Elephant
  (d) Green whale

16. DIMP : CJLQ : : UWZA : ?
  (a) XTYB   (b) TXBY
  (c) XTBY   (d) TXYB

DIRECTION (Q. 17): Find the next term.

---

17. BMRG, DLTF, FKVE, HJXD, __ ?
  (a) JIZC   (b) JZIB
  (c) GIFB   (d) MOLC

DIRECTION(Q. 18): In the following question, which set of letters when sequentially placed at the gaps in the given letter series shall complete it?

---

18. c_ab_ca_bc_a

    (a) b c a b   (b) a b c b

    (c) b a c b   (d) c b a c

19. If 'air' is called 'green', green is called 'blue', 'blue' is called 'sky', 'sky' is called 'yellow', 'yellow' is called 'water' and water is called 'pink' then what is the colour of sky ?

    (a) Yellow   (b) Water

    (c) Sky   (d) Blue

20. How many triangles are there in the given figure?

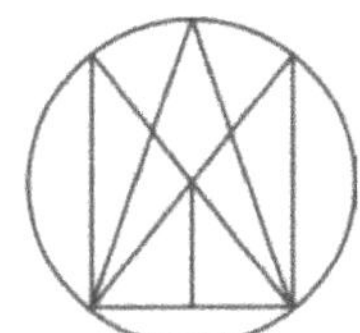

    (a) 10   (b) 12

    (c) 16   (d) 14

21. If a square paper is folded as shown in the question figures and then folded paper is punched. What will be the pattern on opening the paper ?

Question figures :

Paper → First fold → Second fold → Punched

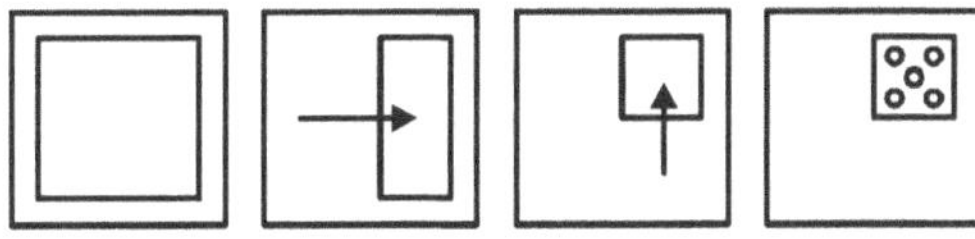

Answer figures :

(a) 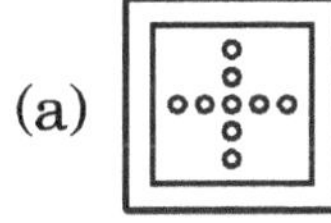   (b) 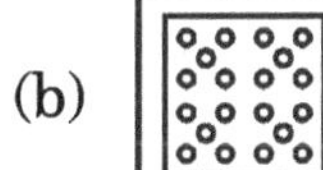

(c) 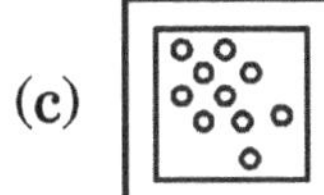   (d) 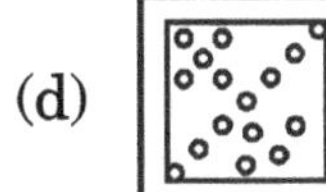

22. One evening, Raja started to walk towards the Sun. After walking a while, he turned to his right and again to his right. After walking a while, he again turned right. Which direction is he facing?

    (a) South   (b) East

    (c) West   (d) North

23. Shankar and Ganesh walked 150 meters towards East. Shankar turned left and walked 100 meters. Ganesh went straight for another 100 meters. Afterwards Ganesh turned to right and Shankar turned left. In which direction are they facing now?

    (a) East and North

    (b) West and South

    (c) North and South

    (d) South and North

24. If the day before yesterday was Sunday, what day will it be three days after the day after tomorrow ?

    (a) Sunday   (b) Monday

    (c) Wednesday   (d) Saturday

25. Roshan is taller than Hardik who is shorter than Susheel. Niza is taller than Harry but shorter than Hardik. Susheel is shorter than Roshan. Who is the tallest ?

    (a) Roshan

    (b) Susheel

    (c) Hardik

    (d) Harry

26. Which figure represents the relationship among Sun, Moon, Molecule?

(a) 

(b) 

(c) 

(d) 

27. Read the figure and find the region representing persons who are educated and employed but not confirmed in job.

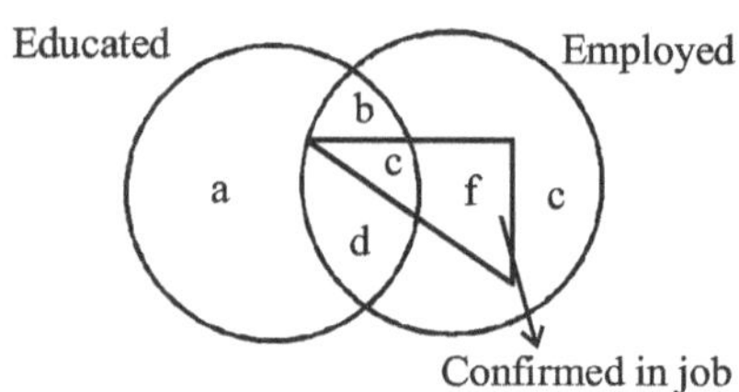

(a) abc
(b) bd
(c) adc
(d) ac

28. If + means ÷, − means ×, × means +, ÷ means −. Give the value for 45 + 9 − 3 × 15 ÷ 2
    (a) 40　　　　　　　(b) 36
    (c) 56　　　　　　　(d) 28

DIRECTION (Q. 29) : In the following question, some equations are solved on the basis of a certain system. On the same basis, find out the correct answer for the unsolved equation.

29. If 235 = 38 and 452 = 45, then 345 =?
    (a) 49
    (b) 66
    (c) 72
    (d) 50

DIRECTION (Q. 30) : In the following question which answer figure will complete the question figure?

30. **Question Figure**

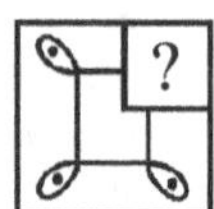

Answer Figures

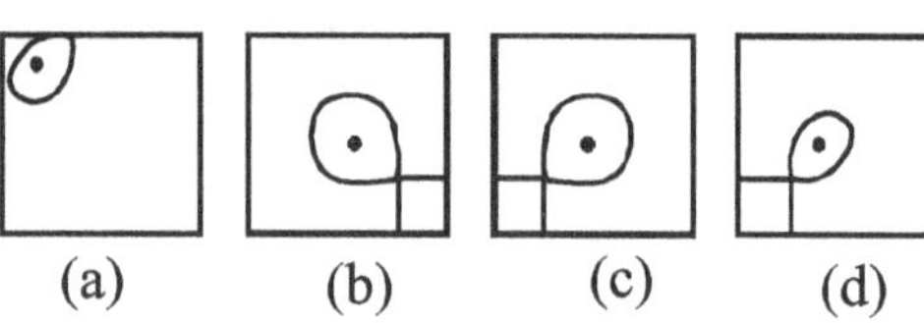

　　(a)　　　　(b)　　　　(c)　　　　(d)

31. Five boys A, B, C, D and E are standing in a row. D is on the right of E. B is on the left of E, but on the right of A. D is on the left of C, who is standing on the extreme right. Who is standing in the middle ?
    (a) D　　　　　　　(b) E
    (b) B　　　　　　　(d) C

32. Pointing to Gauri a person said, "The son of her only brother is the brother of my wife". How is Gauri related to the person?
    (a) Sister-in-law
    (b) Grandmother
    (c) Sister of father-in-law
    (d) None of these

33. A and B are children of D. Who is the father of A?
    To answer this question which of the following statements is/are necessary?
    1. C is the brother of A and the son of E.
    2. F is the mother of B.
    (a) Only (1)
    (b) Only (2)
    (c) Either (1) or (2)
    (d) Both (1) and (2)

34. If the first and second letters in the word DEPRESSION were interchanged, also the third and the fourth letters, the fifth and the sixth letters and so on, which of the following would be the eighth letter from the left?
    (a) R
    (b) O
    (c) S
    (d) I

35. If the alphabet series is arranged in reverse order, which letter will be twelfth to the left of the fourteenth letter from your left?
    (a) Y   (b) W
    (c) M   (d) D

DIRECTION (Q. 36) : Choose the correct mirror image from the given alternatives.

36. QUALITY
    (a) YTIJAUϱ
    (b) YTILAUϱ
    (c) ϬꓵAᒥITY
    (d) YTIᒥAꓵϱ

DIRECTION (Q. 37) : Find the missing number from the given alternatives.

37.

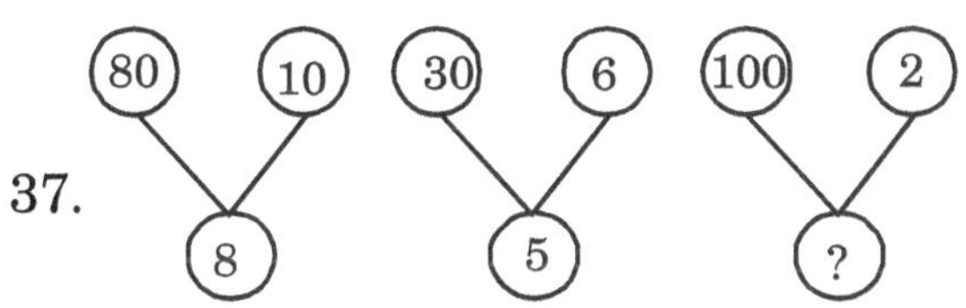

(a) 20   (b) 25
(c) 50   (d) 75

DIRECTION (Q. 38) : In the following question, group the given figures into three classes on the basis of their common properties using each figure only once.

38.

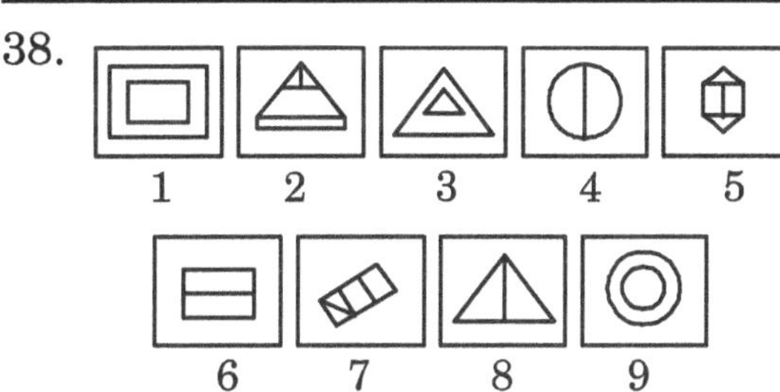

(a) 1, 3, 8; 2, 4, 6; 5, 7, 9
(b) 1, 2, 3; 4, 5, 6; 7, 8, 9
(c) 3, 4, 7; 2, 5, 9; 1, 6, 8
(d) 1, 3, 9; 4, 6, 8; 2, 5, 7

39. The position of how many letters in the word BRAKES remains unchanged when they are arranged in alphabetical order?
    (a) One
    (b) Two
    (c) Three
    (d) More than three

40. Introducing a woman, Sohan said, "She is the mother of the only daughter of my son". How that woman is related to Sohan?
    (a) Daughter
    (b) Sister-in-law
    (c) Wife
    (d) Daughter-in-law

Name : _________

Number of Questions : 40

There is no negative marking in the test.

Max. Marks : 40

Time : 2 Hours

1. A,B,C,D,E,F are sitting on the round table with equal distances. F is sitting opposite to E and between A and D. C is sitting right side of E and opposite to A. Who are the neighbours of A?
   (a) F and D   (b) E and F
   (c) E and C   (d) B and F

2. If '×' means '+', ÷ means '−', + means '÷' and '−' means '×' then what should be the value of the given equation?
   $14 × 4 ÷ 70 + 10 − 2 = ?$
   (a) 10   (b) 15
   (c) 3   (d) 4

DIRECTION (Q. 3): In the question, equation is solved on the basis of a certain system. On the same basis, find out the correct answer for the unsolved equation.

3. If $782 = 20$
   and $671 = 17$, then $884 = ?$
   (a) 26   (b) 23
   (c) 32   (d) 19

DIRECTION (Q. 4): In the following question, which answer figure will complete the question figure?

4. **Question Figure**

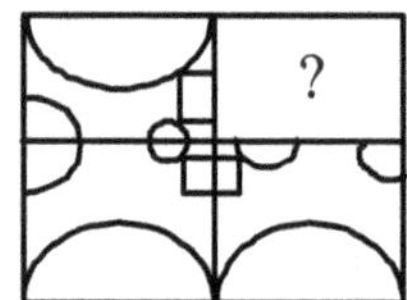

Answer Figures

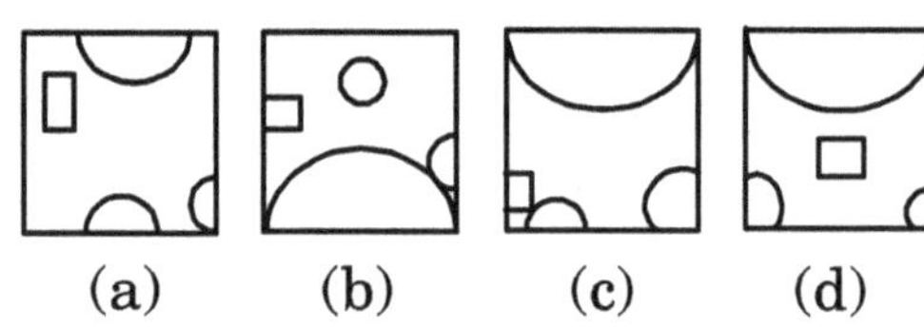

    (a)   (b)   (c)   (d)

5. From the given answer figures, select the one in which the question figure is hidden/embedded.

Question Figure

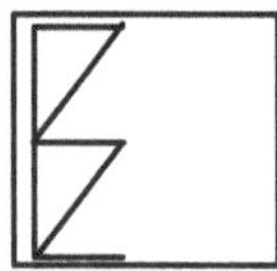

Answer Figures

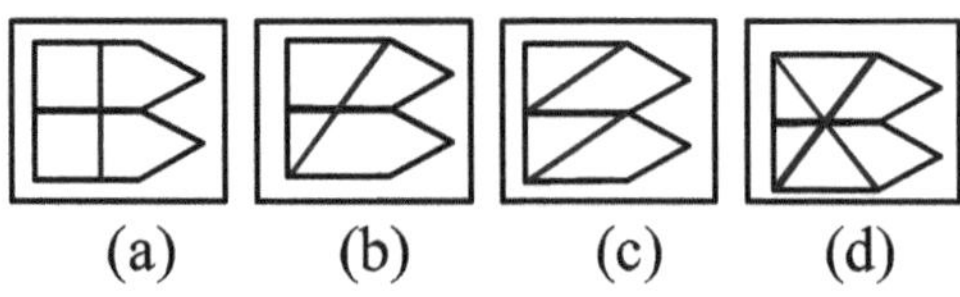

    (a)   (b)   (c)   (d)

6. Find out the figure which best represents the relationship among Garden, Rose and Jasmine.

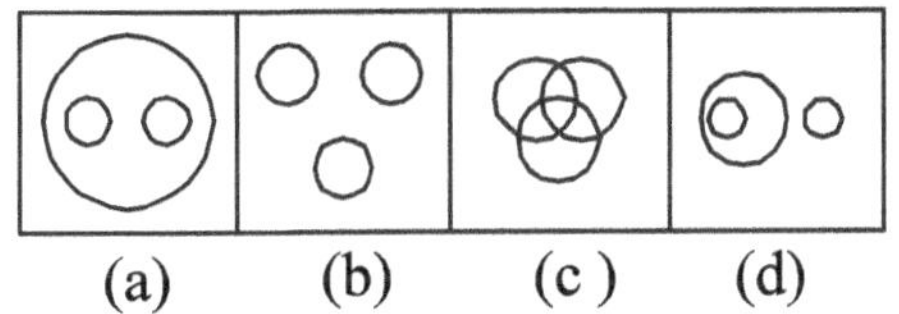

7. The diagram represents Teachers, Singers and Players. Study the diagram and find out how many teachers are also singers.

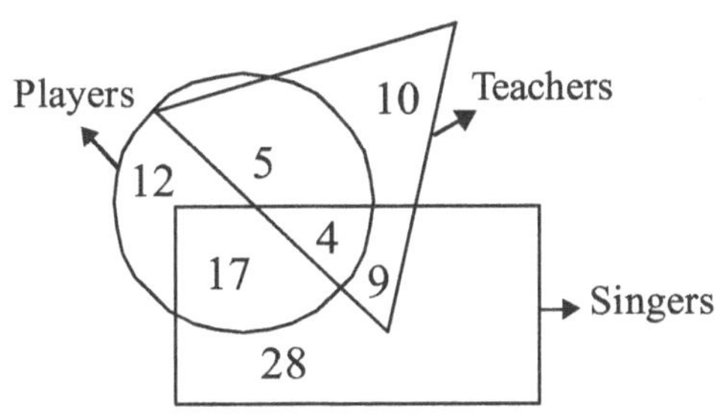

(a) 4
(b) 5
(c) 9
(d) 13

8. Identify the answer figure from which the pieces given in the question figure have been cut.

Question Figure

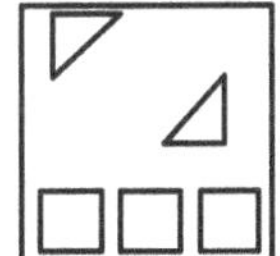

Answer Figures

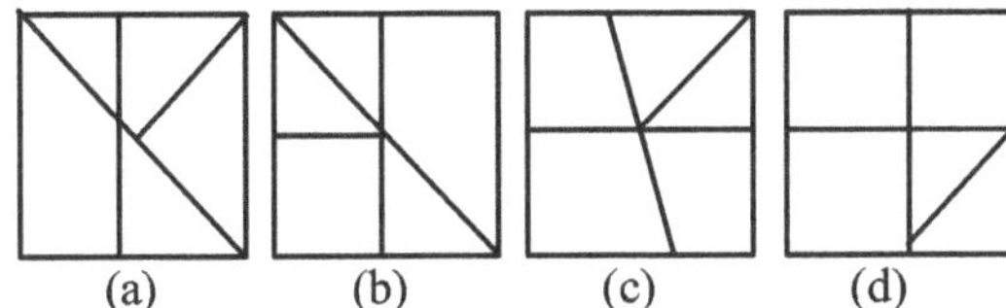

9. Find the number of triangles in the following figure :

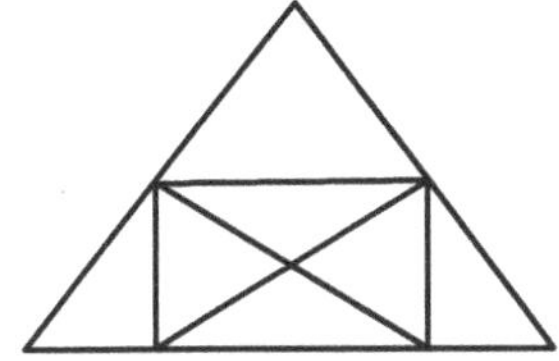

(a) 8
(b) 14
(c) 10
(d) 12

10. Priti scored more than Rahul. Yamuna scored as much as Divya. Lokita scored less than Manju. Rahul scored more than Yamuna. Manju scored less than Divya. Who scored the lowest?
    (a) Yamuna
    (b) Lokita
    (c) Rahul
    (d) Manju

11. If the day-after-tomorrow is Sunday, which day was day-before-yesterday?
    (a) Thursday
    (b) Wednesday
    (c) Tuesday
    (d) Monday

DIRECTION (Q. 12) : In question below, from the given alternative words, select the word which **cannot** be formed using the letters of the given word:

12. ADMINISTRATION
    (a) Station
    (b) Mind
    (c) Ration
    (d) Minister

DIRECTION (Q. 13): In question arrange the following words as per order in the dictionary.

13. 1. Necessary
    2. Navigate
    3. Nautical
    4. Naval
    (a) 3,4,2,1
    (b) 3,2,4,1
    (c) 2,4,3,1
    (d) 4,3,2,1

14. A group of alphabets are given with each being assigned a number. These have to be unscrambled into a meaningful word and correct order of letters may be indicated from the given responses.
    T M H R E O
    5 4 3 2 1 0

(a) 025314   (b) 315402
(c) 405312   (d) 504231

DIRECTIONS (Qs. 15 & 16): Select the related word/number from the given alternatives.

15. 25 : 125 : : 36 : ?
    (a) 180   (b) 206
    (c) 216   (d) 318
16. food : man :: fuel:?
    (a) wood   (b) car
    (c) heat   (d) smoke

17. If the cook is called butler, butler is called manager, manager is called teacher, teacher is called clerk and clerk is called principal, who will teach in the class?

    (a) Cook   (b) Butler

    (c) Manager   (d) Clerk

18. In a certain code language '526' means 'sky is blue'; '24' means 'blue colour' and '436' means 'colour is fun'. Which of the following digit stands for 'fun'?

    (a) 5   (b) 4

    (c) 3   (d) 2

19. If CHAIR is coded as FKDLU then RAID is coded as :

    (a) ULGD   (b) ULKG

    (c) ULDG   (d) UDLG

20. Count the number of cubes in the given figure.

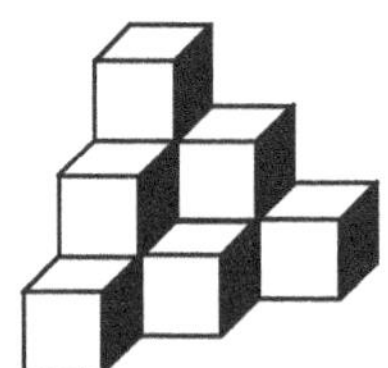

    (a) 14   (b) 12
    (c) 10   (d) 8

DIRECTIONS (Qs. 21 & 22): Find the missing term.

21. 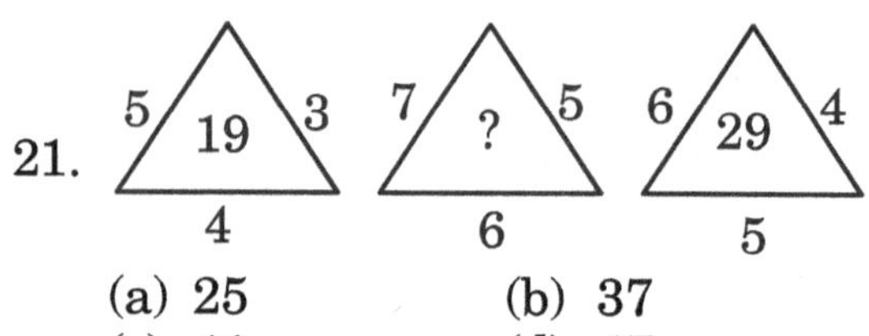

    (a) 25   (b) 37
    (c) 41   (d) 47

22.

A	D	H
F	I	M
?	N	R

    (a) K   (b) N
    (c) O   (d) P

DIRECTION (Q. 23): Find the next figure from the given alternatives.

23. 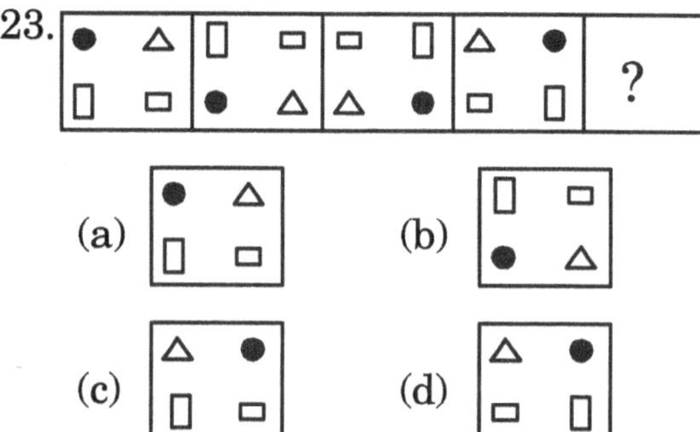

DIRECTION (Q. 24): Find the next term of the given series.

24. 0, 3, 8, 15, 24, 35, 48, 63, ?
    (a) 83   (b) 98
    (c) 79   (d) 80

DIRECTION (Q. 25): In the following question, one term in the number series is wrong. Find out the wrong term.

25. 24, 27, 31, 33, 36, 39,42
    (a) 24   (b) 27
    (c) 31   (d) 33

DIRECTIONS (Qs. 26 to 28) : Identify the one that does not belong to the group of the other three.

26. (a) WUV   (b) ZYX
    (c) TSR   (d) QPO
27. (a) 24   (b) 14
    (c) 48   (d) 18
28. (a) December   (b) February
    (c) March   (d) January

DIRECTION (Q. 29): Choose figure from the options which is different from others.

29. (a) 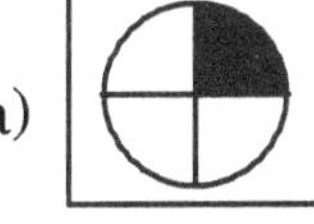   (b) 

   (c) 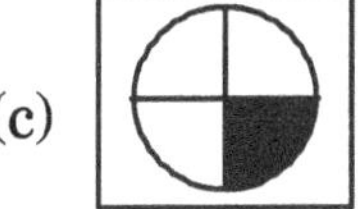   (d) 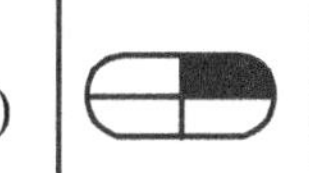

30. A man is facing towards West and turns through 45° clockwise, again 180° clockwise and then turns through 270° anticlockwise. In which direction is he facing now?
   (a) West   (b) North-West
   (c) South   (d) South-West

31. Ankit, Tarun, Rohan and Sohan are friends. They play cards. Partner faces in opposite directions. Ankit faces and Tarun become partners. Sohan faces North. If Ankit faces towards West, then who faces towards South?
   (a) Tarun
   (b) Rohan
   (c) Sohan
   (d) Data inadequate

DIRECTION (Q. 32) : In the following question, arrange the given words in meaningful sequence.

32. 1. Poverty
    2. Population
    3. Death
    4. Unemployment
    5. Lack of food
    (a) 2, 3, 4, 5, 1   (b) 3, 4, 2, 5, 1
    (c) 4, 1, 2, 5, 3   (d) 2, 4, 1, 5, 3

33. If the letters of the word TRANSFORM are rearranged as they appear in the English alphabet, then the position of how many letters will remain unchanged after such rearrangement?
   (a) One   (b) Two
   (c) Three   (d) Four

34. If the first and the third digits in each of the following numbers are interchanged, then which number will be the smallest?
   348 436 652 198 563
   (a) 348   (b) 436
   (c) 652   (d) 198

DIRECTIONS (Qs. 35 & 36) : Read the information given below and answer the questions that follow.

(i)   A, B, C, D, E and F are six members of a family.
(ii)   One couple has parents and their children in the family.
(iii) A is the son of C and E is the daughter of A.
(iv) D is the daughter of F who is the mother of E.

35. Who are the male members in the family?
    (a) A and C
    (b) C and F
    (c) A, B and C
    (d) Can't be determined

36. Which of the following pairs is the parents of the children?
    (a) B and C   (b) C and F
    (c) B and F   (d) A and F

37. How many even digits are there in the series which are followed by an odd digit and preceded by an even digit?

    1 4 5 7 2 5 8 4 9 6 8 2 5 4 1 3 2 7 1
    (a) 1   (b) 2
    (c) 3   (d) 5

DIRECTION (Q. 38) : In the following question, arrange the given words in a meaningful sequence

38. 1. Elephant   2. Cat
    3. Mosquito   4. Tiger
    5. Whale

(a) 5, 3, 1, 2, 4   (b) 3, 2, 4, 1, 5
(c) 1, 3, 5, 4, 2   (d) 2, 5, 1, 4, 3

39. In a group of Friends, two men have wives, one is a bachelor, another's wife is dead, two are divorcees. They take four children with them to a picnic. How many have gone to the picnic?
    (a) 12   (b) 10
    (c) 14   (d) 13

DIRECTION (Q. 40) : Find the missing figure in the given matrix.

40.

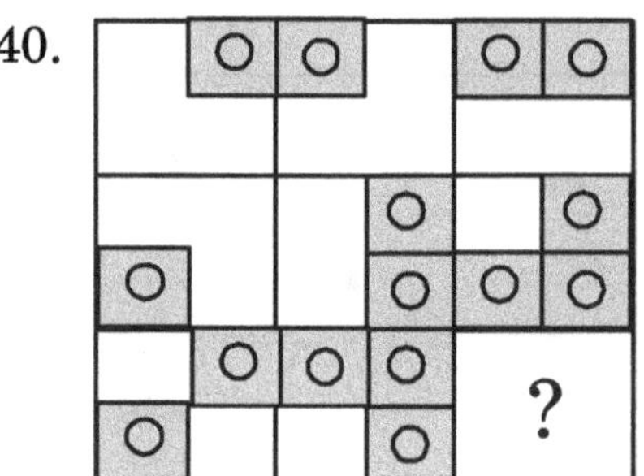

(a)   (b) 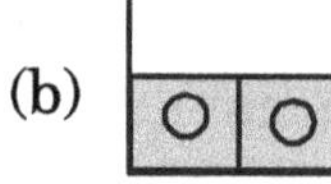

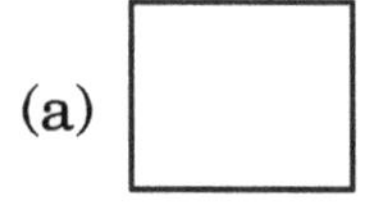

(c) 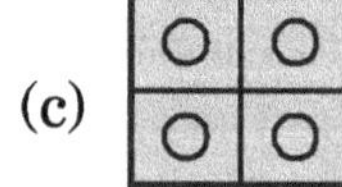   (d) 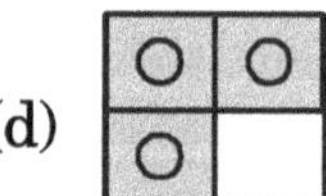

OLYMPIAD
Mock Test 1

Name : __________ **Max. Marks : 25**

Number of Questions : 25 **Time : 1 Hour**

There is no negative marking in the test.

1. Identify the following :
   – It is a device that generates hardcopy outputs.
   – It draw lines on a paper using a commands received from a computer.

   (a) 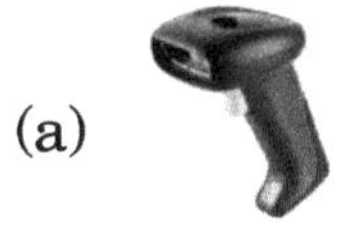 (b) 

   (c)  (d) 

2. Which of the following statements is INCORRECT about an inkjet printer?
   (a) It forms characters and images by separating small drops of link in paper.
   (b) It is commonly used in homes for everyday printing.
   (c) It uses CIJ and Drop – on – Demand printing methods.
   (d) It produces water proof prints.

3. Identify the following :
   – It is typically integrated directly within the CPU chip.
   – It improves processing by acting as a termporary high speed holding area between the main memory and CPU.
   (a) RAM
   (b) CD
   (c) ROM
   (d) Cache Memory

4. Which of the following statements is INCORRECT about an SD card?
   (a) You can lock/unlock the write operation using the write protection notch.
   (b) A direction notch on the card indicates which side should be inserted first in the electronic equipment.
   (c) It is temporary or volatile memory.
   (d) The label of the memory card contains vendor identification.

5. Match the computer types given in Column – I with their descriptions in Column – II.

Column – I		Column – II
(A) Server	(i)	Expensive computer that perform complex calculations extremely rapidly.

(B) Super-computer	(ii) Provides resources to other Computers connected to a network.
(C) Embedded systems	(iii) A small mobile computing device.
(D) PDA	(iv) A self – conatined device which performspre-programmed functions.

(a) (A) – (i), (B) – (iii), (C) – (iv), (D) – (ii)

(b) (A) – (iii), (B) – (i), (C) – (ii), (D) – (iv)

(c) (A) – (ii), (B) – (i), (C) – (iv), (D) – (iii)

(d) (A) – (i), (B) – (iii), (C) – (ii), (D) – (iv)

6. Match the following.

Column – I	Column –II
(A) John Mauchly & J. Presper Eckert	(i) IBM Mark I Computer
(B) Howard H. Aiken	(ii) Invented the Difference Engine and Analytical Engine
(C) Charles Babbage	(iii) Invented electrio-mechanical tabulator to help with the U.S. Census
(D) Herman Hollerith	(iv) Created the ENIAC

(a) (A) – (iv), (B) – (i), (C) – (ii), (D) – (iii)

(b) (A) – (ii), (B) – (iii), (C) – (i), (D) – (iv)

(c) (A) – (iii), (B) – (i), (C) – (ii), (D) – (iv)

(d) (A) – (iv), (B) – (ii), (C) – (iii), (D) – (i)

7. Identify the following :

– It is a feature that allows you to see and manage all external devices from a central location.

– Examples of such devices can be a camera, mobile phone of flash drive.

– This feature can be accessed by going to Devices and Printers option in Control Panel.

(a) Device Show

(b) Device Name

(c) Device Stage

(d) Device View

8. You want to know following information about your computer.

1. Amount of RAM installed

2. Pen and touch input supported by the system

Which of the following options of Control Panel provides you the above listed information?

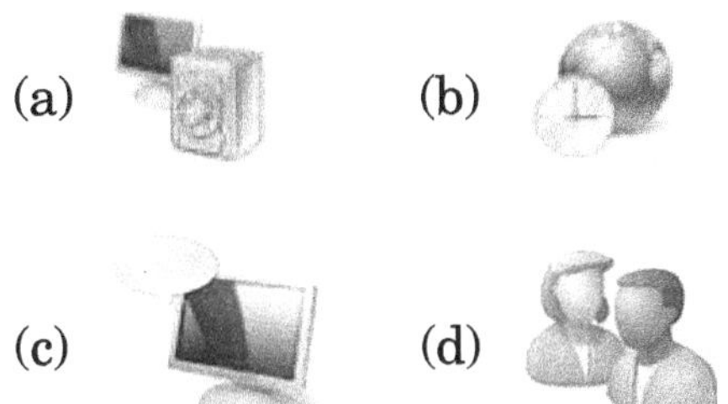

(a)   (b)

(c)   (d)

9. Identify the tool :

   – It is used for referencing information that appears in another location in a document.

   – This information can be headings, figures and tables in various parts of your document.

   – It gets automatically updated if the content is moved to another location.

   (a) Cross – reference

   (b) Hyperlink

   (c) Direct reference

   (d) Indirect reference

10. A theme can be __________.

   (a) Applied to all slides

   (b) Applied to selected slides

   (c) Hidden by right clicking on it

   (d) Both (a) and (b)

11. Using which of the following options, you can share your slide show with anyone over the internet by sharing its URL?

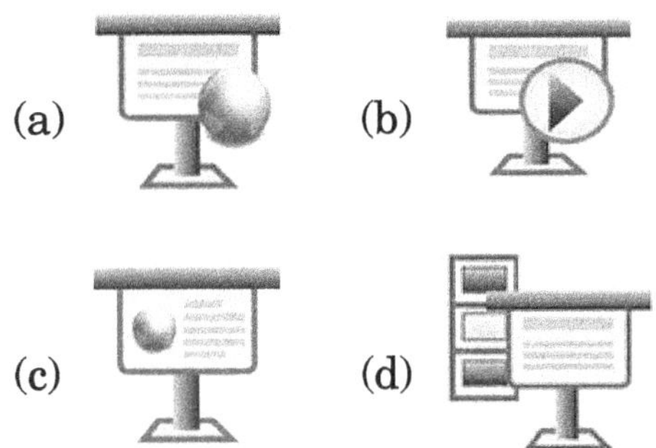

(a)   (b)

(c)   (d)

12. Which of the following statement hold (s) true about the given command button with respect to Header & Footer tools?

Statement 1 : It adds the count of total number of pages in a worksheet to the header or footer.

Statement 2 : The count gets automatically updated as changes are made in the workbook.

   (a) Only Statement 1

   (b) Only Statement 2

   (c) Both Statement 1 and Statement 2

   (d) Neither Statement 1 nor Statement 2

13. Match the QBASIC operator names given is Column – I with their corresponding operators given in Column – II.

Column – I	Column – II
(A) Logical Operators	(i) $+, -, *, /, \wedge$
(B) Relational Operators	(ii) AND, OR, NOT
(C) Arithmetic Operators	(iii) $=, >, <, \leq, \geq$

(a) (A) – (i), (B) – (ii), (C) – (iii)

(b) (A) – (ii), (B) – (i), (C) – (iii)

(c) (A) – (ii), (B) – (iii), (C) – (i)

(d) (A) – (iii), (B) – (i), (C) – (ii)

14. Which of the following statements holds (s) true about client-server architecture?

Statement 1 : In this architecture, the server has more powerful central processor, memory and large disk drives than clients.

Statement 2 : A client/server network is utilised by desktop computers only.

(a) Only statement 1

(b) Only statement 2

(c) Both statement 1 and statement 2

(d) Neither statement 1 nor statement 2

15. Which of the following statements hold(s) true about given service?

Statement 1 : You can connect to this service by using an internet connection.

Statement 2 : It eliminates the difficulty and expenses of maintaining, upgrading your own computer hardware and software.

(a) Only Statement 1

(b) Only Statement 2

(c) Both statement 1 and statement 2

(d) Neither statement 1 nor statement 2

16. To access a mainframe or super computer, users need ______

(a) Node   (b) Laptop

(c) Tablet   (d) Terminal

17. Which of the following is a large and expensive, computer capable of simultaneously processing data for hundreds or thousands of users?

(a) Handheld Computer

(b) Tablet

(c) Personal Computer

(d) Mainframe Computer

18. Computer________ is whatever is typed, submitted, or transmitted to a computer system.

(a) input   (b) output

(c) data   (d) circuitry

19. The most widely used computer device is ______.

(a) solid state disks

(b) external hard disk

(c) internal hard disk

(d) mouse

20. The computer's processor consists of which of the following parts?

    (a) CPU and Main Memory

    (b) Hard Disk and Floppy Drive

    (c) Control Unit and ALU

    (d) Operating system and Applications

21. The fastest component for accessing stored data/information is/are

    (a) cache

    (b) DVDs

    (c) hard disks

    (d) main memory

22. A _______ is a software program used to view Web pages.

    (a) site   (b) host

    (c) link   (d) browser

23. Which of the following is called as protocol in the URL ?

    http://www.xyz.com

    (a) .com

    (b) www

    (c) xyz

    (d) http

24. Windows 10 is in an example of a _______?

    (a) application software

    (b) browser

    (c) operating system

    (d) shareware

25. What is the default file extension for all word documents?

    (a) TXT   (b) WRD

    (c) FIL   (d) DOC

OLYMPIAD
Mock Test 2

Name : _________

Number of Questions : 25

Max. Marks : 25

Time : 1 Hour

There is no negative marking in the test.

1. Which of the following statements is INCORRECT about a registers?
   (a) It is a small high speed storage unit.
   (b) It holds the data and instructions that need to be processed immediately.
   (c) It holds the data permanently.
   (d) Data stored in specific registers have special meaning to the CPU.

2. Unscramble the given word and select the option with which it relatees.

   ROCOPRESS
   (a) Intel Core i7
   (b) Microsoft Edge
   (c) Device Driver
   (d) SATA

3. Which of the following is NOT a difference between Blu-ray disc and DVD?
   (a) The quality of audio and video recorded on Blu-ray disc is higher than DVDs.
   (b) Read only memory type is not available in Blu-ray disc whereas DVD supports read only.
   (c) Blu-ray disc uses violet-blue laser, whereas DVD uses red laser.
   (d) A single layer blu-ray disc can store upto 25 GB data whereas a single layer DVD can store only 4.7 GB of data.

4. First generation computers were replaced by second generation computers because ____________.
   (a) operating speed of first generation computers was higher than second generation computers
   (b) power consumption of first generation computers was higher than second generation computers
   (c) ICs were used as the main component in first generation computers
   (d) they were easily portable than second generation computers

5. You have a computer that runs Windows 7. To view the processes that are currently trying to access a network resource, you should ________.

(a) open Resource Monitor and click the Network tab

(b) open Windows Task Manager and click the Network tab

(c) open event Viewer and examine the Network Profile Operational log

(d) open Performance Monitor and add all the counters for network interface.

6. The given icon can be used to _______________ in a mail-merged document.

(a) view the merged data

(b) make changes to the list of recipients

(c) highlight the field in letter

(d) add a greeting line in letter

7. Which of the following statement holds(s) true about the given option?

Statement 1: It lets you run a program when an object is clicked while viewing a presentation in Slide sorter view.

Statement 2: It can only be used with a Clipart graphic.

(a) Only statement 1

(b) Only statement 2

(c) Both statement 1 and Statement 2

(d) Neither statement 1 nor statement 2

8. Which of the following tasks cannot be done in Slide Master?

(a) Changing the slide orientation

(b) Changing the background styles.

(c) Editing the speakers notes

(d) Editing the name of a layout.

9. Identify the function of the given icon.

(a) It is used for adding up and down arrows

(b) It is used to rotate text diagonally or vertically.

(c) It is used for wrapping text by displaying it on multiple lines.

(d) It is used for adding text effects to a cell.

10. Match the MS - Excel shortcut sequences given in Column - I with their description in Column - II.

Column - I	Column - II
(A) Ctrl + I	(i) Applies or removes bold formatting

(B) Ctrl + @/2   (ii) Applies or removes underling

(C) Ctrl + #/3   (iii) Displays the Format Cells dialog box

(D) Ctrl + $/4   (iv) Applies or removes italic formating

(a) (A) - (ii), (B) - (i), (C) - (iv), (D) - (iii)

(b) (A) - (ii), (B) - (iii), (C) - (i), (D) - (iv)

(c) (A) - (ii), (B) - (iv), (C) - (i), (D) - (iii)

(d) (A) - (iii), (B) - (i), (C) - (iv), (D) - (ii)

11. In this mode, a QBASIC statement is executed as soon as you press the  key. It is the ________.

(a) program mode
(b) status mode
(c) intermediate mode
(d) immediate mode

12. Which of the following statements is true for a Boot Sector Virus?

(a) It infect boot/master boot records on a hard disk.
(b) It is most active while a computer system is booting
(c) Disk Killer is a well known boot virus.
(d) All of these

13. Match the following.

Column - I		Column - II
(A) E - Commerce	(i)	Founder of the World Wide Web
(B) FTP	(ii)	Company that offers Internet service
(C) Tim Berners - Lee	(iii)	Host computer connected to the web that contains data in the form of web pages
(D) ISP	(iv)	Online Trading
(E) Web server	(v)	A protocol used for exchanging files

(a) (A) - (iv), (B) - (v), (C) - (i), (D) - (iii), (E) - (ii)
(b) (A) - (v), (B) - (iv), (C) - (i), (D) - (iii), (E) - (ii)
(c) (A) - (iv), (B) - (v), (C) - (i), (D) - (ii), (E) - (iii)
(d) (A) - (v), (B) - (iv), (C) - (i), (D) - (ii), (E) - (iii)

14. Ctrl, shift and alt are called ________ keys.

(a) adjustment
(b) function
(c) modifier
(d) alphanumeric

15. VLSI technology is used in ________ generation computers.
   - (a) first
   - (b) second
   - (c) third
   - (d) fourth

16. For selecting or highlighting, which of the following device is generally used?
   - (a) Icon
   - (b) Keyboard
   - (c) Mouse
   - (d) Floppy Disk

17. Access control based on a person's fingerprints is an example of
   - (a) biometric identification
   - (b) characteristic identification
   - (c) fingerprint security
   - (d) logistics

18. CD and DVD drives are the examples of
   - (a) coding media drives
   - (b) solid stage storage drives
   - (c) zip drives
   - (d) storage devices

19. The main memory of a computer can also be called
   - (a) primary storage
   - (b) internal memory
   - (c) primary memory
   - (d) all of these

20. Documents on the Web are called ________.
   - (a) web pages
   - (b) web sites
   - (c) web communities
   - (d) web tags

21. What is the storage area for email messages called?
   - (a) A folder
   - (b) A directory
   - (c) A mailbox
   - (d) The hard disk

22. To restart the computer the following combination of keys is used
   - (a) Ctrl + Alt + Del
   - (b) Backspace + Ctrl
   - (c) Esc + Ctrl
   - (d) Insert + Esc

23. File extensions are used in order to——
   - (a) name the file
   - (b) ensure the filename is not lost
   - (c) identify the file
   - (d) identify the file type

24. A(n)______ is a special visual and audio effect applied in Powerpoint to text or content.
   - (a) animation
   - (b) flash
   - (c) wipe
   - (d) dissolve

25. The shortcut key to insert the current date?
   - (a) Alt + Shift + D
   - (b) Alt + Shift + V
   - (c) Alt + Shift + C
   - (d) Alt + Shift + B

Name : _________

Number of Questions : 25

Max. Marks : 25

Time : 1 Hour

There is no negative marking in the test.

1. Match the following.

Column – I	Column – II
(A) OMR	(i) Consists of a flat surface and a stylus
(B) Touch screen	(ii) Performs the job similar to concept keyboard
(C) Graphic Tablet	(iii) A technique for inputting text into a computer by means of a document reader

   (a) (A) – (i), (B) – (iii), (C) – (ii)
   (b) (A) – (ii), (B) – (i) , (C) – (iii)
   (c) (A) – (iii), (B) – (ii), (C) – (i)
   (d) (A) – (ii), (B) – (iii), (C) – (i)

2. Which of the following scanners are commonly used in the publishing industry?
   (a) Low resolution flatbed scanners
   (b) Sheet – fed scanners
   (c) Handheld scanners
   (d) Drum scanners

3. Identify the following :
   – It is a portable storage device.
   – It needs to be spinned to read data stored on it.
   – It has a single spiral track.

4. Second generations computers moved from cryptic binary machine language to symbolic __________ language.
   (a) Assembly
   (b) High level
   (c) Pascal
   (d) Basic

5. Special effects used to introduce slides in a presentation are called
   (a) Effects
   (b) Custom Animations
   (c) Transitions
   (d) Present Animations

6. Which of the following statements is incorrect with respect to MS Excel 2010 functions?
   (a) COUNT () function counts the number of cells in a range that contains number.
   (b) Both, NOW () and TODAY () is used to display the current time.

(c) The ROUND () function is used to round a number to a specified number of digits.

(d) CONCATENATE () function is used to join several strings into one text string.

7. For mail merge, ______________ consists of the list of names and addresses to be printed on labels and envelopes.
   (a) data source
   (b) main document
   (c) new document
   (d) website

8. When we create a custom show in a presentation, even when a custom show already exists for it, then __________.
   (a) previous custom show gets deleted
   (b) previous custom show gets merged with the recent one.
   (c) both the custom shows remain in the presentation
   (d) a copy of the presentation is created with the new custom show.

9. Using [icon] icon of Slide Master view you can __________ in a slide layout.
   (a) insert new text placeholders
   (b) change overall design for your slides
   (c) hide background graphics
   (d) change background styles

10. Which of the following is the CORRECT description of Auto Complete feature?
    (a) It will force MS – Excel to display value in multiple lines within the cell.
    (b) It automatically fills the entry based on other entries that you have already made in a column, when you type the first few letters of the similar text.
    (c) It inserts a series of values or text items in a range of cells.
    (d) None of these

11. Which of the following is the CORRECT command to make a box filled with yellow color in QBASIC?
    (a) SCREEN 13
        LINE (60, 10) – (60, 10), 9, BF
    (b) SCREEN 13
        LINE (10, 60) – (100, 100), 13, B
    (c) SCREEN 13
        LINE (10, 60) – (100, 100), 14, BF
    (d) SCREEN 13
        LINE (60, 10) – (10, 60), 4, BF

12. Which of the following statements holds (s) true about client-server architecture?
    Statement 1 : In this architecture, the server has more powerful central processor, memory and larger disk drives than clients.
    Statement 2 : A client/server network is utilised by desktop computers only.
    (a) Only statement 1
    (b) Only statement 2
    (c) Both statement 1 and statement 2
    (d) Neither statement 1 nor statement 2

13. What is an agribot?

   (a) A robot deployed for agricutural purposes.
   (b) A robot deployed for plant nursing
   (c) A robot working cooperatively
   (d) A robot involved in robotic harvesting
14. Integrated Chips or IC's were started to be in use from which generation of Computers?
   (a) 1st Generation
   (b) 2nd Generation
   (c) 3rd Generation
   (d) 4th Generation
15. First supercomputer developed in India is
   (a) PARAM   (b) ARYA Bhatt
   (c) BUDDHA   (d) SHIVA
16. All the characters that a device can use is called its ?
   (a) Skill Set
   (b) Character Alphabet
   (c) Character Codes
   (d) Keyboard Characters
17. What is the full form of 'RAID'?
   (a) Random Access of Inexpensive disks
   (b) Redundant Array of Inexpensive data
   (c) Random Array of Inexpensive data
   (d) Redundant Array of Inexpensive disks
18. Which of the following is in the ascending order of Data hierarchy?
   (a) Bit – Byte – Record – Field – Database – File
   (b) Byte – Bit – File – Record – Database – Field
   (c) Bit – Byte – Field – Record – File – Database
   (d) Field – Byte – Bit – Record – File– Database
19. What is an E-mail attachment?
   (a) A receipt sent by the recipient
   (b) A separate document from another program sent along with an E-mail message
   (c) A malicious parasite that feeds off, of your messages and destroys the contents
   (d) A list of CC: or BCC: recipients
20. Where is the newly received email stored?
   (a) In your website
   (b) In address-box
   (c) In Inbox
   (d) In your personal laptop
21. Applications are often referred to as
   (a) data file
   (b) executable files
   (c) system software
   (d) the operating system
22. All the deleted files go to
   (a) recycle bin
   (b) task bar
   (c) tool bar
   (d) my computer
23. Which of the following is not a FONT EFFECT?
   (a) Font Color
   (b) Super Script
   (c) Engrave
   (d) Strike Through
24. The Zoom control slider is located in __________.
   (a) title bar   (b) status bar
   (c) formula bar   (d) scroll bar
25. A pixel is
   (a) a computer program that draws picture
   (b) a picture stored in the secondary memory
   (c) the smallest resolvable part of a picture
   (d) a virus

Name : _________

Max. Marks : 40

Number of Questions : 40

Time : 2 Hours

There is no negative marking in the test.

1. This device takes video or still photographs by recording images on an electronic image sensor.

(a)   (b)

(c)   (d)

2. Identify the following :
   – It is a set commands, instructions, rules and syntax.
   – It is used to create a software program.
   (a) Integrated chip
   (b) Software package
   (c) Operating system
   (d) Programming language

3. Which of the following is an online storage service?

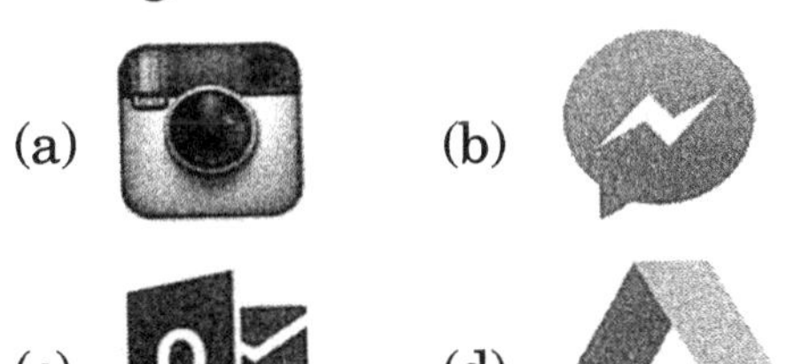

(a)   (b)

(c)   (d)

4. What is the role of an actuator in a hard – disk drive?
   (a) It moves the read – write arm.
   (b) It magnetize the platter
   (c) It rotates the platter at high speed.
   (d) It controls the flow of data to and from the platter.

5. Identify the following :
   – It is larger than microcomputer.
   – CDC – 160A and Micro VAX 3100 are its examples.
   (a) Supercomputer
   (b) Minicomputer
   (c) Mobile PC
   (d) None of these

6. Which of the following statements hold (s) true about Apple Lisa Computer?
   Statement 1 : It was a personal computer with a GUI.
   Statement 2 : It featured drop-down menu and icons.
   (a) Only statement 1
   (b) Only statement 2
   (c) Both statement 1 and statement 2
   (d) Neither statement 1 nor statement 2

7. Which of the following PowerPoint Options allows you to end the slide show with a black slide in MS Powerpoint 2010?
   (a) Language
   (b) General
   (c) Advanced
   (d) Proofing

8. This is a centralized place to view all maintenance and system messages. It is displayed by a flag like icon on the taskbar. It is called the __________.
   (a) action center
   (b) media center
   (c) user account center
   (d) update center

9. Macros can be assigned to __________.
   (a) Command buttons
   (b) Keyboard shortcuts
   (c) Ribbon tabs
   (d) Both (a) and (b)

10. Mail Merge feature of MS – Word does not allow you to ________.
    (a) Select recipients from your phone book
    (b) Specific how to handle errors when completing the mail merge
    (c) Replace the merge fields with actual data from recipient list
    (d) Send mail – merged documents via (e–mail).

11. Which of the following statements is INCORRECT about Themes?
    (a) You can change the colors of the current theme.
    (b) You can change the fonts of the current theme.
    (c) You cannot change the effect of the current theme.
    (d) You can choose the background style for the current theme.

12. To automatically place your school logo at the same position on every slide that uses Title Slide layout, you should use the __________.
    (a) Handout Master
    (b) Notes Master
    (c) Slide Master
    (d) All of these

13. Match the following.

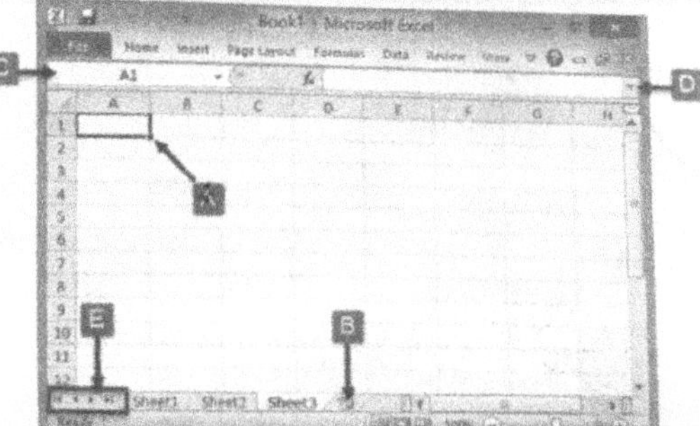

Column – I	Column – II
(A) B	(i) Sheet tab scroll buttons
(B) C	(ii) Name box
(C) D	(iii) Insert Worksheet
(D) E	(iv) Expand Formula Bar

(a) (A) – (ii), (B) – (iii), (C) – (iv), (D) – (i)
(b) (A) – (iii), (B) – (ii), (C) – (iv), (D) – (i)
(c) (A) – (iv), (B) – (i), (C) – (ii), (D) – (iii)
(d) (A) – (iii), (B) – (iv), (C) – (i), (D) – (ii)

14. While entering data in a worksheet, Sita pressed

 +  in a cell, what value will be printed in that cell?

(a) Current Time

(b) Square root of current value in cell

(c) Current Date

(d) Sqaure of current value in cell

15. Select the CORRECT match

(a) PSET (12, 4), 2 – Display a pixel at coordinates (12, 4) in dark green colour

(b) Line (5, 10) – (100, 50), 15 – B – Make a box with white outlined border

(c) Circle (20, 25), 5 Display a red circle with diameter 5

(d) Color 14, 15 – Set the foreground color to yello and background color to purple

16. What will be the value of the variable 'a' after executing the statement, a = abs (–6)?

(a) –6   (b) 0

(c) 6   (d) 1

17. Identify the following:

– It is a software program.

– It records a user's personal information.

– It send the recorded information to third parties without the user's knowledge.

(a) Spyware   (b) Keyloggers

(c) Archiver   (d) None of these

18. Match the following :

(A) Ping Pong   (i) A trojan horse which deletes system files, remains in folders and creates many empty folders

(B) Acid rain   (ii) A boot sector virus

(C) Blaster   (iii) A computer worm that upon execution display two messages, one of which was for Bill Gates.

(a) (A) – (i), (B) – (ii), (C) – (iii)

(b) (A) – (ii), (B) – (i), (C) – (iii)

(c) (A) – (iii), (B) – (i), (C) – (ii)

(d) (A) – (iii), (B) – (ii), (C) – (i)

19. What is meant by e- sensing?

(a) Mechanism/technology that mimics human senses using pattern recognition or sensors.

(b) A device based on human machine interface machanism that works only when the authorised user places its palm on it.

(c) A measurement used to give rating to biometric devices.

(d) Both (a) and (b)

20. Now a days smartphones comes with a feature called geo-tagging. for what purpose it is used?

(a) To insert geographical information into a photo, associating it with the location it was taken at.

(b) To add a keyword into a photo so that whenever you search for the photo you can look up for it by using the keyword.

(c) To add a 3D perspective to a photo, so that as soon as you tap on the photo it starts playing a video

(d) To add color filters to all those photos that were taken at a paticular location.

21. Which printer cannot print more than one character at a time ?
(a) Dot-matrix   (b) Daisy-wheel
(c) Laser   (d) Both (a) and (b)

22. From which language the word "Computer" is derived?
(a) Spanish   (b) English
(c) Latin   (d) Greek

23. Cache and main memory will lose their contents when the power is off. They are __________.
(a) dynamic   (b) static
(c) volatile   (d) non-volatile

24. Data on a floppy disk is recorded in rings called __________.
(a) sectors   (b) ringers
(c) rounders   (d) tracks

25. To be able to "boot", the computer must have a(n)
(a) compiler
(b) loader
(c) operating system
(d) assembler

26. What is a backup?
(a) Restoring the information backup
(b) An exact copy of a system's information
(c) The ability to get a system up and running in the event of a system crash or failure
(d) All of these

27. Which of the following is the first graphical web browser?
(a) MSN   (b) Mozilla
(c) Chrome   (d) Mosaic

28. Which of the following is used for closing a tab on a browser?
(a) Ctrl + Y   (b) Ctrl + A
(c) Ctrl + W   (d) Ctrl + T

29. Which of the following is the first step in sizing a window ?
(a) Point to the title bar
(b) Pull down the View menu to display the toolbar
(c) Point to any corner or border
(d) Pull down the View menu and change to large icons

30. To see the document before the printout is taken, use
(a) insert table
(b) paste
(c) format painter
(d) print preview

31. MBP is a short form for a famous high end notebook from Apple. It is called __________.
(a) Mac Book Programmable
(b) Macintosh Book Pro
(c) Mac-Book Pro
(d) Mountain Book Pro

32. The .... are circular disks having magnetic surface and are also portable and inexpensive.
(a) floppy disks
(b) tape drives
(c) USB drives
(d) all of these

33. Which of the following is/are Windows 7 versions in which you can join an Active Directory domain?

(i)   Windows Professional Edition
(ii) Windows Home Edition
(iii) Windows Enterprise Edition
(iv) Windows Ultimate Edition
(a) Only (i) and (iii)
(b) Only (iv)
(c) Only (i), (iii) and (iv)
(d) All of these

34. What is the function of 'Wrap Text' icon in MS Excel?
   (a) It is used to rotate text to a diagonal angle
   (b) It is used to make all content visible within a cell by displaying it on multiple lines
   (c) It is used to join selected cells into one larger cell
   (d) It is used to highlight interesting cells

35. A computer virus ....
   (a) is a type of malicious software program ("malware") that, when executed, replicates itself by modifying other computer programs and inserting its own code.
   (b) is a green layer which appears on hard drive when it comes in contact of moisture.
   (c) is a type of software program that stop fan spinning of your computer.
   (d) none of these.

36. Stoned is a.........
   (a) worm virus
   (b) boot sector virus
   (c) trojan virus
   (d) bomb virus

37. A browser is an interactive program that permits a user to view web pages on the computer. The browser performs which of the following services?

(a) Receiving new page
(b) Requesting new page from the server
(c) Connecting to the source computer whose address is specified
(d) All of these

38. In MS-Word, which shortcut key is used to increase the font size of text?
   (a) Ctrl + Shift + >
   (b) Ctrl + F
   (c) Ctrl + Alt + F
   (d) Ctrl + Shift + X

39. Match the following virus types given in Column-I with their corresponding examples given in Column-II.

Column-I		Column-II
(A) Macro Virus	(i)	Lamer Exterminator
(B) Boot Sector Virus	(ii)	Melissa
(C) Polymorphic Virus	(iii)	Natas

   (a) A-(ii), B-(i), C-(iii)
   (b) A-(i), B-(ii), C-(iii)
   (c) A-(iii), B-(i), C-(ii)
   (d) A-(iii), B-(ii), C-(i)

40. What is the full form of virus?
   (a) Various idea and resources under seize
   (b) Vital information resources under seize
   (c) Various information resources under seize
   (d) Vital information and resources under supply

Name : __________

Number of Questions : 40

There is no negative marking in the test.

Max. Marks : 40

Time : 2 Hours

1. Select the INCORRECT match.
   (a) World's fastest supercomputer – Sunway TaihuLight
   (b) Example of Hard disk – Floppy disk
   (c) Notebook – Mac Book
   (d) Search engine – Lycos

2. Which of the following statements hold (s) true about machine language?
   Statement 1 : It comprises of only zeros and ones.
   Statement 2 : It is directly understood by a computer.
   (a) Only statement 1
   (b) Only statement 2
   (c) Both statement 1 and statement 2
   (d) Neither statement 1 nor statement 2

3. Identify the following :
   – it is used as main memory in personal computers.
   – Inside its chip, each memory holds one bit of information
   – It is made up of two parts, a transistor and a capacitor.
   (a) Dynamic RAM
   (b) Static RAM
   (c) Video RAM
   (d) Audio RAM

4. You are not able to work with images on your computer. You are also not able to run serval programs easily on your computer. Your computer keeps giving messages like "insufficient memory for this operation".
   Upgrading which of the following components may solve the above problem?
   (a) RAM
   (b) Processor
   (c) CD drive
   (d) Sound card

5. Which of the following statements hold (s) true about first generation of computers?
   Statement 1: They required magnetic drums for memory.
   Statement 2 : The inner working of these computers was quite unsophisticated.
   (a) Only statement 1
   (b) Only statement 2
   (c) Both statement 1 and statement 2
   (d) Neither statement 1 nor statement 2

6. A marvel of technology, the __________ are compounds that perform complex scientific calculations speedily.
   (a) Servers
   (b) Supercomputers
   (c) Laptops
   (d) PDA

7. Which of these is not an MS Excel 2010 valid function?
   (a) COUNTIF
   (b) SUMIF
   (c) COUNTA
   (d) COUNTUP

8. Which of the following statements is true when multiple user accounts have been created on a computer?
   (a) Each user can customize certain account setting
   (b) Each user has administrative rights and an administrator password
   (c) Each account is time limited
   (d) None of these

9. Identify the following :
   – They are used to identify positions in a document
   – These positions can be the beginning of a chapter or a table.
   – They can be used to jump to specific points in a document.
   (a) Bookmarks
   (b) Hyphenation
   (c) Watermarks
   (d) Save points

10. Which of the following options allow you to see what part of your letter will be replaced by information from the recipient list in a mail merged document?
    (a) Rules
    (b) Match Fields
    (c) Find Recipients
    (d) Highlight Merge Fields

11.  is used to __________.
    (a) change the shape of the current drawing
    (b) convert the current drawing into a free-form shape
    (c) insert an embedded object
    (d) add an action to the selected object to specify what should happen when you click on it or hover over it with your mouse

12. Which of the following options will allow you to create a link to the last slide in a presentation?

    (i) 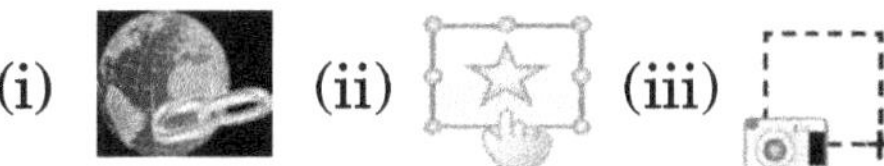 (ii) (iii)

    (a) Only (i)
    (b) Both (i) and (ii)
    (c) Both (i) and (iii)
    (d) Both (ii) and (iii)

13. Match the different Merge options given in Column - I with their corresponding names given in Column – II.

Column – I   **Column – II**

(A) 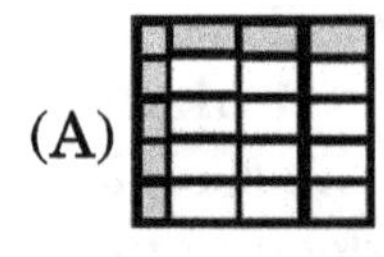   (i) Merge & Centre

(B) 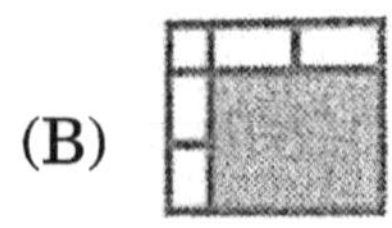   (ii) Unmerge Cells

(C) 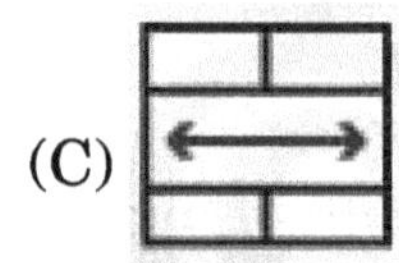   (iii) Merge Cells

(D) 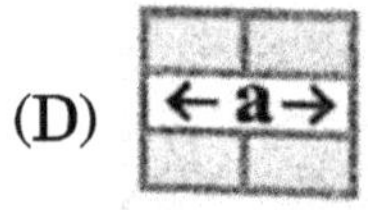   (iv) Merge Across

(a) (A) – (i), (B) – (ii), (C) – (iii), (D) – (iv)
(b) (A) – (ii), (B) – (iii), (C) – (iv), (D) – (i)
(c) (A) – (iv), (B) – (i), (C) – (ii), (D) – (iii)
(d) (A) – (iii), (B) – (iv), (C) – (i), (D) – (ii)

14. Raman has entered the value 1 into cell A1 and 3 into cell A2. Now, he selected both the cells and dragged down the fill handle. What would be the result of this action?
(a) It will create a linear series of even numbers
(b) It will create a number series of odd numbers.
(c) It will copy the values of selected cells into next cells
(d) It is not possible to drag the fill handle downward.

15. Which of the following commands is used to display the graphics on the screen?
(a) CANVAS
(b) RESOLUTION
(c) LOCATE
(d) SCREEN

16. Match the QBASIC variable names given in Column – I with variable types given in Column – II

Column – I   **Column – II**
(A) vara %   (i) String type
(B) varb &   (ii) Integer type
(C) varc#   (iii) Long type
(D) vard$ (iv) Double type

(a) (A) – (i), (B) – (iii), (C) – (iv), (D) – (ii)
(b) (A) – (i), (B) – (ii), (C) – (iv), (D) – (iii)
(c) (A) – (iii), (B) – (ii), (C) – (iv), (D) – (i)
(d) (A) – (ii), (B) – (iii), (C) – (iv), (D) – (i)

17. Identify the following
   – It is one of the services offered by the internet.
   – A search query submitted by user is passed to multiple search engines and then their response is merged into a result list
(a) Negative search
(b) Root search
(c) Metasearch
(d) Megasearch

18. To prevent virus from infecting your computer, you should __________.

(a) equip your PC with a licensed antivirus program
(b) scan flash drives and optical discs before copying data from them
(c) not install pirated software from unknown sources on your computer
(d) all of these

19. Which of the following is a smart TV platform developed by Google?
(a) Google TV+
(b) Android TV
(c) Android L
(d) Smart Andriod

20. Favicon stands for favorite icon that represents a tiny version of a company or web site's logo. Which of the following is a current favicon used for Google?

(a)   (b)
(c)   (d)

21. Which among the following is an important circuitry in a computer system that directs the operation of the processor?
(a) Memory
(b) Address Bus
(c) Accumulator
(d) Control Unit

22. The term __________ refers to data storage systems that make it possible for a computer or electronic device to store and retrieve data.
(a) retrieval technology
(b) input technology
(c) output technology
(d) storage technology

23. What disk is used to cold-boot a PC?
(a) Setup disk
(b) System disk
(c) Diagnostic disk
(d) Program disk

24. A character of information is represented by a(n) __________.
(a) byte   (b) bit
(c) field   (d) attribute

25. Android is a(n) ______
(a) operating system
(b) application
(c) interface
(d) software

26. E-commerce allows companies to __________.
(a) issue important business reports
(b) conduct business over the Internet
(c) support decision making processes
(d) keep track of paper-based transactions

27. Why should you delete unknown e-mail attachments?
(a) It can make you land in jail.
(b) The person could track you down and hurt you.
(c) It is a bad manners.
(d) It might contain a virus that could hurt your computer.

28. Which of the following terms is not related to Internet?
(a) Link
(b) Function key
(c) Browser
(d) Search engine

29. Which among the following key can be used as a shortcut to rename a folder in Microsoft Windows 8 and higher versions?
(a) F2   (b) F4
(c) F6   (d) F9

30. To save a document for the first time, __________ option is used.
(a) Save as   (b) Save
(c) Save on   (d) Copy

31. Match the following output devices given in Column-I with their descriptions given in Column-II.

Column-I

A. Speech

B. Voice Reproduction

C. Voice Response

Column-II

(i) It produces system audio output by selecting an audio output from a set of prerecorded audio response.

(ii) It enables a system computer to talk to a user.

(iii) It converts text synthesizer information into spoken sentences.

(a) A-(iii), B-(i), C-(ii)
(b) A-(i), B-(ii), C-(iii)
(c) A-(iii), B-(ii), C-(i)
(d) A-(i), B-(iii), C-(ii)

32. Which of the following protocol is used for wireless data and voice communication?
(a) TCP
(b) CDMA
(c) IEEE
(d) None of these.

33. SIMM stands for ....
(a) Syntex Internet multipulexing module
(b) Single In-line memory module
(c) Single internatonal multiplexer module
(d) Single instruction multiplier method

34. Modern hard disks come in capacities measured in ....
(a) megabytes
(b) gigabytes
(c) terabytes
(d) both (b) and (c)

35. Choose the correct option for the given sentences.
(i) It is generally the first slide of the presentation.
(ii) It is used to introduce a topic and set the tone for the presentation.
(a) Table slide
(b) Title slide
(c) Graph slide
(d) Bullet slide

36. ___________is a program that may interrupt the normal operation of a computer.
(a) Virus   (b) Routine
(c) Destroyer   (d) Disable

37. Which technology is used in compact disc?
(a) Laser   (b) Electrical
(c) Mechanical   (d) None of these

38. Which one of the following devices contains BIOS (Basic input output system)?
(a) ROM   (b) RAM
(c) CPU   (d) Motherboard

39. The total number of dots present on a monitor is called ___________
(a) SVGA   (b) EGA
(c) Pixels   (d) Resolution

40. The storage devices are of two types: primary and secondary. Which of the following are secondary storage devices?
(a) RAM
(b) Hard disk
(c) Floppy disc
(d) Both (b) and (c)

HINTS AND EXPLANATIONS

ENGLISH

| MOCK TEST 1 |

ANSWER KEY

1	(b)	11	(d)	21	(a)	31	(b)	41	(a)
2	(b)	12	(c)	22	(a)	32	(b)	42	(c)
3	(a)	13	(a)	23	(a)	33	(c)	43	(b)
4	(d)	14	(b)	24	(a)	34	(c)	44	(c)
5	(c)	15	(d)	25	(b)	35	(a)	45	(b)
6	(b)	16	(a)	26	(b)	36	(c)		
7	(a)	17	(d)	27	(a)	37	(c)		
8	(a)	18	(a)	28	(c)	38	(c)		
9	(b)	19	(a)	29	(b)	39	(b)		
10	(a)	20	(a)	30	(a)	40	(c)		

1. **(b)** I wish it would rain! It's too hot.

2. **(b)** The principal spoke **se**parately to each student.

3. **(a)** He was so fast asleep that it was tough to wake him up.

4. **(d)** We regret that we cannot comply with your request.

5. **(c)** She is an M.A. in Geography.

6. **(b)** This is the tallest building in the world.

7. **(a)** The thief broke down when the police started interrogating him.

8. **(a)** My dog barks whenever he hears any noise at the door.

9. **(b)** Joey wanted so many gifts on Christmas.

10. **(a)** The , no article

11. **(d)** I have to reach airport by 9:00, otherwise I will miss my flight.

12. **(c)** You must not be so rude! Why don't you say thanks and please once in a while.

13. **(a)** I met him during my holiday with my family.

14. **(b)** I will wear this suit for today's meeting.

15. **(d)** This is not my book; I just borrowed it.

16. **(a)** This is not my house; it is their house. I have just come here to stay for some time

17. **(d)** I read this book every day before I go to sleep.

18. **(a)** He introduced himself as the manager of the company

19. (a) One should accept life's misfortunes as well as its joys. One should take the bitter with the sweet.

20. (a) My friends told me I would not like the movie, on the contrary, I enjoyed it.

21. (a) You can lead the way.

22. (a) Do not open this letter; it is a private letter.

23. (a) The Harappan script cannot be deciphered. So we cannot tell much about it.

24. (a) He was offered a chauffeur-driven car by his company.

25. (b) with

26. (b) in

27. (a) to

28. (c) would

29. (b) last

30. (a) many

31. (b) This itinerary shows that the payment was made in American Dollar.

32. (b) The traveller is travelling from San Francisco to China on 26th of July in the morning.

33. (c) If someone wants to change his booking request, he will have to visit the site of the airlines.

34. (c) A government issued photo-id.

35. (a) Economy is the opposite of lavish.

36. (c) Initially I found the city very crowded, but now I guess I am used to it.

37. (c) Mr. Harrison started his new job yesterday. Now would work for six days a week.

38. (c) When I lived near that park, I used to play everyday.

39. (b) Where were you? Why were you so late to open the door? I did not hear the doorbell.

40. (c) Peter: Hurray! We won the football match.
Harry: Congratulations!
Peter: Thanks, It's all because of our team's hard work.

41. (a) Tom:Hello, can I speak to George?
Siya: Yes, please hold on for a minute.

42. (c) Roger: Can you please be quiet? I am studying.
James: Sure, sorry for disturbing you.

43. (b) Ginni: why are so late? What took you so long?
Ryan: We halted to buy some fruits.

44. (c) Shyam: Sir, I think that is a better idea.
Sir: Okay, let's consider that one too!

45. (b) Yatin: I am happy to win the first prize.
Gautam: You ought to be happy.

MOCK TEST 2

ANSWER KEY

1	(b)	11	(a)	21	(a)	31	(a)	41	(a)
2	(b)	12	(d)	22	(d)	32	(b)	42	(a)
3	(a)	13	(b)	23	(c)	33	(b)	43	(b)
4	(b)	14	(d)	24	(a)	34	(a)	44	(c)
5	(b)	15	(a)	25	(d)	35	(d)	45	(b)
6	(a)	16	(b)	26	(c)	36	(a)		
7	(a)	17	(a)	27	(b)	37	(c)		
8	(a)	18	(a)	28	(a)	38	(b)		
9	(b)	19	(b)	29	(a)	39	(a)		
10	(a)	20	(b)	30	(b)	40	(b)		

1. **(b)** Horses are often fed on chaff.
2. **(b)** The X-ray showed a fracture of the knee.
3. **(a)** Kial might venture into education. This is a possibility.
4. **(b)** The government has to work hard to provide internet in every home. It might succeed in doing it soon.
5. **(b)** They should have come out of their house, once they felt the earthquake.
6. **(a)** They might shift into their new flat.
7. **(a)** India must pay attention to its infrastructure, if it wants to compete with the developed countries.
8. **(a)** India features prominently on every list of polluted countries.
9. **(b)** Non-violence and non-alignment were cornerstone of India's foreign policy.
10. **(a)** After the recent developments, India has become a force to reckon with.
11. **(a)** A person who measures angles is called surveyor.
12. **(d)** A test to discover something new is experiment.
13. **(b)** 'Pig in a poke' means a deal made with proper research.
14. **(d)** The muscle in his right arm is quite painful.
15. **(a)** Our teacher taught us about gravity.
16. **(b)** Minors are not allowed to vote.
17. **(a)** He has all the luxuries of life.
18. **(a)** India has lost the match against China.
19. **(b)** The concert ended on a high note.
20. **(b)** There are thousands of mice destroying the grain.

21.(a) The thief was arrested by the police.

22.(d) The audience clapped loudly when she finished her song.

23.(c) To treat something as unimportant.

24.(a) You can't walk away when I am talking to you.

25.(d) Northern Railways apologised for the delay caused.

26.(c) Jeremy has been taking many lectures lately, so he does not get free time.

27.(b) Why did you take so much time to reach home. You should not have been so late.

28.(a) What a lame excuse! I expected you to have completed your work.

29.(a) Take up only the amount of work that you can complete. Do not bite off more than you can chew.

30.(b) It may be easy to achieve freedom, however, it is tough to maintain it.

31.(a) Subramanium Chandrashekhar belonged to India.

32.(b) If the mass of the star is less than the Chandrashekhar limit, it will become a white dwarf.

33.(b) Precision means accuracy.

34.(a) The value of Chandrashekhar limit is 1.39 M.

35.(d) It becomes a supernova.

36.(a) Airhostess: Please show me your boarding pass. This way please. Here it is.

37.(c) Sunny: Are they coming?
David: They will reach within half an hour.

38.(b) Robin: What is the time?
Frazer: It's quarter past eight.

39.(a) Ram: Who all are left in the contest?
Shyam: He is the only one left in the contest.

40.(b) I am having food

41.(a) Paul: Did you listen to the Prime Minister's speech?
Smith: Yes, I listened to the whole speech.
Paul: Did you listen to what he spoke about debt relief in developing countries.

42.(a) Mother: It is not good to be violent; you must try to resolve through talks.

43.(b) Saira: I am having a terrible stomach ache.
Ruhi: You must see a doctor immediately.

44.(c) Manager: How's the response to the event?
Employee: It's going good.
Manager: Great! I expected it to be a hit.

45.(b) Johnson: I have made a big cake because I am expecting friends.
Smith: (b) Great! Can I also join?.
Johnson: Sure, even you can join in.

MOCK TEST 3

ANSWER KEY

1	(b)	11	(a)	21	(a)	31	(b)	41	(a)
2	(a)	12	(b)	22	(b)	32	(b)	42	(d)
3	(a)	13	(b)	23	(b)	33	(a)	43	(b)
4	(a)	14	(b)	24	(b)	34	(a)	44	(b)
5	(b)	15	(a)	25	(a)	35	(d)	45	(a)
6	(a)	16	(a)	26	(c)	36	(b)	46	(b)
7	(a)	17	(b)	27	(b)	37	(b)	47	(a)
8	(c)	18	(c)	28	(b)	38	(b)	48	(b)
9	(d)	19	(a)	29	(b)	39	(b)	49	(d)
10	(b)	20	(c)	30	(b)	40	(a)	50	(a)

1. (b) The man and his wife were touring on the coast.

2. (a) Sam is sweeping all the fallen leaves in the garden.

3. (a) He has stacked the books on the two top shelves.

4. (a) He mopped up the dirty water on the floor.

5. (b) It was useless to keep waiting for a delayed train.

6. (a) The officer was annoyed to see corruption in his office.

7. (a) I have known him for a long time .

8. (c) Water in my house is drinkable you can have it directly from the tap.

9. (d) Sam's handwriting is illegible; he himself can't read it.

10. (b) Bob was trying to climb a mountain. But he couldn't.

11. (a) James and I are making pasta for dinner.

12. (b) Animals should not be bathed in rivers or canals. It contaminates water.

13. (b) What route did you take to my house ?

14. (b) Blood is returned to the heart in this vein.

15. (a) The mayor declared a holiday on Monday.

16. (a) Where is he going? He will get late.

17. (b) I cannot tolerate unnecessary waste of time.

18. (c) With only three days left of the session, the government has to pass the law.

19. (a) Do you have any money left to buy sweets?

20. (c) Meg fell from the horse yesterday, so she went to the hospital.

21.(a) Mary told him what had happened to his dog, so he ran home to see how it was.

22.(b) I would like to have some further information.

23.(b) for

24.(b) when

25.(a) in

26.(c) was

27.(b) This

28.(b) an

29.(b) were

30.(b) while

31.(b) Ecologically Sensitive Area

32.(b) Excessive mining, big construction

33.(a) Western Ghats are spread over 6 states namely Gujarat, Maharashtra, Goa, Tamil Nadu, Karnataka, Kerala.

34.(a) Horizontal means parallel to the ground

35.(d) Sustainable development means a development that does not exhaust earth's natural resources and can be sustained. A development that keeps the environment into consideration and wants to preserve the future too .

36.(b) The plan shows value in terms of crores.

37.(b) Flood management comes within the management of states. Centre only provides technical advice and financial assistance.

38.(b) Kerala does not have the largest percentage of works that have been approved. It is Assam.

39.(b) 517 flood control works have been approved.

40.(a) Deadly means lethal.

41.(a) Ram: Yes, it had been raining all night.

42.(d) Rekha: The Sun is appearing on the horizon.

43.(b) Customer:I want to buy cups.

44.(b) Excuse me, would you tell me the way to the bus stop?

45.(a) Which university will you join after passing school?

46.(b) Zoya: Much better, Abid. Thanks for coming to see me.

47.(a) Bank employee: Good Morning, Madam. What can I do for you?

Client: I want to open a Savings account.

48.(b) Bank Employee: Yes, madam! May I have your surname first?

Client: My surname is Handa.

49.(d) Soham: Sorry, you can't go now.

50.(a) Fauzia: I'd love to.

MOCK TEST 4

ANSWER KEY

1	(a)	11	(d)	21	(b)	31	(d)	41	(b)
2	(a)	12	(d)	22	(b)	32	(a)	42	(a)
3	(a)	13	(b)	23	(a)	33	(a)	43	(a)
4	(a)	14	(b)	24	(b)	34	(b)	44	(b)
5	(a)	15	(b)	25	(c)	35	(d)	45	(b)
6	(d)	16	(a)	26	(b)	36	(d)	46	(b)
7	(a)	17	(c)	27	(b)	37	(b)	47	(a)
8	(c)	18	(a)	28	(a)	38	(d)	48	(c)
9	(b)	19	(a)	29	(b)	39	(c)	49	(b)
10	(c)	20	(b)	30	(c)	40	(b)	50	(b)

1. **(a)** Illegal imitation means forgery.

2. **(a)** I would have bought it if it were less expensive.

3. **(a)** My office hours are very inflexible, I have to arrive exactly on time.

4. **(a)** Try to quit somoking, you will feel better.

5. **(a)** Parents must keep an eye on their children, otherwise they tend to lose track.

6. **(d)** The various schemes are formulated to empower women.

7. **(a)** You must go to bed now. This is an order.

8. **(c)** Before we assert our rights, we must fulfil our duties.

9. **(b)** We must wear seat belts while driving.

10. **(c)** We must eat balanced diet to avoid malnutrition.

11. **(d)** The whole nation paid homage to Dr. A.P.J. Abdul Kalam.

12. **(d)** We planted saplings during the tree plantation drive.

13. **(b)** The school conducted an orientation programme for the students of class 7 and 8.

14. **(b)** The rescuers found no sign of the ship which had sunk in the sea.

15. **(b)** It did not take long for the two friends to be back in harmony.

16. **(a)** He gave me a loan of 50,000.

17. **(c)** The chief took a paper and stuck it firmly over the centre of his belt.

18. **(a)** The captain told us to remain calm.

19. **(a)** He goes every day to his office by car.

20. **(b)** He ran very fast to reach the examination centre.

21. **(b)** Nobody has been able to reach the Sun. It is very hot there.

22.(b) They all donated their old books to the orphanage.

23.(a) Rohan and Soham are my brother's two sons. They are my nephews.

24.(b) He broke off negotiations and attacked our country.

25.(c) Now let's close the deal.

26.(b) This is a very different kind of work that you are telling me to do. This is a far cry from whatever I have done up till now.

27.(b) You have to reserve a seat in advance- they get full easily.

28.(a) He can't see anything. He is blind.

29.(b) Expectations that the markets will remain depressed have prompted major producers to drop their projects.

30.(c) Lambert Glacier in East Antarctica holds the world record for being the World's largest glacier.

31.(d) Fiesta is an event marked by celebration.

32.(a) Poster making

33.(a) The last date for registering for the competition before or by 17th March.

34.(b) The event will be held in Lovely International School.

35.(d) Culture means the thoughts, behaviour, languages and customs that we produce and the methods we used to produce them.

36.(d) They deflect sunlight, a single tree provides cooling equal to 10 air conditioners, they also help in reducing pollution.

37.(b) The purpose of this advertisement is to promote tree plantation.

38.(d) Heat island means urban area having higher average temperature; The reasons for it are absorption and retention of heat, Industries and factories polluting air, Various types of fuels that add to the heat.

39.(c) Anytime between 7AM to 4PM on 30th August.

40.(b) This drive will help in planting more trees.

41.(b) Julie: Mr.Shyam, is it your first trip to Tokyo?
Shyam: Yes, everything is new to me.

42.(a) Patient: I feel dizzy and there is a throbbing pain in my head.
Doctor: Have you had this before?

43.(a) Hello, I could hardly recognise you.

44.(b) I had been working in an MNC. What about you?

45.(b) In which class do your children study?.

46.(b) Dennis: I want to buy fruits.

47.(a) Mrs. Vinita: Fill the tank up.

48.(c) Anita: Of course, what's up?
Smita: I am holding a party next weekend. Please come.

49.(b) Siya: I am Siya. May I speak to Sam?

50.(b) Smith: I go out with my friends.

MOCK TEST 5

ANSWER KEY

1	(b)	**11**	(a)	**21**	(b)	**31**	(b)	**41**	(c)
2	(c)	**12**	(a)	**22**	(a)	**32**	(d)	**42**	(c)
3	(c)	**13**	(b)	**23**	(a)	**33**	(d)	**43**	(b)
4	(a)	**14**	(a)	**24**	(a)	**34**	(a)	**44**	(b)
5	(a)	**15**	(c)	**25**	(a)	**35**	(d)	**45**	(a)
6	(a)	**16**	(d)	**26**	(a)	**36**	(b)	**46**	(c)
7	(a)	**17**	(c)	**27**	(b)	**37**	(c)	**47**	(b)
8	(b)	**18**	(a)	**28**	(b)	**38**	(c)	**48**	(b)
9	(a)	**19**	(c)	**29**	(a)	**39**	(a)	**49**	(a)
10	(b)	**20**	(b)	**30**	(b)	**40**	(b)	**50**	(b)

1. (b) We will not oppose you, if you say so.

2. (c) He spent economically.

3. (c) His performance in the competition was better than mine.

4. (a) Shall we reserve tables at Raffles then? This is a suggestion

5. (a) You should enrol into yoga classes. They will definitely help you.

6. (a) You have to start early; you might get stuck in a jam.

7. (a) I have travelled almost the whole of India, now I am in Gangtok.

8. (b) How many chairs do we need for the meeting?

9. (a) We could arrange only a few sponsors for tomorrow's show.

10. (b) Glaciers all over the world are melting at an alarming rate.

11. (a) You seem to be a miser who loves to hoard money.

12. (a) Air is composed of only a small percentage of oxygen.

13. (b) Her coaching was based on instinctive thinking.

14. (a) You'd better take a taxi otherwise you'll be late.

15. (c) She knows some new medicine to cure cancer.

16. (d) No error

17. (c) He fell off the ladder while trying to reach the terrace.

18. (a) Upgrade to the next level of technology.

19. (c) Her salary was not enough to help her repay her loans.

20. (b) This liquid kills germs it is anti-septic.

21. (b) The whole drama came to an end.

22. (a) You must go out of business.

23. (a) It's too late, you don't have a choice now. Don't you know that beggars can't be choosers.

24. (a) I will start up a new enterprise that will help me to complete my other project, too. This way I will, kill two birds with one stone.

25. (a) It takes two to tango.

26. (a) He was trying to find out the details of his case which backfired; and curiosity killed the cat .

27. (b) These tickets should be with us when we go for the show.

28. (b) This parcel should be delivered by tomorrow afternoon.

29. (a) That painting doesn't seem to be real. It could bean an imitation.

30. (b) I saw her crying. She must be really upset.

31. (b) Dr. Bidhan Chandra Roy's birthday is celebrated as the Doctor's Day.

32. (d) Legendary means well-known.

33. (d) To prevent something from coming near you.

34. (a) Paediatricians are doctors that deal with children.

35. (d) Hygiene is important to prevent development of infections and illnesses, to maintain a good life standard and to prevent body odour.

36. (b) Fax

37. (c)

38. (c) Mixed

39. (a) Voice message, Text message, Instant messanger, Fax

40. (b) Instant

41. (c) Student : Please, can I get 5 more minutes?

42. (c) Sahil: That's not a problem, I can pick them up.

43. (b) Neighbour: Sure, I'd love to.

44. (b) Dennis: It was nothing at all. It was pleasure being with you.

45. (a) Salesman: Yes. We have ethnic wear from all parts of the world.

46. (c) Mr. Georg: Of course. It is my pleasure.

47. (b) Bob: Thanks for inviting me.

48. (b) Brian: Thank you for your praise.

49. (a) It is strange that you charge us before we enter.

50. (b) drinks

MATHEMATICS

MOCK TEST-1

ANSWER KEY

1	(d)	11	(b)	21	(c)	31	(c)	41	(d)
2	(a)	12	(c)	22	(c)	32	(b)	42	(b)
3	(d)	13	(a)	23	(c)	33	(a)	43	(d)
4	(c)	14	(a)	24	(c)	34	(d)	44	(b)
5	(a)	15	(a)	25	(b)	35	(b)	45	(a)
6	(a)	16	(c)	26	(c)	36	(d)	46	(b)
7	(d)	17	(b)	27	(b)	37	(b)	47	(d)
8	(c)	18	(d)	28	(c)	38	(d)	48	(b)
9	(b)	19	(c)	29	(c)	39	(a)	49	(c)
10	(a)	20	(d)	30	(b)	40	(c)	50	(b)

1. **(d)** Sum of sides $= \dfrac{11}{15}$

Now, $? = \dfrac{11}{15} - \dfrac{1}{15} - \dfrac{2}{15}$

$? = \dfrac{8}{15}$

2. **(a)** $(-3, 1)$ and $(-5, 7)$

3. **(d)** $\left(\dfrac{4p}{5} - 3\right)\left(\dfrac{5p}{8} - 6\right)$

$= \dfrac{4p}{5} \times \left(\dfrac{5p}{8} - 6\right) + (-3) \times \left(\dfrac{5p}{8} - 6\right)$

$= \dfrac{p^2}{2} - \dfrac{24p}{5} - \dfrac{15p}{8} + 18$

$= \dfrac{p^2}{2} - \dfrac{267}{40}p + 18$

4. **(c)** Let capacity of tank $= C$ litres

$n + \dfrac{e}{100} \times C = C$

$C\left(1 - \dfrac{e}{100}\right) = n$

$C = \dfrac{n \times 100}{100 - e}$ ..... (i)

Suppose x litres should be poured to fill the tank completely.

We have $\dfrac{x \times 100}{e}$

$=$ Capacity $= C$ ...... (ii)

$\therefore$ from (i) and (ii)

$x = \dfrac{ne}{100 - e}$

5. **(a)** Using the changed symbols, we have :

Given expression

$= \dfrac{(36 - 4) \div 8 - 4}{4 \times 8 - 2 \times 16 + 1} = \dfrac{32 \div 8 - 4}{32 - 32 + 1}$

$= \dfrac{4 - 4}{0 + 1} = 0.$

6. **(a)** P represents $\dfrac{7}{3}$,

Q represents $\dfrac{8}{3}$

R represents $\dfrac{-4}{3}$,

S represents $\dfrac{-5}{3}$

7. (d) $\dfrac{280.5}{25.5} = \dfrac{\left(\dfrac{2805}{10}\right)}{2.55 \times 10}$

$= \dfrac{2805}{2.55} \times \dfrac{1}{100} = \dfrac{1100}{100} = 11$

8. (c) C.P. of watch sold at a gain of 10%

$= \dfrac{425 \times 100}{110} = ₹\ 386.36$

C.P. of watch sold at a loss of 10%

$= 425 \times \dfrac{100}{90} = ₹\ 472.22$

Total C.P. – Total S.P.

$= 858.58 - 850 = ₹\ 8.58$

∴ Total loss

$= \dfrac{8.58}{858.58} \times 100\% = 1\%$

(Approximate)

9. (b) $2\pi r - r = 37$

$r = \dfrac{37}{2\pi - 1} = \dfrac{37}{2 \times \dfrac{22}{7} - 1} = 7\ m$

Circumference $= 2\pi r$

$= 2 \times \dfrac{22}{7} \times 7 = 44\ m.$

10. (a) Mean

$= \dfrac{\begin{array}{c}14 \times 5 + 15 \times 8 + 16 \times 15 \\ + 17 \times 10 + 18 \times 2\end{array}}{5 + 8 + 15 + 10 + 2}$

$= \dfrac{70 + 120 + 240 + 170 + 36}{40}$

$= \dfrac{636}{40} = 15.9\ yrs.$

11. (b) Since CD || AB

In △ABC

∴　∠ABE = ∠DCE

(Corresponding angles)

△ABC

Given : ∠B = 3x

$2x + 3x + 4x = 180$

$\Rightarrow 9x = 180 \Rightarrow x = \dfrac{180}{9} = 20$

(By using sum of angles of △ = 180°)

∴ ∠B = 60°

$\Rightarrow$ ∠ABE = ∠DCE = 60° = y.

12. (c) $7(x - 1) = 5(x + 1)$

$7x - 7 = 5x + 5$

$x = 6$

13. (a) Let the transversal t cut the line l at O and the line m at P.

Now, ∠POC = 180°

∴ ∠POA = ∠POC − ∠AOC = 130°

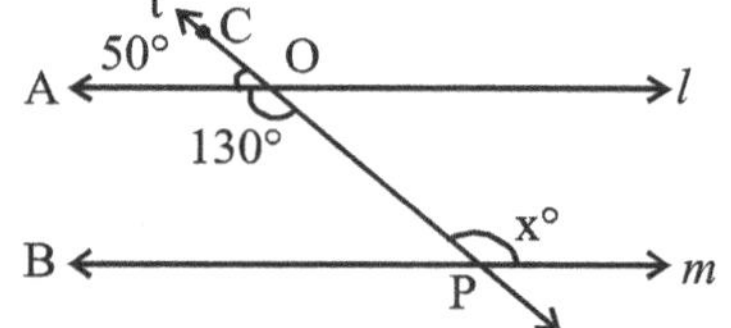

∵ Alternate interior angles are equal.

$\Rightarrow x° = 130°$

14. (a) R = 15 cm, r = 13 cm.

Area of the circulating ring

$= \pi R^2 - \pi r^2$

$= \pi (R^2 - r^2)$

$= \pi (R + r)(R - r)$

$= \dfrac{22}{7}(15 + 13) \times (15 - 13)$

$= \dfrac{22}{7} \times 28 \times 2 = 176\ sq.\ cm.$

15. (a) Ram used (3×10) litres oil in 10 days in total oil used in 10 days = 30 litre % of oil

used $= \dfrac{30}{36} \times 100 = 83.33\%$

16. (c) Speed of the man in still water = 8 kmph.
Let the distance = x km
Speed of the river = 2 kmph
Downstream = 8 + 2 = 10 kmph
Upstream = 8 − 2 = 6 kmph

$\dfrac{x}{10} + \dfrac{x}{6} = \dfrac{48}{60}$

8x = 24
x = 3 km

19. (c) Arrange the given data in ascending order.
We have 33, 35, 41, 46, 55, 58, 64, 77, 87, 90 and 92.
The sixth entry is 58.
Median is 58.

20. (d) All the given statements are true.

(i) In $\triangle ABC$,

$\angle A + \angle B + \angle C = 180°$
$60° + 60° + \angle C = 180°$ (two angles are 60° each)

$\angle C = 180° − 120° = 60°$
∴ If in a triangle, two angles are equal to 60°, then it is equilateral.

(ii) In $\triangle ABC$,

$\angle A + \angle B + \angle C = 180°$
$1x + 1x + 2x = 180°$
$4x = 180° = x = 45°$

Thus, the angles of triangle are 45°, 45° and 90°.
∴ If the angles of a triangle are in the ratio 1 : 1 : 2, then it is a right angled isosceles triangle.

(iii) In $\triangle ABC$,

$\angle A + \angle B + \angle C = 180°$
$1x + 2x + 3x = 180°$
$6x = 180° = x = 30°$
Thus, the angles of triangle are 30°, 60° and 90°.
∴ If the angles of a triangle are in the ratio 1 : 2 : 3, then it is a right angled triangle.

21. (c) Let the number to be multiplies is x.

$\dfrac{-15}{56} * x = \dfrac{-5}{7}$

$x = \dfrac{-56}{15} * \dfrac{-5}{7}$

$x = \dfrac{8}{3}$

22. (c) Ram's rank from last
$= 23 − 13 + 1 = 11^{th}$
Shyam's rank from last
$= 23 − 14 + 1 = 10^{th}$

24. (c)

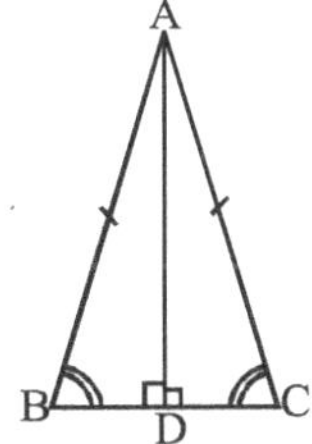

By RHS property
$\triangle ADB \cong \triangle ADC$

25. (b) Mean $= \dfrac{1+2+\ldots\ldots\ldots+10}{10}$

$= \dfrac{55}{10} = \dfrac{11}{2}$

26. (c) Sarita's place from the bottom

$= \left[\begin{array}{cc} \text{Total} & \text{Sarita's place} \\ \text{girls} & \text{from the top} \end{array}\right] + 1$

$= [45 - 11] + 1 = 35^{\text{th}}$

28. (c) Let first prize $= x$

Second prize $= \dfrac{3}{4}\text{x}$

Third prize $= \dfrac{1}{2} \times \dfrac{3\text{x}}{4} = \dfrac{3\text{x}}{8}$

$\text{x} + \dfrac{3\text{x}}{4} + \dfrac{3\text{x}}{8} = 2550$

$\dfrac{17\text{x}}{8} = 2550$

$x = ₹\ 1200$

29. (c) Given T = 8 years
Let A be the Amount
Since the sum doubles itself

$\therefore\ A = 2\,P \Rightarrow \dfrac{A}{P} = 2$

Now $A = P + S.I \Rightarrow A - P = S.I$

$\Rightarrow A - P = \dfrac{P \times R \times T}{100}$

$\Rightarrow \dfrac{A - P}{P} = \dfrac{R \times T}{100} \Rightarrow \dfrac{A}{P} - 1$

$= \dfrac{R \times T}{100} \Rightarrow 2 - 1 = \dfrac{R \times T}{100}$

$\left[\because \dfrac{A}{P} = 2\right]$

$\Rightarrow R \times T = 100$

$\Rightarrow R = \dfrac{100}{T} = \dfrac{100}{8} = 12\dfrac{1}{2}\%$

30. (b) $\left(x^{-1} + y^{-1}\right)^{-1} = \dfrac{1}{(x^{-1} + y^{-1})}$

$\dfrac{1}{(x^{-1} + y^{-1})} = \dfrac{1}{\left(\dfrac{1}{x} + \dfrac{1}{y}\right)}$

$\dfrac{1}{\left(\dfrac{1}{x} + \dfrac{1}{y}\right)} = \dfrac{xy}{x + y}$

31. (c) The perimeter of a triangle is the sum of its side. In an equilateral triangle, all the sides are equal. Hence perimeter is 3 times of side. Let the side of the triangle is s cm.

Perimeter $= \left(x + \dfrac{y}{2} + \dfrac{z}{3}\right)$ cm.

$3s = \left(x + \dfrac{y}{2} + \dfrac{z}{3}\right)$

$s = \left(\dfrac{x}{3} + \dfrac{y}{6} + \dfrac{z}{9}\right)$

32. (b) $\because\ AB = AC$

$\Rightarrow \angle ABC = \angle ACB$

$\angle ACB + \angle ACE = 180°$

$x + x + 40 = 180°$

$2x = 140°$

$x = 70°$

33. (a) As shown in figure, ADE is a triangle.

$\therefore$ By Pythagoras theorem

$\Rightarrow DE^2 = 100 - 64 = 36$

$\Rightarrow DE = \sqrt{36} = 6\,\text{cm}$

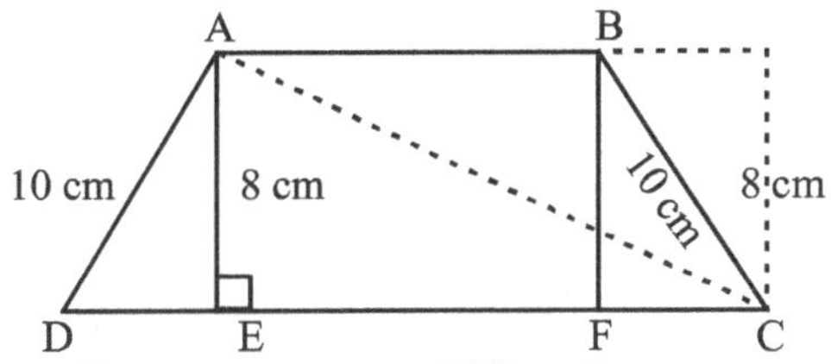

By symmetry, FC = 6 cm.

Let AB = x

Now since perimeter of trapezium = 52

Then,

$(x + 10 + 6 + x + 6 + 10) = 52$

or $2x + 32 = 52$ or $x = 10$ cm.

∴ Area of trapezium

= Area ΔADC + Area ΔABC

$= \left(\dfrac{1}{2} \times 22 \times 8\right) + \left(\dfrac{1}{2} \times 10 \times 8\right)$

$= \dfrac{1}{2}(10 + 22) \times 8 = 128 \text{ cm}^2.$

35. (b) It is clear that all cubes about the edges have either two or three sides painted. Only one central cube in each face as shown in the figure below will have one face painted.

36. (d) Let x be added

$x + (-3p + 7q - 16) = 8$

$x = 8 - (-3p + 7q - 16)$

$= 8 + 3p - 7q + 16$

$= 3p - 7q + 24$

37. (b) Since sum of angles of a quadrilateral $= 360°$

∴ $\angle P + \angle Q + \angle R + \angle S = 360°$

$\Rightarrow 100° + \angle Q + 100° + 75° = 360°$

$\Rightarrow \angle Q = 360° - 275° = 85°.$

38. (d) $6(2a - 1) + 8 = 14$

$12a - 6 + 8 = 14$

$12a = 14 + 6 - 8 = 20 - 8$

$a = \dfrac{12}{12} = 1$

39. (a) $(x - y)(x + y) + (y - z)(y + z) + (z - x)(z + x)$

$= x^2 - y^2 + y^2 - z^2 + z^2 - x^2$

$= 0$

40. (c) Clearly, in the figure there is 1 column containing 3 cubes, 2 columns containing 2 cubes each and 3 columns containing 1 cube each.

Number of cubes in columns of 3 cubes $= 1 \times 3 = 3$;

Number of cubes in columns of 2 cubes $= 2 \times 2 = 4$;

Number of cubes in columns of 1 cube $= 3 \times 1 = 3$;

Therefore, total number of cubes $= 3 + 4 + 3 = 10.$

41. (d) Let the required number be y.

$a : b :: x : y$

$\Rightarrow a \times y = b \times x$

$y = \dfrac{bx}{a}$

42. (b) ∵ $\dfrac{1}{0}$ is not rational, the quotient of two integers is not rational.

43. (d): Divide the equation bc = 99 by ca = 77.

$\dfrac{bc}{ca} = \dfrac{99}{77}$

$$\frac{b}{a} = \frac{9}{7}$$

$$b = \frac{9}{7}a$$

Substitute the obtained value of b in the equation ab = 63.

$$a\left(\frac{9}{7}a\right) = 63$$

$$a \times a = 7 \times 7$$

$$a = 7$$

44. (b) Area of the plot without grass
= area of the rectangle – area of the semi-circle

$$= 60 \times 28 - \frac{1}{2} \times \pi \times \left(\frac{28}{2}\right)^2$$

$$= 60 \times 28 - 11 \times 28$$

$$= 28(60 - 11) = 1372 \text{ m}^2.$$

45. (a) $\because$ PQ = PR

$\Rightarrow \angle Q = \angle R$

Given that $\angle Q = 2\angle P$

We have

$$\angle P + \angle Q + \angle R = 180°$$

$$\frac{\angle Q}{2} + \angle Q + \angle Q = 180°$$

$$\frac{5}{2}\angle Q = 180°$$

$$\angle Q = 72°$$

46. (b) Area of the room = 25 m × 16 m
= 400 m²

Area of the brick = 20 cm × 10 cm

$$= \frac{1}{5}\text{ m} \times \frac{1}{10}\text{ m} = \frac{1}{50}\text{ m}^2$$

$\therefore$ Number of bricks required

$$= \left(400 \div \frac{1}{50}\right) = 20{,}000.$$

47. (d) Area of square ABCD = 16m²
side × side = 16 m²

$\Rightarrow$ side = 4 m.

E₁ F₁ G and H are mid-points

$\therefore$ Area of 4 triangles

$$= 4\left[\frac{1}{2} \times 2 \times 2\right] = 8 \text{ m}^2.$$

Now, area of shaded square = 16 – 8 = 8 m².

48. (b) Mathematics

49. (c) Percentage

$$= \frac{\text{Acquired marks in all subjects}}{\text{Total marks in all subjects}} \times 100$$

$$= \frac{285}{500} \times 100 = 57\%$$

50. (b) Highest marks = 90
Lowest marks = 20
Ratio = 90 : 20 = 9 : 2

MOCK TEST-2

ANSWERS KEY

1	(b)	11	(b)	21	(a)	31	(a)	41	(c)
2	(d)	12	(c)	22	(c)	32	(a)	42	(b)
3	(b)	13	(b)	23	(a)	33	(c)	43	(c)
4	(c)	14	(c)	24	(d)	34	(c)	44	(d)
5	(c)	15	(a)	25	(d)	35	(c)	45	(d)
6	(c)	16	(c)	26	(b)	36	(a)	46	(a)
7	(c)	17	(b)	27	(b)	37	(d)	47	(c)
8	(c)	18	(c)	28	(c)	38	(b)	48	(a)
9	(b)	19	(c)	29	(a)	39	(b)	49	(b)
10	(c)	20	(c)	30	(b)	40	(a)	50	(a)

1. (b) Mean of the data may or may not from the given data.

$$\text{Mean} = \frac{\text{Sum of all observations}}{\text{Number of observations}}.$$

2. (d) Study the following figures:

Let ▯ represent $\frac{1}{4}$m

Then,

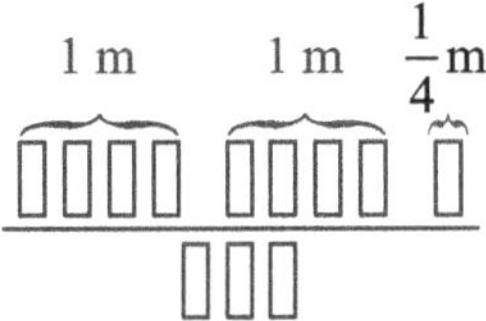

$$= \frac{9 \text{ fourths}}{3 \text{ fourths}} = 3$$

In fact, we calculate that "how many $\frac{3}{4}$ are in $2\frac{1}{4}$?"

And it is calculated as,

$$2\frac{1}{4} \div \frac{3}{4} = \frac{9}{4} \div \frac{3}{4} = \frac{9}{4} \times \frac{4}{3}$$

$$= \frac{9 \times 4}{4 \times 3} = \frac{9}{3} = 3$$

Thus, 3 shirts can be made with $2\frac{1}{4}$m of cloth.

3. (b) Apply the BODMAS rule to simplify the expression.

$$7 - 7 \times 7 + 7 \div 7 = 7 - 7 \times 7 + 1$$

$$7 - 7 \times 7 + 1 = 7 - 49 + 1$$

$$7 - 49 + 1 = -41$$

4. (a) Let the numbers are x, x + 2, x + 4 and x + 6.

$$x + x + 2 + x + 4 + x + 6 = 144$$

$$4x + 12 = 144$$

$$4x = 132$$

$$x = 33$$

The smallest and the largest of the four numbers is 33 and 39 respectively. The product of 33 and 39 is 1287.

5. (c) Through O draw a line EOF parallel to AB and CD.

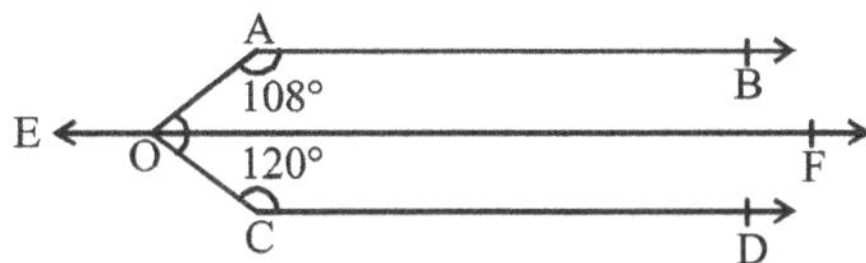

Now, EF || AB and CD || AB.

So, CD || EF

∵ AB || EF and AO is a transversal.

∴ We have ∠AOF + ∠OAB = 180°

∠AOF + 108° = 180°

∠AOF = 72°

∴ EF || CD and OC is a transversal.

So, ∠COF + ∠OCD = 180°

∠COF + 120° = 180°

∠COF = 60°

∴ ∠AOC = ∠AOF + ∠COF

$$= 72° + 60° = 132°$$

6. (c) Let the angles be 3x, 7x, 6x and 4x.

∴ 3x + 7x + 6x + 4x = 360°

or 20x = 360° or x = 18°.

The angles are 54°, 126°, 108°, 72°.

We see that adjacent angles are supplementary but opposite angles are not equal. Clearly, it is a trapezium.

7. (c) Let usual rate be x km/min and distance be y km then time is

18

$\dfrac{y}{x}$ min as per question.

$$\dfrac{y}{x} = \dfrac{\frac{y}{1}}{\frac{7x}{6}} + 4$$

$$\dfrac{y}{x} = \dfrac{6y}{7x} + \dfrac{4}{1}$$

$$\dfrac{y}{x} = \dfrac{6y + 28x}{7x}$$

$$7xy = 6xy + 28x^2$$

$$xy = 28x^2$$

$$\dfrac{y}{x} = 28 \text{ min}$$

8. (c) $\dfrac{2}{x} + 3y = 15$

$$\Rightarrow y = \left(15 - \dfrac{2}{x}\right) \div 3 \qquad .....(i)$$

$$\dfrac{5}{x} - 4y = 3 \qquad ....(ii)$$

Put the value of eqn (i) in eqn (ii)

$$\Rightarrow \dfrac{5}{x} - 4\left(\dfrac{15 - \dfrac{2}{x}}{3}\right) = 3$$

$$\Rightarrow \dfrac{15}{x} - 60 - \dfrac{8}{x} = 9 = \dfrac{15 - 60x - 8}{x} = 9$$

$$\Rightarrow 23 - 60x = 9x \Rightarrow 69x = 23$$

$$\Rightarrow x = \dfrac{23}{69} = \dfrac{1}{3}$$

9. (b)

10. (c) Since no. of girls is twice the no. of boys

$\therefore$ There are 20 boys and 40 girls. Number of students behind Kamal in rank = 60 – 17 = 43

Number of girls ahead of Kamal in rank = 9.

$\therefore$ Number of girls behind Kamal in rank = 40 – 9 = 31.

$\therefore$ Number of boys behind Kamal in rank = 43 – 31 = 12.

11. (b) Sum of the given numbers = –8,

given number is $\dfrac{-17}{9}$

$\therefore$ The other number = (Sum – given number)

$$= -8 - \left(-\dfrac{17}{9}\right)$$

$$= \dfrac{-8}{1} + \dfrac{17}{9} = \dfrac{-8 \times 9 + 17 \times 1}{9}$$

$$= \dfrac{-72 + 17}{9} = \dfrac{-55}{9}.$$

12. (c) Since in vessel I ratio of water and milk is 1 : 2

So, Quantity of water = $\dfrac{1}{3}$ and that of milk = $\dfrac{2}{3}$ Similarly in vessel II, Quantity of water = $\dfrac{2}{7}$ and that of milk = $\dfrac{5}{7}$

From vessel I, $\dfrac{1}{5}$ is taken and from vessel II, $\dfrac{4}{5}$ is taken

Therefore, the ratio of water to milk in the new vessel

$$= \left(\dfrac{1}{3} \times \dfrac{1}{5} + \dfrac{2}{7} \times \dfrac{4}{5}\right) : \left(\dfrac{2}{3} \times \dfrac{1}{5} + \dfrac{5}{7} \times \dfrac{4}{5}\right)$$

$$= \left(\dfrac{1}{15} + \dfrac{8}{35}\right) : \left(\dfrac{2}{15} + \dfrac{20}{35}\right)$$

$$= 31 : 74.$$

13. (b)

Rent (in ₹)	No. of days	No. of cows
370	20	40
111	30	x

Rent is in inverse variation with number of days but rent is in direct variation with number of cows

$$\left.\begin{array}{c}370:111\\30:20\end{array}\right\}::40:x$$

$$x = 40 \times \frac{111}{370} \times \frac{20}{30} = 8.$$

14. (c) As, AB = AC

$7x \times - 5 = 3 \times + 23$

$4x = 28$

$x = 7$

As given, BC = 4 × + 9

Put × = 7 in the equation.

BC = 4(7)+9

BC = 37 cm

15 (a) Required length = H.C.F. of 495 cm, 900 cm and 1665 cm

$495 = 3^2 \times 5 \times 11,$

$900 = 2^2 \times 3^2 \times 5^2,$

$1665 = 3^2 \times 5 \times 37$

∴ H.C.F. $= 3^2 \times 5 = 45$

Hence, required length = 45 cm.

16 (c) Let the retail price be ₹ 100

Then, S.P. = ₹ 80 (after a discount of 20%)

Since, profit = 60%

∴ C.P. $= \dfrac{\text{S.P.}}{1.6} = \dfrac{80}{1.6} = ₹\ 50$

New S.P. = ₹75 (after a commission of 25%)

∴ Profit = ₹(75 − 50) = ₹ 25

Hence, profit $\% = \dfrac{25}{50} \times 100 = 50\%.$

17. (b) $6 : x :: 12 : 36$

$$x = \frac{6 \times 36}{12} = 18.$$

18. (c) $A = P\left(1 + \dfrac{TR}{100}\right)$

$$81 = 72\left(1 + \frac{T \times \dfrac{25}{4}}{100}\right)$$

$$\Rightarrow 81 = 72\left[1 + \frac{25T}{400}\right]$$

$$\Rightarrow \frac{400 + 25T}{400} = \frac{81}{72}$$

$$\frac{16 + T}{16} = \frac{81}{72}$$

$$16 + T = 18$$

$$T = 2 \text{ years.}$$

19. (c) Total students

= [Rakesh's position from the top + Rakesh's position from the bottom] − 1

= [9 + 38] − 1 = 46

20. (c) $25x^2 + 16y^2 + 40xy$

At $x = 1$ and $y = -1$

$25(1)^2 + 16(-1)^2 + 40(1)(-1)$

$= 25 + 16 - 40 = 1.$

21. (a) Here, number of each type of coins is same, hence, we may write,

Number of each type of coin

$$= \frac{\text{Total amount}}{\text{Sum of value of each coin}}$$

∴ Number of each type of coin

$$= \frac{35}{1 + 0.5 + 0.25}$$

= 20 coins of each type.

22. (c) $4y + 5 = -y + 15$

$4y + y = 15 - 5$

$5y = 10$

$$y = \frac{10}{5} = 2$$

23. (a) Zero (0) is a whole number but not a natural number.

24. (d) Let the number of matches India lost = x

Number of matches India won
= x + 4

Total number of matches
= x + x + 4 = 2 × + 4

Matches India won = $\dfrac{3}{5}$ of its total matches

$$x + 4 = \frac{3}{5}\,(2× + 4)$$

$5x + 20 = 6x + 12$

$x = 8$

Total number of matches India played = 2 × + 4

= 2 (8) + 4 = 20

25. (d) Let P = ₹ x

Amount A = ₹ 2x

∴ S.I. = A–P = ₹ 2x – ₹ x = ₹ x

T = 5 years 4 months

$$= 5\frac{4}{12}\text{ years} = 5\frac{1}{3}\text{ years} = \frac{16}{3}\text{ years}$$

Let R be the rate percent per annum.

Using R = $\dfrac{\text{S.I.} \times 100}{P \times T}$,

We get R = $\dfrac{x \times 100}{x \times \dfrac{16}{3}} = \dfrac{300}{16}$

= 18.75

Hence required rate = 18.75% p.a.

26. (b) Let the original fraction be $\dfrac{x}{y}$

Then, $\dfrac{115\% \text{ of } x}{92\% \text{ of } y} = \dfrac{15}{16}$

$\Rightarrow \dfrac{115x}{92y} = \dfrac{15}{16} \Rightarrow \dfrac{x}{y} = \left(\dfrac{15}{16} \times \dfrac{92}{115}\right) = \dfrac{3}{4}.$

28. (c) CP of 110 apples = SP of 100 apples

SP of 1 apple = CP of 1.1 apple

Profit percentage

$$= \frac{SP - CP}{CP} \times 100$$

Profit percentage

$$= \frac{1.1CP - CP}{CP} \times 100$$

Profit percentage

$$= \frac{0.1CP}{CP} \times 100$$

Profit percentage = 10%

29. (a) When the sheet shown in fig. (X) is folded to form a cube, then the face bearing the dot lies opposite to the shaded face, the face bearing a circle (with '+' sign inside it) lies opposite to a blank face and the remaining two blank faces lie opposite to each other. Clearly, the cubes shown in figures (B) and (D) cannot be formed since they have the shaded face adjacent to the face bearing a dot and the cube shown in fig. (C) cannot be formed since it shows all the three blank faces adjacent to each other. Hence, only the cube shown in fig.(A) can be formed.

34. (c) Mean = $\dfrac{\text{Sum of all observations}}{\text{Number of observations}}$

or, $40 = \dfrac{\text{Sum of all observations}}{10}$

So, sum of all observations
= 400

But this is incorrect sum, since one observation was copied wrongly.

So, correct sum = Incorrect sum – Incorrect observation + Correct observation

= 400 – 15 + 45

= 430

Correct Mean

$$= \frac{\text{Correct Sum}}{\text{Number of observations}}$$

$$= \frac{430}{10} = 43$$

35. (c) Let the other number is x

0.56 x = 1.5008

x = 2.68

36. (a) Cost of the car = ₹ 80,000

Decrease at the end of one year
= 20% of 80,000

$$= \frac{20}{100} \times 80,000 = ₹ 16,000$$

Value of the car at the end of one year

= 80,000 – 16,000 = ₹ 64,000

Decrease at the end of 2 years
= 20% of ₹ 64,000

$$= \frac{20}{100} \times 64,000 = ₹ 12,800$$

Value of the car at the end of 2 years

= 64,000 – 12,800 = ₹ 51,200

37. (d) P = ₹ 2400

R = 6% per annum

T = 146 days = $\dfrac{146}{365}$ years

Now, I = $\dfrac{P \times T \times R}{100}$

$$= \frac{2400 \times 146 \times 6}{365 \times 100} = \frac{288}{5}$$

= ₹ 57.60

Interest is ₹ 57.60.

38. (b) Shaded area = Area of the square of side 2 cm – Area of the four quadrants of circle of radius 1 cm

i.e., Shaded area

$$= 2^2 - 4 \times \frac{1}{4} \times \pi . 1^2$$

$$= (4 - \pi) \text{ cm}^2$$

$$= (4 - 3.16) \text{ cm}^2$$

$$= 0.84 \text{ cm}^2$$

39. (b) By verification process,

$$(a) \to \frac{3}{4}, \frac{-2}{1}, \frac{-11}{20}, \frac{-4}{5}$$

$3 \times 1, -2 \times 4,$ correct

$-2 \times 20, -11 \times 1,$

$= -40, -11$ wrong

$$(b) \to \frac{3}{4}, \frac{-11}{20}, \frac{-4}{5}, \frac{-2}{1}$$

$3 \times 20, -11 \times 4 = 60, -44$

$$\frac{3}{4} > \frac{-11}{20}$$

$-11 \times 5, -4 \times 20,$

$$= -55, -80$$

$$\therefore \frac{-11}{20} > \frac{-4}{5}$$

$-4 \times 1, -2 \times 5,$

$= -4, -10$

$$\therefore \frac{-4}{5} > -2$$

40. (a) By definition,

Average

$$= \frac{x + (x+3) + (x+6) + (x+9) + (x+12)}{5}$$

$$= \frac{5x + 30}{5} = x + 6$$

41. (c)

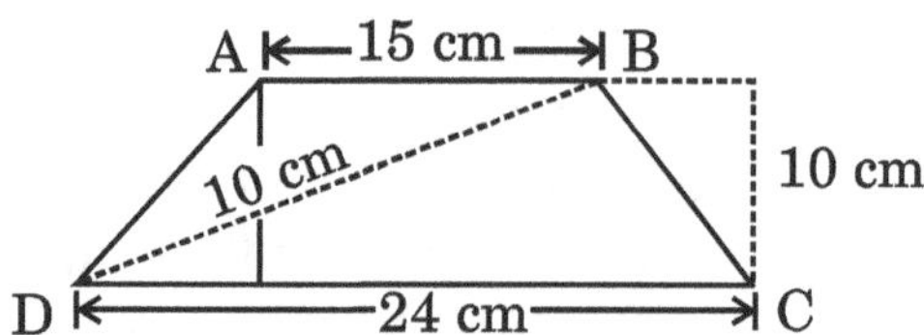

Area of trapezium = Area $\triangle$ABD + Area $\triangle$BCD.

$$= \left(\frac{1}{2} \times 15 \times 10 \right) + \left(\frac{1}{2} \times 24 \times 10 \right)$$

$$= \frac{10}{2}(24 + 15) = 5 \times 39$$

$$= 195 \text{ cm}^2.$$

42. (b) Let ABDC be a circular grass plot whose diameter AD = 70 m

$\Rightarrow$ OD = 35 m

KML is a gravel walk which is 15 m from the edge (i.e., pt. D)

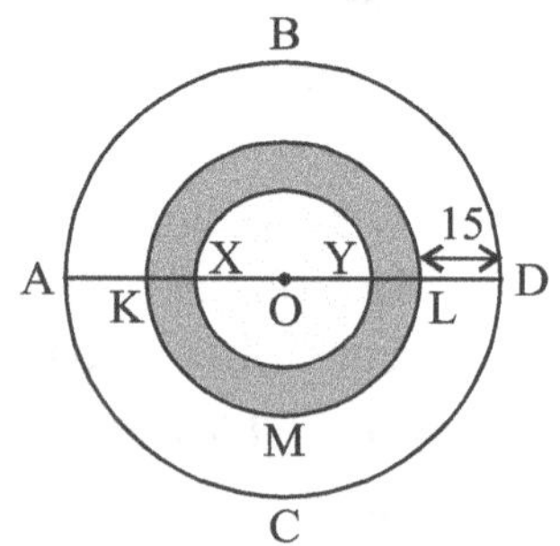

$\Rightarrow$ LD = 15 m

$\Rightarrow$ OL = OD – LD = 35 – 15

   = 20 m

$\therefore$ OY = 20 – 5 = 15 = T

[Since width of gravel walk

= YL = 5 m]

Area of turfing

= Area of grass plot – Area of gravel walk

$$= \pi(35)^2 - \pi\left[(OL)^2 - (OY)^2\right]$$

$$= \pi(35)^2 - \pi\left[(20)^2 - (15)^2\right]$$

$$= \pi(35)^2 - \pi(400 - 225)$$

$$= \pi(35)^2 - \pi \times 175 \text{ m}^2$$

$$= 3300 \text{ m}^2$$

Cost of turfing = Rate / m^2 × Area of turfing

= 2 × 3300 = ₹ 6600

Hence, the cost to turf the grass plot will be ₹ 6600.

43. (c) By definition, x : 8 = 8 : 16

$\Rightarrow$ x × 16 = 8^2

$\therefore$ $x = \dfrac{8^2}{16} = \dfrac{64}{16} = 4.$

44. (d) S.I. = (920 – 800) = ₹ 120

$$120 = \frac{800 \times R \times 3}{100}$$

$\therefore$ R = 5%

Interest at 8% interest

$$= \frac{800 \times 8 \times 3}{100} = ₹ 192$$

$\therefore$ Amount = (800 + 192) = ₹ 992.

45. (d) N = 20, AM = 10

10 = AM

$$= \frac{\text{sum of ages of 20 students}}{20}$$

$\therefore$ Sum of ages of 20 students = 200

Now, the students with mean age of 15 years leave the class

Sum of ages of 5 students.

= AM$_1$ × N$_1$

AM$_1$ = 15, N$_1$ = 5,

sum of ages of 5 students = 75

Remaining sum = 200 – 75 = 125

Remaining number of students

= N – N$_1$

= 20 – 5 = 15

Now, $AM = \dfrac{125}{15} = 8.33$ yrs

47. (c) Length of the road = 90 m

Breadth of the road = 3 m

Area of the road

= 90 × 3 = 270 m^2

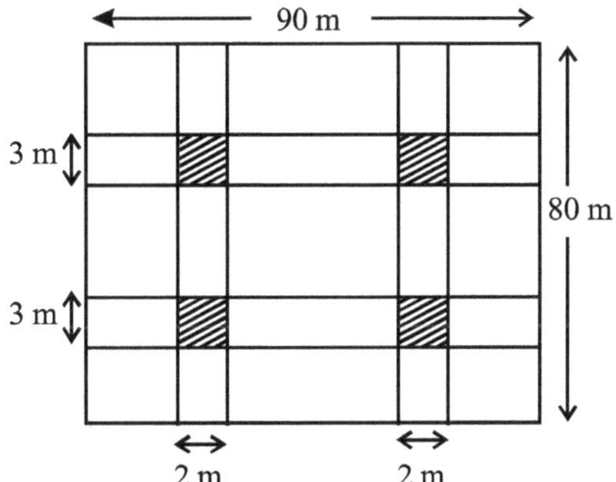

$\therefore$ Total area of the two roads along the length

$$= 2 \times 270 = 540 \text{ m}^2.$$

48. (a) Length of the road = 80 m

Breadth of the road = 2 m

$\therefore$ Area of the road $= (80 \times 2)$
$= 160 \text{ m}^2$

$\therefore$ Total area of the two roads along the breadth $= 2 \times 160$
$= 320 \text{ m}^2.$

49. (b) Total area of the four roads

= Area of four roads – common area

$$= [(540 + 320) - 4 \times (2 \times 3)]\text{m}^2.$$
$$= (860) - 24 = 836 \text{ m}^2.$$

50. (a) Area of the remaining portion of the park

= Area of the park – Area of the roads

$$= (90 \times 80) - 836 = 7200 - 836$$
$$= 6364 \text{ m}^2.$$

MOCK TEST-3

ANSWER KEY

1	(a)	11	(b)	21	(b)	31	(c)	41	(c)
2	(c)	12	(c)	22	(b)	32	(d)	42	(c)
3	(d)	13	(c)	23	(c)	33	(a)	43	(a)
4	(d)	14	(a)	24	(b)	34	(c)	44	(a)
5	(c)	15	(d)	25	(b)	35	(d)	45	(d)
6	(a)	16	(b)	26	(c)	36	(b)	46	(d)
7	(a)	17	(a)	27	(b)	37	(c)	47	(a)
8	(a)	18	(c)	28	(b)	38	(a)	48	(a)
9	(d)	19	(d)	29	(a)	39	(b)	49	(c)
10	(d)	20	(b)	30	(c)	40	(c)	50	(d)

1. (a) Let one angle be x.

So, other angle $= 90° - x$

Thus, $\dfrac{2}{3} \times x = 90° - x$

or $2x = 270° - 3x$

or $2x + 3x = 270°$

or $5x = 270°$

or $x = \dfrac{270}{5} = 54°$

So, one angle = 54° and the other angle $= 90° - 54° = 36°$

2. (c) Mean $= \dfrac{\text{Sum of all observations}}{\text{Number of observations}}$

or $27 = \dfrac{26+28+25+x+24}{5}$

or $27 = \dfrac{103+x}{5}$

or $135 = 103 + x$

or $x = 135 - 103$

So, $x = 32$

3. (d) $\overset{-3}{\frown}\ \overset{-3}{\frown}\ \overset{-3}{\frown}\ \overset{-3}{\frown}\ \overset{-3}{\frown}\ \overset{-3}{\frown}$
11, 8, 5, 2, −1, −4, −7

So, next three consecutive numbers are −1, − 4 and −7.

4. **(d)** $\dfrac{8}{-15}+\dfrac{7}{20}-\dfrac{-11}{35}+\dfrac{1}{5}$

$$=\dfrac{8}{-15}+\dfrac{7}{20}-\dfrac{-11}{35}+\dfrac{1}{5}$$

$$=\dfrac{-8\times28+7\times21+11\times12+1\times84}{420}$$

$$=\dfrac{-224+147+132+84}{420}$$

$$=\dfrac{-224+363}{420}=\dfrac{139}{420}.$$

5. **(c)** We know that,

H.C.F. × L.C.M. = Product of two numbers

$\therefore$ Second number $=\dfrac{16\times240}{48}=80.$

6. **(a)** $\dfrac{3^{12+n}\times9^{2n-7}}{3^{5n}}$

$$=\dfrac{3^{12}.3^{n}\times3^{4n}.3^{-14}}{\left(3^{n}\right)^{5}}=\dfrac{3^{-2}\times3^{5n}}{3^{5n}}$$

$$=3^{-2}=\dfrac{1}{9}$$

7. **(a)** Given : $A + B = 2C$ ....(i)

and $C + D = 2A$ .... (ii)

Adding (i) and (ii) we get :

$A + B + C + D = 2C + 2A \Rightarrow B + D = A + C.$

8. **(a)** $0.125\,P=\dfrac{P\times R\times T}{100}=\dfrac{P\times10\times T}{100}$

$$\dfrac{125}{1000}=\dfrac{T}{10}$$

$$T=\dfrac{10}{8}=1\dfrac{1}{4}\text{ Years}$$

9. **(d)** Bhanu Madhuri

T_1 = 3 years $\quad T_2$ = 10 years

R_1 = 12% $\qquad R_2$ = 24%

$$\dfrac{A_1}{A_2}=\dfrac{100+T_1R_1}{100+T_2R_2}$$

$$=\dfrac{100+3\times12}{100+10\times24}=\dfrac{136}{340}=\dfrac{2}{5}$$

$\therefore$ $A_1 : A_2 = 2 : 5.$

10. **(d)** $\angle B = 180° - (80° + 35°) = 65°$

($\because$ Sum of angles of $\triangle = 180°$)

$\because$ D and E are mid-points of AB and AC, we have DE $||$ BC.

$\because$ $\quad \angle EDB + \angle B = 180°$

$\angle EDB + 65° = 180°$

$\angle EDB = 180° - 65° = 115°.$

11. **(b)** $x \times 4^{-3} = 64$

$$x\times\dfrac{1}{4^{3}}=64$$

$x = 64 \times 4^3 = 2^6 \times (2^2)^3 = 2^6 \times 2^6$
$= 2^{12}.$

12. **(c)** Here, Ak is the height from vertex A, falling outside the triangle.

Area $\triangle ABC = \dfrac{1}{2} \times$ base $\times$ height

$$=\dfrac{1}{2}\times4\times12=24\text{ cm}^2$$

13. **(c)** Let Kajol earned $= ₹\, x$

So, $\dfrac{3}{8}$ of $x = ₹\,75$

$$x \times \dfrac{3}{8} = 75$$

$$x = 75 \times \dfrac{8}{3}$$

$$x = ₹\,200$$

14. **(a)** Let his Salary be ₹ 100

It is increased by 20%, new

salary = ₹ 120

Now, it is decreased by 20%

Now, his salary is

$$= 120 - \frac{20}{100} \times 120 = ₹\ 96$$

∴ his salary is decreased by 4% i.e. (100-96)

15. (d) Smallest number of five digits is 10000

Required number must be divisible by L.C.M. of 16, 24, 36, 54, i.e. 432

On dividing 10000 by 432, we get 64 as remainder

∴ Required number = 10000 + (432 − 64) = 10368.

16. (b) % of sugar in 4 liters solution

$$= \frac{0.04 \times 3}{3+1} \times 100\% = 3\%$$

17. (a) Sum of 5 observations

= 5 × 15 = 75

Sum of first 3 observations

= 3 × 14 = 42.

Sum of the last three observations = 3 × 17 = 51

∴ Third observation

= 42 + 51 − 75 = 93 − 75 = 18

18. (c) Let the initial length and width be l & b respectively.

Then the initial area = l × b

According to the question,

New length and width will be 2l and 2b respectively.

∴ New area = 2l × 2b = 4lb

Increament in area

$$= \frac{4lb - lb}{lb} \times 100\% = 300\%.$$

19. (d) Height of hill = $101\frac{1}{3}$m = $\frac{304}{3}$m

Part of hill covered by water = $\frac{1}{4}$th

Hill covered by water = $\frac{1}{4}$ of $\frac{304}{3}$

$$= \frac{1}{4} \times \frac{304}{3} = \frac{76}{3}$$

Height of hill visible above the water

$$= \frac{304}{3} - \frac{76}{3}$$

$$= \frac{228}{3} = 76\ m$$

20. (b) Let the numbers be 3x and 5x.

$$\Rightarrow \frac{3x+4}{5x+4} = \frac{2}{3} \Rightarrow x = 4$$

∴ Numbers are 12 and 20.

21. (b) $4^{3.5} : 2^5 = 4^{0.5}\ 4^3 : 2^5$

$$2 * 4^3 : 2^5 = 2 * 2^{23} : 2^5$$

$$2 * 2^6 : 2^5 = 4 : 1$$

22. : (b) When × = −8 then |x| = |−8| = 8

x|x| = (−8) (8) = −64

23. (c)

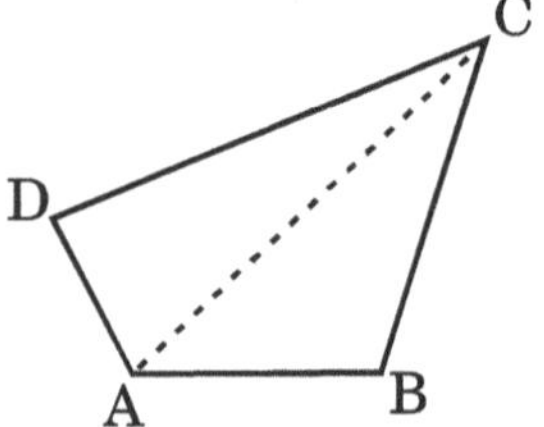

Sum of all angles of quadrilateral = Sum of all angles of △ABC + Sum of all angles of △ADC

= 180° + 180° = 360°

$1x + 4x + 2x + 3x = 360°$

$\Rightarrow x = 36°$

$1x = 36°$; $4x = 144°$; $2x = 72°$; $3x = 108°$

Since, all the angles are different.

Therefore, the quadrilateral is a trapezium.

25. (b) Let breadth = x.

Length = x + 23.

Perimeter = 206 m.

2 (x + 23 + x) = 206

∴ 2x + 23 = 103

$\qquad$ x = 40

Area = $l \times$ b = 63 × 40 = 2520 m^2.

26. (c) Let us make a table to distribute the frequencies:

Marks	30	40	60	75
No. of students (Frequency)	3	8	12	10

Clearly, the maximum students (12) scored 60 marks. Hence, the mode is 60.

27. (b) $A^{+2} \to C$, $C^{+3} \to F$; $E^{+3} \to H$; $H^{+4} \to L$; $M^{+4} \to Q$, $Q^{+5} \to V$.

28. (b) Median from data = $x + 2$

or 21 = x + 2 or x = 21 − 2

or x = 19

29. (a) Let the number be x.

According to the given condition,

$$\frac{1}{3}x - 1 = 1$$

or $\frac{1}{3}x = 1 + 1$

or $\frac{1}{3}x = 2$ or x = 6.

30. (c) First, write the given rational numbers with positive denominators.

$$\frac{7}{-18} = \frac{7 \times (-1)}{-18 \times (-1)} = \frac{-7}{18},$$

$$\frac{5}{-12} = \frac{5 \times (-1)}{-12 \times (-1)} = \frac{-5}{12},$$

$$\frac{-9}{-16} = \frac{-9 \times (-1)}{-16 \times (-1)} = \frac{9}{16}$$

Now, L.C.M. of 18, 12, 16 is:

2 × 2 × 3 × 3 × 4 = 144

and $\dfrac{-7}{18} = \dfrac{-7 \times 8}{18 \times 8} = \dfrac{-56}{144},$

$$\frac{-5}{12} = \frac{-5 \times 12}{12 \times 12} = \frac{-60}{144},$$

$$\frac{9}{16} = \frac{9 \times 9}{16 \times 9} = \frac{81}{144}$$

∴ $\dfrac{-7}{18} + \dfrac{-5}{12} + \dfrac{-9}{16} = \dfrac{-56}{144} + \dfrac{-60}{144} + \dfrac{81}{144}$

$$= \frac{-56 - 60 + 81}{144} = \frac{-35}{144}$$

Alternatively

you could shorten the working by performing the addition as under:

$$\frac{-7}{18} + \frac{-5}{12} + \frac{9}{16} = \frac{-7 \times 8}{18 \times 8} + \frac{-5 \times 12}{12 \times 12} + \frac{9 \times 9}{16 \times 9}$$

$$= \frac{-56 - 60 + 81}{144} = \frac{-35}{144}.$$

31. (c) Given that $\dfrac{C_1}{C_2} = \dfrac{9}{4}$, where C_1 and C_2 are the circumference of both the circles.

Circumference of the circle is given by $2\pi r$, where r is the radius of circle. The circumference is directly proportional to the radius.

Area of circle is given by πr^2. Area of circle is directly proportional to the square of radius.

Hence, $\dfrac{A_1}{A_2} = \dfrac{81}{16}$, where A1 and A_2 are the area of both the circles.

32. (d) Clearly, number of boys in a line

$$= 12 + 4 - 1 = 15$$

∴ Number of boys to be added

$$= 35 - 15 = 20.$$

33. (a) Let the number is x

$$\dfrac{1}{4}\left(\dfrac{2}{5}\right)x = 82$$

$$\dfrac{2}{20}\times x = 82$$

$$x = 410$$

34. (c) $\dfrac{x}{4} + \dfrac{1}{2} = 4$

$$\dfrac{2x+4}{8} = 4$$

$$2x + 4 = 32$$

$$2x = 32 - 4 = 28$$

$$x = \dfrac{28}{2} = 14$$

35. (d) $a\,(b + c) = (a \times b) + (a \times c)$ shows distributive property

36. (b) Arranging in ascending order:

2, 2, 3, 5, 7, 7, 9, 9, 10, 11, 15

Since, number of observations is odd, the middle most value is the median. The middle most value is 7, so median is 7.

37. (c) $\left(-\dfrac{5}{100}\right)\left(\dfrac{5}{100}\right) = \dfrac{-25}{10,000}$

$$\dfrac{-25}{10,000} \times 100\% = 0.25\%$$

decrease

38. (a) Gain %

$$= \dfrac{\text{No. of articles on CP} - \text{No. of articles on SP}}{\text{No. of articles on SP}} \times 100$$

$$= \dfrac{25 - 20}{20} \times 100 = 25\%$$

39. (b) P = 8000, A = 9620, and

$$T = \dfrac{25}{100} \times R = \dfrac{R}{4}$$

$$I = A - P = 9620 - 8000 = 1620$$

$$\Rightarrow I = \dfrac{PTR}{100} \Rightarrow 1620 = \dfrac{8000 \times \dfrac{R}{4} \times R}{100}$$

$$\Rightarrow R = 9\%$$

$$T = \dfrac{R}{4} = \dfrac{9}{4} \Rightarrow T = 2\dfrac{1}{4} \text{ years.}$$

40. (c) September 2003 has 30 days

$$30 \times 3\dfrac{1}{4} = 30 \times \dfrac{13}{4} = 97\dfrac{1}{2} \text{ litres}$$

41. (c) Let $\dfrac{a}{b} = \dfrac{c}{d} = k$

So, a = bk, c = dk

So $\dfrac{ma + nc}{mb + nd} = \dfrac{mbk + ndk}{mb + nd}$

$$= \dfrac{k(mb + nd)}{mb + nd}$$

$$\Rightarrow \quad k = a : b$$

42. (c) Applying factor theorem if 'a' is, the solution of $P(x)$, then $P(a) = 0$.

Now from (ii),

$$4x - 1 - 8$$

$$= 4 \times \frac{9}{5} - 1 - 8$$

$$= \frac{36}{5} - 1 - 8 \Rightarrow \frac{36}{5} - 9$$

$$\Rightarrow \frac{36-45}{5} \Rightarrow \frac{-9}{5} \neq 0.$$

43. (a) Let $\angle EFA = x$

Then, $\angle AFD = x$

It is given that CD intersects line AB at F.

Therefore, $\angle CFB = \angle AFD$

(Vertically opposite angles)

So, $x = 50°$

But, $\angle EFA = \angle AFD$ which give $\angle EFA = 50°$

Now, $\angle CFB + \angle EFA + \angle EFC = 180°$

[As AB is a straight line]

or $50° + 50° + \angle EFC = 180°$

or $\angle EFC = 180° - 100°$

Thus, $\angle EFC = 80°$.

44. (a) Given : In $\triangle$ PQR, PQ = PR

So, PQR is an isosceles triangle and we know, in isosceles $\triangle$, the angles opposite to the equal sides are equal.

$\therefore$ In $\triangle$ PQR, $\angle$ PQR = $\angle$ PRQ

Now, $\angle PRQ = 180° - 100° = 80°$

(Linear pair)

$\therefore \quad \angle PQR = 80°$

$\Rightarrow \quad \angle QPR = 180 - (80° + 80°) = 20°$

45. (d) Area of treapezium is 600 sq.cm.

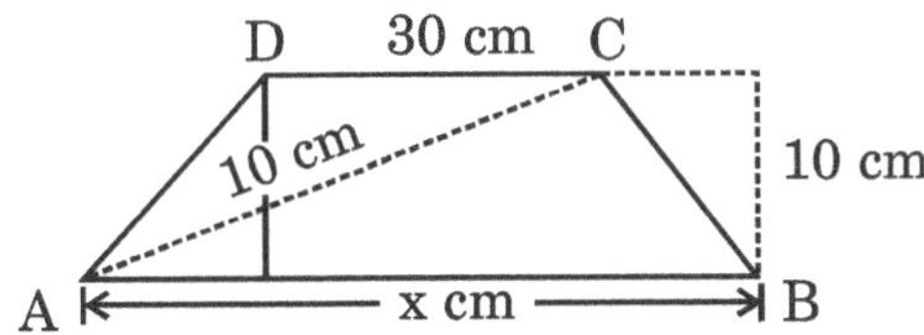

$$600 = \text{Area } (\triangle ABC) + \text{Area } (\triangle ADC)$$

$$\Rightarrow 600 = \left(\frac{1}{2} \times 30 \times 10\right) + \left(\frac{1}{2} \times x \times 10\right)$$

$$\Rightarrow 600 = \frac{1}{2} \times (30 + x) \times 10$$

$$\frac{600 \times 2}{10} = (x + 30)$$

$$120 = x + 30$$

$$\therefore x = 90 \text{ cm}$$

46. (d) All the given statements are false.

47. (a) Use circumference formula

$$c = 2 \times \frac{22}{7} \times 0.77 = 4.84 \text{m}$$

Required distance = 4.84×525
$$= 2.541 \text{ km}$$

48. (a) Height of highest peak
= 8800 m

Height of lowest peak
= 6000 m

Ratio = 8800 : 6000
$$= 22 : 15$$

49. (c) Second highest peak is C.

50. (d) The ascending order of heights is, 6000 m < 6500 m < 7500 m <8200 m < 8600 m < 8800 m

The two middle peaks are 7500m and 8200 m

$$\text{Average} = \frac{7500 + 8200}{2}$$

$$= \frac{15700}{2} = 7850 \text{m}.$$

MOCK TEST-4

ANSWER KEY

1	(a)	11	(c)	21	(c)	31	(a)	41	(c)
2	(d)	12	(c)	22	(c)	32	(b)	42	(a)
3	(b)	13	(b)	23	(d)	33	(a)	43	(c)
4	(d)	14	(c)	24	(c)	34	(c)	44	(b)
5	(d)	15	(c)	25	(a)	35	(a)	45	(a)
6	(b)	16	(c)	26	(d)	36	(a)	46	(a)
7	(c)	17	(a)	27	(d)	37	(a)	47	(c)
8	(b)	18	(b)	28	(b)	38	(b)	48	(b)
9	(d)	19	(b)	29	(a)	39	(a)	49	(b)
10	(a)	20	(b)	30	(a)	40	(a)	50	(c)

1. **(a)** $\dfrac{x}{2} = 3$

$x = 6$

Then, $3x + 2$

$= 3 \times 6 + 2$

$= 18 + 2 = 20$

2. **(d)** Principal = ₹ 75000

Amount = ₹ 80000

Interest = Amount − Principal

$= ₹\ 80000 - ₹\ 75000$

$= ₹\ 5000$

3. **(b)** $\dfrac{-5}{7} = \dfrac{x}{28}$

$\dfrac{-5 \times 28}{7} = x$

$x = -5 \times 4$

$x = -20$

4. **(d)** P = ₹ 25000

R = 20% per annum

T = 1 year

Now, $I = \dfrac{P \times T \times R}{100}$

$= \dfrac{25000 \times 1 \times 20}{100} = ₹\ 5000$

∴ His annual income is ₹ 5000.

5. **(d)** Let his monthly income be ₹100

He spent = ₹82

Money left = $100 - 82 = ₹18$

18% of x = 423

$\dfrac{18}{100} \times x = 423$

$x = 423 \times \dfrac{100}{18} = ₹\ 2350.$

6. **(b)** Quantity of milk = $\dfrac{2}{3} \times 60 = 40$

litres and that of water $= \dfrac{1}{3} \times 60$

= 20 litres

Let x litres of water be added to make the ratio 1 : 2

$\dfrac{40}{20 + x} = \dfrac{1}{2} \Rightarrow x = 60$ litres.

7. (c) $3^{x-2} = \dfrac{3^x}{3^2}$

$\dfrac{3^x}{3^2} = \dfrac{3^x}{9}$

Given that $3^x = 500$

$\dfrac{3^x}{9} = \dfrac{500}{9}$

8. (b) P = ₹ 2500, T = 4 years,
I = ₹ 1500, R = ?

Now, $I = \dfrac{P \times R \times T}{100}$

Therefore, $1500 = \dfrac{2500 \times R \times 4}{100}$

$R = \dfrac{1500 \times 100}{2500 \times 4} = 15$

So, the rate of interest is 15% p.a.

9. (d) $-2\dfrac{3}{4} \times 5\dfrac{6}{7} = \dfrac{-11}{4} \times \dfrac{41}{7}$

Now, product of two rational numbers

$= \dfrac{\text{Product of numerators}}{\text{Product of denominators}}$

So, $-2\dfrac{3}{4} \times 5\dfrac{6}{7} = \dfrac{-11}{4} \times \dfrac{41}{7}$

$= \dfrac{-11 \times 41}{4 \times 7} = \dfrac{-451}{28}.$

10. (a) $M = \left(15 \times \dfrac{20}{100}\right) = 3$ and

$S = \left(15 \times \dfrac{80}{100}\right) = 12$

11. (c) $1 - (-0.3)^3$

$= 1 - [(-0.3) \times (-0.3) \times (-0.3)]$

$= 1 - (-0.027)$

$= 1 + 0.027$

$= 1.027.$

12. (c) Required number = L.C.M. of
12, 15, 20, 27

3	12	15	20	27
4	4	5	20	9
5	1	5	5	9
	1	1	1	9

$\therefore$ L.C.M. $= 3 \times 4 \times 5 \times 9 = 540$

Hence, required number = 540.

13. (b) Let the required angle be $x°$.

Complement of $x° = 90° - x°$

According to the question,

$x° = (90° - x°) + 20°$

$\Rightarrow 2x°$

$= 110°$

$\Rightarrow x° = 55°.$

14. (c) $\left[\left(\dfrac{1}{4}\right)^2 - \left(\dfrac{1}{4}\right)^3\right] \times 2^6$

$= \left(\dfrac{1}{4}\right)^2 \left[1 - \dfrac{1}{4}\right] \times 2^6$

$= \dfrac{1}{16} \times \dfrac{3}{4} \times 64 = 3$

15. (c) $T_r = 11$, $B_r = 31$

$\Rightarrow$ Number of students

$= T_r + B_r - 1$

$= 11 + 31 - 1$

$= 41$

17. **(a)** $\left[(-2)^{(-2)}\right]^{(-3)} = (-2)^6 = 64$

18. **(b)**

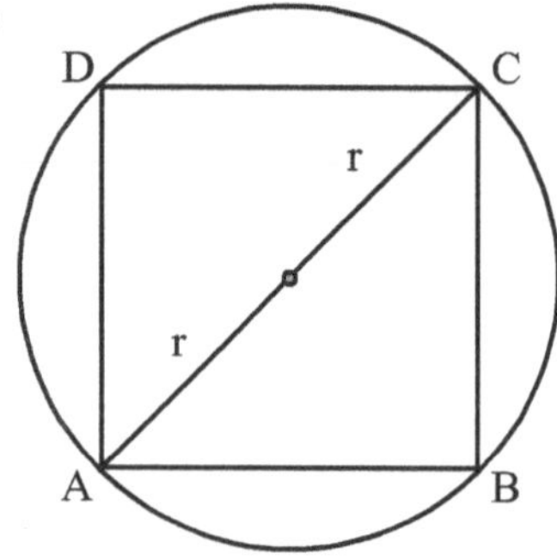

Let r be the radius of the circle in centimetre.

Then its circumference

$= 2\pi r = 100$

$\therefore$ diameter $= 2r = \dfrac{100}{\pi}$

The length of the largest diagonal of the square

= diameter of the circle

$\Rightarrow 2r = \dfrac{100}{\pi}$ cm

$\therefore$ Side of square

$= \dfrac{1}{\sqrt{2}} \times$ largest diagonal

$= \dfrac{1}{\sqrt{2}} \times \dfrac{100}{\pi} = \dfrac{50\sqrt{2}}{\pi}$ cm.

19. **(b)** Given: $p = 95\%$ of $q = \dfrac{95}{100}q$

(To find: q)

$\Rightarrow \dfrac{100}{95}p = q \Rightarrow 1.053\,p = q$

To convert into percentage we multiply it by 100, we get

$q = 105.3\%$ of p.

20. **(b)** 8 edges

21. **(c)** Suman is 17th from the bottom and Raman is 7 ranks ahead of Suman. So Raman is 24th from the last.

$\therefore$ Raman rank from the start is

$39 + 1 - 24$ i.e, 16th

22. **(c)** P = ₹ 8000

$T = 4\dfrac{1}{2}$ years $= \dfrac{9}{2}$ years

R = 8% per annum

Now, $I = \dfrac{P \times T \times R}{100}$

$= \dfrac{8000 \times 9 \times 8}{2 \times 100}$

I = ₹ 2880

Now, amount = Principal + S.I.

= ₹ 8000 + ₹ 2880

= ₹ 10880

$\therefore$ He has to pay ₹ 10880 after $4\dfrac{1}{2}$ years.

23. **(d)** Desired profit = 20%

It means, if

C.P. = ₹ 100, then

Profit (P) = ₹ 20

$\therefore$ S.P. = C.P. + Profit

= ₹ 100 + ₹ 20 = ₹ 120

Now,

C.P.   Profit   S.P. = (C.P.
(₹)   (₹)   + Gain)
100   20   (₹)
                    120

?   3000

$$\text{C.P.} = \frac{3000 \times 100}{120} = ₹\ 2500$$

24. **(c)** AB = AC

BD = DC and AD = AD

By SSS property

$\triangle ADB \cong \triangle ADC$

We have

$\angle ADB + \angle ADC = 180°$

$\Rightarrow \angle ADB = \angle ADC = 90°$

$(\because \triangle ADB \cong \triangle ADC)$

25. **(a)** We have,

Square of diagonal of rectangle = sum of squares of its sides

Let sides of rectangle are a and b

Then, $d^2 = a^2 + b^2$

$100 = a^2 + b^2$

$\Rightarrow \quad a = 8$ cm, b = 6 cm

or $\quad a = 6$ cm, b = 8 cm

26. **(d)** $\dfrac{A}{B} = \dfrac{2}{3}$

$$= \frac{2 \times 5}{3 \times 5} = \frac{10}{15}$$

$$\frac{B}{C} = \frac{5}{6} = \frac{5 \times 3}{6 \times 3} = \frac{15}{18}$$

27. **(d)** Multiply all the numbers around the circle and then divide it by 10 to get the number at the centre, viz.,

$$\frac{7 \times 3 \times 8 \times 5}{10} = 84$$

So, $\dfrac{5 \times 2 \times 6 \times 7}{10} = 42$

28. **(b)** There are 4 blocks in the lower layer close to the ground. Also, there are 3 blocks standing over the lower layer of blocks.

29. **(a)** Removing brackets,

$5x - 15 - 42 + 7x = 24 - 24 + 3x - 3$

Collecting terms,

$12x - 57 = 3x - 3$

Subtracting 3x from each side, we get

$9x - 57 = -3$

Adding 57 to each side, we have

$9x = 54$

Dividing by 9,

$x = 6$

30. **(a)** Total temperature of Monday, Tuesday and Wednesday = 40 × 3 = 120°C.
Total temperature of Tuesday, Wednesday and Thursday = 41 × 3 = 123°C
Temperature of Thursday = 30°C
So, Temperature of Monday = (120 + 30 − 123)°C = 27°C

31. **(a)** Side of the square = $\sqrt{\text{Area}}$

Also 1 hectare = 10000 m

$\therefore$ side of square

$= \sqrt{25 \times 10000}$ m $= 500$ m

Distance to run = Perimeter of the field

$= 4 \times 500$ m $= 2$ km

Time taken by a boy

$= \dfrac{\text{Distance}}{\text{Speed}} = \dfrac{2}{10}$ hr $= 12$ min.

32. (b) The windmill has rotational symmetry of order 4.
Hence
$2K = 4$
$K = 2$

33. (a) $\dfrac{125.625}{0.5} = \dfrac{125625}{1000} \times \dfrac{10}{5} = 251.25$

34. (c) Amount (Principal + Interest) for 2 years = ₹ 1560
Amount (Principal + Interest) for 5 years = ₹ 2100
Hence, interest for 3 years
$= (2100 - 1560) = $ ₹ 540
Simple interest for 2 years
$= $ ₹ 360
$\therefore$ Principal $= (1560 - 360)$
$= $ ₹ 1200

$R = \dfrac{360 \times 100}{1200 \times 2} = 15\%.$ per annum

35. (a) $\dfrac{\sqrt{3}}{2} \times \text{side} = \sqrt{6}$

Side $= 2\sqrt{2}$ cm.

Area $= \dfrac{\sqrt{3}}{4} \times (\text{side})^2$

$= \dfrac{\sqrt{3}}{4} \times (2\sqrt{2})^2$

$= 2\sqrt{3}$ cm^2.

36. (a) If $p + \dfrac{1}{p} = a + b$ and $p - \dfrac{1}{p}$

$= a - b$, then $p = a$ and $\dfrac{1}{p} = b$.

Hence $a \times b = p \times \dfrac{1}{p} = 1$

37. (a) Let the daughter's present age be x years.
Mrs. Kumar's present age
$= 3x$ years
In 5 years time,
Mrs. Kumar's age
$= (3x + 5)$ years
In 5 years time,
her daughter's age $= (x + 5)$ years
Since, their total age in 5 years' time will be 62, we have:
$(3x + 5) + (x + 5) = 62$
$3x + 5 + x + 5 = 62$
$4x = 62 - 10$

$x = \dfrac{52}{4}$

$\therefore$ x = 13
Hence, the daughter's present age is 13 years.

38. (b) only (iv) is correct
Let S be the selling Price
Cost price of T.V. on which there is again of 20%

C.P. $= \dfrac{S \times 100}{100 + 20} = \dfrac{5}{6} S = C_1$

$= \dfrac{5}{4} s = C_2$

Total cost price

$$C = C_1 + C_2 = \left(\frac{5}{4}+\frac{5}{6}\right)S = \frac{25}{12}S$$

Also C.P $= \dfrac{S\times 100}{100-200}$

Total S.P. $= S + S = 2S$

Loss % $= \dfrac{C-S}{C}\times 100$

$$= \frac{\left(\dfrac{25}{12}S\text{-}2S\right)}{\left(\dfrac{25}{12}S\right)}\times 100 \ = \frac{1}{25}\times 100$$

$$= 4\%$$

$$\frac{m}{n}=\frac{40\times 100}{100\times 10}=\frac{4}{1}=4:1$$

39. (a) (i) & (ii)

40. (a) By definition,

$$\frac{6+y+7+x+14}{5}=8$$

or $27 + x + y = 40$ or $x + y = 13$.

41. (c) Area covered by swimming pool
= 30 m × 20 m = 600 m^2
Length of outer rectangle
= (30 + 8 + 8) m = 46 m
and its breadth = (20 + 5 + 5) m
= 30 m
So, the area of outer rectangle
= 46 m × 30 m = 1380 m^2
Area of cemented path
= Area of outer rectangle
     – Area of swimming pool
= (1380 – 600) m^2 = 780 m^2
Cost of cementing 1 m^2 path
= ₹ 200

So, total cost of cementing the path
= ₹ 780 × 200 = ₹ 156000

42. (a) $\dfrac{\pi d^2}{4} = 2464$ \qquad [d is diameter]

$$d^2 = \frac{2464\times 4}{\dfrac{22}{7}} = 3136$$

$d = \sqrt{3136} = 56$ m.

43. (c) Since mode of four numbers is 8 therefore 8 occurs at least two times and 7 is one of them.
So, three observations are 7, 8, 8
Now, Let fourth observations be x.
$\therefore \ 7 + 8 + 8 + x = 4 \times 8 \Rightarrow x = 32 - 23 = 9$

44. (b) Let the number be 'x'.

10% of $x = \dfrac{x}{10}$

Number increased by 10%

i.e. number $= x+\dfrac{x}{10}=\dfrac{11x}{10}$

Now, 10% of $\dfrac{11x}{10}=\dfrac{11x}{100}$

Now, number $\dfrac{11x}{10}$ reduced by 10%

i.e. number $=\dfrac{11x}{10}-\dfrac{11x}{100}$

$$=\frac{110x-11x}{100}$$

$$= \frac{99x}{100} = 99\% \text{ of } x$$

Thus, we get that the number is decreased by 1%.

45. (a) From the table, it is clear that the size corresponding to the maximum frequency (15) is 9. Hence, the mode is 9.

46. (a) $\left(\sqrt{3}x^2y^2 - \sqrt{2}x^3y^2 + \sqrt{2}x^3y^3\right)$

$$x - \sqrt{2}x^2y^2 = -\sqrt{6}x^4y^4 + 2x^5y^4$$

$$-\sqrt{10}x^5y^5$$

47. (c) $\left(x - \frac{1}{x}\right)\left(x + \frac{1}{x}\right)\left(x^2 + \frac{1}{x^2}\right)$

$$= \left(x^2 - \frac{1}{x^2}\right)\left(x^2 + \frac{1}{x^2}\right)$$

$$\left(x^2 - \frac{1}{x^2}\right)\left(x^2 + \frac{1}{x^2}\right) = \left(x^4 - \frac{1}{x^4}\right)$$

48. (b) $(-7xy + 4a^2 + 32 - 5) - (3xy - 4a^2 + 5b^2 + 2)$

$$= -10xy + 8a^2 - 3b^2 - 7$$

49. (b) Total letters in the word = 11

Number of letter M = 2

Probability of getting 'M'

$$= \frac{2}{11}.$$

50. (c) Total letters in the word = 11

Number of consonants = 7

Probability of getting a consonant

$$= \frac{7}{11}.$$

MOCK TEST-5

ANSWER KEY

1	(b)	11	(b)	21	(b)	31	(b)	41	(b)
2	(a)	12	(a)	22	(a)	32	(c)	42	(d)
3	(c)	13	(b)	23	(b)	33	(b)	43	(b)
4	(d)	14	(b)	24	(c)	34	(d)	44	(b)
5	(b)	15	(b)	25	(c)	35	(d)	45	(a)
6	(c)	16	(d)	26	(a)	36	(b)	46	(b)
7	(d)	17	(b)	27	(b)	37	(b)	47	(d)
8	(b)	18	(c)	28	(c)	38	(c)	48	(c)
9	(d)	19	(c)	29	(b)	39	(b)	49	(d)
10	(b)	20	(a)	30	(b)	40	(d)	50	(d)

1. (b) Putting x = 7 in 7x – 1,

$$= 7 \times 7 - 1$$

$$= 49 - 1 = 48$$

$$48 \neq 50$$

2. (a) $\dfrac{A}{B} = \dfrac{7}{9}; \dfrac{B}{C} = \dfrac{6}{7}$

$$\dfrac{A}{C} = \dfrac{A}{B} \times \dfrac{B}{C} = \dfrac{7}{9} \times \dfrac{6}{7} = \dfrac{2}{3}$$

A : C = 2 : 3

3. (c) Here, the base of each number is same (= 3) but indices are different.

So, the required H.C.F. = number with the minimum index, i.e. 3^5.

4. (d) A's age 6 years ago = A's present age – 6

B's age 6 years ago = B's present age – 6

C's age 6 years ago = C's present age – 6

(A + B + C)'s age 6 years ago

= sum of present ages of A, B and C – 6 × 3

= 90 – 6 × 3 = 72

∴ C's age 6 years ago = $\dfrac{3}{(1 + 2 + 3)}$ × 72 = 36

∴ C's present age = 36 + 6 = 42 years.

5. (b) Let the principal be ₹ x, then

$$\text{S.I.} = ₹\,\dfrac{x}{4}$$

T = R, if R = rate per annum

$$\therefore\ \dfrac{x}{4} = \dfrac{x \times R \times R}{100} \Rightarrow R^2 = 25 \Rightarrow R$$

= 5%.

6. (c) Let the dimension of the cube be 'a' cm.

$$\therefore\quad a^3 = 125 \Rightarrow (a)^3 = (5)^3$$

$$\Rightarrow a = 5 \text{ cm}$$

∴ The surface area = $6a^2$

$$= 6(5)^2\ = 150 \text{ cm}^2.$$

7. (c) 20x – 12y = 15y – 9x

21x = 27y

$$\dfrac{x}{y} = \dfrac{27}{21}$$

8. (b) $\triangle$AQC is a right angled triangle

$$(AQ)^2 + (QC)^2 = (AC)^2$$

$$(QC)^2 = (AC)^2 - (AQ)^2$$

$$(QC)^2 = (37)^2 - (12)^2$$

$$(QC)^2 = 1369 - 144 = 1225$$

$$(QC)^2 = (35)^2 \Rightarrow QC = 35$$

BC = BQ + QC = 35 + 35 = 70

[given BQ = QC]

9. (d) A → s; B → p; C → q; D → r

10. (b) Let h be the height of the room in metre, then

Area of four walls = 2(length + breadth) × h

$$77 = 2(7.5 + 3.5) \times h$$

$$\Rightarrow h = \frac{77}{2 \times 11} \Rightarrow h = 3.5 \text{ m}.$$

11. (b) $\dfrac{t}{t+3} = 1\dfrac{1}{4}$

Multiplying both sides by $4(t+3)$, we have:

$$4(t + 3) \times \frac{t}{t+3} = 4(t + 3) \times \frac{5}{4}$$

$$4t = 5(t + 3)$$

$$4t = 5t + 15$$

$$t = -15.$$

12. (a) Statement (i) is true

$$\frac{r_1}{r_2} = \frac{2}{5} \text{ and}$$

$$\frac{\pi r_1^2}{\pi r_2^2} = \left(\frac{r_1}{r_2}\right)^2 = \left(\frac{2}{5}\right)^2 = \frac{4}{25}$$

Statement (ii) is false

Area of square

$$= 14 \times 14 = 196 \text{ cm}^2.$$

Statement (iii) is true:

$$\frac{\pi r_1^2}{\pi r_2^2} = \frac{25}{36}$$

$$\Rightarrow \frac{r_1}{r_2} = \frac{5}{6}$$

Ratio of their circumference

$$= \frac{2\pi r_1}{2\pi r_2} = \frac{r_1}{r_2} = \frac{5}{6}$$

13. (a)

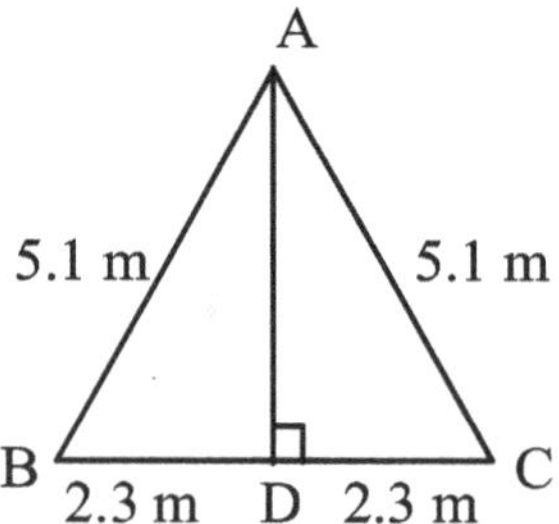

Since area of $DABC = 2 \times$ of $\triangle ADC$

In right angled $\triangle ADC$

$$AD = \sqrt{(5.1)^2 - 2.3^2} = 4.55 \text{ m}$$

$\therefore$ Area of $\triangle ABC = 2.3 \times 4.55$

Since Area of $\triangle ABC = 2 \times$ Area of $\triangle ADC$

$$= 10.47 \text{ sq. m}.$$

14. (b) $0.2(2x - 1) - 0.5(3x - 1) = 0.4$

$$0.4x - 0.2 - 1.5x + 0.5 = 0.4$$

$$-1.1x = 0.1 \quad \text{or} \quad x = \frac{-1}{11}$$

16. (d) Any number divisible by 9 is also divisible by 3.

17. (b) Let $4x$ be the perimeter of the square, so that its area is x^2.

Circumference $= 2\pi r = 4x$

$$\therefore \quad r = \frac{2x}{\pi}$$

$\therefore$ Area

$$= \pi r^2 = \pi\left(\frac{2x}{\pi}\right)^2 = \pi\frac{4}{\pi^2}x^2$$

∴ Ratio of area of the circle and the square

$$= \frac{4}{\pi}x^2 : x^2$$

$$= 4:\pi \text{ or } 4:\frac{22}{7}$$

$$= 28:22 \text{ or } 14:11.$$

18. (c) Let $2A = 3B = 4C = k$

Then, $A = \dfrac{k}{2}$,

$$B = \frac{k}{3}, C = \frac{k}{4}$$

$$A:B:C: \frac{k}{2}:\frac{k}{3}:\frac{k}{4}$$

$$= 6:4:3$$

19. (c) $\dfrac{2}{3}p - \dfrac{5}{2} = \dfrac{7}{2}$

$$\frac{2}{3}p = \frac{7}{2} + \frac{5}{2} \Rightarrow \frac{2}{3}p = 6$$

$$2p = 6 \times 3$$

$$p = \frac{6\times 3}{2} = 9$$

20. (a) Let, $\angle ABC = x$ $\angle CBO = q$

$\angle ACB = y$ $\angle OCB = r$

$\angle BOC = p$

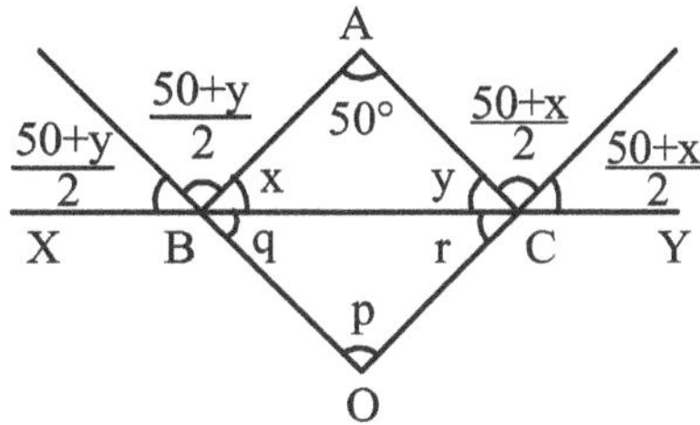

The two interior angles of the triangle are together equal to the exterior angle on the opposite side of the interior angles.

$\Rightarrow$ $50 + y = \angle XBA$

$50 + x = \angle YCA$

But BO and CO are the bisectors of these angles

Hence, $\angle XBA = 2\left(\dfrac{50+y}{2}\right)$ and

$$\angle YCA = 2\left(\frac{50+x}{2}\right)$$

Here, $q = \dfrac{50+y}{2}$

and $r = \dfrac{50+x}{2}$

{vertically opposite angles}

In $\triangle ABC$, $x + y + 50 = 180°$

$x + y = 130°$

In $\triangle BOC$, $q + r + p = 180°$

$$\frac{50+y}{2} + \frac{50+x}{2} + p = 180°$$

$$50 + y + 50 + x + 2p = 360°$$

$$x + y + 2p = 260°$$
$$130° + 2p = 260°$$
$$2p = 130°$$
$$p = 65°$$

21. (b) Let the exterior angle of the polygon be x. Then interior angle of the polygon is $180° - x$.

$$\frac{x}{180° - x} = \frac{1}{4}$$

$$4x = 180° - x$$

$$5x = 180°$$

$$x = 36°$$

Number of side of Polygon =

$$\frac{360°}{\text{exterior angle}}$$

$$\frac{360°}{36°} = 10$$

22. (a) Let the amount taken from each son is ₹ x. Then, 12 − x, 15 − x and 19 − x are in continued proportion.

$$\therefore \quad \frac{12 - x}{15 - x} = \frac{15 - x}{19 - x}$$

$$\Rightarrow (12 - x)(19 - x) = (15 - x)^2$$

or $228 - 12x - 19x + x^2 = 225 - 30x + x^2$

$$\Rightarrow 228 - 31x = 225 - 30x$$

or $228 - 225 = 31x - 30x$

∴ The required amount is ₹ 3.

23. (b) Original price of sofa = ₹ 7,000

Selling price = ₹ 5,500

Decrease in price

$$= 7,000 - 5,500$$

$$= ₹ 1,500$$

Percentage decrease in price

$$= \frac{1500}{7000} \times 100$$

$$= \frac{150}{7} = 21.4\%$$

24. (c) $\dfrac{x}{y} = \dfrac{6}{5}$

$$x = 6k, y = 5k$$

$$\frac{x^2 + y^2}{x^2 - y^2} = \frac{(6k)^2 + (5k)^2}{(6k)^2 - (5k)^2}$$

$$= \frac{61k^2}{11k^2} = \frac{61}{11}$$

26. (a) The seventh day of the month is three days earlier than Friday, which is Tuesday.

So, the fourteenth day is also Tuesday and the nineteenth day is Sunday.

27. (b) $(3x - 4)(5x + 7) = 15x^2 - ax - 28$

$$15x^2 + x - 28$$

$$= 15^2 - ax - 28 \Rightarrow a = -1$$

28. (c) S.P. = ₹ 27.50, Profit = 10%

So, C.P. = ₹ $\left(\dfrac{100}{110} \times 27.50\right) = ₹ 25$

When, S.P. = ₹ 25.75,

Profit = ₹ (25.75 − 25) = ₹ 0.75

$$\therefore \ \text{Profit \%} = \left(\frac{0.75}{25} \times 100\right)\% = 3\%.$$

29. (b) (A) $(3^3)^2 = (3^2)^3 = (9)^3$

(B) $(0^6)^{12} = (0^{18})^{15} = 0$

(C) $(644^3)^0 = 1$ and $(3^0)^{644}$

$= (1)^{644} = 1$

(D) $(2^2)^6 = (4)^6$

$= 4 \times 4 \times 4 \times 4 \times 4 \times 4$

$= 16 \times 16 \times 16 = (16)^3$

30. (b) $-\dfrac{3}{x} = \dfrac{x}{27}$

$x^2 = -81$, which is not a rational number.

31. (b) Situation 2

32. (c) (i), (iii) and (iv)

33. (b) Complementary of $\angle A = 90° - \angle A$

$= 90° - (4x + 2)° = 90° - 4x° - 2°$

$= (88 - 4x)°$

34. (d) From figures (i) and (iv) we conclude that 6, 5, 2 and 3 lie adjacent to 4. It follows that 1 lies opposite to 4.

35. (d) All three outcomes

36. (b) In $\triangle ABC$, $\angle A + \angle B + \angle ACB$

$= 180°$ [Angle sum property]

$60° + 45° + \angle ACB = 180°$

$\angle ACB = 180° - 105° = 75°$

In $\triangle DCE$, $\angle D + \angle E + \angle DCE = 180°$

$80° + \angle E + 75° = 180°$

$\angle E = 180° - 155° = 25°$

37. (b) $a > b < c$

b is the smallest rational number.

38. (c) $\dfrac{10}{100} m = \dfrac{2 \times 20}{100} n$

$m = 4n \Rightarrow m : n = 4 : 1$

39. (b) $2\,C < A + E$, $A + E = C + D$

$\Rightarrow 2C < C + D \Rightarrow C < D$ ...(a)

$A + D = B + C$, $C < D \Rightarrow A < B$

...(b)

$2A > B + D$, $A < B \Rightarrow A > D$

...(c)

$A + E = C + D$, $A > D \Rightarrow E < C$

...(d)

From equations (a), (b), (c) and (d) we get $B > A > D > C > E$

41. (b) Area of the room $= 25\,\text{m} \times 16\,\text{m}$

$= 400\ \text{m}^2$

Area of the brick $= 20\,\text{cm} \times 10\,\text{cm}$

$= \dfrac{1}{5} m \times \dfrac{1}{10} m = \dfrac{1}{50} m^2$

$\therefore$ Number of bricks required

$= \left(400 \div \dfrac{1}{50}\right) = 20{,}000.$

42. (d) Area of parallelogram ABCD

$= AB \times AE$

$= 8 \times 4\ \text{cm}^2 = 32\ \text{cm}^2$

Let altitude corresponding to AD be h. Then,

$h \times AD = 32$

$\Rightarrow h \times 6 = 32$

$\Rightarrow h = \dfrac{32}{6} = \dfrac{16}{3}$

Thus, altitude corresponding to

AD is $\dfrac{16}{3}$ cm.

43. (b) Area of the sign board

= Area of trapezium ABCD −
                      Area of $\triangle$ADE

$= \left[\dfrac{1}{2} \times (6+8) \times (4+3) - \dfrac{1}{2} \times 8 \times 3 \right]$

$= 49 - 12 = 37$ cm^2.

44. (b)

x_i	f_i	$f_i x_i$
44	2	88
58	4	232
74	4	296
61	5	305
62	3	186
	$\sum f_i = 18$	$\sum f_i x_i = 1107$

$\text{Mean} = \dfrac{\sum f_i x_i}{\sum f_i} = \dfrac{1107}{18} = 61.5$

45. (a) In $\triangle$ABC & ADC

$\begin{cases} AB = AD \,(\text{Given}) \\ BC = DC \,(\text{Given}) \\ AC = AC \,(\text{Common}) \end{cases}$

$\triangle$ABC $\cong$ $\triangle$ADC (By SSS)

46. (b) Diameter of circle

$= \sqrt{(8)^2 + (6)^2} = \sqrt{100}$

$= 10 \text{ cm} = r = 5 \text{ cm}$

Required area

= Area of circle − Area of rectangle

$= \dfrac{22}{7}(5)^2 - (6 \times 8)$

$= \dfrac{25 \times 22}{7} - 48$

$= \dfrac{214}{7} = 30.57 \text{ cm}^2$

47. (d) In $\triangle$DBA, DB = DA

$\Rightarrow \angle DBA = \angle BAD = 35°$

In $\triangle$BCD, DC = DB

$\Rightarrow \angle CBD$

$= \angle BCD = 2x$

In $\triangle$ABC, $\angle A + \angle B + \angle C = 180°$

$35° + (35° + 2x) + 2x = 180°$

$4x = 180° - 70° = 110°$

$x = \dfrac{110°}{4} = 27.5°$

48. (c) Total rose production

$= (15 + 12.5 + 12.45 + 20 + 12.4$
$+ 22.5 + 22.4 + 25) \times 1000$

$= 142250$

Now, 10% of total production

$= \dfrac{142250 \times 10}{100} = 14,225.$

Obviously, Haryana, Karnataka and Rajasthan contribute less than 10% in the total production.

49. (d) Total production of rose by all the states = 142250

$$\therefore \text{Average} = \frac{142250}{8}$$

$$= 18 \text{ thousands (Approx.)}$$

50. (d) Total production of states having production below 20,000

$$= 15000 + 12500 + 12450 + 12400 = 52,350$$

$$\therefore \text{Required } \% = \frac{52350}{142250} \times 100$$

$$= 36.8\% \text{ (Approx)}$$

SCIENCE

MOCK TEST-1

ANSWER KEY									
1	(a)	11	(c)	21	(b)	31	(b)	41	(a)
2	(a)	12	(a)	22	(c)	32	(c)	42	(c)
3	(c)	13	(b)	23	(d)	33	(a)	43	(a)
4	(b)	14	(c)	24	(c)	34	(d)	44	(c)
5	(c)	15	(a)	25	(c)	35	(b)	45	(c)
6	(c)	16	(a)	26	(a)	36	(c)	46	(b)
7	(c)	17	(c)	27	(c)	37	(c)	47	(b)
8	(d)	18	(b)	28	(c)	38	(d)	48	(b)
9	(d)	19	(c)	29	(b)	39	(b)	49	(a)
10	(a)	20	(a)	30	(c)	40	(d)	50	(c)

PHYSICS

1. **(a)** Marble tile is a better conductor of heat as compared to a wooden tile.

2. **(a)** The time taken by P is the lowest among the four. It is about $2\frac{1}{2}$ hours, while the others take more time to cover the same distance. Hence, P is the fastest.

3. **(c)** Aluminium foil is a good conductor of heat

4. **(b)** Current carring wire produces magnetic field which deflects the magnetic needle.

5. **(c)** Concave mirror form real images as compared to convex mirror which form virtual images. Plane mirror always forms image of same size as that of object.

6. **(c)** Rotatory motion occurs around a fixed axis.

7. **(c)** $0°\,C = 273\,K$

8. **(d)** Any of the switch can complete the circuit to glow the lamp.

9. **(d)** Different constituents of white light have different wavelengths. So, they travel with different speeds after refraction, though they are traveling with the same speed in air.

10. **(a)** Angle of incidence $= 90° - 65° = 25°$, so angle of incidence $= 25°$.

11. **(c)** Average speed $= \dfrac{2v_1 v_2}{v_1 + v_2}$

$$= \dfrac{2 \times 60 \times 40}{60 + 40}$$

$$= 48\,m/s$$

12. **(a)** Current carrying wire produces magnetic field

13. (b) Distance between object and the image
= 2 × 0.5 = 1 m

14. (c) Steel rod expands on heating.

15. (a) Monsoon is wind carrying water and causese rainfall. Tornado is dark funnel shaped cloud causing storm and heavy rainfall.
Wind is a moving air which can be felt. Thunder storms are a type of lightening in sky during rainy season. Sometimes it causes heavy loss to lives.

CHEMISTRY

16. (a) A - r, B - p, C - s, D - q

17. (c) When an apple slice is cut, oxygen present in oxidises naturally occuring compounds in the apple presence of enzyme.

18. (b) Nylon, acrylic and rayon are artifical fibres while wool and flax are natural fibres.

19. (c) When water evaporates from rivers and seas, liquid water is changed into gaseous water. This is known as water vapour. Water vapour then condenses and forms water droplets which come together to form clouds. Here, gaseous water changes into liquid water. These two parts N and K, of the water cycle involve a change in the state of water. The parts at L and M represent water movement from the clouds back to the Earth. They do not involve any change in states.

20. (a) Weathering is very slow process and loamy soil contain sand, clay and silt.

21. (b) Breaking of plate is a physical change as composition of plate remains the same.

22. (c) Top soil or A - horizon i.e. (i) provides shelter for many living organisms.

23. (d) The process of removing fleece of sheep is called shearing and the person who remove the fleece of sheep is called shearer.

24. (c) Availability of water and minerals in soil for maximum absorption by roots is in the A-horizon.

25. (c) Reaction between an acid and a base is called neutralisation reaction.

26. (a) A - r, B - s, C - q, D - t, E - p

27. (c) A - r, B - q, C - p, D - s

28. (c) Australia and New Zealand.

29. (b) Clayey soil has highest water holding capacity as it is poorly aerated.

30. (c) Water droplets will be formed on inner side of the container due to condensation of water vapour.

BIOLOGY

31. (b) Cyanobacteria are anaerobic photosynthetic bacteria.

32. (c) Earth's weather is caused by un even heating of surface by the radiation of sun.

33. (a) Given plants are producers preparing their own food, by the process of photosynthesis. In this process carbon dioxide is absorbed and oxygen is given out. Most of the animals are heterotrophs.

34. (d) Pholem tissues are responsible for transporting the food prepared in leaves to different parts of the plant.

35. (b) Forests contribute in oxygen production at large scale on the earth. They work as our lungs do in the body.

36. (c) Asthma is not a water born disease. It is a disease related with the function of lungs. It happens due to swelling and deposition of mucus in respiratory tract.

37. (c) Hot and humid climate, abundant rain fall and enough moisture are characteristics of tropical rain forests. That is why a large number of plants and animals find good habitat for survival.

38. (d) Open drain system is a breeding place for different types of vectors like mosquitoes, flies etc. that carry pathogens causing different types of health problems such as diarrhoea, cholera, gastro enteritis etc.

39. (b) (A) - (iv), (B) - (i), (C) - (ii), (D) - (iii)

40. (d) Tropical rain forests support a variety of plants and animals due to availability of enough food and living places. Red eyed frog has sticky pads facilitating to climb on the trees. Toucans are found in South mexico, Central America, Caribbean and tropical regions. They have large and colourful beaks. Its large beak helps in reaching the fruits easily.

41. (a) Option (i), (ii) & (v) are incorrect, the correct statements about these options are as follows–

(i) In insects, circulating body fluids help in osmoregulation, temperature control and transportation of hormones, nutrients and waste products. It has low oxygen carrying capacity.

(ii) Yeasts are microscopic organisms known for fermentation of glucose. Respiration in yeasts takes place in the absence of oxygen.

(v) Maximum capacity of lungs for inhaled air is 3000 mL in a healthy person.

42. (c) Correct options are (i) Liver (ii) Gall bladder (iii) Fats (iv) Fatty acids (v) Glycerol

43. (b) Nevtrophils-

A type of WBC that is an important part of the immune system and help the body fight infection.

44. (c) *Rhizopus* is a fungus. It grows in rainy season or humid atmosphere on breads, pickles and shoes showing brownish, blackish filamentous structure.

45. (c) Reproductive structures of mosses are spores. Underground stems are the reproductive structure of onion which help in vegetative propogation.

46. (b) A → (q), B → (p), C → (s), D → (r)

47. (b) Increase in carbon dioxide will result in global warming.

48. (b) Long hair between the pads on its feet and two thick layers of the fur of polar bear are not meant for hunting prey and getting protection from predators.

49. **(a)** Seeds germinate and give rise to new plants. Pollination leads to fusion of male and female gamete which results in fertilization.

50. **(c)** Gastric Mucous is a hlyco protein that serves two purposes. The lubrication of food masses in order to facilitate movement within the stomach and the formation of a protective layer over the lining epithelium of the stomach cavity.

MOCK TEST-2

ANSWER KEY									
1	(c)	11	(b)	21	(a)	31	(b)	41	(b)
2	(b)	12	(c)	22	(a)	32	(b)	42	(a)
3	(a)	13	(c)	23	(c)	33	(d)	43	(d)
4	(c)	14	(b)	24	(a)	34	(c)	44	(c)
5	(b)	15	(a)	25	(c)	35	(d)	45	(d)
6	(b)	16	(d)	26	(c)	36	(b)	46	(a)
7	(b)	17	(b)	27	(b)	37	(c)	47	(a)
8	(b)	18	(a)	28	(d)	38	(c)	48	(c)
9	(c)	19	(c)	29	(a)	39	(d)	49	(d)
10	(c)	20	(b)	30	(a)	40	(c)	50	(b)

PHYSICS

1. **(c)** Displacement is the shortest distance between the two end points

2. **(b)** When switch is pushed then the circuit is completed and current starts flowing through the electromagnet.

3. **(a)** Iron is a good conductor of heat.

4. **(c)** The energy from the sun is converted to electrical energy by the solar panels, which is then converted to light energy.

5. **(b)** Air is a bad conductor of heat.

6. **(b)** The S.I. unit of time is second, speed is m/s and of distance is metre. The time from one sunrise to the next is called day whereas from one new moon to the next is called month.

7. **(b)** Repulsion is the sure test for magnetism.

8. **(b)** Law of reflection says angle of incidence is equal to angle of reflection

9. **(c)** Thermometer contain a liquid which expand in a uniform manner with temperature.

10. **(c)** Distance between plane mirror and image = 4m

    $\therefore$ Distance between plane mirror and object = 4m
    New distance between plane mirror and object = 3m
    Distance between object and image = $3 \times 2 = 6$m

11. **(b)** Metal expands on heating and contracts on cooling.

12. **(c)** Both the clocks have minute hand so time in minutes can be measured in both clocks.

13. (c) Fuses are safety device which are inserted in the circuit to protect them against excessive flow of current.

14. (b) Concave mirror and convex lens both can produce enlarged image.

15. (a) The fertility depends on neutral state of soil. In coastal areas, the land is generally flooded by sea water which is saline in nature. This decreases the fertility of soil.

CHEMISTRY

16. (d) Both are chemical changes as new substances are formed.

17. (b) Iron sheets are coated with zinc to prevent rusting.

18. (a) Lime water is a solution of $Ca(OH)_2$ in water.

19. (c) A - r, B - q, C - s, D - p

20. (b) Ammonia being basic in nature changes the colour of red litmus to blue.

21. (a) Rock > Gravel > Sand > Silt > Clay

22. (a) Woollen shawl is made up of wool which is obtained from fleece of the sheep without killing them.

23. (c) A - p, B - s, C - r, D - q

24. (a) Window cleaner contains ammonium hydroxide.

25. (c) Substances can be neutral as well. Acids do not turn all indicators red. Lime water being basic turns red litmus to blue.

26. (c) No, it is a physical change and no new substance is formed.

27. (b) Na_2CO_3 is a salt of strong base and weak acid therefore it is basic in nature.

28. (d) Curd and vinegar contain acids

29. (a) Bases have a slippery, soapy feel.

30. (a) The water in the beaker will gain heat.

BIOLOGY

31. (b) *Rhizobium* gets its food from the leguminous plants. It shows symbiotic relation with plant roots.

32. (b) Rainwater harvesting is a process in which rainwater is stored for future use. It helps in supply of drinking water and irrigation.

33. (d) The snowshoe rabbit is adapted for snowy region. White fur of the body of rabbit is helpful to escape from enemy.

34. (c) Suction force causes pulling of water and minerals from the soil. It is a driving force for pulling water upwards.

35. (d) Moist and slimy skin in earthworms and frogs, facilitate the process of respiration.

36. (b) A protective layer is formed by mucus which is secreted by the inner wall of stomach. Due to protective layer, hydro chloric acid has no harmful effect over the wall of stomach.

37. (c) Carbon dioxide present in the blown air turns the lime water into milky.

38. (c) A → (q), B → (p), C → (r), D → (s)

39. (d) Cross pollination requires production of large number of pollen grains for its success.

40. (c) Pollen sacs are found in anther.

41. (b) When you breathe in, or inhale diaphragm contracts and move downwards.

Ribcage moves both upwards and outwards.

42. (a) Villi are finger like projections which are richly supplied with blood vessels. They are present in the inner lining of the small intestine and help in the absorption of nutrients by increasing the surface area for absorption.

43. (d) Symbiosis is a relationship in which two or more than two partners live together causing benefit to each other. For e.g. Relation between roots of pea plant and *Rhizobium.*

44. (c) Fragmentation is a type of reproduction taking place in organism having filamentous structure. In this process, body is divided in many parts each of which creates new similar organisms.

45. (d) Polar bear is adapted for regions full of snow. It is characterized by having fat layer under the skin, curved and sharp claws and thick white fur. Because of these features, it lives in snowy area without any hardships.

46. (a) Burning of forest causes soil erosion creating loss of humidity, reduction of organic matter and porosity of soil. The burnt soil is easily removed by wind and rainfall.

47. (a) Venous blood is dull red in colour.

48. (c) Forests are not responsible for flood condition. They check water current thus preventing soil erosion.

49. (d) P arrow indicates the direction from leaf to other parts of a tree. It is because sugar is formed in leaf during photosynthesis and carried to other parts. **Q** arrow indicates the water supply from roots to leaf for the process of photosynthesis. Water is absorbed by roots and distributed to different parts of the plant.

50. (b)

MOCK TEST-3

ANSWER KEY									
1	(b)	11	(a)	21	(c)	31	(b)	41	(d)
2	(b)	12	(d)	22	(a)	32	(a)	42	(a)
3	(c)	13	(b)	23	(b)	33	(c)	43	(a)
4	(b)	14	(a)	24	(b)	34	(a)	44	(b)
5	(c)	15	(b)	25	(b)	35	(c)	45	(b)
6	(b)	16	(c)	26	(a)	36	(a)	46	(c)
7	(d)	17	(b)	27	(d)	37	(c)	47	(a)
8	(d)	18	(d)	28	(d)	38	(c)	48	(b)
9	(a)	19	(b)	29	(d)	39	(b)	49	(b)
10	(b)	20	(b)	30	(c)	40	(b)	50	(b)

PHYSICS

1. **(b)** Liquid inside the pan is heated by the process of convection.
2. **(b)** If a body covers equal distances in equal intervals of time then body is said to be travelling with uniform speed.
3. **(c)** All the bulbs are in series combination so they glow at same time.
4. **(b)** Size of image in case of plane mirror does not change with distance.
5. **(c)** Both the temperatures are equal because one measures in fahreheit and other in celsius scale. As we know $\dfrac{C}{5} = \dfrac{F-32}{9}$
6. **(b)** Image is called virtual because images are formed in locations where light does not actually reach.
7. **(d)** Battery is based on chemical effect of current.
8. **(d)** A man walks from his home to market with a speed of 5 km/h. Distance = 2.5 km and time = $\dfrac{d}{v} = \dfrac{2.5}{5} = \dfrac{1}{2}$ hr.

   and he returns back with speed of 7.5 km/h in rest of time of 10 minutes.

   Distance = $7.5 \times \dfrac{10}{60} = 1.25 \, km$

   So, Average speed

   $= \dfrac{\text{Total distance}}{\text{Total time}} = \dfrac{(2.5 + 1.25) \, km}{(40/60) \, hr} = \dfrac{45}{8} \, km/hr.$
9. **(a)** Hot air rises up and causes a decrease in air pressure.
10. **(b)** Some amount of light is absorbed at each reflection due to which light intensity decreases after some reflections.
11. **(a)** Iron is a good conductor of heat therefore it conduct away heat given to the paper.
12. **(d)** Time period will be equal to time taken to travel 'AO' and then 'OB' and after that Back to 'A'.
13. **(b)** Rainbow can be seen only when Sun is behind the observer.
14. **(a)** Solid expands on heating.
15. **(b)** Puri is the district head quarter in Odisha. It is situated on the Bay of Bengal. Due to coastal line it is mostly affected by cyclones in monsoon time.

CHEMISTRY

16. **(c)** Iron (Fe) + Oxygen (O_2) + moisture $(H_2O) \rightarrow$ Rust (iron oxide)
17. **(b)** The process in statement (a) is a physical change as the liquid changes to a gaseous state and no new substance is formed.
    In statement (b), LPG burns to form a new substance so it is a chemical change.
18. **(d)** (A) - (i), (B) - (iii), (C) - (ii)
19. **(b)** $HCl \,(X) \xrightarrow{\text{phenolphthalein}}$ colourless

    $NaOH \,(Y) \xrightarrow{\text{phenolphthalein}}$ Pink

    $HCl + NaOH \longrightarrow NaCl + H_2O$
20. **(b)** Soil conservation measures are mainly aimed at protecting top soil.
21. **(c)** Turmeric is an acid-base indicator.

22. (a) Soil is formed by breaking down of rocks.

23. (b) The upper limit of the layer at which all the space between the soil particles and cracks in the rocks are filled with water is called water table.

24. (b) Wool is obtained from sheep. It traps and retain a lot of water and it is suitable for winter wear.

25. (b) Correct sequence of the steps involved in processing of wool are :

Rearing → shearing

→ scouring → sorting

→ removing burr → dyeing

→ making yarn

26. (a) Rusting of iron is a chemical change. Air and water are required for rusting.

Saline water increases the rate of rusting process.

27. (d) Vinegar and curd are acidic in nature Antacid is basic in nature.

28. (d) Carbonic acid is produced by all the given method in the options.

29. (d) Silk fibre is produced by silk worm in pupe stage.

30. (c) Step I involves dissolving of copper sulphate into hot water which is a physical change. In step II crystallisation of copper sulphate occurred which is also a physical change as composition of copper sulphate remains the same.

31. (b) Heat is released when water vapour turns into rain drops during rain formation.

32. (a) Spores are asexual reproductive bodies while gametes are sexual reproductive bodies.

33. (c) Chlorophyll is responsible for the production of starch. Lichen shows the relationship of symbiosis in which two organisms – fungus and alga take part. Fungus provides mineral and shelter to alga and alga prepares food for fungus. Thus both of them survive on bare rock helping each other.

34. (a) Chlorine is used to disinfect water killing certain bacteria and other harmful microbes. It is used for the process of chlorination to purify the water supply.

35. (c) Both have streamlined body.

36. (a) Stomata are small openings found on the lower surface of a leaf. These are responsible for transpiration and exchange of gases.

37. (c) In sewage water, most of the inorganic impurities are related with phosphate compounds derived from different types of detergents. When these materials are discharged in sewage water, they cause phosphate accumulation in polluted water.

38. (c) Yeast is used in wine and beer industries using the process of fermentation. It is a type of fungus which respires anaerobically i.e. without oxygen.

40. (b) Sewerage is the system of a network of pipes used for taking away waste water from houses to the treatment plant.

41. (d) Xylem provides support to plant in transportation of water with minerals and phloem is responsible for carrying food from leaves to different parts of the plant.

42. (a) Starch and sugar are carbohydrates
Cellulose cannot be digested in our digestive system due to lack of appropriate enzyme.

43. (a) When bees collect nectar from the flower, it helps in carrying pollen grains to other places. Bees touch anthers to collect pollen grain from a flower.

45. (b) Tropical region is characterized by rain forest having areas of biodiversity. It has dense vegetation, variety of animals such as– monkeys, birds, elephants, snakes and frog etc.

46. (c) The temperature range of tropical rain forests is 21 to 30°C.

47. (a) $A \rightarrow (r); B \rightarrow (s); C \rightarrow (q); D \rightarrow (p)$

49. (b) Molars and premolars are responsible for grinding the food.

50. (b) Penguins are aquatic animal living mainly in Antarctica region. They are flightless birds but they are good swimmers.

MOCK TEST-4

ANSWER KEY									
1	(b)	11	(c)	21	(d)	31	(b)	41	(c)
2	(a)	12	(a)	22	(a)	32	(d)	42	(d)
3	(c)	13	(b)	23	(d)	33	(c)	43	(a)
4	(c)	14	(b)	24	(c)	34	(a)	44	(d)
5	(b)	15	(d)	25	(d)	35	(b)	45	(d)
6	(a)	16	(d)	26	(d)	36	(d)	46	(c)
7	(b)	17	(a)	27	(b)	37	(d)	47	(a)
8	(a)	18	(b)	28	(c)	38	(c)	48	(a)
9	(c)	19	(a)	29	(b)	39	(c)	49	(d)
10	(b)	20	(b)	30	(d)	40	(c)	50	(a)

PHYSICS

1. (b) Speed while going to school

$$= \frac{\frac{3}{30}}{60} = 6 \text{ km/hr}$$

Speed while coming back home

$$= \frac{\frac{3}{20}}{60} = 9 \text{ km/hr}$$

$$\text{Average speed} = \frac{6+9}{2} = 7.5 \text{ km/hr}$$

2. **(a)** By Joule's law when current is passed through conductor then heat energy is released.

3. **(c)** Particle has same average velocity between 0 to 10 and 10 to 20 seconds but in opposite directions.

4. **(c)** Inside of spoon acts as concave mirror and outer side acts as convex mirror.

5. **(b)** As P is acting as an electromagnet, it should be made of a soft-magnetic material such as soft iron. Q needs to be a magnetic material, such as soft iron, and R is a permanent magnet, thus it is made of steel.

6. **(a)** Prism by the method of dispersion split the white light into its seven constituent colours.

7. **(b)** Cyclist is covering unequal distances in equal intervals of time so he is moving with non-uniform motion.

8. **(a)** Heat always flows from a hotter region to a colder one. Since iron is a good conductor of heat, more heat will flow from our body into it and we will feel it as cold. As paper is a bad conductor less heat will flow from our body.

9. **(c)** Graph (c) represents a body moving with uniform motion which comes to rest suddenly.

10. **(b)** Air moves from a region of high pressure to low pressure.

11. **(c)** Rainbow always shows 'VIBGYOR' from bottom to top.

12. **(a)** Thermometer (i) and (iii) can measure body temprature but (ii) cannot

13. **(b)** Current can flow in a circuit only when it is closed.

14. **(b)** Concave lens always forms virtual erect and diminished size of image.

15. **(d)** Generally cyclones develop due to high temperatures which creates low pressure. It causes attraction of wind towards low pressure zone.

CHEMISTRY

16. **(d)** Painting and greasing iron articles prevent them from rusting.

17. **(a)** Sorter's disease is caused by bacterium *Bacillus anthracis*.

19. **(a)** All alkalies are bases but reverse is not true. Hence option (a) is correct.

20. **(b)** Correct order from (i) to (iv) will be gravel, sand, clay, humus

21. **(d)** Rusting is a phenomen on of formation of oxide layer on metal surface in presence of air and moisture. This process speeds up in the presence of salt.

22. **(a)** A → (r); B→ (q); C → (p); D →(s)

23. **(d)** China rose indicator gives magenta colour in acidic medium, green colour in basic medium and no colour change in neutral medium.

24. **(c)** Rate of evaporation depends on the surface area of the water in the vessel. II vessel has more surface area.

∴ Rate of evaporation will be faster in II and slowest in I. Since each vessel contain equal amount of water initially, therefore (c) represent the correct volume of water in each container after five hours. (volume of water decreases with time in each vessel.)

25. (d)

S.No.	Name of breed	Quality of wool	State where found
1.	Lohi	Good quality wool	Rajasthan, Punjab
2.	Rampur bushair	Brown fleece	Uttar Pradesh, Himachal Pradesh
3.	Nali	Carpet wool	Rajasthan, Haryana, Punjab
4.	Bakharwal	For woollen shawls	Jammu and Kashmir

26. (d) X represents loamy soil which is a mixture of sand, silt and clay. Loamy soil is best suited for cultivation.

27. (b) Eggs → caterpillar → cocoon → pupa → adult moth

28. (c) X is methyl orange as it turns yellow in basic medium i.e. in presence of Y which is basic in nature having H^+ ions < OH^- ions.

29. (b) (i) is a physical change as it involves conversion in state i.e. liquid kerosene into vapour. While (ii) is a chemical change.

BIOLOGY

31. (b) This site is about vermicomposting flush toilets-on-site processing of domestic sewage with earth worms.

32. (d) Sand, fine gravel and medium gravel are used to filter the polluted water. First of all water is passed through medium gravel then fine gravel, then into sand. Upto this level, pollutants and suspensions are filtered maximum.

33. (c) The roots of pea plants have nodules. These nodules contain nitrogen fixing bacteria which fix nitrogen in soil increasing the fertility of farmland.

34. (a) The process of chewing breaks down large part of food into small particles. During this period, saliva mixes with food. It helps in digestion.

35. (b) Autotrophs are known as producers which are mostly plants. Plants prepare food through the process of photosynthesis.

36. (d) After the process of pollination, the stigma, of flower which receives the pollern grains is withered and dropped off.

37. (d) Lactic acid is produced during heavy exercise in our muscle cells. It causes tiredness and we feel the need of relaxation and comfort.

38. (c) Biogas and sludge are products which are formed during treatment of waste water. Biogas is used as fuel.

39. (c) Intestinal villi are finger–like outgrowths which are responsible for absorption of digested food.

40. (c) Pulmonary artery carries blood having CO_2. Pulmonary vein carries blood having O_2.

41. **(c)** Oesophagus is a food pipe reaching stomach. Epiglottis protects the windpipe against entering of food or water.

42. **(d)** Cockroches are insects having flattened body shape helping in crawling between crevices and spaces for habitat and safety.

43. **(d)** The steps involved in human nutrition are as follows. Ingestion $\rightarrow$ digestion $\rightarrow$ absorption $\rightarrow$ assimilation ad egestion

44. **(b)** The sticky pads help the frogs to climb the trees.

45. **(d)** Capillaries are minute tube like structures which link between tissues and arteries– They perform the function of nutrients absorption and exchange of gases such as – CO_2 and O_2.

46. **(c)** The large ears of the elephant help it to keep cool in the hot and humid climate of rain forests.

47. **(a)** The correct sequence of budding in yeast is as follows:– entry of nucleus into bud $\rightarrow$ formation of bud on outer surface of parent cell $\rightarrow$ doubling of nucleus and division $\rightarrow$ partition between parent cell and the bud $\rightarrow$ breaking of bud and evolution of a new daughter cell.

48. **(a)** The digestion of cellulose rich food material does not take place in our intestine. The reason is that there is lack of cellulose digesting enzymes in human body.

49. **(d)** The layer of oil over the water prevents evaporation of water and breeding of mosquitoes. Due to oily layer, the larvae of mosquitoes do not respire properly and get destroyed.

50. **(a)** Scales of snaks help them in protect them from drying and also helps them to crawl.

MOCK TEST-5

ANSWER KEY

1	(c)	11	(b)	21	(a)	31	(d)	41	(c)
2	(a)	12	(c)	22	(a)	32	(a)	42	(a)
3	(d)	13	(a)	23	(a)	33	(a)	43	(d)
4	(a)	14	(c)	24	(b)	34	(b)	44	(a)
5	(b)	15	(b)	25	(a)	35	(d)	45	(c)
6	(c)	16	(a)	26	(a)	36	(b)	46	(a)
7	(a)	17	(c)	27	(a)	37	(b)	47	(a)
8	(d)	18	(a)	28	(c)	38	(b)	48	(a)
9	(a)	19	(b)	29	(a)	39	(c)	49	(d)
10	(c)	20	(c)	30	(d)	40	(d)	50	(b)

PHYSICS

1. **(c)** Kamal is using a plane mirror whereas Tarun is using convex mirror.

2. **(a)** Soil is bad conductor of heat. Metals are good conductor of heat.

3. **(d)** Both are moving with same speed but 'B' will always ahead of 'A' by 20 m.

4. **(a)** Since the shiny aluminium foil is pasted on the outer surface of the ball, this behaves like a convex mirror.

5. **(b)** Distance travelled = Area under graph

$$= \frac{1}{2} \times 3 \times 6$$

$$= 9 \text{ m}$$

6. **(c)** Black colour being a better absorber of heat, bulb X gets more heated due to heat radiated by the electric bulb resulting in the expansion of air inside it. The expanded air requires more space and thus pushes the alcohol towards limb Y.

7. **(a)** Only circuit A provide the closed path for the current to flow and then bulb will glow.

8. **(d)** Mercury is used in thermometer because it is a liquid metal having large coefficient of expansion.

9. **(a)** Time period of simple pendulum remains constant

$$T = 2\pi\sqrt{\frac{\ell}{g}}$$

10. **(c)** Wood is a bad conductor of electricity, if it is dried then it will act as an insulator.

11. **(b)** When two blocks of ice are pressed together little heat is generated due to pressure and friction just melts the outer layers. When that two blocks are melted friction decreases and due to the low temp of both the ice cubes the water just refreezes.

12. **(c)** Normal human body temperature is 37° C

13. **(a)** Concave mirror or convex lens only form real image of the object.

14. **(c)** Electric heater is based on heating effect of current.

15. **(b)** A tornado is a voilent twisting funnel of wind which appears due to low pressure of wind. It causes destruction of plants, trees, animals and humans etc.

CHEMISTRY

17. **(c)** Iron $(Fe) \xrightarrow[(O_2 \text{ and } H_2O)]{\text{moist air}} \underset{\text{Rust}}{Fe_2O_3}$

Process of rusting becomes faster when humidity is high and it can be prevented by applying grease or by depositing a layer of metal like zinc.

19. **(b)** Base (p) + phenolphthalein
(pink solution)

$\xrightarrow{\text{Acid (q)}}$ Colourless solution

$\xrightarrow{\text{Base (r)}}$ Pink solution

20. **(c)** A - iv, B - i, C - iii, D - ii

22. **(a)** Turmeric turns red in basic solution and remains yellow in acidic and neutral solution.

23. **(a)** Shearing involves removing fleece from the body of the

sheep. It does not harm the sheep as only uppermost layer of skin is removed which is made up of dead cells.

24. (b) Percolation rate (mL/min)

$$= \frac{\text{Amount of water percolated(mL)}}{\text{Percolation time (min)}}$$

$$20 \text{ mL/min} = \frac{200 \text{ mL}}{\text{Percolation time}}$$

$$\text{Percolation time} = \frac{200 \text{ mL}}{20 \text{ mL} / \text{min}}$$

$$= 10 \text{ min}$$

$$= 10 \times 60 \text{ second}$$

$$= 600 \text{ s}$$

25. (a) (A) - (ii), (B) - (iii), (C) - (iv), (D) - (i)

26. (a) Forest prevent soil erosion as trees reduce the force and speed of raindrops.

27. (a) Wool is made up of proteins like our hairs.

28. (c) The sting of an ant releases formic acid.

29. (a) Irreversible physical changes
- Cutting a log of wood into pieces
- Punching a hole in a paper

Chemical change
- Breaking down of ozone
- Lime water turns milky
- Digestion of food

Reversible Physical change
- Melting of glaciers.

30. (d) P = aquifer, Q = Soil,
R = Permeable rocks,
S = water table

31. (d) The correct order of the events during digestive process moistening as follows :
I. moistening of food and beginning of starch breakdown
II. liquification of food, breakdown of protein
III. proteins carbohydrates, fats breakdown, absorption of nutrients in blood.
IV. Absorption of water and vitamins.

32. (a) Accumulation of lactic acid causes cramps in muscles. Generally it happens after heavy physical work.

33. (a) Pretending as dead is a good trick to decieve the predators or other enemies. It is a behavioural adaptation shown by hognose snake.

35. (d) In given figure, the organism (X) is (i) Hydra. It adopts predatory mode of nutrition in which prey (Y) is trapped by its tentacles.

37. (b) Gold fish feeds on larvae of mosquitoes present in the pond water. Thus breeding of mosquitoes is prevented.

38. (b) The gills are helpful in breathing. The gills are supplied with blood vessels which absorb O_2 dissolved in water.

39. (c) Saprophytic organisms get their food from decomposing organic matters present in the surrounding.

40. (d) Oily material and fats will block the drainage system and will not help in elimination of water.

41. (c) Ammonia (NH_3) is the excretory product in aquatic animals. It is given out from the body through gaseous exchange during breathing.

42. (a) Due to increase in temperature on land, the winds flow from the land towards the ocean. In winter, the ocean water does not warm easily.

43. (d) Ginger is a farming product which is grown in farms where as gum, honey and catechu are obtained from forest.

44. (a) The correct order of the process of nutrition in Numinants is as follows–
Swallowing of food → incomplete food digestion → chewing of cud (half chewed food/grass) → complete digestion.

45. (c) With the help of urine test, a doctor diagnoses some diseases in the patient such as – presence of pathogens, presence of some harmones etc. It does not indicate the function of various organs in the body.

46. (a) The amount of CO_2 in exhaled air is high. It is due to production of CO_2 during respiration process taking place within the tissues of body.

47. (a) Germination occurs when the favourable conditions are available so that the dormant embryo present within a seed is activated.

48. (a) Polar region is the coldest part of the earth. It is due to axial tilt of the earth. This region receives very low sunlight.

49. (d) • Phloem tubes are responsible for transportation of food from leaves to different part of the plant. These are found throughout plant body. An adult human contains 5-6 litres blood in the body.
• The number of Red blood cells is higher than white blood cells.

50. (b) A turkey bird is resident of North America. Its wings are underdeveloped and body weight is comparatively more. So it is unable to fly.

GENERAL KNOWLEDGE

MOCK TEST-1

ANSWER KEY

1	(b)	4	(b)	7	(d)	10	(a)	13	(c)	16	(a)	19	(d)	22	(a)	25	(c)
2	(c)	5	(a)	8	(a)	11	(c)	14	(a)	17	(a)	20	(b)	23	(a)		
3	(c)	6	(c)	9	(b)	12	(d)	15	(c)	18	(c)	21	(d)	24	(a)		

1. **(b)** Nose is the prominent feature of proboscis monkey.

2. **(c)** Siberian Husky is a dog which was initially used as sled animal.

3. **(c)** The science of classification of animals and plants on the basis of characterstics is called taxonomy.

4. **(b)** We provide electricity by turning on plug to the washing machine and it performs mechanical work by washing clothes.

5. **(a)** A → (q), B → (r), C → (s), D → (p)

6. **(c)** Cutting of wood is a physical change as no new substance is formed. Conversion of manure from leaves is a chemical change.

7. **(d)** Algae and fungi live in a symbiotic relationship. The fungus provides water and minerals to the algae. The algae in turn provides prepared food to the fungus both depend on each other.

8. **(a)** During digestion food is broken down into simple substances so that the nutrients are easily absorbed by blood.

9. **(b)** Tropical rain forests are found on either side of equator. They receive heavy rainfall and have equal duration of day and night.

10. **(a)** The correct order is:
Nostrils → larynx → trachea

11. **(c)** Vegetative propagation occurs in vegetative parts of plants; stems, roots and leaves.

12. **(d)** All these things should not be thrown in the drain as they may cause chobing of the drain.

13. **(c)** Mughal empire started with : Babur (1526-1530) followed by Humayun (1530-1540), (1555-1556), Akbar (1556-1605) ,Jahangir (1605-1627) , Shah Jahan 1627-1658 and Aurangzeb (1658-1707).

17. **(a)** Kushwant Singh has written the novel 'Train to Pakistan'.

18. **(c)** World Hand Hygiene Day is observed every year on May 5 globally. The day is organized by the World Health Organization (WHO). The main aim of the day is to make people across the globe more aware of the importance of hand hygiene in health care facilities, thus protecting health care workers and patients from infections. Theme for the year 2020: "SAVE LIVES: Clean your hands".

19. **(d)** Eminent Historian Hari Shankar Vasudevan passed away at the age of 68 in a private hospital at Kolkata after testing positive for novel coronavirus on May 6th 2020.

20. **(b)** Kiara scored good marks because she was consistent in her studies.

21. **(d)** Indian professional tennis player Sania Mirza (33) has created new history by becoming the 1st Indian to win Fed Cup Heart Award 2020 for Asia/Oceania zone. She decided to give a prize money of $ 2000 to the Telangana Chief Minister Relief Fund to help battle against coronavirus.

22. **(a)** International Nurses Day (IND) is an international event observed every year on May 12 globally to commemorate the birth anniversary of Florence Nightingale. She was also known as 'The Lady with the

Lamp'. This year the day marks the 202th birth anniversary of Florence Nightingale. Theme for the year 2022: Nurses: A voice to lead- Nursing the World to Health.

23. (a) Karnataka government and Congress Vice President Rahul Gandhi had launched 'Indra Canteen' in Bengaluru to reach out to the poorer sections of the society.

24. (a) According to WHO, a person can take precautions by covering the nose and mouth while sneezing via tissue or an elbow. Then, immediately throw the tissue into a closed dustbin.

25. (c) Coronavirus may cause illness from the common cold to more other serious diseases like Middle East Respiratory Syndrome (MERS-CoV) and Severe Acute Respiratory Syndrome (SARS-CoV).

MOCK TEST-2

ANSWER KEY

1	(b)	4	(d)	7	(b)	10	(c)	13	(a)	16	(d)	19	(b)	22	(c)	25	(b)
2	(c)	5	(c)	8	(d)	11	(a)	14	(d)	17	(a)	20	(b)	23	(d)		
3	(a)	6	(b)	9	(d)	12	(c)	15	(d)	18	(b)	21	(a)	24	(d)		

1. (b) Oology is the study of bird eggs, nest and breeding behaviour.

2. (c) Okapi is a zebra-like animal that is native to Democratic Republic of Congo in Central Africa.

3. (a) Maharashtra is the largest producer of cashews in India.

4. (d) Zinc is used in electroplating to make objects rust-free.

5. (c) In deserts the sand radiates heat very quickly as compared to earth and so deserts have cooler nights.

6. (b) In an electric motor, electrical energy gets connected to mechanical energy.

7. (b) A → (r), B → (p), C → (q), D → (s)

8. (d) Correct sequence is
Shearing → Scouring → Sorting → Picking of burrs → Grading → Dyeing

9. (d) Excessive use of insecticides and fertilizers causes soil pollution.

10. (c) A pitcher plant has a pitcher shaped leaf, with the apex of leaf forming the lid of the pitcher.

11. (a) Photosynthesis is the only process through which green plants prepare food. All other organisms are dependent on green plants directly or indirectly.

12. (c) Saline contains enzyme which breaks down starch into sugars.

13. (a) Polar bears have strong sense of smell which help then to locate their prey.

14. (d) Water table of a place depends on rainfall and water seepage.

15. (d) (a) and (b) refer to sewage.

16. (d) Moth ki Masjid was built during the rule of Sikandar Lodhi by his wazir in Delhi.

17. (a) A - II, B - IV, C - I, D - III

19. (b) The book 'River of Smoke'is not written by V.S. Naipaul.

20. (b) U.S Polo Assn. is an American luxury clothing brand.

21. (a) 22 balls are there on the table at the start of a snooker game.

22. (c) Dress code is the rule for wearing clothes at a particular place.

23. (d) According to the World Economic Forum (WEF)'s global Energy Transition Index (ETI) 2022, India has moved up two places from rank 87th Sweden

(74.2%) topped for the 3rd consecutive time followed by Switzerland (73.4%) and Finland (72.4%). The index is a composite score of 40 indicators, benchmarks 115 countries on the current performance of their energy system, and readiness for transition to a secure, sustainable, affordable, and inclusive future energy system.

24. (d) Israel named a street in Tel Aviv after Indian poet Rabindranath Tagore on his 159th birth anniversary to honor his valuable contributions in the field and to mankind. He was born on May 7, 1861, in Calcutta. In Bengal Rabindra Jayanti is celebrated on the 25th day of the Bengali month of Boishakh.

25. (b) China has won the 1st edition of FIDE Chess.com online Nations Cup 2020 chess tournament took place from 5-10 May 2020, through a chess.com platform. China's team, which won the prize money of $48,000, became the champion on the basis of scoring the most points in the league stage despite playing a 2-2 draw against the US (United States) in the final.

MOCK TEST-3

ANSWER KEY

1	(c)	4	(d)	7	(d)	10	(a)	13	(c)	16	(d)	19	(d)	22	(c)	25	(c)
2	(b)	5	(a)	8	(b)	11	(d)	14	(b)	17	(a)	20	(b)	23	(d)		
3	(d)	6	(b)	9	(d)	12	(c)	15	(c)	18	(d)	21	(b)	24	(c)		

1. (c) Giant panda is an endangered species which feeds on bamboo and is found in China.

2. (b) Sharks are cartilaginous fish which live in deep sea.

3. (d) All these statements are Correct.

4. (d) Baking soda forms CO_2 when mixed with vinegar and forms bubbles. It also makes dough rise while baking. It neutralizes acidic odours.

5. (a) Michael Faraday discovered link between electricity and magnetism called electro-magnetism.

7. (d) Vandhe Bharat mission is the massive repatriation operation planned by the Indian government to bring back stranded Indians in different parts of the world in the wake of the coronavirus crisis. In the first phase that started on May 7, more than 60 "non-scheduled, commercial" flights will operate from about 12 countries to bring back 15,000 citizens. The second phase of the Vandhe Bharat mission in the third week of May is expected to cover European nations.

8. (b) Oxides of nitrogen and sulphur dissolves in rain water to form corresponding acids. This result into acid rain.

9. (d) Muddy water is a mixture of mud and water.

10. (a) (b) and (c) are incomplete

11. (d) Meteorological department issues about alerts cyclone etc.

12. (c) A $\rightarrow$ s, B $\rightarrow$ p, C $\rightarrow$ q, D $\rightarrow$ r.

13. (c) We should use sewers for removal of urban waste and we should not excrete in open these measures can prevent water pollution.

16. (d) Midday meal scheme is a school meal programme of the Government of India designed to improve the nutritional status of school children.

17. (a) Earthquake starts from the epicenter in the earth's crust.

21. (d) Benjamin Netanyahu has been sworn as the Israel Prime Minister (PM) for the 6th time.

23. (d) The International Cricket Council (ICC) Cricket Committee, chaired by former Indian cricketer & commentator, Anil Kumble has recommended a ban on the use of saliva to make the ball shine due to the Covid-19 (Coronavirus) pandemic. However, the committee considered ball-shining as safe from the use of sweat.

24. (c) In view of the ongoing lockdown in the country due to Coronavirus (COVID-19), Kotak Mahindra Bank has become the 1st bank in India to allow video Know your customer (KYC) facility for its customers opening savings account (SA) on Kotak 811 platform.

MOCK TEST-4

ANSWER KEY

1	(b)	5	(b)	9	(c)	13	(b)	17	(b)	21	(b)	25	(c)	29	(b)	33	(a)	37	(b)
2	(a)	6	(b)	10	(b)	14	(b)	18	(d)	22	(b)	26	(b)	30	(b)	34	(b)	38	(a)
3	(c)	7	(b)	11	(b)	15	(c)	19	(b)	23	(d)	27	(a)	31	(a)	35	(b)	39	(a)
4	(b)	8	(a)	12	(b)	16	(b)	20	(c)	24	(d)	28	(d)	32	(a)	36	(a)	40	(a)

3. (b) A tropical reinforest has four distinct layers.

(i) **Emergent layer** - This layer is at the top and only giant trees reach this level. This layer is very sunny.

(ii) **Canopy** - This is the thickest layer and most trees grow to this height.'

(iii) **Understorey** - This layer consisto of herbs and shrubs. Not much sunlight reaches this layer due to dense canopy.

(iv) **Forest floor**- This layer is dark, damp and full of dead leaves, plants and twigs.

6. (b) Baliapal movement started in Odisha against testing of missiles on fertile land.

7. (b) 1 Hour = 3600 seconds

1 nanosecond = 10^{-9} seconds

1 microsecond = 10^{-6} seconds

1 light year = 9.4×10^{15} m

Nanosecond is the smallest unit

9. (c) Convex mirror is used for this purpose.

11. (b) The appointments committee of the union cabinet appointed Govinda Rajulu Chintala as Chairman of National Bank for Agriculture and Rural Development (NABARD). He was the successor of Harsh Kumar Bhanwala. Shaji K V and P.V.S Suryakumar have been appointed as Deputy Managing Directors (DMD) of NABARD.

13. (b) No new products are formed in a physical change.

14. (b) Pitcher plant is an insectivorous plant which derives its nutrition from insects. They eat insects to fulfill their protein requirement.

18. (d) The Karnataka State Mango Department and Marketing Corporation Ltd. (KSMD&MCL) and Flipkart signed a memorandum of understanding (MoU) to support the mango farmers in this mango season to sell their produce through the online platform of Flipkart.

20. (c) A powerful super-cyclone Amphan, making landfall at 2.30 p.m. between Digha in West Bengal and Hatiya island in Bangladesh with winds of about 120mph (190km/h), has killed at least 22 people and destroying thousands of homes. "Amphan", pronounced as "Um-pun", means sky. The name was given by Thailand in 2004.

26. (b) The practice of sati was prevalent in the Rajput community Now this practice has been banned and made illegal under the Prevention of Sati Act of 1987.

31. (a) The transfer of water from one system to another and back again is called the water cycle.

37. (b) Indian classical dance form Sattriya belongs to Assam.

38 (a) He was a Brazilian footballer Socrates.

39. (a) The World Bank named former Bear Stearns executive Carmen Reinhart as its new Vice President (VP) and chief economist, tapping an expert on financial crises who also serves on the advisory board of the New York Federal Reserve. Reinhart's appointment is effective on June 15, 2020.

MOCK TEST- 5

ANSWER KEY

1	(a)	5	(a)	9	(a)	13	(a)	17	(c)	21	(d)	25	(d)	29	(c)	33	(d)	37	(b)
2	(a)	6	(d)	10	(c)	14	(c)	18	(d)	22	(c)	26	(c)	30	(b)	34	(a)	38	(c)
3	(a)	7	(a)	11	(c)	15	(d)	19	(c)	23	(a)	27	(d)	31	(c)	35	(b)	39	(d)
4	(c)	8	(c)	12	(a)	16	(d)	20	(c)	24	(b)	28	(b)	32	(a)	36	(c)	40	(b)

1. (a) Cinchona bark contains quinine, which is a medicine used to treat *malaria*. It also contains quinidine which is a medicine used to treat heart palpitations

2. (a) The smallest of all canids, fennec foxes sport extraordinarily large ears that help them hunt at night.

4. (c) Priestley pursued his investigations of gases. On 1st August 1774, hediscovered oxygen.

6. (d) The weak zones where earthquakes are more likely to occur are called as seismic zones. These zones are also called as fault zones.

7. (a) One person, Linus Pauling, has won two undivided Nobel Prizes. In 1954 he won the Prize for Chemistry. Eight years later he was awarded the Peace Prize for his opposition to weapons of mass destruction.

8. (c) India's first manned space flight - Gaganyaan - is expected to send three persons into the space for seven days and the spacecraft will be placed in a low earth orbit of 300-400 km.

10. (c) Rashtriya Vayoshri Yojana is scheme for providing Physical Aids and Assisted-living Devices for Senior citizens belonging to BPL category. This is a Central Sector Scheme, fully funded by the Central Government. Rashtriya Vayoshri Yojana in Nellore District of Andhra Pradesh.

11. (c) Potential energy is the energy possessed by an object due to its position. Since, water stored in a dam is present at a greater height with respect to ground, it possesses potential energy.

12. (a) Thorny bushes are found in dry and hot subtropical areas with seasonal rainfall as low as 500 millimeters. The rainfall is very low and therefore these areas are usually deserts. The bushes shed their leaves seasonally to avoid loss of water.

13. (a) A→ s, B → p, C → q, D → r

14. (c) Tungsten is used in bulbs due to its high melting point and resistivity.

15. (d) In the Philippines and Japan, it is called the 'typhoon'.

16. (d) The industrial disease usually associated with wool textiles is anthrax.

17. (c) Antacids act as neutralizing agents. These agents treat stomach acidity by neutralizing gastric hydrochloric acid or preventing the secretion of acid.

18. (d) *Manipur's* "Khudol" has been listed among the top 10 global initiatives for an inclusive fight against the COVID-19 pandemic.

19. (c)   20.   (c)   21.   (d)

22. (c) Elephants have long ears that help keep them cool in hot and humid climates.

23. (a) A → r, B → s, C → q, D → p

24. (b)

25. (d) Thanjavur, Madurai and Somnath are some examples of temple towns. These cities and towns feature a form of urbanisation where the town is developed around a prominent temple.

26. (c) The Kolkata Port (KoPT), located on the left bank of Hugli River is the first major as well as the only riverine port in India.

27. (d) I, II, III and IV

28. (b) On *May 24, 2020*Uttarakhand became the 1ststate to release a report highlighting its conservation efforts to save over 1,100 rare plants from extinction.

29. (c) A sonnet is a poem of 14 lines that reflects upon a single issue or idea.

30. (b) The Blue Umbrella is a 1980 Indian novel written by Ruskin Bond.

31. (c) It'll be a long time before The Simpsons is dethroned as the longest-running scripted primetime series in the history of American television.

32. (a) Lady Gaga, is an American singer, songwriter and actress. She is known for her image reinventions and musical versatility. Gaga began performing as a teenager, singing at open mic nights and acting in school plays.

34. (a) The Ickabog is a fairy tale by J. K. Rowling. The story was published in installments by Rowling online, before its official publication in November 2020. The Ickabog is Rowling's first children's book since Harry Potter and the Deathly Hallows was published in 2007.

35. (b) MalalaYousafzai, 19 has been appointed United Nations (UN) Messenger of Peace by the UN Secretary-General, Antonio Gutteres, on April 10th, 2017 and became the youngest person ever to receive the distinction.

38. (c) The 2024 Summer Olympics officially the Games of the XXXIII Olympiad and commonly known as Paris 2024, is an upcoming international multi-sport event that is scheduled to take place from 26 July to 11 August 2024 with Paris as its main host city.

39. (d) VikasAbhaya is the name of the scheme launched by Karnataka VikasGrameena Bank to provide loan to Micro, Small and Medium Enterprises.

40. (b)

LOGICAL REASONING

MOCK TEST-1

ANSWER KEY

1	(a)	6	(d)	11	(c)	16	(a)	21	(b)
2	(b)	7	(c)	12	(a)	17	(b)	22	(d)
3	(c)	8	(c)	13	(c)	18	(b)	23	(b)
4	(b)	9	(c)	14	(b)	19	(d)	24	(c)
5	(a)	10	(d)	15	(c)	20	(c)	25	(a)

1. **(a)** The pattern is $\times 4 - 2$, $\times 4 - 2$, ... So, $88 - 2 = 86$

2. **(b)** The pattern is $+6 - 3$, $+6 - 3$, ... So, $27 - 3 = 24$

3. **(c)** In each next step, the pin rotates 90° CW and the arrow rotates 90° ACW.

4. **(b)** $\dfrac{27 \times 1}{3} = 9; \dfrac{6 \times 7}{3} = 14;$

$\dfrac{9 \times 7}{3} = 21$

5. **(a)** The position of the alphabets from the beginning and the last is the same.

6. **(d)** 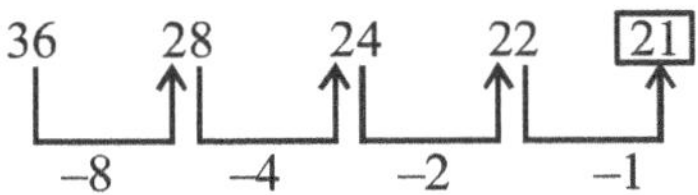

7. **(c)** Except Veranda, all others are surrounded by four walls.

8. **(c)** The pattern is as follows :

$$36 \quad 28 \quad 24 \quad 22 \quad \boxed{21}$$
$$-8 \qquad -4 \qquad -2 \qquad -1$$

9. **(c)** The pattern is as follows :

$$D \xrightarrow{+4} H \xrightarrow{+4} L \xrightarrow{+4} P \xrightarrow{+4} T$$
$$A \xrightarrow{+4} E \xrightarrow{+4} I \xrightarrow{+4} M \xrightarrow{+4} Q$$

10. **(d)** There is no 'A' letter in the given word.

11. **(c)** Arrangement of words as per dictionary:

1. Latch
↓
2. Latitude
↓
3. Laugh
↓
4. Laurels

12. **(a)** The first letter of the word is moved one step forward to obtain the first letter of the code, while the other letters remain unaltered.

13. **(c)**

R	O	S	E	C	H	A	I	P
6	8	2	1	7	3	4	5	9

From the coding pattern, it is clear that codes for S, E, A, R, C and H are 2, 1, 4, 6, 7 and 3 respectively.

14. (b) This group of items can be represented as in the figure given below.

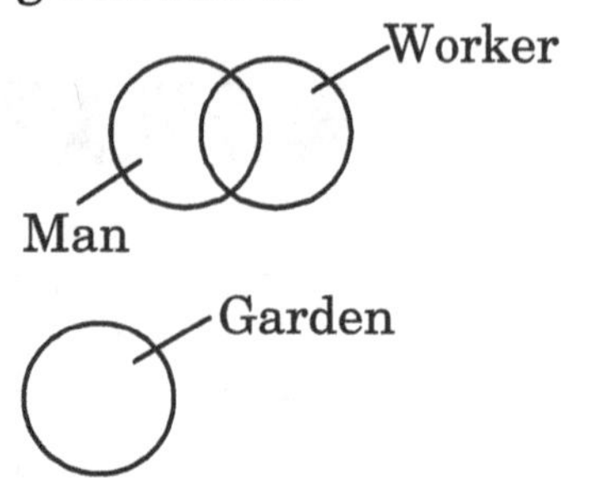

15. (c) Raman's rank from the start
= (Total number of students) − (Raman's rank from the end) + 1
= 39 − 24 + 1
= 16 th.

16. (a) S is the father of Q's mother. Hence, S is Maternal grandfather of Q.

17. (b) The movements of the cat and the distance the cat covers from point to point are shown in the diagram. The cat finally comes at G. So, the cat is finally facing North.

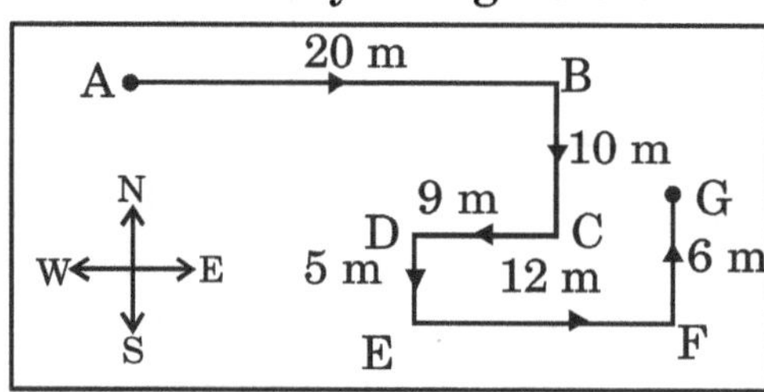

18. (b) Given expression = (10 × 4) + (4 × 4) − 6
= 40 + 16 − 6 = 50

19. (d) Number of triangles = 14

Triangles are: ABH, BCI, BIH, BCH, DFG, DEF, DFJ, GFJ, ACH, BDJ, FIH, BDF, BHF, EFB.

20. (c)

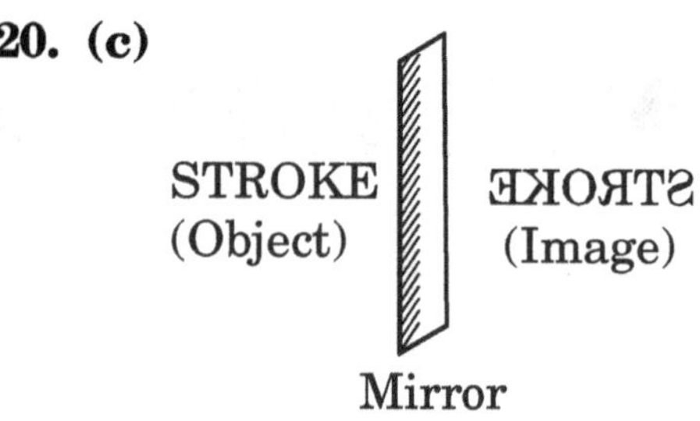

21. (b)

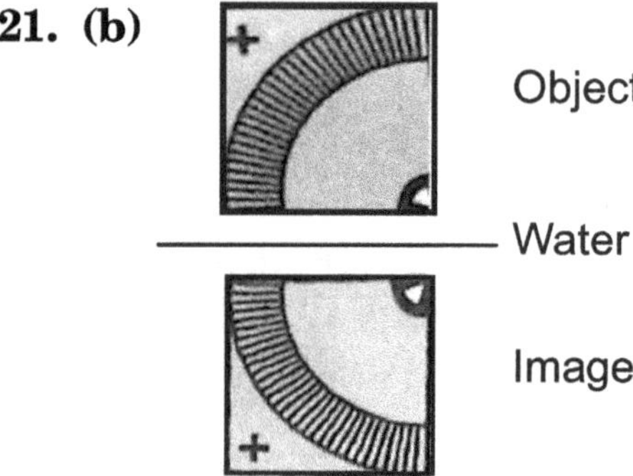

22. (d)

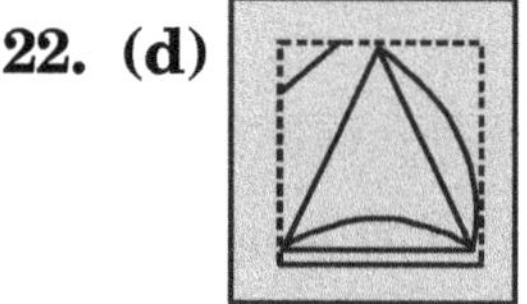

23. (b)

24. (c) Adjacent faces of the face with 1 dot are with 5 dots, 2 dots, 3 dots and 4 dots. Fig (ii) is obtained by rotationing fig (i) two times keeping 1 dot unchanged. So, number opposite to 3 is 6.

25. (a) Consider row-wise. The bar doubles in number and then stick to the opposite side. The other element doubles in number and shifts equally to the corners of opposite diagonal.

MOCK TEST-2

ANSWER KEY

1	(b)	6	(c)	11	(d)	16	(c)	21	(c)
2	(d)	7	(b)	12	(b)	17	(b)	22	(d)
3	(c)	8	(c)	13	(d)	18	(b)	23	(b)
4	(a)	9	(c)	14	(c)	19	(c)	24	(c)
5	(b)	10	(c)	15	(c)	20	(c)	25	(d)

1. **(b)** The number '3' space represents Indian teachers who are also advocates as this number is common to given condition.

2. **(d)**

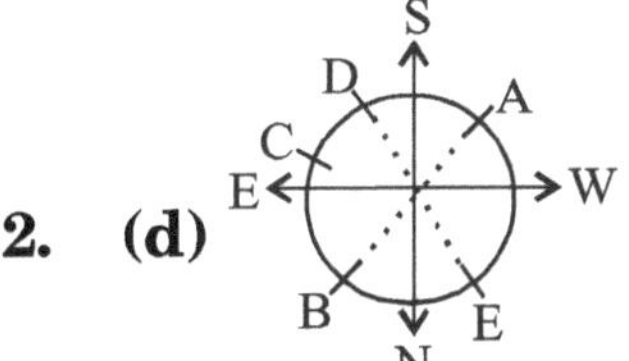

   So, C is facing towards East.

3. **(c)**

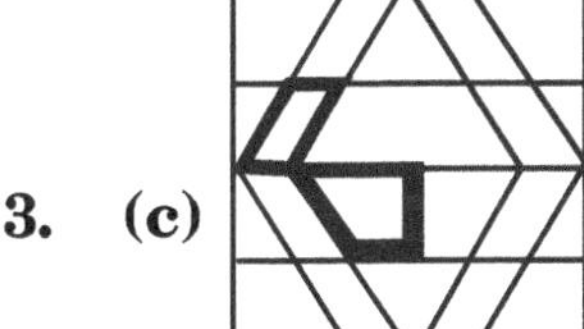

4. **(a)**

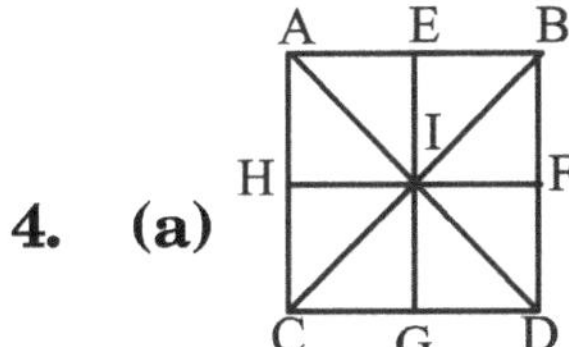

   The triangles are :
   ΔAIH; ΔAIE; ΔEIB; ΔBFI;
   ΔIHC; ΔIGC; ΔIGD; ΔDFI;
   ΔIAB; ΔIBD; ΔICD; ΔIAC;
   ΔBAC; ΔACD; ΔBDC; ΔBDA
   Total triangles = 16

5. **(b)** Perk > Pick > Pile > Pith > Pour
       4   1   3   2   5

6. **(c)** NATION as a letter A is not there in word CONTENTION.

7. **(b)** As, H O N E S T Y
   ↓ ↓ ↓ ↓ ↓ ↓ ↓
   5 1 3 2 4 6 8

   and, P O V E R T Y
   ↓ ↓ ↓ ↓ ↓ ↓ ↓
   7 1 9 2 0 6 8

   Therefore,

   H O R S E
   ↓ ↓ ↓ ↓ ↓
   5 1 0 4 2

8. **(c)** Except Subtract, all others are Nouns. The Noun for subtract (Verb) is Subtraction.

9. **(c)** 27 is perfect cube. All other numbers are prime number.

10. **(c)** Here, Writer uses pen for writting. Similarly, painter uses brush for painting.

11. **(d)**

12. **(b)** Except (b), in all other figures, the number of dots is five.

13. **(d)** B is the daughter of C.

14. **(c)** 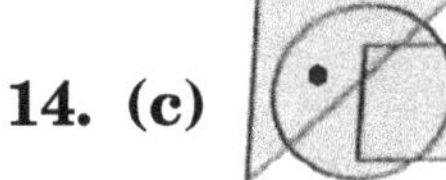

15. (c) Opposite faces are (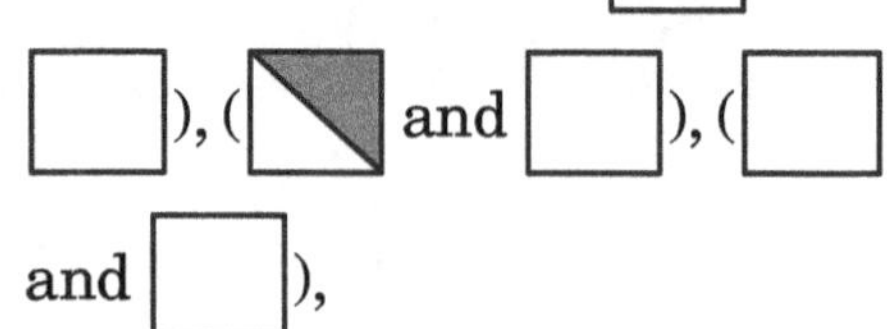 and

These conditions of opposite faces are applicable in boxes (2) and (3) only.

16. (c) A diagram is made according to the directions given in the question. Clearly, X is in South-West of Z.

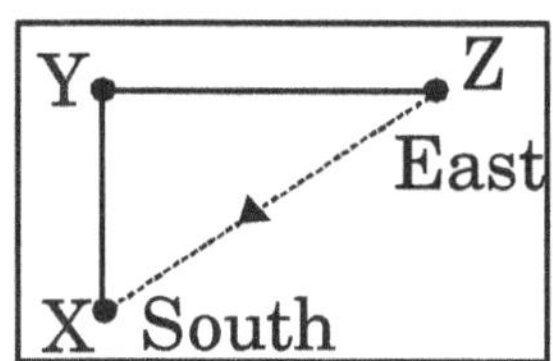

17. (b)
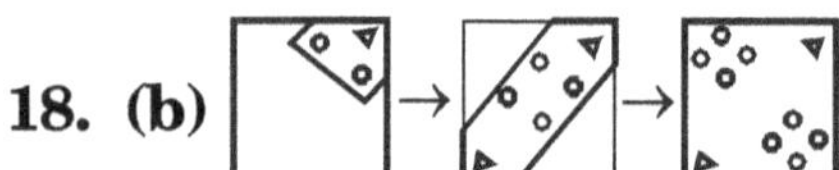

18. (b)
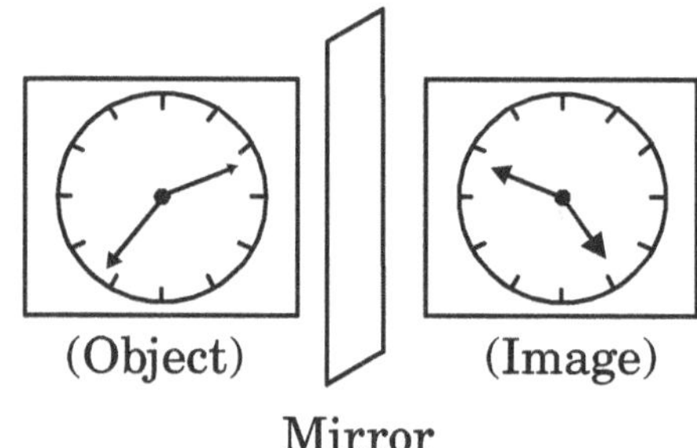

19. (c) A member is a part of family, and also family is a part of community.

Hence, the correct order is Member, Family, Community, Locality, Country.

20. (c) In each column, the top and bottom figures are the water images of each other.

21. (c) Given expression $= 18 \times 12 \div 4 + 5 - 6 \Rightarrow 18 \times 3 + 5 - 6 = 53$

22. (d)

23. (b)

24. (c) $\dfrac{\text{FAMILY}}{\text{FAMILY}}$ Object — Water layer — Image

25. (d) The total number of students in the class $= 7 + 28 - 1 = \boxed{34}$

MOCK TEST-3

ANSWER KEY

1	(b)	6	(b)	11	(d)	16	(c)	21	(b)
2	(d)	7	(c)	12	(b)	17	(a)	22	(c)
3	(d)	8	(d)	13	(b)	18	(a)	23	(b)
4	(a)	9	(a)	14	(b)	19	(a)	24	(a)
5	(d)	10	(d)	15	(a)	20	(c)	25	(b)

1. **(b)** As, paper is product of Tree. Similarly, glass is a product of sand.

2. **(d)** The relationship between the numbers is :
$x : (x^2 - 1)$
$(9)^2 - 1 = 81 - 1 = 80$
$(100)^2 - 1 = 10000 - 1 = 9999$

3. **(d)** As, $49 - 33 = 16$, $62 - 46 = 16$
$83 - 67 = 16$ But, $70 - 55 = 15$

4. **(a)** Except Flute, all others are stringed musical instruments.

5. **(d)** The pattern is as follows :

$$A \xrightarrow{+2} C \xrightarrow{+2} E \xrightarrow{+2} \boxed{G}$$
$$Z \xrightarrow{-2} X \xrightarrow{-2} V \xrightarrow{-2} \boxed{T}$$

6. **(b)** The pattern is as follows:

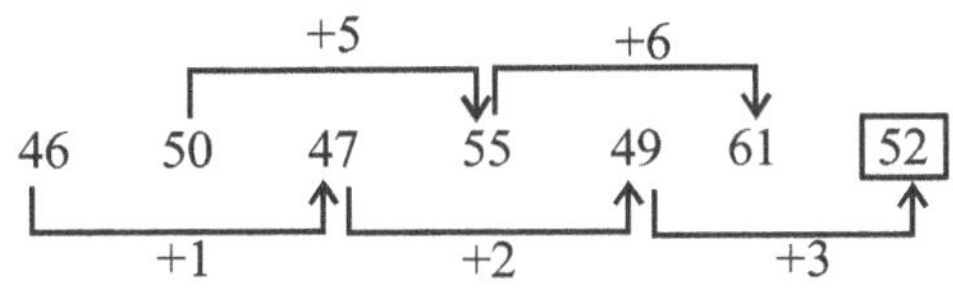

46   50   47   55   49   61 $\boxed{52}$

7. **(c)** Arrangement of words according to Dictionary :
B. Toronto → C. Torped → E. Torsel → A. Tortoise → D. Torus

8. **(d)** TRACTOR is the word which cannot be formed from the given word as 'T' does not comes twice in the original word.

9. **(a)** 2 ⑤ △₃ ⇒ △books are
(old)
⑤ 4 6 ⇒ man is (old)

△₃ 7 8 ⇒ buy good △books
Codes are :
5 ⇒ old   4 ⇒ man or is
8 ⇒ buy or good
3 ⇒ books   6 ⇒ man or is
2 ⇒ are   7 ⇒ buy or good
So, 2 stands for "are" in that code.

10. **(d)** As, $5 + 4 = 9$ and $9 \times 2 = 18$
$6 + 3 = 9$ and $9 \times 3 = 27$
$12 + 4 = 16$ and ? $16 \times \boxed{6} = 96$

11. **(d)**

12. **(b)** Except (b), in all other circles both the dark shaded regions are nearer to each other.

13. **(b)** Letters of DELHI are reduced by $-1, -2, -3, -4$ and -5 respectively. Based on that code for 'BOMBAY' would be 'AMJXVS'.

14. **(b)** The lower layer bears 10 blocks. Hence. total number of blocks $= 10 + 4 = 14$.

15. (a) Half shaded faces could not appear as shown in boxes (2) and (3).

16. (c) Abhishek is the only brother of Anshu and Neeta is sister-in-law of Anshu. So, Neeta is wife of Abhishek.

17. (a) 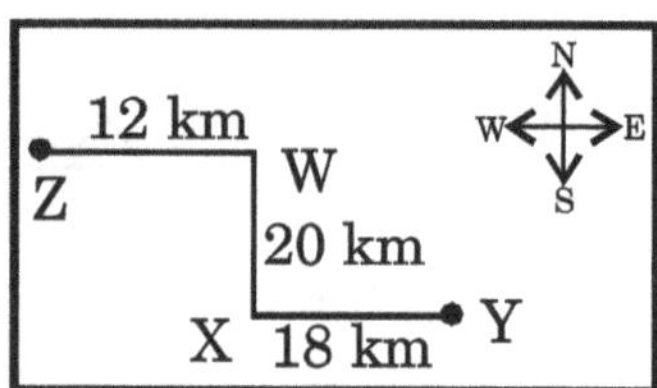

18. (a) From the figure, it is clear that Y and Z denote the starting and finishing points, respectively. Z is to the North-West of point Y.

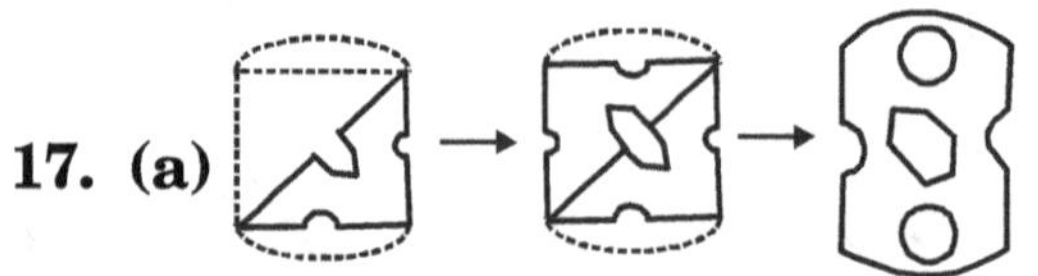

19. (a) The 3rd figure in each row is the uncommon parts of lines in first two figures.

20. (c) Both men and trees are living beings.

21. (b)

22. (c) Monday falls on 1th, 8th, 15th, 22nd and 29th. So, 5th day from 21st which is 26th is Friday.

23. (b)

P $\Rightarrow$ ÷	Q $\Rightarrow$ ×
R $\Rightarrow$ +	S $\Rightarrow$ –

20 Q 12P6 R5 S13 = ?
$$20 \times 12 \div 6 + 5 - 13$$
$$= 20 \times 2 + 5 - 13$$
$$= 40 + 5 - 13$$
$$= 45 - 13 = 32$$

24. (a)

Left ●———+———+———+———+———● Right
　　　　　M　R　P　L　O

Hence, P coach is in the middle of the five coaches.

25. (b)

MOCK TEST-4

ANSWER KEY

1	(b)	9	(c)	17	(a)	25	(a)	33	(b)
2	(c)	10	(d)	18	(c)	26	(d)	34	(c)
3	(a)	11	(b)	19	(c)	27	(b)	35	(a)
4	(c)	12	(d)	20	(c)	28	(d)	36	(a)
5	(c)	13	(b)	21	(b)	29	(d)	37	(c)
6	(a)	14	(d)	22	(a)	30	(d)	38	(d)
7	(b)	15	(c)	23	(b)	31	(b)	39	(b)
8	(b)	16	(d)	24	(a)	32	(c)	40	(d)

1. (b) The first, third and fifth letters are each moved one step backward, while the second, fourth and sixth letters are each moved one step forward to obtain the corresponding letters of the code.

2. (c)

Letter	B	R	A	I	N	T	E
Code	*	%	÷	#	×	$	+

The code for RENT is % + × $.

3. (a) The words in all other pairs are antonyms.

4. (c) It is the set of all prime numbers.

5. (c) Using the proper signs, we get:
$$= 36 - 8 \div 4 + 6 \div 2 \times 3$$
$$= 36 - 2 + 3 \times 3$$
$$= 36 - 2 + 9 = 45 - 2 = 43.$$

6. (a) The number in the center of each figure is the cube of the number of sides of the figure

7. (b) $16 + 12 - 1 = 27$

8. (b) When the sheet in fig. (X) is folded to form a cube, then 'F' appears opposite 'B' and 'A' appears opposite 'D'. Therefore, the cube in fig. (A) which shows 'F' adjacent to 'B', the cube in fig.(C) which shows 'E' adjacent to 'C' and the cube in fig. (D) which shows 'A' adjacent to 'D' cannot be formed.

9. (c) c, e, a, d, b

10. (d)

11. (b)

12. (d) 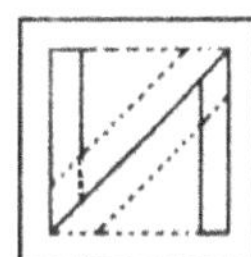

13. (b) There is no 'V' letter in the given word.

14. (d) Arrangement of words as per dictionary:

(i) Forge
↓
(ii) Forget
↓
(iv) Forgive
↓
(iii) Forgo
↓
(iv) Format

15. (c) As Blue whale is heaviest animal in the sea. Similarly, Elephant is heaviest animal on the land.

16. (d)

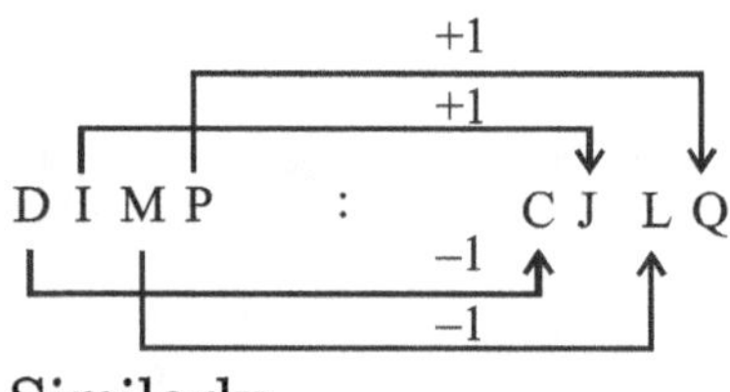

Similarly,

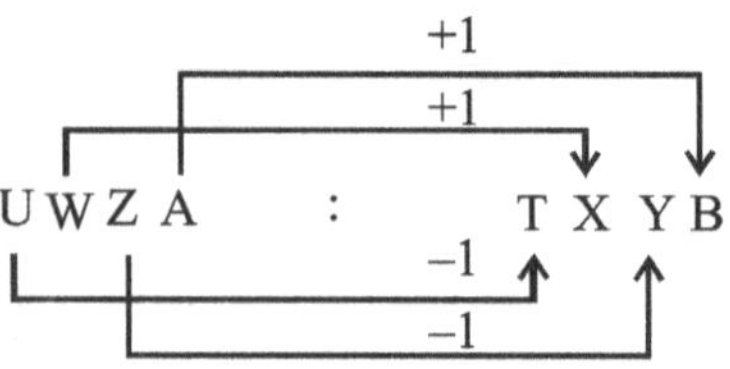

17. (a) The pattern is as follows :

$$B \xrightarrow{+2} D \xrightarrow{+2} F \xrightarrow{+2} H \xrightarrow{+2}$$
$$M \xrightarrow{-1} L \xrightarrow{-1} K \xrightarrow{-1} J \xrightarrow{-1}$$
$$R \xrightarrow{+2} T \xrightarrow{+2} V \xrightarrow{+2} X \xrightarrow{+2}$$
$$G \xrightarrow{-1} F \xrightarrow{-1} E \xrightarrow{-1} D \xrightarrow{-1}$$

J I Z C

So, JIZC will complete the series.

18. (c) c b a / b a c / a c b / c b a

19. (c) The colour of sky is blue. But blue is called sky. Hence, option (c) is correct choice.

20. (c)

There are 16 triangles in the given figure. These are AHO, ACB, BHO, BAD, ABE, BEF, BAF, ABG, AOF, AFD, BOG, BGC, ADO BOC, FBE and AEG

21. (b)

22. (a) The direction diagram is as follows:

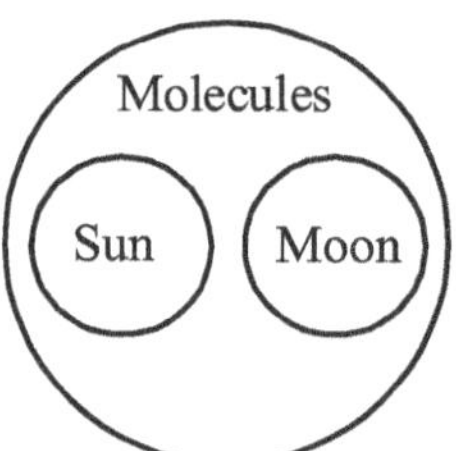

So, Raja is facing south-direction.

23. (b)

Shankar is facing to west-direction & Ganesh is facing to south-direction.

24. (a) Day before yesterday was Sunday.
Therefore, today is Tuesday.
Day after tomorrow will be Thursday.
Thursday + 3 = Sunday

25. (a) Roshan > Susheel > Hardik
Hardik > Niza > Harry
Roshan > Susheel
Roshan > Susheel > Hardik
> Niza > Harry
Therefore, Roshan is the tallest.

26. (d) Every thing is composed of molecules. Sun is different from Moon.

27. (b) The letters 'b' and 'd' are present in both the circles.

28. (d)

+ ⇒ ÷	− ⇒ ×
× ⇒ +	÷ ⇒ −

$45 + 9 - 3 \times 15 \div 2$
$\Rightarrow ? = 45 \div 9 \times 3 + 15 - 2$
$\Rightarrow ? = 5 \times 3 + 15 - 2$
$\Rightarrow ? = 30 - 2 = \boxed{28}$

29. (d) $235 \Rightarrow (2)^2 + (3)^2 + (5)^2 = 38$

$452 \Rightarrow (4)^2 + (5)^2 + (2)^2 = 45$

$345 \Rightarrow (3)^2 + (4)^2 + (5)^2 = \boxed{50}$

30. (d)

31. (b)

32. (c) Gauri's brother is the father-in-law of the person.

33. (b) D is the father of both A and B.

34. (c) Givon word : D E P R E S S I O N
The new letter sequence is E D R P S E I S N O
Now, the 8th letter from the left is 'S'.

35. (a) We obtain the following letter series on reversing the order of the alphabets.
Z Y X W V U T S R Q P O N M L K J I H G F E D C B A
Required letter = (14 − 13) + 1 = 2nd letter from your left in the rearrangement.

36. (a)

37. (c)

$80 \div 10 = 8; 30 \div 6 = 5; 100 \div 2 = 50$

38. (d)

39. (b) Arranging the letters in alphabetical order:
B R A $\boxed{K}$ E $\boxed{S}$
A B E $\boxed{K}$ R $\boxed{S}$

40. (d) The woman is his son's wife that is, daughter-in-law.

MOCK TEST-5

ANSWERS KEY

1	(d)	9	(b)	17	(d)	25	(c)	33	(a)
2	(d)	10	(b)	18	(c)	26	(a)	34	(c)
3	(b)	11	(b)	19	(d)	27	(b)	35	(d)
4	(c)	12	(d)	20	(c)	28	(b)	36	(d)
5	(c)	13	(a)	21	(c)	29	(c)	37	(b)
6	(a)	14	(c)	22	(a)	30	(d)	38	(b)
7	(d)	15	(c)	23	(a)	31	(b)	39	(a)
8	(d)	16	(b)	24	(d)	32	(d)	40	(c)

1. (d)

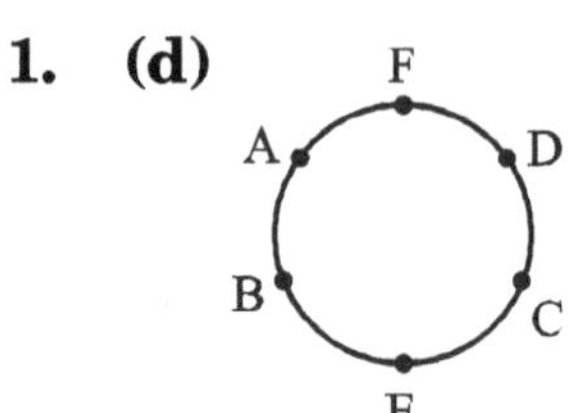

B and F are neighours of A

2. (d)

$\times \Rightarrow +$	$\div \Rightarrow -$
$+ \Rightarrow \div$	$- \Rightarrow \times$

$14 \times 4 \div 70 + 10 - 2 = ?$

$\Rightarrow ? = 14 + 4 - 70 \div 10 \times 2$

$\Rightarrow ? = 14 + 4 - 7 \times 2$

$\Rightarrow ? = 18 - 14 = \boxed{4}$

3. (b)

⑦ + ⑧ + ②

$17 + 3 = 20$

⑥ + ⑦ + ①

$14 + 3 = 17$

⑧ + ⑧ + ④

$20 + 3 = 23$

4. (c)

5. (c)

6. (a) Best representation of the relationship is :

7. (d) Number of teachers who are also singers = 9 + 4 = 13

8. (d)   9. (b)

10. (b) Priti > Rahul

Rahul > Yamuna = Divya

Manju > Lokita

Divya > Manju

Now, Priti > Rahul > Yamuna = Divya > Manju > Lokita

Therefore, Lokita scored the lowest.

11. (b) Wednesday was the day before yesterday. Below figure shows the days pattern:

Wednesday ← day before yesterday

Friday ← day (current)

Sunday ← day after tomorrow

12. (d) Minister cannot be formed as there is no 'E' in the word 'ADMINISTRATION'.

13. (a) Words as per order in dictionary Nautical > Naval > Navigate >

Necessary

So, correct order is 3, 4, 2, 1

14. (c)

$$\begin{array}{cccccc} 4 & 0 & 5 & 3 & 1 & 2 \\ \downarrow & \downarrow & \downarrow & \downarrow & \downarrow & \downarrow \\ M & O & T & H & E & R \end{array}$$

15. (c) The relationship between the numbers is :

$x^2 : x^3$

$(5)^2 = 25; (5)^3 = 125$

$(6)^2 = 36; (6)^3 = 216$

16. (b) Food is necessary for man. Similarly, fuel is necessary for car.

17. (d) A teacher teaches in a class and as given 'teacher' is called 'clerk'. So a 'clerk' will teach in the class.

18. (c) In the first and the third statements '6' means 'is'. In the second and third statements we get '4' means 'colour'. Thus in the third statement, '3' means 'fun'.

19. (d) The word is coded by moving the letters three steps forward.

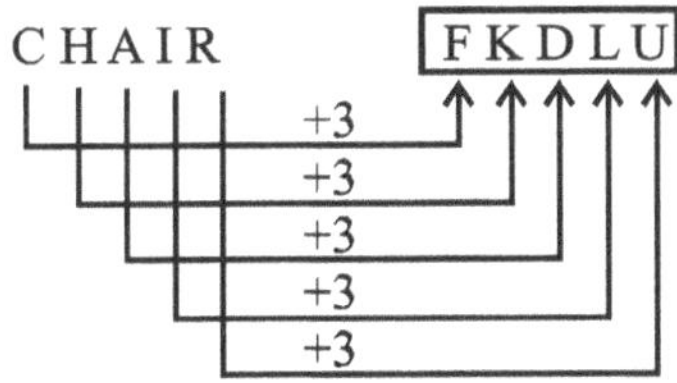

Similarly,

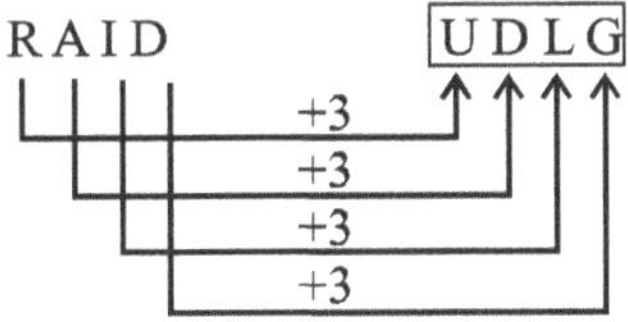

20. (c) Clearly, in the figure there are—1 column containing

3 cubes, 2 columns containing 2 cubes each and 3 columns containing 1 cube each.

Number of cubes in columns of

3 cubes = $1 \times 3 = 3$;

Number of cubes in columns of 2 cubes = $2 \times 2 = 4$;

Number of cubes in columns of 1 cubes = $3 \times 1 = 3$;

Therefore, total number of cubes = $3 + 4 + 3 = 10$.

21. (c) The pattern is : $5 \times 3 + 4 = 19$, and $6 \times 4 + 5 = 29$

Similarly, $7 \times 5 + 6 = 41$.

22. (a) The letters in the second and third rows are five steps ahead of corresponding letters in the first and second rows respectively.

23. (a) $\triangle$ and $\square$ are moving CW while ● and $\square$ are moving ACW one step each. So next figure is in option (a).

24. (d) The given sequence is $1^2 - 1 = 0, 2^2 - 1 = 3, 3^2 - 1 = 8, ...$ so on. So, $9^2 - 1 = 81 - 1 = 80$.

25. (c) Each next term in the series is 3 more than the preceding term. So the wrong term is 31 as $27 + 3 = 30$

26. (a) Three letters are not in order as in the reverse order of the English alphabets.

27. (b) 14 is the only number that is not divisible by 3 or 6.

28. (b) All except February are months with 31 days, while February has 28 or 29 days.

29. (c) In all other figures, the upper right quarter portion is shaded.

30. (d) As shown in the figure, the man initially faces in the direction OA. On moving 45° clockwise, the man faces in the direction OB. On further moving 180° clockwise, he faces in the direction OC. Finally on moving 270° anticlockwise, he faces in the direction OD, which is South-West.

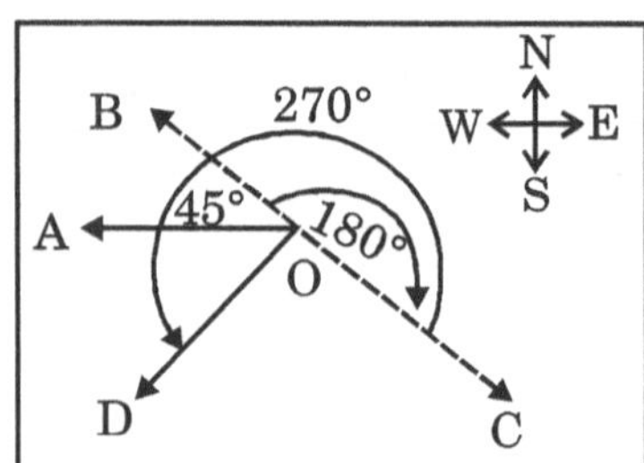

31. **(b)** The arrangement of four friends is as following:

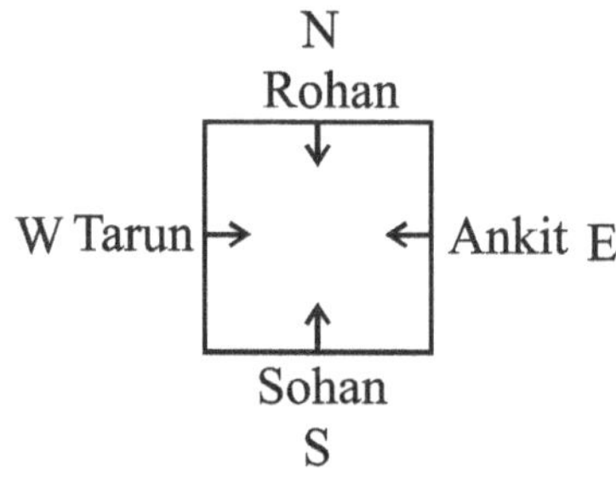

So, if Ankit towards west, then Rohan faces towards south.

32. **(d)** Population → Unemployment → Poverty → Lack of food → Death

33. **(a)** After rearrangement in alphabetical order:

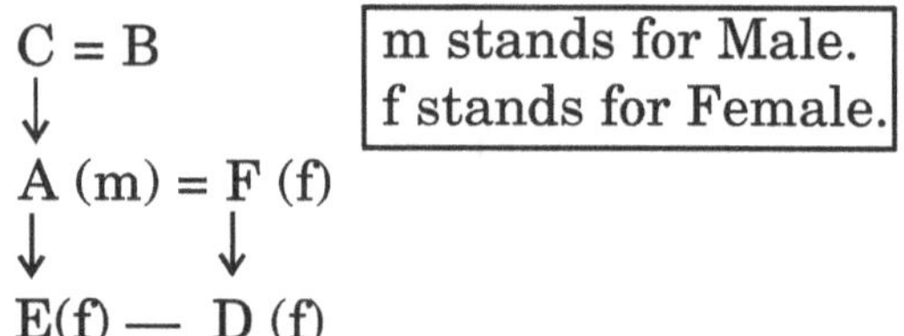

35. **(d)**

$$C = B$$
$$\downarrow$$
$$A\,(m) = F\,(f)$$
$$\downarrow \qquad \downarrow$$
$$E(f) — D\,(f)$$

m stands for Male.
f stands for Female.

Can't be determined

36. **(d)**

37. **(b)** 1457258 $\boxed{4}$ 968 $\boxed{2}$ 5413271

38. **(b)** Mosquito, Cat, Tiger, Elephant, Whale.

39. **(a)** Two couples → 4 persons
One Bachelor + One Widower + Two Divorcees = 4 Persons
4 children.
Therefore 12 persons went to the picnic.

40. **(c)** In each row/column, the 3rd figure is the combination of the 1st and 2nd figure.

CYBER

MOCK TEST-1

ANSWERS KEY

1	(c)	6	(a)	11	(a)	16	(d)	21	(a)
2	(d)	7	(c)	12	(c)	17	(d)	22	(d)
3	(d)	8	(c)	13	(c)	18	(a)	23	(d)
4	(c)	9	(a)	14	(a)	19	(c)	24	(c)
5	(c)	10	(d)	15	(c)	20	(c)	25	(d)

1. (c) A pen plotter draw vector graphics on paper based on commands received from the computer.

2. (d) Inkjet printer produces prints by spraying ink through tiny nozzles. So, it does not produce waterproof prints

14. (a) Client server network can be utilized by any type computers. So, only statement 1 is true.

15. (c) Given logo is of Dropbox which is an online file hosting service. It is used for saving files on the clouds.

MOCK TEST-2

ANSWER KEY

1	(c)	6	(b)	11	(d)	16	(c)	21	(c)
2	(a)	7	(a)	12	(d)	17	(a)	22	(a)
3	(b)	8	(c)	13	(c)	18	(d)	23	(d)
4	(b)	9	(b)	14	(c)	19	(c)	24	(a)
5	(a)	10	(d)	15	(d)	20	(a)	25	(a)

1. (c) It holds data temporarily.

2. (a) Unscrambled word is PROCESSOR and among the given option Intel COre i7 is a processor.

8. (c) In slide master, you can only set the format of the slides, no changes can be made to its content.

9. (b) Orientation option is used for labeling narrow columns. It rotates text diagonally and vertically.

MOCK TEST-3

ANSWER KEY

1	(c)	6	(b)	11	(c)	16	(d)	21	(c)
2	(d)	7	(a)	12	(a)	17	(d)	22	(a)
3	(a)	8	(c)	13	(a)	18	(c)	23	(a)
4	(a)	9	(a)	14	(c)	19	(b)	24	(b)
5	(c)	10	(b)	15	(a)	20	(c)	25	(c)

3. (a) To read the content of a CD, laser beam is shined on thedisc and to move the laser to right part of CD, the CD is spinned.

5. (c) Personalization option allows you to changes desktop background, screensaver and taskbar and windows border color.

MOCK TEST-4

ANSWER KEY									
1	(a)	9	(d)	17	(a)	25	(c)	33	(c)
2	(d)	10	(a)	18	(b)	26	(d)	34	(b)
3	(d)	11	(c)	19	(a)	27	(d)	35	(a)
4	(a)	12	(c)	20	(a)	28	(c)	36	(b)
5	(b)	13	(b)	21	(d)	29	(c)	37	(d)
6	(c)	14	(c)	22	(c)	30	(d)	38	(a)
7	(c)	15	(b)	23	(c)	31	(c)	39	(a)
8	(a)	16	(c)	24	(d)	32	(a)	40	(b)

6. (c) Apple Lisa was the first computer to have drop-down menu, clickable buttons and menu like screen interface.

7. (c) The advanced option allows you to end the slide show with a black slide in MS Powerpoint.

8. (a) Action center is used to resolve problem related to security issue in computer.

11. (c) Like colors and fonts, effects of theme an also be changed.

16. (c) abs function turns a negative number into positive number, thus returning its absolute value.

MOCK TEST-5

ANSWER KEY									
1	(b)	9	(a)	17	(c)	25	(a)	33	(b)
2	(c)	10	(d)	18	(d)	26	(b)	34	(d)
3	(a)	11	(d)	19	(b)	27	(d)	35	(b)
4	(a)	12	(b)	20	(a)	28	(b)	36	(a)
5	(b)	13	(b)	21	(d)	29	(a)	37	(a)
6	(b)	14	(b)	22	(d)	30	(a)	38	(a)
7	(d)	15	(d)	23	(b)	31	(a)	39	(c)
8	(a)	16	(d)	24	(b)	32	(b)	40	(d)

1. (b) Floppy disk is a magnetic storage medium placed inside a plastic carrier. It is not an example of hard disk.

6. (b) Supercomputers are high speed computers whose performance is measured in FLOPS.

8. (a) When there is a different account for each user then the user is given certain permission to manage his account.

11. (d) Action feature helps you add an action to perform when an object is clicked or mouse is hovered it.

33. (b) A SIMM, or single in-line memory module, is a type of memory module containing random access memory used in computers from the early 1980s to the late 1990s.